Modern Art and Modernism:
A Critical Anthology

Modern Art and Modernism:
A Critical Anthology

Edited by Francis Frascina and Charles Harrison
with the assistance of Deirdre Paul
at the Open University

Harper and Row, Publishers
in association with
The Open University

Harper & Row, Publishers
London

Cambridge
Hagerstown
Philadelphia
New York

San Francisco
Mexico City
Sao Paulo
Sydney

Harper & Row Ltd
28 Tavistock Street
London WC2E 7PN

British Library Cataloguing in Publication Data

Modern art and modernism.
  1. Modernism (Art)
  I. Frascina, Francis, *1950–*
  II. Harrison, Charles
  709'.03'4   N6490

  ISBN 0-06-318-2343
  ISBN 0-06-318-2335 Pbk

Typeset by Inforum Ltd, Portsmouth
Printed and bound at The Pitman Press Ltd, Bath

Contents

Introduction

In giving this book the title of *Modern Art and Modernism* we mean to draw attention to the relationship between the art of the modern period and the forms of criticism which have been developed to interpret and explain it. Art does not develop independently of criticism. Such writers as Baudelaire, Fry and Greenberg have often been seen as influential figures who have helped to determine the course of art. It is hoped that this book will provide some material for consideration of the inter-relationship between art and ideas about art.

This anthology was originally compiled as a reader for an Open University course on *Modern Art and Modernism: Manet to Pollock*. The selection was therefore designed primarily to serve specific needs and interests in relation to other teaching material. This also helps to account for the five main headings under which the texts are grouped. It should be recognized that there is considerable overlap between them. The aim of the course is to consider the history of modern art in the light of the prevailing body of theory, which we identify as 'Modernism', and to test the explanatory power of this theory in the light of alternative forms of explanation and interpretation. In particular, the intention has been to examine both the circumstances under which modern art has been produced, and those under which critical theories and forms of interpretation have themselves been produced.

A work of criticism inevitably reflects a response at a particular historical moment and in the light of particular commitments and interests. Yet influential critical interpretations have often tended to establish the terms of reference for interpretation and appraisal during subsequent generations. In offering a selection of critical and theoretical texts covering the span of the modern period in art, we have hoped to encourage study of the historical – and historically specific – nature of debate about the meaning of art.

We have not attempted to produce a coherent selection or to map out a coherent development. The criticism of modern art has itself proceeded unevenly, and often in terms of the competition between different types of interpretation, expressing different interests, and variously connected to art itself. What we have attempted to do is to select some vivid and typical examples of Modernist criticism at different stages of its development (Denis, Bell, Fry, Cheney, Greenberg), and also of types of art theory and criticism which stand outside this principal current, either because they derive from consciously opposed points of view (Trotsky, Brecht, Benjamin), or because they represent the interests of movements outside the Modernist mainstream (Tarabukin, Eluard), or by virtue of their roots in other methods and disciplines (Goodman). Some of the typical examples of modern art criticism are typically opaque and confusing (Worringer, Bahr, Rebay). That this does not seem to have counted against their authority and influence is in itself of interest. One issue which does seem to distinguish Modernist theories from those critical texts and methods which we have grouped under the heading of 'Art and Society', is that the issue of the class character of culture is seen as crucial in the latter, while it is generally not raised at all in the former.

Debate will continue about the meaning of art and about meaning in art. The issues at stake have their roots both in the history of art and in the history of art criticism. The concept of art itself is handed down to us through a history of interpretations. It is hoped that this anthology will provide material for study of the ways in which that concept has been formed, argued over, and transformed in the modern period.

The majority of these articles and extracts have been abbreviated as appropriate to the overall theme and purpose of this collection. Substantial excisions are marked [. . .]. Minor excisions which leave the flow of the text unchanged have been left unmarked. Texts are otherwise free from editing, and authors' original usages have been maintained. Original illustrations and footnotes have been included only where necessary for reference, or at the express wishes of individual authors.

Among colleagues at the Open University who have also been engaged in preparation of the course to which this anthology relates, we would like to thank Nigel Blake, Briony Fer, Gill Perry, Aaron Scharf, Sara Selwood and Belinda Thomson for their assistance in selecting and preparing this material. We would also like to express our gratitude to those authors who have agreed to the inclusion and editing of their material. Particular thanks are due to Dr Deirdre Paul for invaluable editorial assistance.

F. F.
C. H.

Introductory Texts

1   Modernist Painting

Clement Greenberg

Modernism includes more than just art and literature. By now it includes almost the whole of what is truly alive in our culture. It happens, also, to be very much of a historical novelty. Western civilization is not the first to turn around and question its own foundations, but it is the civilization that has gone furthest in doing so. I identify Modernism with the intensification, almost the exacerbation, of this self-critical tendency that began with the philosopher Kant. Because he was the first to criticize the means itself of criticism, I conceive of Kant as the first real Modernist.

The essence of Modernism lies, as I see it, in the use of the characteristic methods of a discipline to criticize the discipline itself – not in order to subvert it, but to entrench it more firmly in its area of competence. Kant used logic to establish the limits of logic, and while he withdrew much from its old jurisdiction, logic was left in all the more secure possession of what remained to it.

The self-criticism of Modernism grows out of but is not the same thing as the criticism of the Enlightenment. The Enlightenment criticized from the outside, the way criticism in its more accepted sense does; Modernism criticizes from the inside, through the procedures themselves of that which is being criticized. It seems natural that this new kind of criticism should have appeared first in philosophy, which is critical by definition, but as the nineteenth century wore on it made itself felt in many other fields. A more rational justification had begun to be demanded of every formal social activity, and Kantian self-criticism was called on eventually to meet and interpret this demand in areas that lay far from philosophy.

We know what has happened to an activity like religion that has not been able to avail itself of 'Kantian' immanent criticism in order to justify itself. At first glance the arts might seem to have been in a situation like religion's. Having been denied by the Enlightenment all tasks they could take seriously, they looked as though they were going to be assimilated to entertainment pure and simple, and entertainment itself looked as though it was going to be assimilated, like religion, to therapy. The arts could save themselves from this leveling down only by demonstrating that the kind of experience they provided was valuable in its own right and not to be obtained from any other kind of activity.

Each art, it turned out, had to effect this demonstration on its own account. What had to be exhibited and made explicit was that which was unique and irreducible not only in art in general, but also in each particular art. Each art had to determine, through the operations peculiar to itself, the effects peculiar and exclusive to itself. By doing this each art would, to be sure, narrow its area of competence, but at the same time it would make its possession of this area all the more secure.

It quickly emerged that the unique and proper area of competence of each art coincided with all that was unique to the nature of its medium. The task of self-criticism became to eliminate from the effects of each art any and every effect

Source: Art and Literature no. 4, spring 1965, pp. 193–201. Reprinted by permission of the author.

that might conceivably be borrowed from or by the medium of any other art. Thereby each art would be rendered 'pure', and in its 'purity' find the guarantee of its standards of quality as well as of its independence. 'Purity' meant self-definition, and the enterprise of self-criticism in the arts became one of self-definition with a vengeance.

Realistic, illusionist art had dissembled the medium, using art to conceal art. Modernism used art to call attention to art. The limitations that constitute the medium of painting – the flat surface, the shape of the support, the properties of pigment – were treated by the Old Masters as negative factors that could be acknowledged only implicitly or indirectly. Modernist painting has come to regard these same limitations as positive factors that are to be acknowledged openly. Manet's paintings became the first Modernist ones by virtue of the frankness with which they declared the surfaces on which they were painted. The Impressionists, in Manet's wake, abjured underpainting and glazing, to leave the eye under no doubt as to the fact that the colors used were made of real paint that came from pots or tubes. Cézanne sacrificed verisimilitude, or correctness, in order to fit drawing and design more explicitly to the rectangular shape of the canvas.

It was the stressing, however, of the ineluctable flatness of the support that remained most fundamental in the processes by which pictorial art criticized and defined itself under Modernism. Flatness alone was unique and exclusive to that art. The enclosing shape of the support was a limiting condition, or norm, that was shared with the art of the theater; color was a norm or means shared with sculpture as well as the theater. Flatness, two-dimensionality, was the only condition painting shared with no other art, and so Modernist painting oriented itself to flatness as it did to nothing else.

The Old Masters had sensed that it was necessary to preserve what is called the integrity of the picture plane: that is, to signify the enduring presence of flatness under the most vivid illusion of three-dimensional space. The apparent contradiction involved – the dialectical tension, to use a fashionable but apt phrase – was essential to the success of their art, as it is indeed to the success of all pictorial art. The Modernists have neither avoided nor resolved this contradiction; rather, they have reversed its terms. One is made aware of the flatness of their pictures before, instead of after, being made aware of what the flatness contains. Whereas one tends to see what is *in* an Old Master before seeing it as a picture, one sees a Modernist painting as a picture first. This is, of course, the best way of seeing any kind of picture, Old Master or Modernist, but Modernism imposes it as the only and necessary way, and Modernism's success in doing so is a success of self-criticism.

It is not in principle that Modernist painting in its latest phase has abandoned the representation of recognizable objects. What it has abandoned in principle is the representation of the kind of space that recognizable, three-dimensional objects can inhabit. Abstractness, or the non-figurative, has in itself still not proved to be an altogether necessary moment in the self-criticism of pictorial art, even though artists as eminent as Kandinsky and Mondrian have thought so. Representation, or illustration, as such does not abate the uniqueness of pictorial art; what does do so are the associations of the things represented. All recognizable entities (including pictures themselves) exist in three-dimensional space, and the barest suggestion of a recognizable entity suffices to call up associations of that kind of space. The fragmentary silhouette of a human figure, or of a teacup, will do so, and by doing so alienate pictorial space from the two-dimensionality which is the guarantee of painting's independence as an art. Three-dimensionality is the province of sculpture, and for the sake of its own autonomy painting has had above all to divest itself of everything it might share with sculpture. And it is in the course of its effort to do this, and not so much – I repeat – to exclude the representational or the 'literary', that painting has made itself abstract.

At the same time Modernist painting demonstrates, precisely in its resistance to the sculptural, that it continues tradition and the themes of tradition, despite all appearances to the contrary. For the resistance to the sculptural begins long before the advent of Modernism. Western painting, insofar as it strives for realistic illusion, owes an enormous debt to sculpture, which taught it in the beginning how to shade and model towards an illusion of relief, and even how to dispose that illusion in a complementary illusion of deep space. Yet some of the greatest feats of Western painting came as part of the effort it has made in the last four centuries to suppress and dispel the sculptural. Starting in Venice in the sixteenth century and continuing in Spain, Belgium, and Holland in the seventeenth, that effort was carried on at first in the name of color. When David, in the eighteenth century, sought to revive sculptural painting, it was in part to save pictorial art from the decorative flattening-out that the emphasis on color seemed to induce. Nevertheless, the strength of David's own best pictures (which are predominantly portraits) often lies as much in their color as in anything else. And Ingres, his pupil, though subordinating color far more consistently, executed pictures that were among the flattest, least sculptural done in the West by a sophisticated artist since the fourteenth century. Thus by the middle of the nineteenth century all ambitious tendencies in painting were converging (beneath their differences) in an anti-sculptural direction.

Modernism, in continuing this direction, made it more conscious of itself. With Manet and the Impressionists, the question ceased to be defined as one of color versus drawing, and became instead a question of purely optical experience as against optical experience modified or revised by tactile associations. It was in the name of the purely and literally optical, not in that of color, that the Impressionists set themselves to undermining shading and modeling and everything else that seemed to connote the sculptural. And in a way like that in which David had reacted against Fragonard in the name of the sculptural, Cézanne, and the Cubists after him, reacted against Impressionism. But once again, just as David's and Ingres' reaction had culminated in a kind of painting even less sculptural than before, so the Cubist counter-revolution eventuated in a kind of painting flatter than anything Western art had seen since before Cimabue – so flat indeed that it could hardly contain recognizable images.

In the meantime the other cardinal norms of the art of painting were undergoing an equally searching inquiry, though the results may not have been equally conspicuous. It would take me more space than is at my disposal to tell how the norm of the picture's enclosing shape or frame was loosened, then tightened, then loosened once again, and then isolated and tightened once more by successive generations of Modernist painters; or how the norms of finish, of paint texture, and of value and color contrast, were tested and retested. Risks have been taken with all these, not only for the sake of new expression, but also in order to exhibit them more clearly as norms. By being exhibited and made explicit they are tested for their indispensability. This testing is by no means finished, and the fact that it becomes more searching as it proceeds accounts for the radical simplifications, as well as radical complications, in which the very latest abstract art abounds.

Neither the simplifications nor the complications are matters of license. On the contrary, the more closely and essentially the norms of a discipline become defined the less apt they are to permit liberties ('liberation' has become a much abused word in connection with avant-garde and Modernist art). The essential norms or conventions of painting are also the limiting conditions with which a marked-up surface must comply in order to be experienced as a picture. Modernism has found that these limiting conditions can be pushed back indefinitely before a picture stops being a picture and turns into an arbitrary object; but it has also found that the further back these limits are pushed the more explicitly they have to be observed. The intersecting black lines and colored rectangles of a Mondrian may seem hardly enough to make a picture out of, yet by echoing the picture's enclosing shape so self-evidently they impose that shape as a regulating norm with a new force and a new completeness. Far from incurring the danger of arbitrariness in the absence of a model in nature, Mondrian's art proves, with the passing of time, almost too disciplined, too convention-bound in certain respects; once we have become used to its utter abstractness we realize that it is more traditional in its color, as well as in its subservience to the frame, than the last paintings of Monet are.

It is understood, I hope, that in plotting the rationale of Modernist art I have had to simplify and exaggerate. The flatness towards which Modernist painting orients itself can never be an utter flatness. The heightened sensitivity of the picture plane may no longer permit sculptural illusion, or *trompe-l'oeil*, but it does and must permit optical illusion. The first mark made on a surface destroys its virtual flatness, and the configurations of a Mondrian still suggest a kind of illusion of a kind of third dimension. Only now it is a strictly pictorial, strictly optical third dimension. Where the Old Masters created an illusion of space into which one could imagine oneself walking, the illusion created by a Modernist is one into which one can only look, can travel through only with the eye.

One begins to realize that the Neo-Impressionists were not altogether misguided when they flirted with science. Kantian self-criticism finds its perfect expression in science rather than in philosophy, and when this kind of self-criticism was applied in art the latter was brought closer in spirit to scientific method than ever before – closer than in the early Renaissance. That visual art should confine itself exclusively to what is given in visual experience, and make no reference to anything given in other orders of experience, is a notion whose only justification lies, notionally, in scientific consistency. Scientific method alone asks that a situation be resolved in exactly the same kind of terms as that in which it is presented – a problem in physiology is solved in terms of physiology, not in those of psychology; to be solved in terms of psychology, it has to be presented in, or translated into, these terms first. Analogously, Modernist painting asks that a literary theme be translated into strictly optical, two-dimensional terms before becoming the subject of pictorial art – which means its being translated in such a way that it entirely loses its literary character. Actually, such consistency promises nothing in the way of aesthetic quality or aesthetic results, and the fact that the best art of the past seventy or eighty years increasingly approaches such consistency does not change this; now as before, the only consistency which counts in art is aesthetic consistency, which shows itself only in results and never in methods or means. From the point of view of art itself its convergence of spirit with science happens to be a mere accident, and neither art nor science gives or assures the other of anything more than it ever did. What their convergence does show, however, is the degree to which Modernist art belongs to the same historical and cultural tendency as modern science.

It should also be understood that the self-criticism of Modernist art has never been carried on in any but a spontaneous and subliminal way. It has been altogether a question of practice, immanent to practice and never a topic of theory. Much has been heard about programs in connection with Modernist art, but there has really been far less of the programmatic in Modernist art than in Renaissance or Academic art. With a few untypical exceptions, the masters of Modernism have betrayed no more of an appetite for fixed ideas about art than Corot did. Certain inclinations and emphases, certain refusals and abstinences seem to become necessary simply because the way to stronger, more expressive art seems to lie through them. The immediate aims of Modernist artists remain individual before anything else, and the truth and success of their work is individual before it is anything else. To the extent that it succeeds as art Modernist art partakes in no way of the character of a demonstration. It has needed the accumulation over decades of a good deal of individual achievement to reveal the self-critical tendency of Modernist painting. No one artist was, or is yet, consciously aware of this tendency, nor could any artist work successfully in conscious awareness of it. To this extent – which is by far the largest – art gets carried on under Modernism in the same way as before.

And I cannot insist enough that Modernism has never meant anything like a break with the past. It may mean a devolution, an unraveling of anterior tradition, but it also means its continuation. Modernist art develops out of the past without gap or break, and wherever it ends up it will never stop being intelligible in terms of the continuity of art. The making of pictures has been governed, since pictures first began to be made, by all the norms I have mentioned. The Paleolithic painter or engraver could disregard the norm of the frame and treat the surface in both a literally and a virtually sculptural way because he made images rather than pictures, and worked on a support whose limits could be disregarded because (except in the case of small objects like a bone or horn) nature gave them to the artist in an unmanageable way. But the making of pictures, as against images in the flat, means the deliberate choice and creation of limits. This deliberateness is what Modernism harps on: that is, it spells out the fact that the limiting conditions of art have to be made altogether human limits.

I repeat that Modernist art does not offer theoretical demonstrations. It could be said, rather, that it converts all theoretical possibilities into empirical ones, and in doing so tests, inadvertently, all theories about art for their relevance to the actual practice and experience of art. Modernism is subversive in this respect alone. Ever so many factors thought to be essential to the making and experiencing of art have been shown not to be so by the fact that Modernist art has been able to dispense with them and yet continue to provide the experience of art in all its essentials. That this 'demonstration' has left most of our old *value* judgments intact only makes it the more conclusive. Modernism may have had something to do with the revival of the reputations of Uccello, Piero, El Greco, Georges de la Tour, and even Vermeer, and it certainly confirmed if it did not start other revivals like that of Giotto; but Modernism has not lowered thereby the standing of Leonardo, Raphael, Titian, Rubens, Rembrandt or Watteau. What Modernism has made clear is that, though the past did appreciate masters like these justly, it often gave wrong or irrelevant reasons for doing so.

Still, in some ways this situation has hardly changed. Art criticism lags behind Modernist as it lagged behind pre-Modernist art. Most of the things that get written about contemporary art belong to journalism rather than criticism properly speaking. It belongs to journalism – and to the millennial complex from which so many journalists suffer in our day – that each new phase of Modernism should be hailed as the start of a whole new epoch of art making a decisive break with all the customs and conventions of the past. Each time, a kind of art is expected that will be so unlike previous kinds of art and so 'liberated' from norms of practice or taste, that everybody, regardless of how informed or uninformed, will be able to have his say about it. And each time, this expectation is disappointed, as the phase of Modernism in question takes its place, finally, in the intelligible continuity of taste and tradition, and as it becomes clear that the same demands as before are made on artist and spectator.

Nothing could be further from the authentic art of our time than the idea of a rupture of continuity. Art is, among many other things, continuity. Without the past of art, and without the need and compulsion to maintain past standards of excellence, such a thing as Modernist art would be impossible.

2   Historical Interpretation

Sir Karl Popper

It can be argued that Modernism is a doctrine of the kind we now call historicist (and that historicism is an intellectual error). The philosopher Karl Popper made the word 'historicism' his own when he published The Poverty of Historicism, *and we now use the word in this sense. Popper uses the word to characterize 'a theory (about the course of historical development) which has often been put forward, but perhaps never in a fully developed form'. He continued, 'This is why I have deliberately chosen the somewhat unfamiliar label "historicism". By introducing it I hope I shall avoid merely verbal quibbles: for nobody, I hope, will be tempted to question* [our emphasis] . . . *what the word "historicism" really or properly or essentially means.' (*The Poverty of Historicism, *pp. 3–4.)*

Popper defined historicism for his own use thus: '. . . I mean by "historicism" an approach to the social sciences which assumes that historical prediction *is their principal aim, and which assumes that this aim is attainable by discovering the "rhythms" or the "patterns", the "laws" or the "trends" that underlie the evolution of history.' (*The Poverty of Historicism, *p. 3.) To say that Modernism is historicist is to say that it sees artistic developments in the modern era as growing out of each other in accordance with rhythms, patterns, laws or trends.*

In this extract from The Poverty of Historicism, *Popper outlines an argument against historicism in general. It is important to note, however, that he does not argue against the 'interested' writing of history.*

[Editors]

Is there nothing whatever in the historicist demand for a reform of history – for a sociology which plays the role of a theoretical history, or a theory of historical development? Is there nothing whatever in the historicist idea of 'periods'; of the 'spirit' or 'style' of an age; of irresistible historical tendencies; of movements which captivate the minds of individuals and which surge on like a flood, driving, rather than being driven by, individual men? Nobody who has read, for example, the speculations of Tolstoy in *War and Peace* – historicist, no doubt, but stating his motives with candour – on the movement of the men of the West towards the East and the counter-movement of the Russians towards the West, can deny that historicism answers a real need. We have to satisfy this need by offering something better before we can seriously hope to get rid of historicism.

Tolstoy's historicism is a reaction against a method of writing history which implicitly accepts the truth of the principle of leadership; a method which attributes much – too much, if Tolstoy is right, as he undoubtedly is – to the great man, the leader. Tolstoy tries to show, successfully I think, the small influence of the actions and decisions of Napoleon, Alexander, Kutuzov, and the other great leaders of 1812,

Source: Sir Karl Popper, 'Situational Logic in History. Historical Interpretation' in *The Poverty of Historicism* (Routledge and Kegan Paul, 1961), pp. 147–152. First published in 1957. Footnotes have been omitted.

in the face of what may be called the logic of events. Tolstoy points out, rightly, the neglected but very great importance of the decisions and actions of the countless unknown individuals who fought the battles, who burned Moscow, and who invented the partisan method of fighting. But he believes that he can see some kind of historical determination in these events – fate, historical laws, or a plan. In his version of historicism, he combines both methodological individualism and collectivism; that is to say, he represents a highly typical combination – typical of his time, and, I am afraid, of our own – of democratic-individualist and collectivist-nationalistic elements.

This example may remind us that there are *some* sound elements in historicism; it is a reaction against the naïve method of interpreting political history merely as the story of great tyrants and great generals. Historicists rightly feel that there may be something better than this method. It is this feeling which makes their idea of 'spirits' – of an age, of a nation, of an army – so seductive.

Now I have not the slightest sympathy with these 'spirits' – neither with their idealistic prototype nor with their dialectical and materialistic incarnations – and I am in full sympathy with those who treat them with contempt. And yet I feel that they indicate, at least, the existence of a lacuna, of a place which it is the task of sociology to fill with something more sensible, such as an analysis of problems arising within a tradition. There is room for a more detailed analysis of the *logic of situations*. The best historians have often made use, more or less unconsciously, of this conception: Tolstoy, for example, when he describes how it was not decision but 'necessity' which made the Russian army yield Moscow without a fight and withdraw to places where it could find food. Beyond this *logic of the situation*, or perhaps as a part of it, we need something like an analysis of social movements. We need studies, based on methodological individualism, of the social institutions through which ideas may spread and captivate individuals, of the way in which new traditions may be created, and of the way in which traditions work and break down. In other words, our individualistic and institutionalist models of such collective entities as nations, or governments, or markets, will have to be supplemented by models of political situations as well as of social movements such as scientific and industrial progress. These models may then be used by historians, partly like the other models, and partly for the purpose of explanation, along with the other universal laws they use. But even this would not be enough; it would still not satisfy all those real needs which historicism attempts to satisfy.

If we consider the historical sciences in the light of our comparison between them and the theoretical sciences, then we can see that their lack of interest in universal laws puts them in a difficult position. For in theoretical science laws act, among other things, as centres of interest to which observations are related, or as points of view from which observations are made. In history the universal laws, which for the most part are trivial and used unconsciously, cannot possibly fulfil this function. It must be taken over by something else. For undoubtedly there can be no history without a point of view; like the natural sciences, history must be *selective* unless it is to be choked by a flood of poor and unrelated material. The attempt to follow causal chains into the remote past would not help in the least, for every concrete effect with which we might start has a great number of different partial causes; that is to say, initial conditions are very complex, and most of them have little interest for us.

The only way out of this difficulty is, I believe, consciously to introduce a *preconceived selective point of view* into one's history; that is, to write *that history which interests us*. This does not mean that we may twist the facts until they fit into a framework of preconceived ideas, or that we may neglect the facts that do not fit. On the contrary, all available evidence which has a bearing on our point of view should be considered carefully and objectively (in the sense of 'scientific objectivity'). But it means that we need not worry about all those facts and aspects which have no bearing upon our point of view and which therefore do not interest us.

Such selective approaches fulfil functions in the study of history which are in some ways analogous to those of theories in science. It is therefore understandable that they have often been taken for theories. And indeed, those rare ideas inherent in these approaches which can be formulated in the form of *testable hypotheses*, whether singular or universal, may well be treated as scientific hypotheses. But as a rule, these historical 'approaches' or 'points of view' *cannot be tested*. They cannot be refuted, and apparent confirmations are therefore of no value, even if they are as numerous as the stars in the sky. We shall call such a selective point of view or focus of historical interest, if it cannot be formulated as a testable hypothesis, a *historical interpretation*.

Historicism mistakes these interpretations for theories. This is one of its cardinal errors. It is possible, for example, to interpret 'history' as the history of class struggle, or of the struggle of races for supremacy, or as the history of religious ideas, or as the history of the struggle between the 'open' and the 'closed' society, or as the history of scientific and industrial progress. All these are more or less interesting points of view, and *as such* perfectly unobjectionable. But historicists do not present them as such; they do not see that there is necessarily a plurality of interpretations which are fundamentally on the same level of both suggestiveness and arbitrariness (even though some of them may be distinguished by their *fertility* – a point of some importance). Instead, they present them as doctrines or theories, asserting that 'all history is the history of class struggle', etc. And if they actually find that their point of view is fertile, and that many facts can be ordered and interpreted in its light, then they mistake this for a confirmation, or even for a proof, of their doctrine.

On the other hand, the classical historians who rightly oppose this procedure are liable to fall into a different error. Aiming at objectivity, they feel bound to avoid any selective point of view; but since this is impossible, they usually adopt points of view without being aware of them. This must defeat their efforts to be objective, for one cannot possibly be critical of one's own point of view, and conscious of its limitations, without being aware of it.

The way out of this dilemma, of course, is to be clear about the necessity of adopting a point of view; to state this point of view plainly, and always to remain conscious that it is one among many, and that even if it should amount to a theory, it may not be testable.

SECTION ONE

Modern Life, Modernité and Modernism

3   The Salon of 1846: On the Heroism of Modern Life

Charles Baudelaire

Many people will attribute the present decadence in painting to our decadence in behaviour. This dogma of the studios, which has gained currency among the public, is a poor excuse of the artists. For they had a vested interest in ceaselessly depicting the past; it is an easier task, and one that could be turned to good account by the lazy.

It is true that the great tradition has been lost, and that the new one is not yet established.

But what *was* this great tradition, if not a habitual, everyday idealization of ancient life – a robust and martial form of life, a state of readiness on the part of each individual, which gave him a habit of gravity in his movements, and of majesty, or violence, in his attitudes? To this should be added a public splendour which found its reflection in private life. Ancient life was a great *parade*. It ministered above all to the pleasure of the eye, and this day-to-day paganism has marvellously served the arts.

Before trying to distinguish the epic side of modern life, and before bringing examples to prove that our age is no less fertile in sublime themes than past ages, we may assert that since all centuries and all peoples have had their own form of beauty, so inevitably we have ours. That is in the order of things.

All forms of beauty, like all possible phenomena, contain an element of the eternal and an element of the transitory – of the absolute and of the particular. Absolute and eternal beauty does not exist, or rather it is only an abstraction skimmed from the general surface of different beauties. The particular element in each manifestation comes from the emotions: and just as we have our own particular emotions, so we have our own beauty.[. . .]

As for the garb, the outer husk, of the modern hero, although the time is past when every little artist dressed up as a grand panjandrum and smoked pipes as long as duck-rifles, nevertheless the studios and the world at large are still full of people who would like to poeticize *Antony* with a Greek cloak and a parti-coloured vesture.*

But all the same, has not this much-abused garb its own beauty and its native charm? Is it not the necessary garb of our suffering age, which wears the symbol of a perpetual mourning even upon its thin black shoulders? Note, too, that the dress-coat and the frock-coat not only possess their political beauty, which is an expression of universal equality, but also their poetic beauty, which is an expression of the

---

* Dumas the elder's prose-drama *Antony* was produced in 1831. The central character became a powerful hero-figure of the times, and young men who cast themselves for this rôle in real life were popularly known as 'Antonys'.

Source: 'The Salon of 1846', translated by J. Mayne, *Art in Paris* (Phaidon, 1965), pp. 116–120. Some footnotes have been omitted. Baudelaire's review originally appeared as a booklet on 13 May 1846.

public soul – an immense cortège of undertaker's mutes (mutes in love, political mutes, bourgeois mutes . . .). We are each of us celebrating some funeral.

A uniform livery of affliction bears witness to equality; and as for the eccentrics, whose violent and contrasting colours used easily to betray them to the eye, today they are satisfied with slight nuances in design in cut, much more than in colour. Look at those grinning creases which play like serpents around mortified flesh – have they not their own mysterious grace? [. . .]

Let not the tribe of colourists be too indignant. For if it is more difficult, their task is thereby only the more glorious. Great colourists know how to create colour with a black coat, a white cravat and a grey background.

But to return to our principal and essential problem, which is to discover whether we possess a specific beauty, intrinsic to our new emotions, I observe that the majority of artists who have attacked modern life have contented themselves with public and official subjects – with our victories and our political heroism. Even so, they do it with an ill grace, and only because they are commissioned by the government which pays them. However there are private subjects which are very much more heroic than these.

The pageant of fashionable life and the thousands of floating existences – criminals and kept women – which drift about in the underworld of a great city; the *Gazette des Tribunaux* and the *Moniteur* all prove to us that we have only to open our eyes to recognize our heroism.

Suppose that a minister, baited by the opposition's impertinent questioning, has given expression once and for all – with that proud and sovereign eloquence which is proper to him – to his scorn and disgust for all ignorant and mischief-making oppositions. The same evening you will hear the following words buzzing round you on the Boulevard des Italiens: 'Were you in the Chamber today? and did you see the minister? Good Heavens, how handsome he was! I have never seen such scorn!'

So there *are* such things as modern beauty and modern heroism! [. . .]

The life of our city is rich in poetic and marvellous subjects. We are enveloped and steeped as though in an atmosphere of the marvellous; but we do not notice it.

The *nude* – that darling of the artists, that necessary element of success – is just as frequent and necessary today as it was in the life of the ancients; in bed, for example, or in the bath, or in the anatomy theatre. The themes and resources of painting are equally abundant and varied; but there is a new element – modern beauty.

For the heroes of the Iliad are but pigmies compared to you, Vautrin, Rastignac and Birotteau!* – and you, Fontanarès,† who dared not publicly declaim your sorrows in the funereal and tortured frock-coat which we all wear today! – and you, Honoré de Balzac, you the most heroic, the most extraordinary, the most romantic and the most poetic of all the characters that you have produced from your womb!

* Well-known characters from Balzac's novels.
† The hero of Balzac's play *Les ressources de Quinola* (1842), which was set in the sixteenth century – the period of doublet and hose.

4　　The Salon of 1859: The Modern Public and Photography

Charles Baudelaire

[. . .] For us the natural painter, like the natural poet, is almost a monster. The exclusive taste for the True (so noble a thing when it is limited to its proper applications) oppresses and stifles the taste of the Beautiful. Where one should see nothing but Beauty (I mean in a beautiful painting, and you can easily guess what is in my mind), our public looks only for Truth. The people are not artists, not naturally artists; philosophers perhaps, moralists, engineers, connoisseurs of instructive anecdotes, whatever you like, but never spontaneously artists. They feel, or rather they judge, in stages, analytically. Other more fortunate peoples feel immediately, all at once, synthetically.

I was speaking just now of artists who seek to astonish the public. The desire to astonish and to be astonished is very proper. 'It is a happiness to wonder'; but also 'it is a happiness to dream' [Poe, *Morella*]. The whole question, then, if you insist that I confer upon you the title of artist or connoisseur of the fine arts, is to know by what process you wish to create or feel wonder. Because the Beautiful is *always* wonderful, it would be absurd to suppose that what is wonderful is *always* beautiful. Now our public, which is singularly incapable of feeling the happiness of dreaming or of marvelling (a sign of its meanness of soul), wishes to be made to wonder by means which are alien to art, and its obedient artists bow to its taste; they try to strike, to surprise, to stupefy it by means of unworthy tricks, because they know that it is incapable of ecstasy in front of the natural devices of true art.

During this lamentable period, a new industry arose which contributed not a little to confirm stupidity in its faith and to ruin whatever might remain of the divine in the French mind. The idolatrous mob demanded an ideal worthy of itself and appropriate to its nature – that is perfectly understood. In matters of painting and sculpture, the present-day *Credo* of the sophisticated, above all in France (and I do not think that anyone at all would dare to state the contrary), is this: 'I believe in Nature, and I believe only in Nature (there are good reasons for that). I believe that Art is, and cannot be other than, the exact reproduction of Nature (a timid and dissident sect would wish to exclude the more repellent objects of nature, such as skeletons or chamber-pots). Thus an industry that could give us a result identical to Nature would be the absolute of art.' A revengeful God has given ear to the prayers of this multitude. Daguerre was his Messiah. And now the faithful says to himself: 'Since Photography gives us every guarantee of exactitude that we could desire (they really believe that, the mad fools!), then Photography and Art are the same thing.'

Source: 'The Salon of 1859', translated by J. Mayne, *Art in Paris* (Phaidon, 1965), pp. 149–155. Footnotes have been omitted. The whole review was originally published in four instalments between 10 June and 20 July 1859 in the *Revue Française*

From that moment our squalid society rushed, Narcissus to a man, to gaze at its trivial image on a scrap of metal. A madness, an extraordinary fanaticism took possession of all these new sun-worshippers. Strange abominations took form. By bringing together a group of male and female clowns, got up like butchers and laundry-maids at a carnival, and by begging these *heroes* to be so kind as to hold their chance grimaces for the time necessary for the performance, the operator flattered himself that he was reproducing tragic or elegant scenes from ancient history. Some democratic writer ought to have seen here a cheap method of disseminating a loathing for history and for painting among the people, thus committing a double sacrilege and insulting at one and the same time the divine art of painting and the noble art of the actor. A little later a thousand hungry eyes were bending over the peepholes of the stereoscope, as though they were the attic-windows of the infinite. The love of pornography, which is no less deep-rooted in the natural heart of man than the love of himself, was not to let slip so fine an opportunity of self-satisfaction. And do not imagine that it was only children on their way back from school who took pleasure in these follies; the world was infatuated with them. [. . .]

As the photographic industry was the refuge of every would-be painter, every painter too ill-endowed or too lazy to complete his studies, this universal infatuation bore not only the mark of a blindness, an imbecility, but had also the air of a vengeance. I do not believe, or at least I do not wish to believe, in the absolute success of such a brutish conspiracy, in which, as in all others, one finds both fools and knaves; but I am convinced that the ill-applied developments of photography, like all other purely material developments of progress, have contributed much to the impoverishment of the French artistic genius, which is already so scarce. In vain may our modern Fatuity roar, belch forth all the rumbling wind of its rotund stomach, spew out all the undigested sophisms with which recent philosophy has stuffed it from top to bottom; it is nonetheless obvious that this industry, by invading the territories of art, has become art's most mortal enemy, and that the confusion of their several functions prevents any of them from being properly fulfilled. Poetry and progress are like two ambitious men who hate one another with an instinctive hatred, and when they meet upon the same road, one of them has to give place. If photography is allowed to supplement art in some of its functions, it will soon have supplanted or corrupted it altogether, thanks to the stupidity of the multitude which is its natural ally. It is time, then, for it to return to its true duty, which is to be the servant of the sciences and arts – but the very humble servant, like printing or shorthand, which have neither created nor supplemented literature. Let it hasten to enrich the tourist's album and restore to his eye the precision which his memory may lack; let it adorn the naturalist's library, and enlarge microscopic animals; let it even provide information to corroborate the astronomer's hypotheses; in short, let it be the secretary and clerk of whoever needs an absolute factual exactitude in his profession – up to that point nothing could be better. Let it rescue from oblivion those tumbling ruins, those books, prints and manuscripts which time is devouring, precious things whose form is dissolving and which demand a place in the archives of our memory – it will be thanked and applauded. But if it be allowed to encroach upon the domain of the impalpable and the imaginary, upon anything whose value depends solely upon the addition of something of a man's soul, then it will be so much the worse for us!

I know very well that some people will retort, 'The disease which you have just been diagnosing is a disease of imbeciles. What man worthy of the name of artist, and what true connoisseur, has ever confused art with industry?' I know it; and yet I will ask them in my turn if they believe in the contagion of good and evil, in the action of the mass on individuals, and in the involuntary, forced obedience of the individual to the mass. It is an incontestable, an irresistible law that the artist should act upon the public, and that the public should react upon the artist; and besides, those terrible witnesses, the facts, are easy to study; the disaster is verifiable. Each day art further diminishes its self-respect by bowing down before external reality; each day the painter becomes more and more given to painting not what he dreams but what he sees. Nevertheless *it is a happiness to dream*, and it used to be a glory to express what one dreamt. But I ask you! does the painter still know this happiness?

Could you find an honest observer to declare that the invasion of photography and the great industrial madness of our times have no part at all in this deplorable result? Are we to suppose that a people whose eyes are growing used to considering the results of a material science as though they were the products of the beautiful, will not in the course of time have singularly diminished its faculties of judging and of feeling what are among the most ethereal and immaterial aspects of creation?

special nature of present-day beauty. The draperies of Rubens or Veronese will in no way teach you how to depict *moire antique, satin à la reine* or any other fabric of modern manufacture, which we see supported and hung over crinoline or starched muslin petticoat. In texture and weave these are quite different from the fabrics of ancient Venice or those worn at the court of Catherine. Furthermore the cut of skirt and bodice is by no means similar; the pleats are arranged according to a new system. Finally the gesture and the bearing of the woman of today give to her dress a life and a special character which are not those of the woman of the past. In short, for any 'modernity' to be worthy of one day taking its place as 'antiquity', it is necessary for the mysterious beauty which human life accidentally puts into it to be distilled from it. [. . .]

I have remarked that every age had its own gait, glance and gesture. The easiest way to verify this proposition would be to betake oneself to some vast portrait-gallery, such as the one at Versailles. But it has an even wider application. Within that unity which we call a Nation, the various professions and classes and the passing centuries all introduce variety, not only in manners and gesture, but even in the actual form of the face. Certain types of nose, mouth and brow will be found to dominate the scene for a period whose extent I have no intention of attempting to determine here, but which could certainly be subjected to a form of calculation. Considerations of this kind are not sufficiently familiar to our portrait-painters; the great failing of M. Ingres, in particular, is that he seeks to impose upon every type of sitter a more or less complete, by which I mean a more or less despotic, form of perfection, borrowed from the repertory of classical ideas.

In a matter of this kind it would be easy, and indeed legitimate, to argue *a priori*. The perpetual correlation between what is called the 'soul' and what is called the 'body' explains quite clearly how everything that is 'material', or in other words an emanation of the 'spiritual', mirrors, and will always mirror, the spiritual reality from which it derives. If a painstaking, scrupulous, but feebly imaginative artist has to paint a courtesan of today and takes his 'inspiration' (that is the accepted word) from a courtesan by Titian or Raphael, it is only too likely that he will produce a work which is false, ambiguous and obscure. From the study of a masterpiece of that time and type he will learn nothing of the bearing, the glance, the smile or the living 'style' of one of those creatures whom the dictionary of fashion has successively classified under the coarse or playful titles of 'doxies', 'kept women', *lorettes* or *biches*.

The same criticism may be strictly applied to the study of the military man and the dandy, and even to that of animals, whether horses or dogs; in short, of everything that goes to make up the external life of this age. Woe to him who studies the antique for anything else but pure art, logic and general method! By steeping himself too thoroughly in it, he will lose all memory of the present; he will renounce the rights and privileges offered by circumstance – for almost all our originality comes from the seal which Time imprints on our sensations. I need hardly tell you that I could easily support my assertions with reference to many objects other than women. What would you say, for example, of a marine painter (I am deliberately going to extremes) who, having to depict the sober and elegant beauty of a modern vessel, were to tire out his eyes by studying the overcharged, involved forms and the monumental poop of a galleon, or the complicated rigging of the sixteenth century? Again, what would you think if you had commissioned an artist to paint the portrait of a thoroughbred, famed in the annals of the turf, and he then proceeded to confine

5   The Painter of Modern Life

Charles Baudelaire

Modernity

[. . .] Be very sure that this man [Constantin Guys], such as I have depicted him – this solitary, gifted with an active imagination, ceaselessly journeying across the great human desert – has an aim loftier than that of a mere *flâneur*, an aim more general, something other than the fugitive pleasure of circumstance. He is looking for that quality which you must allow me to call 'modernity'; for I know of no better word to express the idea I have in mind. He makes it his business to extract from fashion whatever element it may contain of poetry within history, to distil the eternal from the transitory. Casting an eye over our exhibitions of modern pictures, we are struck by a general tendency among artists to dress all their subjects in the garments of the past. Almost all of them make use of the costumes and furnishings of the Renaissance, just as David employed the costumes and furnishings of Rome. There is however this difference, that David, by choosing subjects which were specifically Greek or Roman, had no alternative but to dress them in antique garb, whereas the painters of today, though choosing subjects of a general nature and applicable to all ages, nevertheless persist in rigging them out in the costumes of the Middle Ages, the Renaissance or the Orient. This is clearly symptomatic of a great degree of laziness; for it is much easier to decide outright that everything about the garb of an age is absolutely ugly than to devote oneself to the task of distilling from it the mysterious element of beauty that it may contain, however slight or minimal that element may be. By 'modernity' I mean the ephemeral, the fugitive, the contingent, the half of art whose other half is the eternal and the immutable. Every old master has had his own modernity; the great majority of fine portraits that have come down to us from former generations are clothed in the costume of their own period. They are perfectly harmonious, because everything – from costume and coiffure down to gesture, glance and smile (for each age has a deportment, a glance and a smile of its own) – everything, I say, combines to form a completely viable whole. This transitory, fugitive element, whose metamorphoses are so rapid, must on no account be despised or dispensed with. By neglecting it, you cannot fail to tumble into the abyss of an abstract and indeterminate beauty, like that of the first woman before the fall of man. If for the necessary and inevitable costume of the age you substitute another, you will be guilty of a mistranslation only to be excused in the case of a masquerade prescribed by fashion. (Thus, the goddesses, nymphs and sultanas of the eighteenth century are still convincing portraits, *morally* speaking.)

It is doubtless an excellent thing to study the old masters in order to learn how to paint; but it can be no more than a waste of labour if your aim is to understand the

Source: *The Painter of Modern Life and Other Essays*, translated by J. Mayne (Phaidon, 1964); pp. 12–15 'Modernity' and pp. 34–38 'Women and prostitutes'. The whole essay was originally published in instalments in *Figaro*, 26 and 28 November and 3 December 1863. Footnotes have been omitted.

his researches to the Museums and contented himself with a study of the horse in the galleries of the past, in Van Dyck, Borgognone or Van der Meulen? [. . .]

Women and prostitutes

Having taken upon himself the task of seeking out and expounding the beauty in *modernity*, Monsieur G. [Constantin Guys] is thus particularly given to portraying women who are elaborately dressed and embellished by all the rites of artifice, to whatever social station they may belong. Moreover in the complete assemblage of his works, no less than in the swarming ant-hill of human life itself, differences of class and breed are made immediately obvious to the spectator's eye, in whatever luxurious trappings the subjects may be decked.

At one moment, bathed in the diffused brightness of an auditorium, it is young women of the most fashionable society, receiving and reflecting the light with their eyes, their jewelry and their snowy, white shoulders, as glorious as portraits framed in their boxes. Some are grave and serious, others blonde and brainless. Some flaunt precocious bosoms with an aristocratic unconcern, others frankly display the chests of young boys. They tap their teeth with their fans, while their gaze is vacant or set; they are as solemn and stagey as the play or opera that they are pretending to follow.

Next we watch elegant families strolling at leisure in the walks of a public garden, the wives leaning calmly on the arms of their husbands, whose solid and complacent air tells of a fortune made and their resulting self-esteem. Proud distinction has given way to a comfortable affluence. Meanwhile skinny little girls with billowing petticoats, who by their figures and gestures put one in mind of little women, are skipping, playing with hoops or gravely paying social calls in the open air, thus rehearsing the comedy performed at home by their parents.

Now for a moment we move to a lowlier theatrical world where the little dancers, frail, slender, hardly more than children, but proud of appearing at last in the blaze of the limelight, are shaking upon their virginal, puny shoulders absurd fancy-dresses which belong to no period, and are their joy and their delight.

Or at a café door, as he lounges against the windows lit from within and without, we watch the display of one of those half-wit peacocks whose elegance is the creation of his tailor and whose head of his barber. Beside him, her feet supported on the inevitable footstool, sits his mistress, a great baggage who lacks practically nothing to make her into a great lady – that 'practically nothing' being in fact 'practically everything', for it is *distinction*. Like her dainty companion, she has an enormous cigar entirely filling the aperture of her tiny mouth. These two beings have not a single thought in their heads. Is it even certain that they can see? Unless, like Narcissuses of imbecility, they are gazing at the crowd as at a river which reflects their own image. In truth, they exist very much more for the pleasure of the observer than for their own.

And now the doors are being thrown open at Valentino's, at the Prado or the Casino – those Bedlams where the exuberance of idle youth is given free rein. Women who have exaggerated the fashion to the extent of perverting its charm and totally destroying its aims, are ostentatiously sweeping the floor with their trains and the fringes of their shawls; they come and go, pass and repass, opening an astonished eye like animals, giving an impression of total blindness, but missing nothing.

Against a background of hellish light, or if you prefer, an *aurora borealis* – red, orange, sulphur-yellow, pink (to express an idea of ecstasy amid frivolity), and sometimes purple (the favourite colour of canonesses, like dying embers seen through a blue curtain) – against magical backgrounds such as these, which remind one of variegated Bengal Lights, there arises the Protean image of wanton beauty. Now she is majestic, now playful; now slender, even to the point of skinniness, now cyclopean; now tiny and sparkling, now heavy and monumental. She has discovered for herself a provocative and barbaric sort of elegance, or else she aspires, with more or less success, towards the simplicity which is customary in a better world. She advances towards us, glides, dances, or moves about with her burden of embroidered petticoats, which play the part at once of pedestal and balancing-rod; her eye flashes out from under her hat, like a portrait in its frame. She is a perfect image of the savagery that lurks in the midst of civilization. She has her own sort of beauty, which comes to her from Evil always devoid of spirituality, but sometimes tinged with a weariness which imitates true melancholy. She directs her gaze at the horizon, like a beast of prey; the same wildness, the same lazy absent-mindedness, and also, at times, the same fixity of attention. She is a sort of gipsy wandering on the fringes of a regular society, and the triviality of her life, which is one of warfare and cunning, fatally grins through its envelope of show. The following words of that inimitable master, La Bruyère, may be justly applied to her: 'Some women possess an artificial nobility which is associated with a movement of the eye, a tilt of the head, a manner of deportment, and which goes no further.'

These reflections concerning the courtesan are applicable within certain limits to the actress also; for she too is a creature of show, an object of public pleasure. Here however the conquest and the prize are of a nobler and more spiritual kind. With her it is a question of winning the heart of the public not only by means of sheer physical beauty, but also through talents of the rarest order. If in one aspect the actress is akin to the courtesan, in another she comes close to the poet. We must never forget that quite apart from natural, and even artificial, beauty, each human being bears the distinctive stamp of his trade, a characteristic which can be translated into physical ugliness, but also into a sort of 'professional' beauty.

In that vast picture-gallery which is life in London or Paris, we shall meet with all the various types of fallen womanhood – of woman in revolt against society – at all levels. First we see the courtesan in her prime, striving after patrician airs, proud at once of her youth and the luxury into which she puts all her soul and all her genius, as she delicately uses two fingers to tuck in a wide panel of silk, satin or velvet which billows around her, or points a toe whose over-ornate shoe would be enough to betray her for what she is, if the somewhat unnecessary extravagance of her whole toilette had not done so already. Descending the scale, we come down to the poor slaves of those filthy stews which are often, however, decorated like cafés; hapless wretches, subject to the most extortionate restraint, possessing nothing of their own, not even the eccentric finery which serves as spice and setting to their beauty.

Some of these, examples of an innocent and monstrous self-conceit, express in their faces and their bold, uplifted glances an obvious joy at being alive (and indeed, one wonders why). Sometimes, quite by chance, they achieve poses of a daring and nobility to enchant the most sensitive of sculptors, if the sculptors of today were sufficiently bold and imaginative to seize upon nobility wherever it was to be found, even in the mire; at other times they display themselves in hopeless attitudes of boredom, in bouts of tap-room apathy, almost masculine in their brazenness, killing time with cigarettes, orientally resigned – stretched out, sprawling on settees, their skirts hooped up in front and behind like a double fan, or else precariously balanced on stools and chairs; sluggish, glum, stupid, extravagant, their eyes glazed with brandy and their foreheads swelling with obstinate pride. We have climbed down to the last lap of the spiral, down to the *femina simplex* [unadorned woman] of the Roman satirist [Juvenal, *Satire VI*]. And now, sketched against an atmospheric background in which both tobacco and alcohol have mingled their fumes, we see the emaciated flush of consumption or the rounded contours of obesity, that hideous health of the slothful. In a foggy, gilded chaos, whose very existence is unsuspected by the chaste and the poor, we assist at the Dervish dances of macabre nymphs and living dolls whose childish eyes betray a sinister glitter, while behind a bottle-laden counter there lolls in state an enormous Xanthippe [wife of Socrates, notorious for her ill nature] whose head, wrapped in a dirty kerchief, casts upon the wall a satanically pointed shadow, thus reminding us that everything that is consecrated to Evil is condemned to wear horns.

Please do not think that it was in order to gratify the reader, any more than to scandalize him, that I have spread before his eyes pictures such as these; in either case this would have been to treat him with less than due respect. What in fact gives these works their value and, as it were, sanctifies them is the wealth of thoughts to which they give rise – thoughts however which are generally solemn and dark. If by chance anyone should be so ill-advised as to seek here an opportunity of satisfying his unhealthy curiosity, I must in all charity warn him that he will find nothing whatever to stimulate the sickness of his imagination. He will find nothing but the inevitable image of vice, the demon's eye ambushed in the shadows or Messalina's shoulder gleaming under the gas; nothing but pure art, by which I mean the special beauty of evil, the beautiful amid the horrible. In fact, if I may repeat myself in passing, the general feeling which emanates from all this chaos partakes more of gloom than of gaiety. It is their moral fecundity which gives these drawings their special beauty. They are heavy with suggestion, but cruel, harsh suggestion which my pen, accustomed though it is to grappling with the plastic arts, has perhaps interpreted only too inadequately.

6   Edouard Manet

Emile Zola

The man and the artist

Edouard Manet was born in Paris in 1833. I have only a few biographical details concerning him. In this orderly police state of ours, an artist's life is the same as that of any quiet bourgeois; he paints his pictures in his studio as others sell pepper over their counters. The long-haired types of 1830, thank heavens, have completely disappeared, and our painters have become what they ought to be – people living the same life as everyone else.

After spending some years with the Abbé Poiloup at Vaugirard, Edouard Manet finished his education at the Collège Rollin. At the age of seventeen, on leaving college, he fell in love with painting. What a terrible love that is – parents tolerate a mistress, even two; they will close their eyes if necessary to a straying heart and senses. But the Arts! Painting for them is the Scarlet Woman, the Courtesan, always hungry for flesh, who must drink the blood of their children, who clutches them, panting, to her insatiable lips. Here is Orgy unforgivable, Debauchery – the bloody spectre which appears sometimes in the midst of families and upsets the peace of the domestic hearth. [. . .]

Contemporary fools, who earn their living by making the public laugh, have turned Manet into a sort of Bohemian character, a rogue, a ridiculous bogey, and the public has accepted the jokes and the caricatures as so much truth. The truth is far removed from these dummies, created in the imagination of penny-a-line humorists, and it is in order to present the real man that I write these lines.

The artist has confessed to me that he adores society and that he found secret pleasure in the perfumed and glittering refinement of *soirées*. He was drawn to them by his love of bold and vivid colour [. . .] Then he returns to his home and there tastes the quiet pleasures of the modern bourgeois. [. . .]

I really *had* to write these lines before speaking of Manet as an artist. I feel it is much easier now to tell people who are already prejudiced what I believe to be the truth. I hope that people will cease to treat this man, whose portrait I have attempted to trace in a few lines, as a slovenly dauber, and that they will pay polite attention to the unbiased opinions which I am going to give on a sincere and dedicated artist. [. . .]

This is how I explain the birth of a true artist, Edouard Manet, for example. Feeling that he was making no progress by copying the masters, or by painting

Source: 'Une nouvelle manière en peinture: Edouard Manet' first appeared on 1 January 1867 in the *Revue du XIX Siècle*; then for a second time under the title *Edouard Manet, Étude Biographique et Critique* (Dentu, Paris) on the occasion of Manet's one-man show which he opened in Paris at the end of May 1867. This extract is from P. Courthion and P. Cailler, *Portrait of Manet by Himself and his Contemporaries*, translated by M. Ross (Cassell, 1960), pp. 116–139.

Nature as seen through the eyes of individuals who differed in character from himself, he came to understand, quite naturally, one fine day, that it only remained to him to see Nature as it really is, without looking at the works or studying the opinions of others. From the moment he conceived this idea, he took some object, person or thing, placed it at the end of his studio and began to reproduce it on his canvas in accordance with his own outlook and understanding. He made an effort to forget everything he had learned in museums; he tried to forget all the advice that he had been given and all the paintings that he had ever seen. All that remained was a singular gifted intelligence in the presence of Nature, translating it in its own manner.

Thus the artist produced an *œuvre* which was his own flesh and blood. Certainly, this work was linked with the great family of works already created by mankind; it resembled, more or less, certain among them. But it had in a high degree its own beauty – I should say vitality and personal quality. The different components, taken perhaps from here and there, of which it was composed, combined to produce a completely new flavour and personal point of view; and this combination, created for the first time, was an aspect of things hitherto unknown to human genius. From then onwards Manet found his direction; or to put it better, he had found himself. He was seeing things with his own eyes, and in each of his canvases he was able to give us a translation of Nature in that original language which he had just found in himself. [. . .]

Here is the popular opinion concerning art. There is an 'absolute' of beauty which is regarded as something outside the artist or, to express it better, there is a perfect ideal for which every artist reaches out, and which he attains more or less successfully. From this it is assumed that there is a common denominator of beauty. This common denominator is applied to every picture produced, and according to how far the work approaches or recedes from this common denominator, the work is declared good or less good. Circumstances have elected that the Classical Greek should be regarded as the standard of beauty, so that all works of art created by mankind have ever since been judged on their greater or lesser resemblance to Greek works of art. [. . .]

Here, then, is what I believe concerning art. I embrace all humanity that has ever lived and which at all times, in all climates, under all circumstances, has felt, in the presence of Nature, an imperious need to create and reproduce objects and people by means of the arts. Thus I have a vast panorama, each part of which interests and moves me profoundly. Every great artist who comes to the fore gives us a new and personal vision of Nature. Here 'reality' is the fixed element, and it is the differences in outlook of the artists which has given to works of art their individual characteristics. For me, it is the different outlooks, the constantly changing viewpoints, that give works of art their tremendous human interest. I would like all the pictures of all the painters in the world to be assembled in one vast hall where, picture by picture, we would be able to read the epic of human creation. The theme would always be this self-same 'nature', this self-same 'reality' and the variations on the theme would be achieved by the individual and original methods by which artists depict God's great creation. In order to pronounce fair judgment on works of art, the public should stand in the middle of the vast hall. Here beauty is no longer 'absolute' – a ridiculous common denominator. Beauty becomes human life itself; the human element, mixed with the fixed element of 'reality' giving birth to a creation which belongs to mankind. Beauty lies within us, and not without. What is the use of philosophic abstractions! Of what use is a perfection dreamed up by a little group of men! It is humanity that interests me. What moves me, what gives me exquisite pleasure is to find in each of the creations of man an artist, a brother, who shows me with all his strength and with all his tenderness the face of Nature under a different guise.

A work of art, seen in this way, tells me the story of flesh and blood; it speaks to me of civilizations and of countries. And when in the midst of the vast hall I cast an eye over the immense collection, I see before me the same poem in a thousand different languages, and I never tire of re-reading it in each different picture, enchanted by the delivery or strength of each dialect. [. . .]

The ridiculous common denominator does not exist any more; the critic studies a picture for what it is, and pronounces it a great work when he finds in it a vital and original interpretation of reality. He can then state that to the genesis of human creation another page has been added; that an artist has been born who has given Nature a new soul and new horizons. Our creation stretches from the past into an infinite future. Every society will produce its artists, who will bring with them their own points of view. No systems, no theories can hold back life in these unceasing productions.

Our task then, as judges of art, is limited to establishing the language and the characters; to study the languages and to say what new subtlety and energy they possess. The philosophers, if necessary, will take it on themselves to draw up formulas. I only want to analyse facts, and works of art are nothing but simple facts.

Thus I put the past on one side – I have no rules or standards – I stand in front of Edouard Manet's pictures as if I were standing in front of something quite new which I wish to explain and comment upon.

What first strikes me in these pictures, is how true is the delicate relationship of tone values. Let me explain. . . . Some fruit is placed on a table and stands out against a grey background. Between the fruit, according to whether they are nearer or further away, there are gradations of colour producing a complete scale of tints. If you start with a 'note' which is lighter than the real note, you must paint the whole in a lighter key; and the contrary is true if you start with a note which is lower in tone. Here is what I believe is called 'the law of values'. I know of scarcely anyone of the modern school, with the exception of Corot, Courbet and Edouard Manet, who constantly obeys this law when painting people. Their works gain thereby a singular precision, great truth and an appearance of great charm.

Manet usually paints in a higher key than is actually the case in Nature. His paintings are light in tone, luminous and pale throughout. An abundance of pure light gently illuminates his subjects. There is not the slightest forced effect here; people and landscapes are bathed in a sort of gay translucence which permeates the whole canvas.

What strikes me is due to the exact observation of the law of tone values. The artist, confronted with some subject or other, allows himself to be guided by his eyes which perceive this subject in terms of broad colours which control each other. A head posed against a wall becomes only a patch of something more, or less, grey; and the clothing, in juxtaposition to the head, becomes, for example, a patch of colour which is more, or less, white. Thus a great simplicity is achieved – hardly any details, a combination of accurate and delicate patches of colour, which, from a few paces away, give the picture an impressive sense of relief.

I stress this characteristic of Edouard Manet's works, because it is their dominating feature and makes them what they are. The whole of the artist's personality consists in the way his eye functions: he sees things in terms of light colour and masses.

What strikes me in the third place is his elegance – a little dry but charming. Let us understand each other. I am not referring to the pink and white elegance of the heads of china dolls, I am referring to a penetrating and truly human elegance. Edouard Manet is a man of the world and in his pictures there are certain exquisite lines, certain pretty and graceful *attitudes* which testify to his love for the elegance of the salons. Therein the unconscious element, the true nature of the painter is revealed. And here I take the opportunity to deny the existence of any relationship (as has been claimed) between the paintings of Edouard Manet and the verses of Charles Baudelaire. I know that a lively sympathy has brought painter and poet together, but I believe that the former has never had the stupidity, like so many others, to put 'ideas' into his painting. The brief analysis of his talent which I have just made, proves with what lack of affectation he confronts Nature. [. . .]

It has been said that Edouard Manet's canvases recall the 'penny-plain, twopence-coloured' pictures from Epinal. There is a lot of truth in this joke which is in fact a compliment. Here and there the manner of working is the same, the colours are applied in broad patches, but with this difference, that the workmen of Epinal employ primary colours without bothering about values, while Edouard Manet uses many more colours and relates them exactly. It would be much more interesting to compare this simplified style of painting with Japanese engravings, which resemble Manet's work in their strange elegance and magnificent bold patches of colour.

One's first impression of a picture by Edouard Manet is that it is a trifle 'hard'. One is not accustomed to seeing reproductions of reality so simplified and so sincere. But as I have said, they possess a certain stiff but surprising elegance. To begin with one's eye only notices broad patches of colour, but soon objects become more defined and appear in their correct place.

After a few moments, the whole composition is apparent as something vigorous; and one experiences a real delight in studying this clear and serious painting which, if I may put it this way, renders Nature in a manner both gentle *and* harsh.

On coming close to the picture, one notices that the technique is more delicate than bold; the artist uses only a brush and that with great caution; there is no heavy impasto, only an even coat of paint. This bold painter, who has been so hounded, works in a very calculated manner, and if his works are in any way odd, this is only due to the very personal way in which he sees and translates objects on to canvas.

In a word, if I were interrogated, if I were asked what new language Manet was speaking, I would answer, 'He speaks in a language which is composed of simplicity and truth.' The note which he strikes in his pictures is a luminous one which fills his canvas with light. The rendering which he gives us is truthful and simplified, obtained by composing his pictures in large masses.

I cannot repeat too often that, in order to understand and savour his talent, we must forget a thousand things. It is not a question, here, of seeking for an 'absolute' of beauty. The artist is neither painting history nor his soul. What is termed 'composition' does not exist for him, and he has not set himself the task of representing some abstract idea or some historical episode. And it is because of this that he should neither be judged as a moralist nor as a literary man. He should be judged simply as a painter. He treats figure subjects in just the same way as still-life subjects are treated in art schools; what I mean to say is that he groups figures more or less fortuitously, and after that he has no other thought than to put them down on canvas as he sees them, in strong contrast to each other. Don't expect anything of him except a truthful and literal interpretation. He neither sings nor philosophizes. He knows how to paint and that is all. He has his own personal gift, which is to appreciate the delicacy of the dominant tones and to model objects and people in simplified masses. He is a child of our age. I see him as an analyst painter. All problems have been re-examined; science requires solid foundations and this has been achieved by accurate observation of facts. This approach is not confined to the world of science alone. In all branches of knowledge and in all the works of mankind, man has tended to find basic and definitive principles in reality.

Compared with our historical and *genre* painters, our modern landscape artists have achieved much more, because they have studied our countryside, content to interpret the first corner of a forest they came upon. Manet uses this same method in each of his works; while others break their heads trying to compose a new picture of *The Death of Cæsar* or *Socrates Drinking Hemlock*, he quietly places some objects or poses some people in a corner of his studio and begins to paint. I repeat, he is merely an analyst. His work is much more interesting than the plagiarisms of his colleagues. Art as practised by him leads to ultimate truth. This artist is an interpreter of things as they are, and, for me, his works have the great merit of being accurate descriptions, rendered in an original and human language.

He has been reproached for imitating the Spanish Masters. I agree that in his first works, there is a resemblance – one must be somebody's child. But after painting his *Le Déjeuner sur l'Herbe*, he has, it seems to me, established definitely that personality which I have tried to explain and upon which I have briefly commented. Perhaps the truth is that the public, seeing him paint Spanish scenes and costumes, decided that he was taking his models from beyond the Pyrenees, and, this being the case, the accusation of plagiarism soon followed.

But it is as well to know that if Edouard Manet painted his *espada* and *majo*, it was because he had Spanish costumes in his studio and found their colours beautiful. It was only in 1865 that he travelled across Spain; his canvases are too individual in character for him to be taken as nothing more than an illegitimate child of Velazquez or Goya.

His works

[. . .] I am only going to speak of the pictures which seem to me to be the flesh and blood of Edouard Manet. To begin with there are the pictures of 1863 which, when exhibited at Martinet's in the Boulevard des Italiens, caused a veritable uproar. As usual, hissing and cat-calls announced the fact that a new and original artist had just revealed himself. There were fourteen pictures exhibited; we will find them again at the Universal Exhibition. [. . .]

As far as *Lola de Valence* is concerned, she is extolled in Charles Baudelaire's quatrain which was hissed and treated in much the same way as the picture itself:

> *Entre tant de beautés que partout on peut voir,*
> *Je comprends bien, amis, que le désir balance*
> *Mais on voit scintiller dans Lola de Valence*
> *Le charme inattendu d'un bijou rose et noir.* *

I don't pretend to defend this verse but, for me, it has the great merit of summing up in rhyme the whole of the artist's individuality. It is perfectly true that *Lola de Valence* is a *bijou rose et noir*. The painter by now is already working only in masses [*taches*] and his Spanish woman is painted largely in bold contrasts. The whole canvas is painted in only two tones.

The picture which I prefer amongst these is *La Chanteuse des Rues*. A young woman, well known on the heights of the Panthéon, is making her exit from a brasserie, eating cherries which she holds in a sheet of paper. The whole work is in a soft pale grey. The subject here seems to me to have been analysed with extreme simplicity and accuracy. A work such as this has, apart from its subject, a dignity which makes it appear larger than it really is. One is aware of the search for truth and the conscientiousness of a man who, above all, is setting down honestly what he sees. [. . .]

In the Salon des Refusés, in 1863, Edouard Manet exhibited three paintings. I do not know whether it was because he was a persecuted man, but, on this occasion, the artist did find some people to come to his defence and even some admirers. It must be admitted that his contribution to the exhibition was one of the most outstanding; it consisted of *Le Déjeuner sur l'Herbe*, *Portrait de Jeune Homme en Costume de Majo* and *Portrait de Mademoiselle V . . . en Costume d'Espada*.

These last two pictures were considered to be quite outrageous, but they were painted with unusual vigour and were extremely strong in tone. I consider that here the painter showed himself more of a colourist than usual. The paint is always fresh – but savagely and startlingly fresh. The separate masses are applied thickly and boldly and stand out from the background with all the vividness of Nature.

Le Déjeuner sur l'Herbe is Edouard Manet's largest picture, in which he has realized the dream of all painters – to pose life-size figures in a landscape. One knows how skilfully he has overcome this problem. There is some foliage, a few tree trunks, and in the background a river in which a woman in a shift is bathing. In the foreground two young men are seated facing a second woman who has just emerged from the water and who is drying her naked body in the open air. This nude woman has shocked the public which has been unable to see anything but her in the picture. Good heavens! How indecent! What! A woman without a stitch of clothing seated between two fully clad men! Such a thing has never been seen before! But this belief

---

* Which may be roughly translated as:
    Among so many beauties, everywhere to be seen,
    I well know, friends, desire swings to and fro,
    But one sees sparkling in Lola of Valencia
    The unexpected charm of a rose and black jewel.

[Editors' translation]

is a gross error; in the Musée du Louvre there are more than fifty pictures in which clothed people mix with the naked. But no one goes to the Louvre to be shocked. Besides, the public has taken good care not to judge *Le Déjeuner sur l'Herbe* as a true work of art. The only thing it has noticed is that some people are eating, seated on the grass after bathing. It was considered that the artist's choice of subject was obscene and showy, whereas all that the artist had sought to do was to obtain an effect of strong contrasts and bold masses. Artists, especially Manet, who is an analytical painter, do not have this preoccupation with subject matter which, more than anything else, worries the public. For example the nude woman in *Le Déjeuner sur l'Herbe* is undoubtedly only there to give the artist an opportunity of painting flesh. What you have to look for in the picture is not just a picnic on the grass, but the whole landscape, with its bold and subtle passages, its broadly painted solid foreground, its light and delicate background and that firm flesh modelled in broad areas of light, those supple and strong materials, and, particularly that delicate splash of white among the green leaves in the background; in fact to look at the whole of this vast, airy composition, at this attention to Nature, rendered with such accurate simplicity – at the whole of this admirable work, in which the artist has concentrated his unique and rare gifts. [. . .]

In 1865, Manet was still admitted to the Salon where he exhibited *Jésus Insulté par les Soldats* and his masterpiece, *Olympia*. I say 'masterpiece' and I don't retract the word. I maintain that this painting is the veritable flesh and blood of the painter. It contains everything the artist has in him and nothing but the artist. It will remain as the most characteristic example of his talent, his greatest achievement. In it I descried the personality of Edouard Manet, and when I made an analysis of the artist's character, it was precisely this picture, which incorporates all his characteristics, that I had in my mind's eye. Here we have one of those 'penny-plain, twopence-coloured' pictures as the professional humorists say. Olympia, lying on white linen sheets, appears as a large pale mass against a black background. In this black background is seen the head of a Negress carrying a bouquet of flowers, and that famous cat which so diverted the public. At first sight one is aware of only two tones in the picture – two violently contrasting tones. Moreover, all details have disappeared. Look at the head of the young girl: the lips are just two thin pink lines, the eyes are reduced to a few black strokes. Now look closely at the bouquet, I beg you. Simple masses of rose colour, blue and green. Everything is simplified, and if you want to reconstruct reality, move back a few paces. Then a strange thing happens – each object falls into correct relation, the head of Olympia stands out in astonishing relief from the background, the bouquet becomes a marvel of brilliance and freshness. Accuracy of vision and simplicity of handling have achieved this miracle. The artist has worked in the same manner as Nature, in large, lightly coloured masses, in large areas of light, and his work has the slightly crude and austere look of Nature itself. But the artist has his *partis pris* [prejudices]: for art can only exist by enthusiasm. These *partis pris* consist of precisely that elegant dryness and those violent contrasts which I have pointed out. Here is the personal touch, which gives his works their peculiar flavour. Nothing is more exquisitely delicate than the pale tones of the different white of the linen on which Olympia reclines: in the juxtaposition of these whites an immense difficulty has been overcome. The pale colouring of the child's body is charming. She is a young girl of sixteen, no doubt a model whom Edouard Manet calmly painted just as she was. And yet everybody cried out in protest: the nude body was found to be indecent – but naturally, because here was flesh – a naked girl whose charms are already a little faded, whom the artist had thrown on to canvas. When our artists give us a Venus, they 'correct' Nature, but Edouard Manet has asked himself, 'Why lie, why not tell the truth?' He has made us acquainted with Olympia, a contemporary girl, the sort of girl we meet every day on the pavements, with thin shoulders wrapped in a flimsy faded woollen shawl. The public as usual has taken good care not to understand the painter's intentions. Some people tried to find a philosophic meaning in the picture, others, more light-hearted, were not displeased to attach an obscene significance to it.

Ho there! proclaim out loud to them, *cher Maître*, that you are not at all what they imagine, and a picture for you is simply an excuse for an exercise in analysis. You needed a nude woman and you chose Olympia, the first-comer. You needed some clear and luminous patches of colour, so you added a bouquet of flowers; you found it necessary to have some dark patches so you placed in a corner a Negress and a cat. What does all this amount to – you scarcely know, no more do I. But I know that you have succeeded admirably in doing a painter's job, the job of a great painter; I mean to say you have forcefully reproduced in your own particular idiom the truths of light and shade and the reality of objects and creatures.

I come now to the last works, those which the public does not know. Note the inconstancy of human beings: Edouard Manet, accepted by the Salon twice consecutively, is flatly rejected in 1866. The strangely original *Olympia* is accepted, but neither *Le Joueur de Fifre* nor *L'Acteur Tragique* [. . .] One of our great modern landscape painters has said that this picture [*Le Joueur de Fifre*] is a 'tailor's shop-sign', and I agree with him if by that he meant that the costume of the young musician is treated with the simplicity of a poster. The yellow of the braid, the blue-black of the tunic, the red of the trousers, are here again no more than flat patches of colour. This simplification, produced by the acute and perceptive eye of the artist, has resulted in a picture full of light and *naïveté*, charming to the point of delicacy, yet realistic to the point of ruggedness. [. . .]

Such is the work of Edouard Manet, such is the *ensemble* which, I hope, the public will be invited to see in the galleries of the Universal Exhibition. I cannot believe that the public will remain blind and mocking when they see this harmonious and perfect collection which I have just briefly discussed. There will be such a manifestation of originality and humanity, that truth must be finally victorious. And it is most important that the public should bear in mind that these pictures represent only six years' effort and that the artist is hardly thirty-three years of age. The future lies before him – personally, I dare not confine him to the present.

The public

[. . .] Put ten people of average intelligence in front of a new and original picture and these people, all ten, will behave in the most childish way. They will nudge each other and comment on the picture in the drollest way imaginable. The artistic history of our times is there to tell how such purblind fools and scoffers gathered in front of the first paintings by Decamps, Delacroix and Courbet. For jesting is catching, and one fine morning Paris awakes to find it has acquired a new plaything. [. . .]

We will see that it is simply the more or less original appearance of the picture which has induced this idiotic mirth. The pose is excruciatingly funny! This colour makes you cry with laughter! This line has made more than a hundred people sick! All that the public has seen is a subject – a subject treated in a certain manner. They look at works of art in the same way as children look at picture books – to amuse themselves, to get some fun out of them. Ignorant people laugh with complete self-assurance; knowledgeable people – those who have studied art in moribund schools – are annoyed, on examining the new work, not to discover in it the qualities in which they believe and to which their eyes have become accustomed. No one thinks of looking at it objectively. The former understands nothing about it, the latter make comparisons. None of them can 'see', and hence they are roused to mirth or anger. I repeat, it is simply the superficial way the work presents itself to the eye that is the cause of all this. The public never tries to probe further. They have stuck, as it were, on the surface. What is shocking and irritating to them is not the inner meaning of the work, but the general superficial aspect of it. If it were possible, the public would willingly accept the same subject matter, presented differently.

Originality! That's what shocks. We are all more or less, without knowing it, creatures of habit who obstinately follow the same beaten path to which we are accustomed. Every new path alarms us, we shy at unknown precipices and refuse to go forward. We always want to have the same horizon before us; we laugh at, or are irritated by the things we don't understand. That is why we are quite happy to accept originality when it is watered down but reject violently anything that upsets our preconceived ideas. As soon as someone with individuality appears on the scene, we become defiant and scared; we are like suspicious horses that rear at a fallen tree across the road because they can't comprehend either the nature or the cause of this obstacle and don't seek any further to explain it to themselves. [. . .]

The public will never be fair towards true artists so long as it fails to regard a work of art solely as a free and original interpretation of Nature. Is it not sad to remember, today, that Delacroix was hissed in his time and that his genius was despised and was triumphant only after his death? What do his detractors think now, and why don't they speak out and admit that they were blind and unintelligent? That should be a lesson to them. Perhaps it would teach them to understand that there is no 'common denominator', nor rules, nor obligations of any sort – only living men, bringing with them a liberal expression of life, giving their flesh and blood, becoming more glorious as they become more personal and perfect. In that case one should make straight away for the pictures which are strange and bold – those would be the ones which should be attentively and seriously studied, in order to see if therein human genius is apparent. One would then disdainfully dismiss the copies and stutterings of spurious painters, and all those pictures worth twopence-ha'penny which are merely the products of a skilful hand. What one needs to look for, above all, in a work of art, is the human touch, a living corner of creation, a new manifestation of humanity in the face of the realities of Nature.

But there is nobody to guide the public, and what do you expect the public to do today in the midst of all this hubbub? Art, in a manner of speaking, is split up. The great kingdom, split into pieces, has formed itself into a host of small republics. Each artist has attracted his public, flattering it, giving it what it likes, gilded and decorated toys with rosy favours – this art, with us, has become one vast sweet-shop where there are *bonbons* for all tastes. Painters háve merely become pathetic decorators who ornament our terrible modern apartments. The best of them have become antiquaries stealing a bit of this or that from the dead masters, and apart from the landscape painters, these narrow-minded and bourgeois decorators have made the deuce of a noise: each one has his own feeble theory, each tries to please and conquer. The mob, fawned upon, goes from one to the other, enjoying today the whimsies of this painter, and tomorrow the bogus strength of that. And all this disgraceful business, flattery and admiration of trumpery, is carried on in the so-called sacred name of Art. Greece and Italy are staked against chocolate soldiers, beauty is spoken of in the way one speaks of a gentleman acquaintance with whom one is on very friendly terms.

Then come the critics to cast still more trouble into this tumult. Art critics are like musicians who all play their own tunes simultaneously, hearing only their own instruments in the appalling hubbub that they are producing. One wants colour, another drawing, a third intellectual quality. I could name one who polishes his phrases and is only happy when he is able to describe a picture in the most picturesque terms possible, and another, who apropos of a woman lying supine finds occasion to write a discourse on democracy; and yet another who frames his ridiculous opinions in the form of rhyming music-hall couplets. The mob, completely at a loss, doesn't know to whom to turn. Peter says 'white', Paul says 'black'! If one believes the former, the landscape of this picture should be effaced, if one believes the latter, it is the figures that should be effaced, so that in the end nothing remains but the frame, which would be an excellent thing. There is not the slightest analysis in this approach. Truth is not a whole; these are only digressions, more or less. Each looks at the same picture in a different frame of mind, and each one criticizes it according to circumstances or his mood.

So the mob, seeing how little in accord are those who have pretentions of guiding them, allow themselves to admire or jeer as they please. There is no common point of view. A word pleases them, or displeases them – that's all. And note, what pleases them is always the most commonplace, something they have seen every year. Our artists do not spoil them; they have so accustomed them to insipidity, to pretty lies, that they reject the real truth with all their might. It is simply a question of education. When a Delacroix appears on the scene, he is hissed. Why doesn't he look like the others! [. . .]

And that is how, one day, a gang of urchins met Edouard Manet in the street and started the rumpus which brought me to a halt – me, a fastidious and unbiased passer-by. I laid information against them as well as I could, asserting that the urchins were in the wrong, and sought to snatch the artist from their grasp and lead him to a safe place. There were some policemen – I beg your pardon, I mean art critics – present, who assured me that the man was being stoned because he had outrageously desecrated the Temple of Beauty. I answered them that Destiny had undoubtedly already chosen the future setting in the Louvre for *Olympia* and *Le Déjeuner sur l'Herbe*. No one listened, and I retired as the urchins were now beginning to cast sullen looks at me.

7   The Impressionists and Edouard Manet

Stéphane Mallarmé

[. . .] Let us take a short glimpse backward on art history. Rarely do our annual
exhibitions abound with novelty, and some few years back such years of abundance
were still more rare; but about 1860 a sudden and a lasting light shone forth when
Courbet began to exhibit his works. These then in some degree coincided with that
movement which had appeared in literature, and which obtained the name of
Realism; that is to say, it sought to impress itself upon the mind by the lively
depiction of things as they appeared to be, and vigorously excluded all meddlesome
imagination. It was a great movement, equal in intensity to that of the Romantic
school, just then expiring under the hands of the landscape painters; and it then
moved many on a new and contemporaneous path. But in the midst of this, there
began to appear, sometimes perchance on the walls of the Salon, but far more
frequently and certainly on those of the galleries of the rejected, curious and singular
paintings – laughable to the many, it is true, from their very faults, but nevertheless
very disquieting to the true and reflective critic, who could not refrain from asking
himself what manner of man is this? and what the strange doctrine he preaches? For
it was evident that the preacher had a meaning; he was persistent in his reiteration,
unique in his persistency, and his works were signed by the then new and unknown
name of *Edouard Manet*. There was also at that time, alas! that it should have to be
written in the past tense, an enlightened amateur, one who loved all arts and lived for
one of them. These strange pictures at once won his sympathy; an instinctive and
poetic foresight made him love them; and this before their prompt succession and
the sufficient exposition of the principles they inculcated had revealed their meaning
to the thoughtful few of the public many. But this enlightened amateur died too soon
to see these, and before his favourite painter had won a public name. That amateur
was our last great poet, Charles Baudelaire.

Following in appreciative turn came the then coming novelist Emile Zola. With
that insight into the future which distinguishes his own works, he recognized the
light that had arisen, albeit that he was yet too young to then define that which we
today call Naturalism, to follow the quest, not merely of that reality which impresses
itself in its abstract form on all, but of that absolute and important sentiment which
Nature herself impresses on those who have voluntarily abandoned conventional-
ism.

In 1867 a special exhibition of the works of Manet and some few of his followers,
gave to the then nameless school of recent painting which thus grew up, the
semblance of a party, and party strife grew high. The struggle with this resolute
intruder was preached as a crusade from the rostrum of each school. For several

Source: Art Monthly Review vol. 1, no. 9, 1876. (Translator uncertain, no known original French source
exists.)

years a firm and implacable front was formed against its advance; until at length vanquished by its good faith and persistency, the jury recognized the name of Manet, welcomed it, and so far recovered from its ridiculous fears, that it reasoned and found that it must either declare him a self-created sovereign pontiff, charged by his own faith with the cure of souls, or condemn him as a heretic and a public danger. [. . .]

Wearied by the technicalities of the school in which, under Couture, he studied, Manet, when he recognized the inanity of all he was taught, determined either not to paint at all or to paint entirely from without himself. Yet, in his self-sought insulation, two masters – masters of the past – appeared to him, and befriended him in his revolt. Velazquez, and the painters of the Flemish school, particularly impressed themselves upon him, and the wonderful atmosphere which enshrouds the compositions of the grand old Spaniard, and the brilliant tones which glow from the canvases of his northern compeers, won the student's admiration, thus presenting to him two art aspects which he has since made himself the master of, and can mingle as he pleases. It is precisely these two aspects which reveal the truth, and give the paintings based upon them living reality instead of rendering them the baseless fabric of abstracted and obscure dreams. These have been the tentatives of Manet, and curiously, it was to the foreigner and the past that he turned for friendly council in remedying the evils of his country and his time. And yet truth bids me say that Manet had no pressing need for this; an incomparable copyist, he could have found his game close to hand had he chosen his quarry there; but he sought something more than this, and fresh things are not found all at once; freshness, indeed, frequently consists – and this is especially the case in these critical days – in a co-ordination of widely scattered elements.

The pictures in which this reversion to the traditions of the old masters of the north and south are found constitute Manet's first manner. Now the old writers on art expressed by the word 'manner', rather the lavish blossoming of genius during one of its intellectual seasons than the fact fathered, found or sought out by the painter himself. But that in which the painter declares most his views is the choice of his subjects. Literature often departs from its current path to seek for the aspirations of an epoch of the past, and to modernise them for its own purpose, and in painting Manet followed a similarly divergent course, seeking the truth, and loving it when found, because being true it was so strange, especially when compared with old and worn-out ideals of it. Welcomed on his outset, as we have said, by Baudelaire, Manet fell under the influence of the moment, and, to illustrate him at this period, let us take one of his first works, *Olympia*; that wan, wasted courtesan, showing to the public, for the first time, the non-traditional, unconventional nude. The bouquet, yet enclosed in its paper envelope, the gloomy cat (apparently suggested by one of the prose poems of the author of the *Fleurs du Mal*) and all the surrounding accessories, were truthful, but not immoral – that is, in the ordinary and foolish sense of the word – but they were undoubtedly intellectually perverse in their tendency. Rarely has any modern work been more applauded by some few, or more deeply damned by the many, than was that of this innovator.

If our humble opinion can have any influence in this impartial history of the work of the chief of the new school of painting, I would say that the transition period in it is by no means to be regretted. Its parallel is found in literature, when our sympathies are suddenly awakened by some new imagery presented to us; and this is what I like in Manet's work. It surprised us all as something long hidden, but suddenly revealed. Captivating and repulsive at the same time, eccentric, and new, such types as he gave us were needed in our ambient life. In them, strange though they were, there was nothing vague, general, conventional or hackneyed. Often they attracted attention by something peculiar in the physiognomy of his subject, half hiding or sacrificing to those new laws of space and light he set himself to inculcate, some minor details which others would have seized upon.

Bye and bye, if he continues to paint long enough, and to educate the public eye – as yet veiled by conventionality – if that public will then consent to see the true beauties of the people, healthy and solid as they are, the graces which exist in the bourgeoisie will then be recognised and taken as worthy models in art, and then will come the time of peace. As yet it is but one of struggle – a struggle to render those truths in nature which for her are eternal, but which are as yet for the multitude but new.

The reproach which superficial people formulate against Manet, that whereas once he painted ugliness now he paints vulgarity, falls harmlessly to the ground, when we recognise the fact that he paints the truth, and recollect those difficulties he encountered on his way to seek it, and how he conquered them.

[. . . The painter's aim] was not to make a momentary escapade or sensation, but by steadily endeavouring to impress upon his work a natural and a general law, to seek out a type rather than a personality, and to flood it with light and air: and such air!, air which despotically dominates over all else. And before attempting to analyse this celebrated picture I should like to comment somewhat on that truism of tomorrow, that paradox of today, which in studio slang is called 'the theory of open air' or at least on that which it becomes with the authoritative evidence of the later efforts of Manet. But here is first of all an objection to overcome. Why is it needful to represent the open air of gardens, shore or street, when it must be owned that the chief part of modern existence is passed within doors? There are many answers; among these I hold the first, that in the atmosphere of any interior, bare or furnished, the reflected lights are mixed and broken and too often discolour the flesh tints. For instance, I would remind you of a painting in the Salon of 1873 which our painter justly called a *Rêverie*. There a young woman reclines on a divan exhaling all the lassitude of summer time; the jalousies of her room are almost closed, the dreamer's face is dim with shadow, but a vague, deadened daylight suffuses her figure and her muslin dress. This work is altogether exceptional and sympathetic.

Woman is by our civilisation consecrated to night, unless she escape from it sometimes to those open air afternoons by the seaside or in an arbour, affectionated by moderns. Yet I think the artist would be in the wrong to represent her among the artificial glories of candle-light or gas, as at that time the only object of art would be the woman herself, set off by the immediate atmosphere, theatrical and active, even beautiful, but utterly inartistic. Those persons much accustomed, whether from the habit of their calling or purely from taste, to fix on a mental canvas the beautiful remembrance of woman, even when thus seen amid the glare of night in the world or at the theatre, must have remarked that some mysterious process despoils the noble phantom of the artificial prestige cast by candelabra or footlights, before she is admitted fresh and simple to the number of everyday haunters of the imagination. The complexion, the special beauty which springs from the very source of life, changes with artificial lights, and it is probably from the desire to preserve this grace in all its integrity, that painting – which concerns itself more about this flesh-pollen than any other human attraction – insists on the mental operation to which I have lately alluded, and demands daylight – that is, space with the transparence of air alone. The natural light of day penetrating into and influencing all things, although itself invisible, reigns also on this typical picture called *The Linen* [. . .]

The search after truth, peculiar to modern artists, which enables them to see Nature and reproduce her, such as she appears to just and pure eyes, must lead them to adopt air almost exclusively as their medium, or at all events to habituate themselves to work in it freely and without restraint: there should at least be in the revival of such a medium, if nothing more, an incentive to a new manner of painting. This is the result of our reasoning, and the end I wish to establish. As no artist has on his palette a transparent and neutral colour answering to open air, the desired effect can only be obtained by lightness or heaviness of touch, or by the regulation of tone. Now Manet and his school use simple colour, fresh, or lightly laid on, and their results appear to have been attained at the first stroke, that the ever-present light blends with and vivifies all things. As to the details of the picture, nothing should be absolutely fixed in order that we may feel that the bright gleam which lights the picture, or the diaphanous shadow which veils it, are only seen in passing, and just when the spectator beholds the represented subject, which being composed of a harmony of reflected and ever-changing lights, cannot be supposed always to look the same, but palpitates with movement, light and life.

But will not this atmosphere – which an artifice of the painter extends over the whole of the object painted – vanish, when the completely finished work is as a repainted picture? If we could find no other way to indicate the presence of air than the partial or repeated application of colour as usually employed, doubtless the representation would be as fleeting as the effect represented, but from the first conception of the work, the space intended to contain the atmosphere has been indicated, so that when this is filled by the represented air, it is as unchangeable as the other parts of the picture. Then composition (to borrow once more the slang of the studio) must play a considerable part in the aesthetics of a master of the Impressionists? No; certainly not; as a rule the grouping of modern persons does not suggest it, and for this reason our painter is pleased to dispense with it, and at the same time to avoid both affectation and style. Nevertheless he must find something on which to establish his picture, though it be but for a minute – for the one thing needful is the time required by the spectator to see and admire the representation with that promptitude which just suffices for the connection of its truth. If we turn to natural perspective (not that utterly and artificially classic science which makes our eyes the dupes of a civilized education, but rather that artistic perspective which we learn from the extreme East – Japan, for example) – and look at these sea-pieces of Manet, where the water at the horizon rises to the height of the frame, which alone interrupts it, we feel a new delight at the recovery of a long obliterated truth.

The secret of this is found in an absolutely new science, and in the manner of cutting down the pictures, and which gives to the frame all the charm of a merely financial boundary, such as that which is embraced at one glance of a scene framed in by the hands, or at least all of it found worthy to preserve. This is the picture, and the function of the frame is to isolate it; though I am aware that this is running counter to prejudice. For instance, what need is there to represent this arm, this hat, or that river bank, if they belong to someone or something exterior to the picture; the one thing to be attained is that the spectator accustomed among a crowd or in nature to isolate one bit which pleases him, though at the same time incapable of entirely forgetting the abjured details which unite the part to the whole, shall not miss in the work of art one of his habitual enjoyments, and whilst recognizing that he is before a painting half believes he sees the mirage of some natural scene. Some will probably object that all of these means have been more or less employed in the past, that dexterity – though not pushed so far – of cutting the canvas off so as to produce an illusion – perspective almost conforming to the exotic usage of barbarians – the light touch and fresh tones uniform and equal, or variously trembling with shifting lights – all these ruses and expedients in art have been found more than once in the English school, and elsewhere. But the assemblage for the first time of all these relative processes for an end, visible and suitable to the artistic expression of the needs of our times, this is no inconsiderable achievement in the cause of art, especially since a mighty will has pushed these means to their uttermost limits. [. . .]

If we try to recall some of the heads of our argument and to draw from them possible conclusions, we must first affirm that Impressionism is the principal and real movement of contemporary painting. The only one? No; since other great talents have been devoted to illustrate some particular phase or period of bygone art; among these we must class such artists as Moreau, Puvis de Chavannes, etc.

At a time when the romantic tradition of the first half of the century only lingers among a few surviving masters of that time, the transition from the old imaginative artist and dreamer to the energetic modern worker is found in Impressionism.

The participation of a hitherto ignored people in the political life of France is a social fact that will honour the whole of the close of the nineteenth century. A parallel is found in artistic matters, the way being prepared by an evolution which the public with rare prescience dubbed, from its first appearance, 'intransigeant', which in political language means radical and democratic.

The noble visionaries of other times, whose works are the semblance of worldly things seen by unworldly eyes (not the actual representations of real objects), appear as kings and gods in the far dream-ages of mankind; recluses to whom were given the genius of a dominion over an ignorant multitude. But today the multitude demands to see with its own eyes; and if our latter-day art is less glorious, intense and rich, it is not without the compensation of truth, simplicity and child-like charm.

At that critical hour for the human race when Nature desires to work for herself, she requires certain lovers of hers – new and impersonal men placed directly in communion with the sentiment of their time – to loose the restraint of education, to let hand and eye do what they will, and thus through them, reveal herself.

For the mere pleasure of doing so? Certainly not, but to express herself, calm, naked, habitual, to those newcomers of tomorrow, of which each one will consent to be an unknown unit in the mighty numbers of a universal suffrage, and to place in their power a newer and more succinct means of observing her.

Such, to those who can see in this the representative art of a period which cannot isolate itself from the equally characteristic politics and industry, must seem the meaning of the manner of painting which we have discussed here, and which although marking a general phase of art has manifested itself particularly in France.

Now in conclusion I must hastily re-enter the domain of aesthetics, and I trust we shall thoroughly have considered our subject when I have shown the relation of the present crisis – the appearance of the Impressionists – to the actual principles of painting – a point of great importance.

In extremely civilized epochs the following necessity becomes a matter of course, the development of art and thought having nearly reached their far limits – art and thought are obliged to retrace their own footsteps, and to return to their ideal source, which never coincides with their real beginnings. English Pre-Raphaelitism, if I do not mistake, returned to the primitive simplicity of mediaeval ages. The scope and aim (not proclaimed by authority of dogmas, yet not the less clear) of Manet and his followers is that painting shall be steeped again in its cause, and its relation to nature. But what, except to decorate the ceilings of salons and palaces with a crowd of idealized types in magnificent foreshortening, what can be the aim of a painter before everyday Nature? To imitate her? Then his best efforts can never equal the original with the inestimable advantages of life and space – 'Ah no! this fair face, that green landscape, will grow old and wither, but I shall have them always, true as nature, fair as remembrance, and imperishably my own; or the better to satisfy my creative artistic instinct, that which I preserve through the power of Impressionism is not the material portion which already exists, superior to any mere representation of it, but the delight of having recreated nature touch by touch. I leave the massive and tangible solidity to its fitter exponent, sculpture. I content myself with reflecting on the clear and durable mirror of painting, that which perpetually lives yet dies every moment, which only exists by the will of Idea, yet constitutes in my domain the only authentic and certain merit of nature – the Aspect. It is through her that when rudely thrown at the close of an epoch of dreams in the front of reality, I have taken from it only that which properly belongs to my art, an original and exact perception which distinguishes for itself the things it perceives with the steadfast gaze of a vision restored to its simplest perfection.'

8   'L'Exposition des Indépendants' in 1880

J. K. Huysmans

On Degas

I do not recall having ever felt as moved as I was when, in 1876, I first came upon the works of this master. This was a real feeling of 'possession' for me, since I had, until then, been solely attracted towards the paintings of the Dutch school, which satisfied my needs for reality and intimacy. The modern, which I had sought in vain in the exhibitions of the time, and which only broke through in places, piecemeal, suddenly appeared in front of me, in its entirety. When I made my writing début in a weekly rag called the *Gazette des Amateurs*, produced by M. Bachelin-Deflorenne, I wrote the following lines:

> M. Degas exhibits two oil paintings which depict ballet dancers from the *Opéra*: three women in yellow tulle skirts are folded in each other's arms; behind them, the backdrop is being raised to reveal the pink costumes of the corps de ballet; there's an extraordinary realism about the way these three women are set firmly on their hips and their points.
>
> They don't have artificial creamy skin but rather real flesh, just a little faded by the layers of powder and ointments. It is all absolutely real and truly beautiful. I would also recommend a look at the painting above this one, which shows the body of a woman, leaning forward, as well as two drawings on pink paper in which one ballerina is seen from behind whilst the other ties up her shoe. Both are captured with an unusual suppleness and strength.

The joy I first felt as a novice has since increased at every exhibition in which Degas' paintings have been shown.

A painter of modern life had been born, moreover a painter who derived from and resembled no other, who brought with him a totally new artistic flavour, as well as totally new skills. Washerwomen in their shops, dancers at rehearsals, café-concert singers, theatres, race-horses, portraits, cotton dealers in America, women stepping out of their bath, boudoir and dressing-room impressions, all these diverse topics have been treated by this artist though he is generally reputed to have only painted ballet dancers!

But in this year's exhibition, it is paintings of the ballet that predominate. And, if it were possible, he has surpassed himself here, this delicate man with his nervous sensitive temperament, whose eye is so strangely haunted and preoccupied by the human figure in motion, be it under the artificial glare of gas lamps or in the wan daylight of rooms lit by the sad rays coming from a courtyard.

Look at this dance examination, one ballet dancer bent over to tie a lace and another, her head on her chest, with her roman nose bulging from beneath her red

Source: L'Art Moderne (Paris, 1883), translated by Martine Moon and Belinda Thomson. *L'Art Moderne* was reissued in 1969 by Gregg International, England.

hair. Close to them a friend in street dress, a common girl, with freckled cheeks, whose unkempt hair is pulled back under a hat bristling with red feathers, and some mother or other wearing a cap and flowered shawl, her face like that of a concierge, chat during the intervals. What truth! What life! How light are all these shapes and how rightly the light bathes the scene; look how successfully the expressions of those faces, the boredom of an arduous mechanical task, the piercing looks of the mother whose hopes rise even when she sees her daughter wearing herself to a shadow and her friend's indifference to a tiredness they have all felt are accentuated, noted with the shrewdness of an analyst who can be at one and the same time both cruel and subtle.

Another of his paintings is gloomy: in the large practice room, a woman slumps her chin in her fists, a statue embodying boredom and fatigue, while a friend, the back of her skirt puffed over the back of the chair on which she is sitting, looks in a bemused fashion at groups hopping about to the thin notes of a violin.

Now we see them resuming their clownish antics again. The break is over, the music screeches, the torturing of limbs begins all over again. And in these paintings where the characters are often cut off by the frame as in some Japanese pictures, the exercises are speeding up, legs are raised in rhythm, hands cling to the bars which run along the walls, the tips of the shoes beat the floor in a frantic way, lips smile automatically. The illusion becomes so exact that, staring at these jumping girls, they become alive and quiver and one can almost hear the teacher's shouts above the bitter noise of the small violin: 'Heels forward, hips tucked in, wrists firm, keep apart'; at this last order the girls perform their *grand développé*, foot lifted up, resting tensely on the highest bar, carrying the puffed skirts with it.

Then the metamorphosis is complete. The giraffes who could not break themselves in, the elephants whose joints refused to move, are now supple. The training period is over, and now we see them appear on the stage, before an audience, pirouetting round and round, flying about, toes dancing to and fro, in splashes of gas and electric lights. And here again M. Degas sticks them, full of life, in front of the stage, catches them at the second they leap or curtsey on both sides, blowing kisses to the audience, pending the time when they become box attendants, palmists or walkers-on.

The observation is so accurate that a physiologist could study the human body in every one of this series of girls. Here we see the butch woman who's being licked into shape and whose colours fade on a miserable diet of Italian cheese and *vin ordinaire*; there, the original anaemic waifs of girls lying in attic rooms, exhausted by the demands of their calling, by the exercises for which they are too young; there again, the dry, nervous girls whose muscles bulge under their costumes, genuine goats built to jump, real dancers with steel springs and iron knee tendons.

How charming some of these girls are! Radiating a special beauty made of the mixture of gutter commonness and grace! How exquisite, almost divine, are some of these untidy little girls, who iron or carry the washing, or some of these gaping-mouthed singers who wear black gloves, some of these acrobats being hoisted up into the vault of a circus!

What a study of the effects of light! I must mention in this context a theatre box, in pastel, a vacant box close to the stage, with a cherry red half-lifted screen and a darker background of crimson wallpaper; a woman's profile leans from the balcony above, watching the yelping 'hams'. The tones of her cheeks and ears, warmed red by the heat of the hall and the blood that has rushed to them, then becoming paler on her temples, are caught with an extraordinary exactitude as the light strikes them.

M. Degas' exhibition is this year made up of about ten works. I have already talked about a number of these, but I would like to mention two superb drawings: one of a woman's head which would be quite worthy of a place among the drawings of the French School in the Louvre; the other a portrait of the late lamented Duranty in front of which I shall now pause for a while.

It goes without saying that M. Degas has avoided the ridiculous backgrounds that painters love, the scarlet, olive-green or gentle blue curtains, or the purple, brownish, green and ash-grey stains which are such monstrous hindrances to truth. For one should after all paint a portrait in the environment of the sitter, in the street, in a real setting, anywhere, rather than in the middle of a polished layer of empty colours.

M. Duranty sits there, in front of his table surrounded by his prints and books, and his nervous tapering fingers, his sharp and mocking eyes, his probing and acute appearance, his English comedian's tight-lipped smile, his little dry laugh into the stem of his pipe, all come back to my mind when I see the canvas in which the character of this inquisitive analyst is so accurately reproduced.

It is difficult to convey in writing even the vaguest idea of what M. Degas' paintings are about. Only literature can give a fair analogy. If a comparison between these two art forms were possible I would say that the execution of M. Degas recalls in many aspects the literary art of the Goncourt brothers.

They will all have to be considered, in their own ways, the most refined and accomplished artists of this century. Just as Jules and Edmond de Goncourt had to forge a cutting and powerful tool, create a new palette of colours, an original vocabulary and a new language in order to make visible, almost tangible, the external visual form of 'the human animal' in its natural habitat, to dismantle the mechanism of its passions, to explain the stage-by-stage progress of its thoughts, the aberration of its devotions, the natural blossoming of its vices, and to express its most transitory feelings; so, in the same way, M. Degas had to design himself an instrument that was both fine and expansive, flexible and firm, in order to express the vision of beings and things in an atmosphere which belongs to them, to show the movements, postures, gestures, the slight alterations of physiognomy, the different aspects of features and clothes, depending on the dimming or glowing of lights, and to translate effects hitherto misunderstood or deemed impossible to represent in painting.

He too had to borrow from all the languages of painting, combine the various elements of oil and turpentine, of water colour and pastel, of distemper and gouache, forge new colours, break the accepted rules of subject matter.

Daring and remarkable painting which tries to depict weightlessness, the breeze which lifts the muslin of costumes, the currents of air rising from *entrechats* and separating the layers of tulle skirts; clever yet simple painting, which tackles the boldest, most complicated body postures, muscles working then relaxing, the most unpredictable effects of perspective; painting which dares to convey the precise visual sensation of following Miss Lola as she climbs by the strength of her teeth up to the top of the Fernando Hall, by making the ceiling of the circus seem to lean to one side!

How far we now are from all the traditional processes used to represent contours and shadows, from all the old artificial colours mixed on the palette, from all the ancient tricks taught down the centuries! And since Delacroix's time there hasn't been such a new way of applying the rules of optical mixing, that is, obtaining on the canvas by the juxtaposition of two other colours a tone that is absent from the palette.

Here in Duranty's portrait, there are almost garish pink dabs on the forehead, touches of green in the beard, blue in the velvet of the collar; the fingers are made up of yellow bordered with bishop's purple. Seen close, it all looks slashed together, a hatching of strident conflicting colours, which seem to encroach on one another; seen from a few steps back everything harmonizes, merges into a precise flesh tone, flesh that palpitates, and lives, in a way that no one else in France today knows how to make it.

The same goes for his dancers. The dancer I mentioned previously, the ginger-haired girl with the roman nose inclined onto her chest, has green shadows on her neck and her ankles outlined in purple. When one looks closely, the costume looks like crushed pink crayon; from a distance we see cotton stretched over a muscled leg.

No other painter since Delacroix, whom he has studied at length and who is his true master, has understood as M. Degas does the marriage and adultery of colours; no other painter at this time has a drawing style of such precision and yet breadth, or such a delicate array of colours; no one else has achieved, in a different art form, the exquisite touch the de Goncourts gave to their prose; no one else has fixed in a similar way, in a deliberate and personal style, the most ephemeral feelings, the most fleeting subtleties and nuances.

At this stage a question should be asked. When will this painter achieve the high ranking in contemporary art that is owed to him? When shall we understand that this man is the greatest artist we possess today in France? I am not a prophet, but I know the folly of the enlightened classes; for many years these people have spurned Delacroix, have yet to realize that Baudelaire is the poetic genius of the nineteenth century, standing a hundred feet above all others, Hugo included, and that Flaubert's *L'Education Sentimentale* is the masterpiece of the modern novel; and it is said that literature is the art form which the masses most easily comprehend! Judging by this, I would not be surprised if the truth about M. Degas, to which I am the only writer bearing witness today, was not recognized for many years to come.

It would however be true to say that there has been some change of attitude. The public that was once convulsed with laughter when the *intransigeants* first exhibited, without the slightest touch of sympathy for the attempts that had obviously misfired, for the ravages produced by colour blindness or other eye afflictions, having failed to realize that pathological cases should not be laughed at but make interesting case studies; these people now walk peacefully through the exhibition rooms. They are still frightened and irritated by certain works whose newness confuses them, being quite unaware of the unfathomable abyss which separates M. Degas and M. Caillebotte's concept of the modern and the fabrications of MM. Bastien Lepage and Henri Gervex. Nevertheless in spite of their ignorance, they stop and they look surprised and even a little shaken by the sincerity that comes through these works.

We could almost feel that today the visitors' laughter would tend to be provoked by certain canvases which have been put in this exhibition by error, by mediocre paintings which are neither Impressionist nor modern; and I would like to hope, *en passant*, that the group will be purified and that these nonentities which have inexplicably escaped from the official salons will be swept away.

One can only hope that at the same time as these worthless objects are taken away, new talents will emerge to join the group. The whole of modern life is still to be studied: only a few of its many aspects have begun to be noticed and noted. Everything remains to be done: official galas, salons, balls, corners of family life, of artisan and bourgeois life, shops, markets, restaurants, cafés, bars, in other words the whole of humanity, whichever social class it belongs to or whatever function it performs, at home, in hospitals, dancing halls, theatres, gardens, in poor streets or those large boulevards whose American aspect is the necessary frame for the needs of our era.

Then if a few of the painters who interest us have here and there reproduced a number of episodes of contemporary life, who is the artist who will now re-create the imposing grandeur of factory towns, who will follow in the German Menzel's steps and enter the vast iron works, the railway halls? Admittedly M. Claude Monet has already tried to paint the latter but with his flickering sketches he hasn't succeeded in giving a sense of the colossal size of the stations and locomotives. Where is the landscape artist who will convey the terrifying and impressive solemnity of the high furnaces which burn in the night, the tops of their gigantic chimneys crowned by pale flames?

All the work done by man in manufacturing industries and factories; the whole modern fever of industrial activity, the magnificence of machines, all these remain to be painted and will be painted, provided the modernists worthy of the name agree not to allow themselves to be belittled or mummified by the eternal reproduction of the same monotonous subjects.

Ah! What a chance lies ahead of them! Cabanel's and Gérôme's most recent students will go on patching up the moth-eaten costumes of antiquity in order to obtain a medal; while a few more successful ones have, like prostitutes, been provided with a home from which they sell themselves through their vulgar paintings for the benefit of a picture dealer.

Yet others display their wares for their own benefit, titillating the interest of bourgeois buyers by selling them the sentimental nonsense they adore.

To conclude, French art is in a bad way; it all has to be rebuilt; but never before has a more glorious task been entrusted to talented artists like those whose works I have just been examining in the *Salle des Pyramides*.

9   From Gauguin and Van Gogh to Classicism

Maurice Denis

The great gust of wind that gave new life to French art in about 1890 blew from the shop of père Tanguy, a colour merchant on the rue Clauzel and from the auberge Gloanec at Pont-Aven [. . .]

Bernard, Van Gogh, Anquetin, Toulouse-Lautrec were rebels from the Cormon studio; we, that is Bonnard, Ibels, Ranson, Denis, grouped round Sérusier, were the rebels of the Julian studio. Sympathetic to everything that seemed new and subversive, we were drawn to them, as they were making a clean sweep not only of academic teaching but also, and above all, of naturalism, whether romantic or photographic, which was then universally accepted as the only theory worthy of an age of science and democracy. We met at the first shows of the *Indépendants*, where the influence of Seurat and Signac was already making itself felt.

To the boldnesses of the Impressionists and the divisionists, the newcomers added an awkwardness of execution and an almost caricatural simplification of form: and that was symbolism. The syntheses of the Japanese decorators were not enough to satisfy our demand for simplification. Primitive or oriental idols, Breton calvaries, *'images d'Epinal'*, figures from tapestry and stained glass, all these were mingled with recollections of Daumier, with the awkward Poussinesque style of Cézanne's *Bathers*, with the clumsy peasant subjects of Pissarro. For those who witnessed the 1890 movement, there are no surprises left: the most absurd, the most incomprehensible efforts of the artists now known as the '*Fauves*' can do no more than re-awaken our memories of the extravagances of our own generation [. . .]

No doubt there had been preparations for the new wave of 1890. These artists whose appearance caused a scandal were products of their time and their circumstances; it would be unjust to isolate them from their elders, the Impressionists: in particular it seems that Camille Pissarro had a considerable influence on them. Besides, one couldn't reproach them for failing to recognize their immediate predecessors; from the outset they showed the greatest respect for the artists who had set them on the right track: not only Camille Pissarro, Cézanne, Degas and Odilon Redon, but also Puvis de Chavannes whose official honours might easily have been off-putting to their youthful intransigence. Thus they were the necessary outcome – action and reaction combined – of the great Impressionist movement. Everything has been said on this subject: the absence of all rules, the ineptitude of academic teaching, the triumph of naturalism and the influence of Japanese art had caused the joyous birth of an art which appeared to be free from all constraint. The new motifs of sunlight, artificial lighting and the whole picturesqueness of modern

Source: L'Occident, May 1909, translated by Belinda Thomson.

life had been admitted to the domain of art. Literature was combining the vulgarities of a waning realism with the refinements of symbolism; 'the slice of life' was served up raw; at the same time in poetry the lyricism of young writers was being tried to the limit by the elitist love of the rare word, the novel state of mind, and obscurity. What we required of Cézanne, Gauguin and Van Gogh, they discovered in Verlaine, Mallarmé and Laforgue.

[. . .] Everywhere new ideas were fermenting. But then one has to admit that in the plastic arts, the idea of art, which was limited to begin with to the idea of imitation, rested solely on the naturalist preconception of the temperament or, to be more precise, the individual sensation. 'That's the way they see things', said the critics. We took our scorn for conventions to the limit, with no other object in view than that of being negative: the 'right to do anything' knew no bounds. It was the excess of this anarchy which brought about, as a reaction, the desire for system and the taste for theories. Seurat was the first who tried to substitute a considered working method for this more or less haphazard improvisation on nature. He tried to introduce some order, to create the new doctrine everyone was waiting for. He had the merit of attempting to make rules for Impressionism. [. . .]

[. . .] This period of confusion and renaissance was brilliantly resolved in Van Gogh and Gauguin. Alongside Seurat's scientific Impressionism, they represented barbarism, revolution and turmoil – and in the end wisdom. At first their efforts escaped all classifications, and there was little to distinguish their theories from old-style Impressionism. Art for them, as for their predecessors, was the rendering of a sensation, the exaltation of the individual sensibility. They began by aggravating all the excessive, disorganized elements belonging to Impressionism, and it was only gradually that they became aware of their innovatory role, and realized that their synthesism or symbolism was the precise antithesis of Impressionism.

It was the brutal and paradoxical side of their work that had such an influence [. . .] Without the destructive and negative anarchism of Gauguin and Van Gogh, Cézanne's example, with all it comprised in the way of tradition, restraint and order, would not have been understood. The constructive elements in their work were carried along by the revolutionary elements. And yet for the attentive observer, even in 1890, it was easy to detect in the extremism of their works and the paradoxes of their theories the symptoms of a classical reaction. The salient fact is that since that time there has been an evolution in favour of order, even among those who took part in the 1890 movement, or among those who identify with that movement.

Along with its elders, the younger generation has become resolutely classical. The enthusiasm of this new generation for the seventeenth century, for Italy, for Ingres, is well known: Versailles is fashionable; Poussin praised to the skies; Bach fills the concert halls; romanticism is ridiculed. In literature and in politics, the young are passionate for order. The return to tradition and discipline is as unanimous as the cult of the individual and the spirit of revolt were in our youth. I might cite as evidence the fact that in the avant-garde critics' vocabulary, the word 'classic' is the highest form of praise, and as a result is used to designate 'progressive' tendencies. Impressionism, these days, is considered as a period of 'ignorance and frenzy' which is contrasted with 'a nobler, more measured, more ordered and more cultivated art'. (In fact it's the art of M. Braque that's under discussion!)[1]

In short the moment arrived when a choice had to be made, as Barrès put it, between traditionalism and the intellectual point of view. Syndicalists or *Action*

Torrentius: *Still-Life-Allegory of Temperance*, 1614, Rijksmuseum, Amsterdam

Illusionist stage: The Teatro Olimpico, Vicenza, completed in 1584

The Colonnade of the Uffizi, Florence. Photograph courtesy of the Courtauld
Institute of Art

Pablo Picasso: *Table, Glasses, Cups and Mandolin*, 1911, c S.P.A.D.E.M.
Paris, 1912

Royalist print from the French Revolution. c. 1793

Pavel Tchelitchew: *Tree into Hand and Foot*, Watercolour and ink, 14 x 9¾"
1939. Collection of the Museum of Modern Art, New York. Mrs Simon
Guggenheim Fund

M C Escher: *Day and Night*, Woodcut, 1938, c S.P.A.D.E.M. Paris and Beeldrecht, Amsterdam, 1982

M C Escher: *Solid and Hollow*, lithograph, 1955, c S.P.A.D.E.M. Paris and
Beeldrecht, Amsterdam, 1982

M C Escher: *Belvedere,* lithograph, 1958, c S.P.A.D.E.M. Paris and
Beeldrecht, Amsterdam, 1982

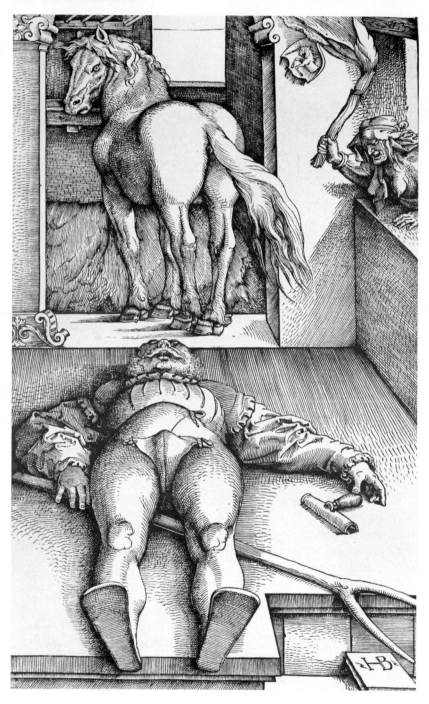

Hans Baldung Grien: *Bewitched Stableboy,* Woodcut, 1544, The
Metropolitan Museum of Art, Rogers Fund, 1917

Josef Albers, *Structural Constellation*, machine engraving on vinylite, 48 x 65 cm. Reproduced by permission of Mrs Anni Albers and the Josef Albers Foundation Inc.

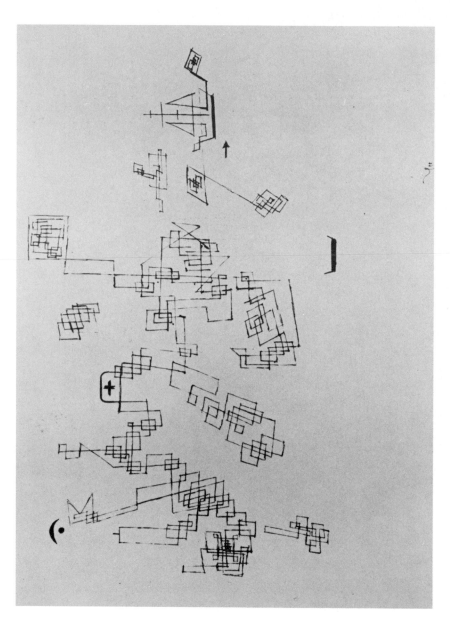

Paul Klee: *Aktivität der Seestadt* (Bustling Harbour) Drawing, 1927, c ADAGP
Paris and Cosmopress, Geneva, 1982

Wassily Kandinsky: *Ruhe* (At Rest) 1928 From the collection of Mr Nathan Cummings, New York.

From *Le Journal Amusant* of 2 March 1867

– Ma fille, on m'a dit que le jeune-homme qui demeure en face t'avait embrassé !!....
– C'est vrai, maman ; mais c'était parcequ'il trouvait que ses chemises étaient bien repassées ,...
et il m'a donné un baiser pour la peine .....
    – S'il est content de son linge, ce n'est pas toi qu'il doit embrasser, mais bien moi ...,qui suis la
maîtresse de la maison .....

From *Le Charivari* of 12 April 1859

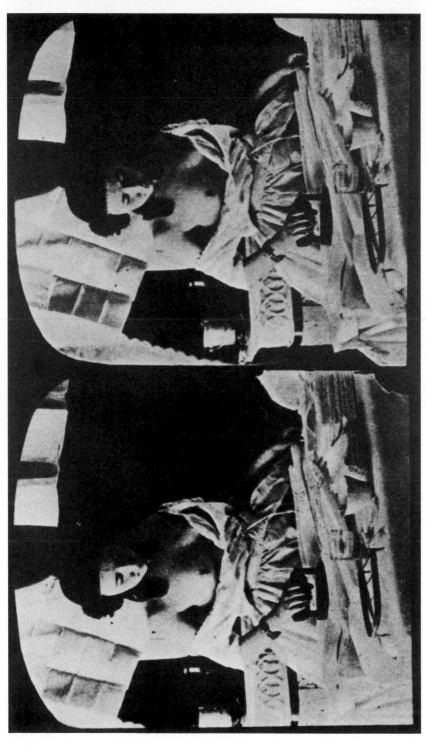

Stereoscopic Photograph of the 1870s

Française monarchists, both brought down to earth from their liberal or libertarian clouds, are striving to keep to the logic of facts, to construct their arguments on reality alone: but the monarchist theory, integral nationalism, among its other advantages has that of taking into account the *successful* experiences of the past. And if we painters have evolved towards classicism it is because we were fortunate enough to take the right approach to the dual aesthetic and psychological problem facing art. We replaced the idea of 'nature seen through a temperament' with the theory of equivalence and of the symbol: we asserted that the feelings or states of mind evoked by such and such a spectacle carried with them in the artist's imagination symbols or plastic equivalents capable of reproducing those emotions or states of mind without his needing to produce a *copy* of the initial spectacle; for every state of our sensibility there had to be a corresponding objective harmony capable of translating it.[2]

Art is no longer just a visual sensation that we set down, a photograph, however refined it may be, of nature. No, art is a creation of our imagination of which nature is only the occasion. Instead of 'working outwards from the eye, we explored the mysterious centre of thought', as Gauguin used to say. In this way the imagination becomes once more the queen of the faculties, in accordance with Baudelaire's wish. And thus we set free our sensibility; art, instead of being a *copy*, became the subjective deformation of Nature.

From the objective point of view, the decorative, aesthetic and rational composition, overlooked by the Impressionists because it went against their taste for improvisation, became the counterpart, the necessary corrective to the theory of equivalents. In the name of expression the latter theory authorized all transformations, even caricatural ones, all excesses of character: but *objective deformation* in its turn obliged the artist to transform everything into Beauty. To sum up, the expressive synthesis, the symbol of a sensation had to be both an eloquent transcription of that sensation and at the same time an object arranged for the pleasure of the eye.

Infinitely bound up in the work of Cézanne, those two tendencies are to be found in varying forms in the work of Van Gogh, Gauguin, Bernard and all the former synthetists. Their thinking is paralleled and the essence of their theory is well summed up in the reduction to the idea of the two deformations. But whereas decorative deformation is what habitually preoccupies Gauguin, on the contrary it is subjective deformation that gives Van Gogh's painting its character and lyricism. You find in the work of the former, beneath rustic or exotic appearances, and alongside a rigorous logic, certain compositional artifices, in which there lingers, dare I say it, a bit of Italian rhetoric. The latter on the contrary, who comes to us from the land of Rembrandt, is a frustrated romantic: the picturesque and the pathetic affect him much more than plastic beauty or arrangement. So they represent an exceptional instance of the double classical and romantic movement. Let us look for a few concrete images by these two masters of our youth to illustrate an article that is too abstract and perhaps obscure.

In Van Gogh's fiery and jerky execution, in his search for brilliancy and in the violence of his tones I can see what it is that attracts the young *tachistes* [i.e. *Fauves*], and the reason why they are satisfied with patches of pure colour or a few stripes. They admire his aggressive attitude in the face of nature, his abnormal, exasperated but truly lyrical vision of things; his determination to say everything he feels, the insistence with which he asserts the most capricious ups and downs of his sensibility – and with what rudimentary means! – with an infuriated slash, with a great lump of impasto. He has that fierce way of attacking the canvas that the last romantics considered a sign of genius; look at the clumsy caricature of a painter of this type Zola made in *L'Œuvre*. There are traces of the naive and trivial influence or naturalism in the work of this mystic, this refined poet, traces I can still see in the present generation. The word 'temperament' and all it implies in the way of bestiality, maintains its prestige. Van Gogh, in short, has caused the young to relapse into romanticism [. . .]

[. . . With Gauguin] we are dealing with a decorator: the man for whom Aurier in the past so imperiously demanded walls! The man who decorated the living room of the inn at Le Pouldu, as well as his gourd and his clogs! The man who, in Tahiti, in spite of worries, illness and poverty, cared about nothing so much as the decoration of his hut. Italian critics call him the '*Frescante*'. He liked the matt appearance of fresco, which is why he prepared his canvases with thick layers of white distemper. Yet he knew nothing about the Quattrocentists; and we see that like them he made use of the flat application of colour and the precise contour. His art has more in common with tapestry and stained glass than with oil painting.

[. . .] For all the incoherent mess he made of his life, Gauguin would not tolerate any in his paintings. He loved order, a sign of intelligence. The reconstruction of art undertaken by Cézanne with the raw material of Impressionism was continued by Gauguin, with less sensitivity and breadth, but with more theoretical rigour. He rendered Cézanne's thinking more explicit. By reinvigorating it with the sources of art, by seeking out the first principles that he called *the eternal laws of beauty*, he gave it a greater force. 'For me, barbarism is rejuvenation', he wrote. 'I have gone a long way back, beyond the horses of the Parthenon . . . back to the "dada" of my childhood, that good wooden horse.'

We are indebted to the barbarians, to the primitives of 1890, for bringing certain essential truths back into focus. Not to *reproduce* nature and life by approximations or by improvised *trompe-l'oeils*, but on the contrary to reproduce our emotions and our dreams by *representing* them with harmonious forms and colours – that, I continue to believe, was a new way of posing the problem of art – at least for our time; and it's an idea that still bears fruit.

In all this discourse I haven't attempted to throw light on the enigma of the genius [. . .] The evolution from Symbolism to Classicism that I have tried to demonstrate and explain is not intended to diminish the spontaneity of the artist. If we wish there to be certain limits to the artist's freedom and for his sensibility to submit to his reasoned judgement, to be sure it's because we hope these restrictions will strengthen his quality, and that, restrained by just rules, his genius will gain in concentration, force and depth. It is true that I am tired of the individualistic state of mind, with its characteristic rejection of all tradition, teaching and discipline and tendency to regard the artist as some sort of demi-god governed by caprice rather than by rules; it is true that this error, which was my own to begin with, has become insupportable to me. Yet from the Symbolist point of view I continue to consider the work of art as a general translation of individual feelings. So the new order that we are beginning to see and that, as we saw, the experiences and theories of 1890 gave birth to, out of anarchy itself, rests on a systematic subordination of the faculties; at the base of this there still lies the sensation: it's a move from individual sensibility to general reason. The inspiration for the work of art will continue to be found in the intuition of the individual only, in the spontaneous perception of a connection, an equivalence between certain states of mind and certain plastic signs which must of necessity translate them. What is new is thinking that symbolism of this kind, far from being incompatible with the classical method, can in fact renew its effectiveness and develop it in an admirable way. And not the least advantage of this system is that of basing a very objective art, an extremely general, plastic language, in short a classical art, on the most subjective and subtle aspect of the human soul, on the most mysterious workings of our inner life.

References

1   Quotation taken from the preface to the Georges Braque catalogue, written by G. Apollinaire, 1908.
2   I have already given this definition of symbolism many times before. It is less metaphysical than Aurier's . . . but Aurier's was never understood by painters . . . The emotion that a beautiful work of art evokes is in every way similar to the religious emotion which hits us when we enter a Gothic nave: such is the power of the proportions, the colours and the forms brought together by genius that they necessarily impose upon the viewer, whoever he may be, the state of mind of their creator.

10   Cézanne

Maurice Denis

There is something paradoxical in Cézanne's celebrity; and it is scarcely easier to explain than to explain Cézanne himself. The Cézanne question divides inseparably into two camps those who love painting and those who prefer to painting itself the literary and other interests accessory to it. I know indeed that it is the fashion to like painting. The discussions on this question are no longer serious and impassioned. Too many admirations lend themselves to suspicion. 'Snobbism' and speculation have dragged the public into painters' quarrels, and it takes sides according to fashion or interest. Thus it has come about that a public naturally hostile, but well primed by critics and dealers, has conspired to the apotheosis of a great artist, who remains nevertheless a difficult master even for those who love him best.

I have never heard an admirer of Cézanne give me a clear and precise reason for his admiration; and this is true even among those artists who feel most directly the appeal of Cézanne's art. I have heard the words – quality, flavour, importance, interest, classicism, beauty, style. . . . Now of Delacroix or Monet one could briefly formulate a reasoned appreciation which would be clearly intelligible. But how hard it is to be precise about Cézanne!

The mystery with which the Master of Aix-en-Provence surrounded his life has contributed not a little to the obscurity of the explanations, though his reputation has benefited thereby. He was shy, independent, solitary. Exclusively occupied with his art, he was always restless and usually ill-satisfied with himself. He evaded up to his last years the curiosity of the public. Even those who professed his methods remained for the most part ignorant of him. The present writer admits that about 1890, at the period of his first visit to Tanguy's shop, he thought that Cézanne was a myth, perhaps the pseudonym of some artist well known for other efforts, and that he disbelieved in his existence. Since then he has had the honour of seeing him at Aix; and the remarks which he there gathered, collated with those of M. E. Bernard, may help to throw some light upon Cézanne's aesthetics.

At the moment of his death, the articles in the press were unanimous upon two points; and, wherever their inspiration was derived from, they may fairly be considered to reflect the average opinion. The obituaries, then, admitted first of all that Cézanne influenced a large section of the younger artists; and secondly that he made an effort towards style. We may gather, then, that Cézanne was a sort of classic, and that the younger generation regards him as a representative of classicism. [. . .]

Gauguin used to say, thinking of Cézanne: 'Nothing is so much like a *croûte* [daub, badly painted picture] as a real masterpiece.' *Croûte* or masterpiece, one can only understand it in opposition to the mediocrity of modern painting. And already we grasp one of the certain characteristics of the classic, namely, *style*, that is to say

Source: *Burlington Magazine*, XVI January 1910, pp. 207-219 (part I) and February 1910, pp. 275-280 (part II), translated by Roger Fry. Originally published in *L'Occident*, September 1907.

synthetic order. In opposition to modern pictures, a Cézanne inspires by itself, by its qualities of unity in composition and colour, in short by its painting. The actualities, the illustrations to popular novels or historical events, with which the walls of our supposed museum are lined, seek to interest us only by means of the subject represented. Others perhaps establish the virtuosity of their authors. Good or bad, Cézanne's canvas is truly a *picture*.

Suppose now that we put together three works of the same family, three *natures-mortes* [still-lifes], one by Manet, one by Gauguin, one by Cézanne. We shall distinguish at once the objectivity of Manet; that he imitates nature 'as seen through his temperament', that he translates an artistic sensation. Gauguin is more subjective. His is a decorative, even a hieratic interpretation of nature. Before the Cézanne we think only of the picture; neither the object represented nor the artist's personality holds our attention. We cannot decide so quickly whether it is an imitation or an interpretation of nature. We feel that such an art is nearer to Chardin than to Manet and Gauguin. And if at once we say: this is a picture and a classic picture, the word begins to take on a precise meaning, that, namely, of an equilibrium, a reconciliation of the objective and subjective. [. . .]

Thus we arrive at our first estimate of Cézanne as reacting against modern painting and against Impressionism.

When he was first feeling his way out of the tradition of Delacroix, Daumier and Courbet, it was already the old masters of the museums that guided his steps. The revolutionaries of his day never came under the attraction of the old masters. He copied them, and one sees with surprise in his father's house at the Jas de Bouffan a large interpretation of a Lancret and a *Christ in Hades* after Navarete. We must, however, distinguish between this first manner, inspired by the Spanish and Bolognese, and his second fresh and delicately accented manner.

In the first period one sees what Courbet, Delacroix, Daumier and Manet became for him, and by what spontaneous power of assimilation he transmuted in the direction of style certain of their classic tendencies. [. . .]

The same interesting conflict, this combination of style and sensibility, meets us again in Cézanne's second period, only it is the Impressionism of Monet and Pissarro that provides the elements, provokes the reaction to them and causes the transmutation into classicism. With the same vigour with which in his previous period he organized the oppositions of black and white, he now disciplines the contrasts of colour introduced by the study of open air light, and the rainbow iridescences of the new palette. At the same time he substitutes for the summary modelling of his earlier figures the reasoned colour-system found in the figure-pieces and *natures-mortes* of this second period, which one may call his 'brilliant' manner.

Impressionism – and by that I mean much more the general movement, which has changed during the last twenty years the aspect of modern painting, than the special art of a Monet or a Renoir – Impressionism was synthetic in its tendencies, since its aim was to translate a sensation, to realize a mood; but its methods were analytic, since colour for it resulted from an infinity of contrasts. For it was by means of the decomposition of the prism that the Impressionists reconstituted light, divided colour and multiplied reflected lights and gradations; in fact, they substituted for varying greys as many different positive colours. Therein lies the fundamental error of Impressionism. The *Fifre* of Manet in four tones is necessarily more synthetic than the most delicious Renoir, where the play of sunlight and shadow creates the widest range of varied half-tones. Now there is in a fine Cézanne as much simplicity, austerity and grandeur as in Manet, and the gradations retain the freshness and lustre which give their flower-like brilliance to the canvases of Renoir. Some months before his death Cézanne said: 'What I wanted was to make of Impressionism something solid and durable, like the art of the museums.' It was for this reason also that he so much admired the early Pissarros, and still more the early Monets. Monet was, indeed, the only one of his contemporaries for whom he expressed great admiration.

Thus, at first guided by his Latin instinct and his natural inclination, and later with full consciousness of his purpose and his own nature, he set to work to create out of Impressionism a certain classic conception.

In constant reaction against the art of his time, his powerful individuality drew from it none the less the material and pretext for his researches in style; he drew from it the sustaining elements of his work. At a period when the artist's sensibility was considered almost universally to be the sole motive of a work of art, and when improvisation – 'the spiritual excitement provoked by exaltation of the senses' – tended to destroy at one blow both the superannuated conventions of the academies and the necessity for method, it happened that the art of Cézanne showed the way to substitute reflection for empiricism without sacrificing the essential *rôle* of sensibility. Thus, for instance, instead of the chronometric notation of appearances, he was able to hold the emotion of the moment even while he elaborated almost to excess, in a calculated and intentional effort, his studies after nature. He *composed* his *natures-mortes*, varying intentionally the lines and the masses, disposing his draperies according to premeditated rhythms, avoiding the accidents of chance, seeking for plastic beauty; and all this without losing anything of the essential *motive* – that initial motive which is realized in its essentials in his sketches and watercolours. I allude to the delicate symphony of juxtaposed gradations, which his eye discovered at once, but for which at the same moment his reason spontaneously demanded the logical support of composition, of plan and of architecture.

There was nothing less artificial, let us note, than this effort towards a just combination of style and sensibility. That which others have sought, and sometimes found, in the imitation of the old masters, the discipline that he himself in his earlier works sought from the great artists of his time or of the past, he discovered finally in himself. And this is the essential characteristic of Cézanne. His spiritual conformation, his *genius*, did not allow him to profit directly from the old masters: he finds himself in a situation towards them similar to that which he occupied towards his contemporaries. His originality grows in his contact with those whom he imitates or is impressed by; thence comes his persistent *gaucherie* [awkwardness], his happy *naïveté*, and thence also the incredible clumsiness into which his sincerity forced him. For him it is not a question of imposing style upon a study as, after all, Puvis de Chavannes did. He is so naturally a painter, so spontaneously classic. [. . .]

Painting oscillates perpetually between invention and imitation: sometimes it copies and sometimes it imagines. These are its variations. But whether it reproduces objective nature or translates more specifically the artist's emotion, it is bound to be an art of concrete beauty, and our senses must discover in the work of art itself – abstraction made of the subject represented – an immediate satisfaction, a pure aesthetic pleasure. The painting of Cézanne is literally the essential art, the definition of which is so refractory to criticism, the realization of which seems impossible.

It imitates objects without any exactitude and without any accessory interest of sentiment or thought. When he imagines a sketch, he assembles colours and forms without any literary preoccupation; his aim is nearer to that of a Persian carpet weaver than of a Delacroix, transforming into coloured harmony, but with dramatic or lyric intention, a scene of the Bible or of Shakespeare. A negative effort, if you will, but one which declares an unheard of instinct for painting.

He is the man who paints. Renoir said to me one day: 'How on earth does he do it? He cannot put two touches of colour on to a canvas without its being already an achievement.'

It is of little moment what the pretext is for this sampling of colour: nudes improbably grouped in a non-existent landscape, apples in a plate placed awry upon some commonplace material – there is always a beautiful line, a beautiful balance, a sumptuous sequence of resounding harmonies. The gift of freshness, the spontaneity and novelty of his discoveries, add still more to the interest of his slightest sketches. [. . .]

That is surely an important lesson. Have we not confused all the methods of art – mixed together music, literature, painting? In this, too, Cézanne is in reaction. He is a simple artisan, a primitive who returns to the sources of his art, respects its first postulates and necessities, limits himself by its essential elements, by what constitutes exclusively the art of painting. He determines to ignore everything else, both equivocal refinements and deceptive methods. In front of the *motive* he rejects everything that might distract him from painting, might compromise his *petite sensation* as he used to say, making use of the phraseology of the aesthetic philosophy of his youth: he avoids at once deceptive representation and literature. [. . .]

It is a touching spectacle that a canvas of Cézanne presents; generally unfinished, scraped with a palette-knife, scored over with *pentimenti* [literally 'regrets': evidence of the painter's alteration or correction] in turpentine, many times repainted, with an *impasto* that approaches actual relief. In all this evidence of labour, one catches sight of the artist in his struggle for style and his passion for nature; of his acquiescence in certain classic formulae and the revolt of an original sensibility; one sees reason at odds with inexperience, the need for harmony conflicting with the fever of original expression. [. . .]

Let us admit that it gives rise sometimes, with Cézanne, to chaotic results. We have unearthed a classic spontaneity in his very sensations, but the realization is not reached without lapses. Constrained already by his need for synthesis to adopt disconcerting simplifications, he deforms his design still further by the necessity for expression and by his scrupulous sincerity. It is herein that we find the motives for the *gaucherie* with which Cézanne is so often reproached, and herein lies the explanation of that practice of *naïveté* and ungainliness common to his disciples and imitators. [. . .]

What astonishes us most in Cézanne's work is certainly his research for form, or, to be exact, for deformation. It is there that one discovers the most hesitation, the most *pentimenti* on the artist's part. The large picture of the *Baigneuses*, left unfinished in the studio at Aix, is from this point of view typical. Taken up again, numberless times during many years, it has varied but little in general appearance and colour, and even the disposition of the brush-strokes remains almost permanent. On the other hand the dimensions of the figures were often readjusted; sometimes they were life-size, sometimes they were contracted to half; the arms, the torsos, the legs were enlarged and diminished in unimaginable proportions. It is just there that lies the variable element in his work; his sentiment for form allowed neither of silhouette nor of fixed proportions.

For, to begin with, he did not comprehend drawing by line and contour. In spite of the exclamation reported by M. V. during the sittings for his portrait, 'Jean Dominique is strong!', it is certain that he did not love M. Ingres. He used to say, 'Degas is not enough of a painter; he has not enough of *that!*' – and, with a nervous gesture, he imitated the stroke of an Italian decorator. He often talked of the caricaturists, of Gavarni, of Forain, and above all of Daumier. He liked exuberance of movement, relief of muscular forms, impetuosity of hand, bravura of handling. He used to draw from Puget. He demanded always ease and vehemence in execution. He preferred, one cannot doubt, the *chic* drawing of the Bolognese to the conciseness of Ingres.

On the walls of Jas de Bouffan, covered up now with hangings, he has left improvisations, studies painted as the inspiration came, and which seem carried through at a sitting. They make one think, in spite of their fine pictorial quality, of the fanfaronnades of Claude in Zola's *L'Œuvre*, and of his declamations upon 'temperament'. The models of his choice at this period are engravings after the Spanish and Italian artists of the seventeenth century. When I asked him what had led him from this vehemence of execution to the patient technique of the separate brush-stroke, he replied, 'It is because I cannot render my sensation at once; hence I put on colour again, *I put it on as best I can*. But when I begin I endeavour always to paint with a full impasto like Manet, *giving the form with the brush.*'

'There is no such thing as line,' he said, 'no such thing as modelling, there are only contrasts. When colour attains its richness form attains its plenitude.' [Quoted by Emile Bernard.]

Thus, in his essentially concrete perception of objects, form is not separated from colour; they condition one another, they are indissolubly united. And in consequence in his execution he wishes to realize them as he sees them, by a single brush-stroke. If he fails it is certainly in part from the imperfection of his craft, of which he used to complain, but also and above all from his scruples as a colorist, as we shall see presently.

All his faculty for abstraction – and we see how far the painter dominates the theorist – all his faculty for abstraction permits him to distinguish only among notable forms 'the sphere, the cone and the cylinder'. All forms are referred to those which he is alone capable of thinking. The multiplicity of his colour schemes varies them infinitely. But still he never reaches the conception of the circle, the triangle, the parallelogram; those are abstractions which his eye and brain refuse to admit. *Forms* are for him *volumes*.

Hence all objects were bound to tell for him according to their relief, and to be situated according to planes at different distances from the spectator within the supposed depth of the picture. A new antinomy, this, which threatens to render highly accidental 'that plane surface covered with colours arranged in a determined order'. Colorist before everything, as he was, Cézanne resolves this antinomy by chromatism – the transposition, that is, of values of black and white into values of colour.

'I want,' he told me, following the passage from light to shade on his closed fist – 'I want to do with colour what they do in black and white with the stump.' He replaces light by colour. This shadow is a colour, this light, this half-tone are colours. The white of this table-cloth is a blue, a green, a rose; they mingle in the shadows with the surrounding local tints; but the crudity in the light may be harmoniously translated by dissonant blue, green and rose. He substitutes, that is, contrasts of tint for contrasts of tone. He disentangles thus what he used to call 'the confusion of sensations'. In all this conversation, of which I here report scraps, he never once mentioned the word 'values'. His system assuredly excludes relations of values in the sense accepted in the schools.

Volume finds, then, its expression in Cézanne in a gamut of tints, a series of touches; these touches follow one another by contrast or analogy according as the form is interrupted or continuous. This was what he was fond of calling *modulating* instead of modelling. We know the result of this system, at once shimmering and forcible; I will not attempt to describe the richness of harmony and the gaiety of illumination of his pictures. It is like silk, like mother-of-pearl and like velvet. Each *modulated* object manifests its contour by the greater or less exaltation of its colour. If it is in shadow its colour shares the tints of the background. This background is a tissue of tints sacrificed to the principal motive which they accompany. But on any and every pretext the same process recurs on chromatic scales where the colours contrast and interweave in tones and half-tones. The whole canvas is a tapestry where each colour *plays* separately and yet at the same time fuses its sonority in the total effect. The characteristic aspect of Cézanne's pictures comes from this juxta-position, from the mosaic of separate and slightly fused tones. 'Painting', he used to say, 'is the registration of one's coloured sensations' (E. Bernard). Such was the exigence of his eye that he was compelled to have recourse to this refinement of technique in order to preserve the quality, the flavour of his sensations, and satisfy his need of harmony. Bachaumont in 1767 wrote of Chardin: 'His method of painting is singular. He poses his colours one after another, almost without mixing them, in such a way that his work somewhat resembles a mosaic or patchwork like the needlework tapestry called cross-stitch.'

The fruit-pieces of Cézanne and his unfinished figures afford the best examples of this method, the idea of which was perhaps taken from Chardin: a few decisive touches declare the roundness of the form by their juxtaposition with softened tints, the contour does not come till the last, as a vehement accent, put in with turpentine to underline and isolate the form already realized by the gradation of colour.

In this assemblage of tints with an aim at grandeur of style, perspective disap-pears; values too (in the school of art sense) and values of atmosphere are attenuated and equalized. The decorative effect and the balance of the composition appear all the more complete owing to this sacrifice of aerial perspective. Venetian painting with a more enveloping chiaroscuro offers frequently this fine aspect of unity of plane. It is curious that it is this which most struck the first symbolists, Gauguin, Bernard, Anquetin – those, in fact, who were the first to love and imitate Cézanne. Their synthetic system admitted only flat tints and a hard contour; thence arose a whole series of decorative works which I, certainly, do not wish to decry; but how much more synoptic, how much more concrete and vital were the syntheses of Cézanne!

Synthesis does not necessarily mean simplification in the sense of suppression of certain parts of the object; it is simplifying in the sense of *rendering intelligible*. It is, in short, creating a hierarchy: submitting each picture to a single rhythm, to a dominant; sacrificing, subordinating – generalizing. It is not enough to *stylize* an object (as they say in the school of Grasset), to make some sort of copy of it, and then to underline the external contour with a thick stroke. Simplification so obtained is not synthesis. [. . .]

And this, again, is one of the points wherein he touches the classics; he never compromises by abstraction the just equilibrium between nature and style. All his labour is devoted to preserving his sensation; but this sensation implies the identity of colour and form; his sensibility implies his style. Naturally and instinctively he unites, in his spirit if not on his canvas, the grace and brilliance of modern colorists with the robustness of the old masters. Doubtless the realization is not reached without labour nor without lapses. But the order which he discovers is for him a necessity of expression.

He is at once the climax of the classic tradition and the result of the great crisis of liberty and illumination which has rejuvenated modern art. He is the Poussin of Impressionism. He has the fine perception of a Parisian, and he is splendid and exuberant like an Italian decorator. He is orderly as a Frenchman and feverish as a Spaniard. He is a Chardin of the decadence and at times he surpasses Chardin. There is something of El Greco in him and often the healthfulness of Veronese. But such as he is he is so naturally, and all the scruples of his will, all the assiduity of his effort have only aided and exalted his natural gifts. [. . .]

He liked to speak, with an appearance of modesty, of his 'little sensation', of his 'little sensibility'. He complained that Gauguin had taken it from him and *'l'eut promenée dans tous les paquebots'*. In truth his art is so concise and so natural, so living and so spontaneous, that it is difficult to get inspiration from his technical methods without carrying off with them something of himself as well. For Félibien, speaking of painters, the sensation is: 'The application of things to the spirit *or* the judgment which the spirit passes on them.' The two operations, the *Aspect* and *Prospect*, as Poussin says, are no longer separate with Cézanne. To organize one's sensations was a discipline of the seventeenth century; it is the preconceived limitation of the artist's receptivity. But the true artist is like the true *savant*, 'a child-like and serious nature'. He accomplishes this miracle – to preserve amidst his efforts and his scruples all his freshness and *naïveté*.

SECTION TWO

The Development of Modernism

11 The Aesthetic Hypothesis

Clive Bell

It is improbable that more nonsense has been written about aesthetics than about anything else: the literature of the subject is not large enough for that. It is certain, however, that about no subject with which I am acquainted has so little been said that is at all to the purpose. The explanation is discoverable. He who would elaborate a plausible theory of aesthetics must possess two qualities – artistic sensibility and a turn for clear thinking. Without sensibility a man can have no aesthetic experience, and, obviously, theories not based on broad and deep aesthetic experience are worthless. Only those for whom art is a constant source of passionate emotion can possess the data from which profitable theories may be deduced; but to deduce profitable theories even from accurate data involves a certain amount of brain-work, and, unfortunately, robust intellects and delicate sensibilities are not inseparable. As often as not, the hardest thinkers have had no aesthetic experience whatever. I have a friend blessed with an intellect as keen as a drill, who, though he takes an interest in aesthetics, has never during a life of almost forty years been guilty of an aesthetic emotion. So, having no faculty for distinguishing a work of art from a handsaw, he is apt to rear up a pyramid of irrefragable argument on the hypothesis that a handsaw is a work of art. [. . .]

On the other hand, people who respond immediately and surely to works of art, though, in my judgment, more enviable than men of massive intellect but slight sensibility, are often quite as incapable of talking sense about aesthetics. Their heads are not always very clear. They possess the data on which any system must be based; but, generally, they want the power that draws correct inferences from true data. Having received aesthetic emotions from works of art, they are in a position to seek out the quality common to all that have moved them, but, in fact, they do nothing of the sort. I do not blame them. Why should they bother to examine their feelings when for them to feel is enough? Why should they stop to think when they are not very good at thinking? Why should they hunt for a common quality in all objects that move them in a particular way when they can linger over the many delicious and peculiar charms of each as it comes? So, if they write criticism and call it aesthetics, if they imagine that they are talking about Art when they are talking about particular works of art or even about the technique of painting, if, loving particular works they find tedious the consideration of art in general, perhaps they have chosen the better part. If they are not curious about the nature of their emotion, nor about the quality common to all objects that provoke it, they have my sympathy, and, as what they say is often charming and suggestive, my admiration too. Only let no one suppose that what they write and talk is aesthetics; it is criticism, or just 'shop'.

The starting-point for all systems of aesthetics must be the personal experience of

Source: Clive Bell, 'The Aesthetic Hypothesis' in *Art* (Chatto and Windus, 1931), pp. 3–30. First published in 1914. Footnotes have been omitted. Reprinted by permission of Quentin Bell and Chatto and Windus Limited; and G. P. Putnam's Sons.

a peculiar emotion. The objects that provoke this emotion we call works of art. All sensitive people agree that there is a peculiar emotion provoked by works of art. I do not mean, of course, that all works provoke the same emotion. On the contrary, every work produces a different emotion. But all these emotions are recognizably the same in kind; so far, at any rate, the best opinion is on my side. That there is a particular kind of emotion provoked by works of visual art, and that this emotion is provoked by every kind of visual art, by pictures, sculptures, buildings, pots, carvings, textiles, etc., etc., is not disputed, I think, by anyone capable of feeling it. This emotion is called the aesthetic emotion; and if we can discover some quality common and peculiar to all the objects that provoke it, we shall have solved what I take to be the central problem of aesthetics. We shall have discovered the essential quality in a work of art, the quality that distinguishes works of art from all other classes of objects.

For either all works of visual art have some common quality, or when we speak of 'works of art' we gibber. Everyone speaks of 'art', making a mental classification by which he distinguishes the class 'works of art' from all other classes. What is the justification of this classification? What is the quality common and peculiar to all members of this class? Whatever it be, no doubt it is often found in company with other qualities; but they are adventitious – it is essential. There must be some one quality without which a work of art cannot exist; possessing which, in the least degree, no work is altogether worthless. What is this quality? What quality is shared by all objects that provoke our aesthetic emotions? What quality is common to Sta. Sophia and the windows at Chartres, Mexican sculpture, a Persian bowl, Chinese carpets, Giotto's frescoes at Padua, and the masterpieces of Poussin, Piero della Francesca and Cézanne? Only one answer seems possible – significant form. In each, lines and colours combined in a particular way, certain forms and relations of forms, stir our aesthetic emotions. These relations and combinations of lines and colours, these aesthetically moving forms, I call 'significant form'; and 'significant form' is the one quality common to all works of visual art.

At this point it may be objected that I am making aesthetics a purely subjective business, since my only data are personal experiences of a particular emotion. It will be said that the objects that provoke this emotion vary with each individual, and that therefore a system of aesthetics can have no objective validity. It must be replied that any system of aesthetics which pretends to be based on some objective truth is so palpably ridiculous as not to be worth discussing. We have no other means of recognising a work of art than our feeling for it. [. . .] A good critic may be able to make me see in a picture that had left me cold things that I had overlooked, till at last, receiving the aesthetic emotion, I recognise it as a work of art. To be continually pointing out those parts, the sum, or rather the combination, of which unite to produce significant form, is the function of criticism. But it is useless for a critic to tell me that something is a work of art; he must make me feel it for myself. This he can do only by making me see; he must get at my emotions through my eyes. Unless he can make me see something that moves me, he cannot force my emotions. I have no right to consider anything a work of art to which I cannot react emotionally; and I have no right to look for the essential quality in anything that I have not *felt* to be a work of art. The critic can affect my aesthetic theories only by affecting my aesthetic experience. All systems of aesthetics must be based on personal experience – that is to say, they must be subjective.

Yet, though all aesthetic theories must be based on aesthetic judgments, and ultimately all aesthetic judgments must be matters of personal taste, it would be rash to assert that no theory of aesthetics can have general validity. For, though A, B, C, D are the works that move me, and A, D, E, F the works that move you, it may well be that x is the only quality believed by either of us to be common to all the works in his list. We may all agree about aesthetics, and yet differ about particular works of art. We may differ as to the presence or absence of the quality x. My immediate object will be to show that significant form is the only quality common and peculiar to all the works of visual art that move me; and I will ask those whose aesthetic experience does not tally with mine to see whether this quality is not also, in their judgment, common to all works that move them, and whether they can discover any other quality of which the same can be said.

Also at this point a query arises, irrelevant indeed, but hardly to be suppressed: 'Why are we so profoundly moved by forms related in a particular way?' The question is extremely interesting, but irrelevant to aesthetics. In pure aesthetics we have only to consider our emotion and its object: for the purposes of aesthetics we have no right, neither is there any necessity, to pry behind the object, into the state of mind of him who made it. Later, I shall attempt to answer the question; for by so doing I may be able to develop my theory of the relation of art to life. I shall not, however, be under the delusion that I am rounding off my theory of aesthetics. For a discussion of aesthetics, it need be agreed only that forms arranged and combined according to certain unknown and mysterious laws do move us in a particular way, and that it is the business of an artist so to combine and arrange them that they shall move us. These moving combinations and arrangements I have called, for the sake of convenience and for a reason that will appear later, 'significant form'.

A third interruption has to be met.

'Are you forgetting about colour?' someone inquires. Certainly not; my term 'significant form' included combinations of lines and of colours. The distinction between form and colour is an unreal one; you cannot conceive a colourless line or a colourless space; neither can you conceive a formless relation of colours. In a black and white drawing the spaces are all white and all are bounded by black lines; in most oil paintings the spaces are multi-coloured and so are the boundaries; you cannot imagine a boundary line without any content, or a content without a boundary line. Therefore, when I speak of significant form, I mean a combination of lines and colours (counting white and black as colours) that moves me aesthetically.

Some people may be surprised at my not having called this 'beauty'. Of course, to those who define beauty as 'combinations of lines and colours that provoke aesthetic emotion', I willingly concede the right of substituting their word for mine. But most of us, however strict we may be, are apt to apply the epithet 'beautiful' to objects that do not provoke that peculiar emotion produced by works of art. Everyone, I suspect, has called a butterfly or a flower beautiful. Does anyone feel the same kind of emotion for a butterfly or a flower that he feels for a cathedral or a picture? Surely, it is not what I call an aesthetic emotion that most of us feel, generally, for natural beauty. I shall suggest, later, that some people may, occasionally, see in nature what we see in art, and feel for her an aesthetic emotion; but I am satisfied that, as a rule, most people feel a very different kind of emotion for birds and flowers and the wings of butterflies from that which they feel for pictures, pots, temples and statues. Why these beautiful things do not move us as works of art move us is another, and not an aesthetic, question. For our immediate purpose we have to discover only what quality is common to objects that do move us as works of art. In the last part of this chapter, when I try to answer the question – 'Why are we so profoundly moved by some combinations of lines and colours?' I shall hope to offer an acceptable explanation of why we are less profoundly moved by others.

Since we call a quality that does not raise the characteristic aesthetic emotion 'beauty', it would be misleading to call by the same name the quality that does. To make 'beauty' the object of the aesthetic emotion, we must give to the word an over-strict and unfamiliar definition. Everyone sometimes uses 'beauty' in an unaesthetic sense; most people habitually do so. To everyone, except perhaps here and there an occasional aesthete, the commonest sense of the word is unaesthetic. Of its grosser abuse, patent in our chatter about 'beautiful huntin' ' and 'beautiful shootin' ', I need not take account; it would be open to the precious to reply that they never do so abuse it. Besides, here there is no danger of confusion between the aesthetic and the non-aesthetic use; but when we speak of a beautiful woman there is. When an ordinary man speaks of a beautiful woman he certainly does not mean that she moves him aesthetically; but when an artist calls a withered old hag beautiful he may sometimes mean what he means when he calls a battered torso beautiful. The ordinary man, if he be also a man of taste, will call the battered torso beautiful, but he will not call a withered hag beautiful because, in the matter of women, it is not to the aesthetic quality that the hag may possess, but to some other quality that he assigns the epithet. Indeed, most of us never dream of going for aesthetic emotions to human beings, from whom we ask something very different. This 'something', when we find it in a young woman, we are apt to call 'beauty'. We live in a nice age. With the man-in-the-street 'beautiful' is more often than not synonymous with 'desirable'; the word does not necessarily connote any aesthetic reaction whatever, and I am tempted to believe that in the minds of many the sexual flavour of the word is stronger than the aesthetic. I have noticed a consistency in those to whom the most beautiful thing in the world is a beautiful woman, and the next most beautiful thing a picture of one. The confusion between aesthetic and sensual beauty is not in their case so great as might be supposed. Perhaps there is none; for perhaps they have never had an aesthetic emotion to confuse with their other emotions. The art that they call 'beautiful' is generally closely related to the women. A beautiful picture is a photograph of a pretty girl; beautiful music, the music that provokes emotions similar to those provoked by young ladies in musical farces; and beautiful poetry, the poetry that recalls the same emotions felt, twenty years earlier, for the rector's daughter. Clearly the word 'beauty' is used to connote the objects of quite distinguishable emotions, and that is a reason for not employing a term which would land me inevitably in confusions and misunderstandings with my readers.

On the other hand, with those who judge it more exact to call these combinations and arrangements of form that provoke our aesthetic emotions, not 'significant form', but 'significant relations of form', and then try to make the best of two worlds, the aesthetic and the metaphysical, by calling these relations 'rhythm', I have no quarrel whatever. Having made it clear that by 'significant form' I mean arrangements and combinations that move us in a particular way, I willingly join hands with those who prefer to give a different name to the same thing.

The hypothesis that significant form is the essential quality in a work of art has at least one merit denied to many more famous and more striking – it does help to explain things. We are all familiar with pictures that interest us and excite our admiration, but do not move us as works of art. To this class belongs what I call 'descriptive painting' – that is, painting in which forms are used not as objects of emotion, but as means of suggesting emotion or conveying information. Portraits of psychological and historical value, topographical works, pictures that tell stories and suggest situations, illustrations of all sorts, belong to this class. That we all recognize the distinction is clear, for who has not said that such and such a drawing was excellent as illustration, but as a work of art worthless? Of course many descriptive pictures possess, amongst other qualities, formal significance, and are therefore works of art: but many more do not. They interest us; they may move us too in a hundred different ways, but they do not move us aesthetically. According to my hypothesis they are not works of art. They leave untouched our aesthetic emotions because it is not their forms but the ideas or information suggested or conveyed by their forms that affect us.

Few pictures are better known or liked than Frith's *Paddington Station*; certainly I should be the last to grudge it its popularity. Many a weary forty minutes have I whiled away disentangling its fascinating incidents and forging for each an imaginary past and an improbable future. But certain though it is that Frith's masterpiece, or engravings of it, have provided thousands with half-hours of curious and fanciful pleasure, it is not less certain that no one has experienced before it one half-second of aesthetic rapture – and this although the picture contains several pretty passages of colour, and is by no means badly painted. *Paddington Station* is not a work of art; it is an interesting and amusing document. In it line and colour are used to recount anecdotes, suggest ideas and indicate the manners and customs of an age: they are not used to provoke aesthetic emotion. Forms and the relations of forms were for Frith not objects of emotion, but means of suggesting emotion and conveying ideas.

The ideas and information conveyed by *Paddington Station* are so amusing and so well presented that the picture has considerable value and is well worth preserving. But, with the perfection of photographic processes and of the cinematograph, pictures of this sort are becoming otiose. Who doubts that one of those *Daily Mirror* photographers in collaboration with a *Daily Mail* reporter can tell us far more about 'London day by day' than any Royal Academician? For an account of manners and fashions we shall go, in future, to photographs, supported by a little bright journalism, rather than to descriptive painting. Had the imperial academicians of Nero, instead of manufacturing incredibly loathsome imitations of the antique, recorded in fresco and mosaic the manners and fashions of their day, their stuff, though artistic rubbish, would now be an historical gold-mine. If only they had been Friths instead of being Alma Tademas! But photography has made impossible any such transmutation of modern rubbish. Therefore it must be confessed that pictures in the Frith tradition are grown superfluous; they merely waste the hours of able men who might be more profitably employed in works of a wider beneficence. Still, they are not unpleasant, which is more than can be said for that kind of descriptive painting of which *The Doctor* is the most flagrant example. [A painting of 1891 by Sir Luke Fildes, now in the Tate Gallery, showing a well-dressed doctor attending a sick child in a working-class cottage. It achieved considerable notoriety when shown in the Royal Academy.] Of course *The Doctor* is not a work of art. In it form is not used as an object of emotion, but as a means of suggesting emotions. This alone suffices to make it nugatory; it is worse than nugatory because the emotion it suggests is false. What it suggests is not pity and admiration but a sense of complacency in our own pitifulness and generosity. It is sentimental. Art is above morals, or, rather, all art is moral because, as I hope to show presently, works of art are immediate means to good. Once we have judged a thing a work of art, we have judged it ethically of the first importance and put it beyond the reach of the moralist. But descriptive pictures which are not works of art, and, therefore, are not necessarily means to good states of mind, are proper objects of the ethical philosopher's attention. Not being a work of art, *The Doctor* has none of the immense ethical value possessed by all objects that provoke aesthetic ecstasy; and the state of mind to which it is a means, as illustration, appears to me undesirable. [. . .]

Most people who care much about art find that of the work that moves them most the greater part is what scholars call 'primitive'. Of course there are bad primitives. [. . .But] as a rule primitive art is good – and here again my hypothesis is helpful – for, as a rule, it is also free from descriptive qualities. In primitive art you will find no accurate representation; you will find only significant form. Yet no other art moves us so profoundly. [. . .] In every case we observe three common characteristics – absence of representation, absence of technical swagger, sublimely impressive form. Nor is it hard to discover the connection between these three. Formal significance loses itself in preoccupation with exact representation and ostentatious cunning.

Naturally, it is said that if there is little representation and less saltimbancery in primitive art, that is because the primitives were unable to catch a likeness or cut intellectual capers. The contention is beside the point. There is truth in it, no doubt, though, were I a critic whose reputation depended on a power of impressing the public with a semblance of knowledge, I should be more cautious about urging it than such people generally are. For to suppose that the Byzantine masters wanted skill, or could not have created an illusion had they wished to do so, seems to imply ignorance of the amazingly dexterous realism of the notoriously bad works of that age. Very often, I fear, the misrepresentation of the primitives must be attributed to what the critics call 'wilful distortion'. Be that as it may, the point is that, either from want of skill or want of will, primitives neither create illusions, nor make display of extravagant accomplishment, but concentrate their energies on the one thing needful – the creation of form. Thus have they created the finest works of art that we possess.

Let no one imagine that representation is bad in itself; a realistic form may be as significant, in its place as part of the design, as an abstract. But if a representative form has value, it is as form, not as representation. The representative element in a work of art may or may not be harmful; always it is irrelevant. For, to appreciate a work of art we need bring with us nothing from life, no knowledge of its ideas and affairs, no familiarity with its emotions. Art transports us from the world of man's activity to a world of aesthetic exaltation. For a moment we are shut off from human interests; our anticipations and memories are arrested; we are lifted above the stream of life. The pure mathematician rapt in his studies knows a state of mind which I take to be similar, if not identical. He feels an emotion for his speculations which arises from no perceived relation between them and the lives of men, but springs, inhuman or superhuman, from the heart of an abstract science. I wonder, sometimes, whether the appreciators of art and of mathematical solutions are not even more closely allied. Before we feel an aesthetic emotion for a combination of forms, do we not perceive intellectually the rightness and necessity of the combination? If we do, it would explain the fact that passing rapidly through a room we recognize a picture to be good, although we cannot say that it has provoked much emotion. We seem to have recognized intellectually the rightness of its forms without staying to fix our attention, and collect, as it were, their emotional significance. If this were so, it would be permissible to inquire whether it was the forms themselves or our perception of their rightness and necessity that caused aesthetic emotion. But I do not think I need linger to discuss the matter here. I have been inquiring why certain combinations of forms move us; I should not have travelled by other roads had I enquired, instead, why certain combinations are perceived to be right and necessary, and why our perception of their rightness and necessity is moving. What I have to say is this: the rapt philosopher, and he who contemplates a work of art, inhabit a world with an intense and peculiar significance of its own; that significance is unrelated to the significance of life. In this world the emotions of life find no place. It is a world with emotions of its own.

To appreciate a work of art we need bring with us nothing but a sense of form and colour and a knowledge of three-dimensional space. That bit of knowledge, I admit, is essential to the appreciation of many great works, since many of the most moving forms ever created are in three dimensions. To see a cube or a rhomboid as a flat pattern is to lower its significance, and a sense of three-dimensional space is essential to the full appreciation of most architectural forms. Pictures which would be insignificant if we saw them as flat patterns are profoundly moving because, in fact, we see them as related planes. If the representation of three-dimensional space is to be called 'representation', then I agree that there is one kind of representation which is not irrelevant. Also, I agree that along with our feeling for line and colour we must bring with us our knowledge of space if we are to make the most of every kind of form. Nevertheless, there are magnificent designs to an appreciation of which this knowledge is not necessary: so, though it is not irrelevant to the appreciation of some works of art it is not essential to the appreciation of all. What we must say is that the representation of three-dimensional space is neither irrelevant nor essential to all art, and that every other sort of representation is irrelevant.

That there is an irrelevant representative or descriptive element in many great works of art is not in the least surprising. Why it is not surprising I shall try to show elsewhere. Representation is not of necessity baneful, and highly realistic forms may be extremely significant. Very often, however, representation is a sign of weakness in an artist. A painter too feeble to create forms that provoke more than a little aesthetic emotion will try to eke that little out by suggesting the emotions of life. To evoke the emotions of life he must use representation. Thus a man will paint an execution, and, fearing to miss with his first barrel of significant form, will try to hit with his second by raising an emotion of fear or pity. But if in the artist an inclination to play upon the emotions of life is often the sign of a flickering inspiration, in the spectator a tendency to seek, behind form, the emotions of life is a sign of defective sensibility always. It means that his aesthetic emotions are weak or, at any rate, imperfect. Before a work of art people who feel little or no emotion for pure form find themselves at a loss. They are deaf men at a concert. They know that they are in the presence of something great, but they lack the power of apprehending it. They know that they ought to feel for it a tremendous emotion, but it happens that the particular kind of emotion it can raise is one that they can feel hardly or not at all. And so they read into the forms of the work those facts and ideas for which they are capable of feeling emotion, and feel for them the emotions that they can feel – the ordinary emotions of life. When confronted by a picture, instinctively they refer back its forms to the world from which they came. They treat created form as though it were imitated form, a picture as though it were a photograph. Instead of going out on the stream of art into a new world of aesthetic experience, they turn a sharp corner and come straight home to the world of human interests. For them the significance of a work of art depends on what they bring to it; no new thing is added to their lives, only the old material is stirred.

A good work of visual art carries a person who is capable of appreciating it out of life into ecstasy: to use art as a means to the emotions of life is to use a telescope for reading the news. You will notice that people who cannot feel pure aesthetic emotions remember pictures by their subjects; whereas people who can, as often as not, have no idea what the subject of a picture is. They have never noticed the representative element, and so when they discuss pictures they talk about the shapes of forms and the relations and quantities of colours. Often they can tell by the quality of a single line whether or not a man is a good artist. They are concerned only with lines and colours, their relations and quantities and qualities; but from these they win an emotion more profound and far more sublime than any that can be given by the description of facts and ideas. [. . .]

12   The Debt to Cézanne

Clive Bell

That with the maturity of Cézanne a new movement came to birth will hardly be disputed by anyone who has managed to survive the 'nineties'; that this movement is the beginning of a new slope is a possibility worth discussing, but about which no decided opinion can yet be held. In so far as one man can be said to inspire a whole age, Cézanne inspires the contemporary movement: he stands a little apart, however, because he is too big to take a place in any scheme of historical development; he is one of those figures that dominate an age and are not to be fitted into any of the neat little pigeon-holes so thoughtfully prepared for us by evolutionists. He passed through the greater part of life unnoticed, and came near creeping out of it undiscovered. No one seems to have guessed at what was happening. It is easy now to see how much we owe to him, and how little he owed to anyone; for us it is easy to see what Gauguin and Van Gogh borrowed – in 1890, the year in which the latter died, it was not so. They were sharp eyes, indeed, that discerned before the dawn of the new century that Cézanne had founded a movement.

That movement is still young. But I think it would be safe to say that already it has produced as much good art as its predecessor. Cézanne, of course, created far greater things than any Impressionist painter; and Gauguin, Van Gogh, Matisse, Rousseau, Picasso, de Vlaminck, Derain, Herbin, Marchand, Marquet, Bonnard, Duncan Grant, Maillol, Lewis, Kandinsky, Brancuzi, von Anrep, Roger Fry, Friesz, Goncharova, L'Hôte, are Rolands for the Olivers of any other artistic period. They are not all great artists, but they all are artists. If the Impressionists raised the proportion of works of art in the general pictorial output from about one in five hundred thousand to one in a hundred thousand, the Post-Impressionists (for after all it is sensible to call the group of vital artists who immediately follow the Impressionists by that name) have raised the average again. Today, I daresay, it stands as high as one in ten thousand. Indeed, it is this that has led some people to see in the new movement the dawn of a new age; for nothing is more characteristic of a 'primitive' movement than the frequent and widespread production of genuine art. Another hopeful straw at which the sanguine catch is the admirable power of development possessed by the new inspiration. As a rule, the recognition of a movement as a movement is its death. As soon as the pontiffs discovered Impressionism, some twenty years after its patent manifestation, they academized it. They set their faces against any sort of development and drove into revolt or artistic suicide every student with an ounce of vitality in him. Before the inspiration of Cézanne had time to grow stale, it was caught up by such men as Matisse and Picasso; by them it was moulded into forms that suited their different temperaments, and already it

Source: Clive Bell, 'The Debt to Cézanne' in *Art* (Chatto and Windus, 1931), pp. 199–214. First published in 1914. Footnotes have been omitted. Reprinted by Quentin Bell and Chatto and Windus, and G. P. Putnam's Sons.

shows signs of taking fresh shape to express the sensibility of a younger generation.
[. . .]

It may be because the nineteenth century was preparing Europe for a new epoch, that it understood better its destructive critics than its constructive artists. At any rate before that century ended it had produced one of the great constructive artists of the world, and overlooked him. Whether or no he marks the beginning of a slope, Cézanne certainly marks the beginning of a movement the main characteristics of which it will be my business to describe. For, though there is some absurdity in distinguishing one artistic movement from another, since all works of art, to whatever age they belong, are essentially the same; yet these superficial differences which are the characteristics of a movement have an importance beyond that dubious one of assisting historians. The particular methods of creating form, and the particular kinds of form affected by the artists of one generation, have an important bearing on the art of the next. For whereas the methods and forms of one may admit of almost infinite development, the methods and forms of another may admit of nothing but imitation. For instance, the fifteenth-century movement that began with Masaccio, Uccello and Castagno opened up a rich vein of rather inferior ore; whereas the school of Raphael was a blind alley. Cézanne discovered methods and forms which have revealed a vista of possibilities to the end of which no man can see; on the instrument that he invented thousands of artists yet unborn may play their own tunes.

What the future will owe to Cézanne we cannot guess: what contemporary art owes to him it would be hard to compute. Without him the artists of genius and talent who today delight us with the significance and originality of their work might have remained port-bound for ever, ill-discerning their objective, wanting chart, rudder and compass. Cézanne is the Christopher Columbus of a new continent of form. In 1839 he was born at Aix-en-Provence, and for forty years he painted patiently in the manner of his master Pissarro. To the eyes of the world he appeared, so far as he appeared at all, a respectable, minor Impressionist, an admirer of Manet, a friend, if not a protégé, of Zola, a loyal, negligible disciple. He was on the right side, of course – the Impressionist side, the side of the honest, disinterested artists, against the academic, literary pests. He believed in painting. He believed that it could be something better than an expensive substitute for photography or an accompaniment to poor poetry. So in 1870 he was for science against sentimentality.

But science will neither make nor satisfy an artist: and perhaps Cézanne saw what the great Impressionists could not see, that though they were still painting exquisite pictures their theories had led art into a *cul de sac*. So while he was working away in his corner of Provence, shut off completely from the aestheticism of Paris, from Baudelairism and Whistlerism, Cézanne was always looking for something to replace the bad science of Claude Monet. And somewhere about 1880 he found it. At Aix-en-Provence came to him a revelation that has set a gulf between the nineteenth century and the twentieth: for, gazing at the familiar landscape, Cézanne came to understand it, not as a mode of light, nor yet as a player in the game of human life, but as an end in itself and an object of intense emotion. Every great artist has seen landscape as an end in itself – as pure form, that is to say; Cézanne has made a generation of artists feel that compared with its significance as an end in itself all else about a landscape is negligible. From that time forward Cézanne set himself to create forms that would express the emotion that he felt for what he had learnt to see. Science became as irrelevant as subject. Everything can be seen as pure form, and behind pure form lurks the mysterious significance that thrills to ecstasy. The rest of Cézanne's life is a continuous effort to capture and express the significance of form.

I have tried to say in another place that there are more roads than one by which a man may come at reality. Some artists seem to have come at it by sheer force of imagination, unaided by anything without them; they have needed no material ladder to help them out of matter. They have spoken with reality as mind to mind, and have passed on the message in forms which owe nothing but bare existence to the physical universe. Of this race are the best musicians and architects; of this race is not Cézanne. He travelled towards reality along the traditional road of European painting. It was in what he saw that he discovered a sublime architecture haunted by that Universal which informs every Particular. He pushed further and further towards a complete revelation of the significance of form, but he needed something concrete as a point of departure. It was because Cézanne could come at reality only through what he saw that he never invented purely abstract forms. Few great artists have depended more on the model. Every picture carried him a little further towards his goal – complete expression; and because it was not the making of pictures but the expression of his sense of the significance of form that he cared about, he lost interest in his work so soon as he had made it express as much as he had grasped. His own pictures were for Cézanne nothing but rungs in a ladder at the top of which would be complete expression. The whole of his later life was a climbing towards an ideal. For him every picture was a means, a step, a stick, a hold, a stepping-stone – something he was ready to discard as soon as it had served his purpose. He had no use for his own pictures. To him they were experiments. He tossed them into bushes, or left them in the open fields to be stumbling-blocks for a future race of luckless critics.

Cézanne is a type of the perfect artist; he is the perfect antithesis of the professional picture-maker, or poem-maker, or music-maker. He created forms because only by so doing could he accomplish the end of his existence – the expression of his sense of the significance of form. When we are talking about aesthetics, very properly we brush all this aside, and consider only the object and its emotional effect on us; but when we are trying to explain the emotional effectiveness of pictures we turn naturally to the minds of the men who made them, and find in the story of Cézanne an inexhaustible spring of suggestion. His life was a constant effort to create forms that would express what he felt in the moment of inspiration. The notion of uninspired art, of a formula for making pictures, would have appeared to him preposterous. The real business of his life was not to make pictures, but to work out his own salvation. Fortunately for us he could only do this by painting. Any two pictures by Cézanne are bound to differ profoundly. He never dreamed of repeating himself. He could not stand still. That is why a whole generation of otherwise dissimilar artists have drawn inspiration from his work. That is why it implies no disparagement of any living artist when I say that the prime characteristic of the new movement is its derivation from Cézanne.

The world into which Cézanne tumbled was a world still agitated by the quarrels of Romantics and Realists. The quarrel between Romance and Realism is the quarrel of people who cannot agree as to whether the history of Spain or the number of pips is the more important thing about an orange. The Romantics and Realists were deaf men coming to blows about the squeak of a bat. The instinct of a Romantic invited to say what he felt about anything was to recall its associations. A rose, for instance, made him think of old gardens and young ladies and sundials, and a thousand quaint and gracious things that, at one time or another, had befallen him or someone else. A rose touched life at a hundred pretty points. A rose was interesting because it had a past. 'Bosh,' said the Realist, 'I will tell you what a rose is; that is to say, I will give you a detailed account of the properties of *Rosa setigera*, not forgetting to mention the urn-shaped calyx-tube, the five imbricated lobes, or the open corolla of five obovate petals.' To a Cézanne one account would appear as irrelevant as the other, since both omit the thing that matters – what philosophers used to call 'the thing in itself', what now, I imagine, they call 'the essential reality'. For, after all, what is a rose? What is a tree, a dog, a wall, a boat? What is the particular significance of anything? Certainly the essence of a boat is not that it conjures up visions of argosies with purple sails, nor yet that it carries coals to Newcastle. Imagine a boat in complete isolation, detach it from man and his urgent activities and fabulous history, what is it that remains, what is that to which we still react emotionally? What but pure form, and that which, lying behind pure form, gives it its significance. It was for this Cézanne felt the emotion he spent his life in expressing. And the second characteristic of the new movement is a passionate interest, inherited from Cézanne, in things regarded as ends in themselves. In saying this I am saying no more than that the painters of the movement are consciously determined to be artists. Peculiarity lies in the consciousness – the consciousness with which they set themselves to eliminate all that lies between themselves and the pure forms of things. To be an artist, they think, suffices. How many men of talent, and even of genius, have missed being effective artists because they tried to be something else?

13   An Essay in Aesthetics

Roger Fry

A certain painter, not without some reputation at the present day, once wrote a little book on the art he practises, in which he gave a definition of that art so succinct that I take it as a point of departure for this essay.

'The art of painting', says that eminent authority, 'is the art of imitating solid objects upon a flat surface by means of pigments.' It is delightfully simple, but prompts the question – Is that all? And, if so, what a deal of unnecessary fuss has been made about it. Now, it is useless to deny that our modern writer has some very respectable authorities behind him. Plato, indeed, gave a very similar account of the affair, and himself put the question – is it then worth while? And, being scrupulously and relentlessly logical, he decided that it was not worth while, and proceeded to turn the artists out of his ideal republic. For all that, the world has continued obstinately to consider that painting was worth while, and though, indeed, it has never quite made up its mind as to what, exactly, the graphic arts did for it, it has persisted in honouring and admiring its painters.

Can we arrive at any conclusions as to the nature of the graphic arts, which will at all explain our feelings about them, which will at least put them into some kind of relation with the other arts, and not leave us in the extreme perplexity, engendered by any theory of mere imitation? For, I suppose, it must be admitted that if imitation is the sole purpose of the graphic arts, it is surprising that the works of such arts are ever looked upon as more than curiosities, or ingenious toys, are ever taken seriously by grown-up people. Moreover, it will be surprising that they have any recognizable affinity with other arts, such as music or architecture, in which the imitation of actual objects is a negligible quantity.

To form such conclusions is the aim I have put before myself in this essay. Even if the results are not decisive, the inquiry may lead us to a view of the graphic arts that will not be altogether unfruitful.

I must begin with some elementary psychology, with a consideration of the nature of instincts. A great many objects in the world, when presented to our senses, put in motion a complex nervous machinery, which ends in some instinctive appropriate action. We see a wild bull in a field; quite without our conscious interference a nervous process goes on, which, unless we interfere forcibly, ends in the appropriate reaction of flight. The nervous mechanism which results in flight causes a certain state of consciousness, which we call the emotion of fear. The whole of animal life, and a great part of human life, is made up of these instinctive reactions to sensible objects, and their accompanying emotions. But man has the peculiar faculty of calling up again in his mind the echo of past experiences of this kind, of going over it

Source: Roger Fry, *Vision and Design* (Pelican, 1961), pp. 23–29. 'An Essay in Aesthetics' first published in *New Quarterly*, 1909. *Vision and Design* first published in 1920 by Chatto and Windus. This is an edited extract and footnotes have been omitted. Reprinted by permission of Mrs Pamela Diamand and Chatto and Windus Ltd. Copyright © Mrs Pamela Diamand 1920. *Vision and Design* was re-issued in 1981 by Oxford University Press.

again, 'in imagination' as we say. He has, therefore, the possibility of a double life; one the actual life, the other the imaginative life. Between these two lives there is this great distinction, that in the actual life the processes of natural selection have brought it about that the instinctive reaction, such, for instance, as flight from danger, shall be the important part of the whole process, and it is towards this that the man bends his whole conscious endeavour. But in the imaginative life no such action is necessary, and, therefore, the whole consciousness may be focused upon the perceptive and the emotional aspects of the experience. In this way we get, in the imaginative life, a different set of values, and a different kind of perception.

We can get a curious side-glimpse of the nature of this imaginative life from the cinematograph. This resembles actual life in almost every respect, except that what the psychologists call the conative part of our reaction to sensations, that is to say, the appropriate resultant action is cut off. If, in a cinematograph, we see a runaway horse and cart, we do not have to think either of getting out of the way or heroically interposing ourselves. The result is that in the first place we *see* the event much more clearly; see a number of quite interesting but irrelevant things, which in real life could not struggle into our consciousness, bent, as it would be, entirely upon the problem of our appropriate reaction. [. . .]

In the second place, with regard to the visions of the cinematograph, one notices that whatever emotions are aroused by them, though they are likely to be weaker than those of ordinary life, are presented more clearly to the consciousness. If the scene presented be one of an accident, our pity and horror, though weak, since we know that no one is really hurt, are felt quite purely, since they cannot, as they would in life, pass at once into actions of assistance.

A somewhat similar effect to that of the cinematograph can be obtained by watching a mirror in which a street scene is reflected. If we look at the street itself we are almost sure to adjust ourselves in some way to its actual existence. We recognize an acquaintance, and wonder why he looks so dejected this morning, or become interested in a new fashion in hats – the moment we do that the spell is broken, we are reacting to life itself in however slight a degree, but, in the mirror, it is easier to abstract ourselves completely, and look upon the changing scene as a whole. It then, at once, takes on the visionary quality, and we become true spectators, not selecting what we will see, but seeing everything equally, and thereby we come to notice a number of appearances and relations of appearances, which would have escaped our notice before, owing to that perpetual economizing by selection of what impressions we will assimilate, which in life we perform by unconscious processes. The frame of the mirror, then, does to some extent turn the reflected scene from one that belongs to our actual life into one that belongs rather to the imaginative life. The frame of the mirror makes its surface into a very rudimentary work of art, since it helps us to attain to the artistic vision. For that is what, as you will already have guessed, I have been coming to all this time, namely that the work of art is intimately connected with the secondary imaginative life, which all men live to a greater or less extent.

That the graphic arts are the expression of the imaginative life rather than a copy of actual life might be guessed from observing children. Children, if left to them-selves, never, I believe, copy what they see, never, as we say, 'draw from nature', but express, with a delightful freedom and sincerity, the mental images which make up their own imaginative lives.

Art, then, is an expression and a stimulus of this imaginative life, which is separated from actual life by the absence of responsive action. Now this responsive action implies in actual life moral responsibility. In art we have no such moral responsibility – it presents a life freed from the binding necessities of our actual existence.

What then is the justification for this life of the imagination which all human beings live more or less fully? To the pure moralist, who accepts nothing but ethical values, in order to be justified, it must be shown not only *not* to hinder but actually to forward right action, otherwise it is not only useless but, since it absorbs our energies, positively harmful. To such a one two views are possible, one the Puritanical view at its narrowest, which regards the life of the imagination as no better or worse than a life of sensual pleasure, and therefore entirely reprehensible. The other view is to argue that the imaginative life does subserve morality. And this is inevitably the view taken by moralists like Ruskin, to whom the imaginative life is yet an absolute necessity. It is a view which leads to some very hard special pleading, even to a self-deception which is in itself morally undesirable.

But here comes in the question of religion, for religion is also an affair of the imaginative life, and, though it claims to have a direct effect upon conduct, I do not suppose that the religious person if he were wise would justify religion entirely by its effect on morality, since that, historically speaking, has not been by any means uniformly advantageous. He would probably say that the religious experience was one which corresponded to certain spiritual capacities of human nature, the exercise of which is in itself good and desirable apart from their effect upon actual life. And so, too, I think the artist might if he chose take a mystical attitude, and declare that the fullness and completeness of the imaginative life he leads may correspond to an existence more real and more important than any that we know of in mortal life.

And in saying this, his appeal would find a sympathetic echo in most minds, for most people would, I think, say that the pleasures derived from art were of an altogether different character and more fundamental than merely sensual pleasures, that they did exercise some faculties which are felt to belong to whatever part of us there may be which is not entirely ephemeral and material.

It might even be that from this point of view we should rather justify actual life by its relation to the imaginative, justify nature by its likeness to art. I mean this, that since the imaginative life comes in the course of time to represent more or less what mankind feels to be the completest expression of its own nature, the freest use of its innate capacities, the actual life may be explained and justified by its approximation here and there, however partially and inadequately, to that freer and fuller life.

Before leaving this question of the justification of art, let me put it in another way. The imaginative life of a people has very different levels at different times, and these levels do not always correspond with the general level of the morality of actual life. Thus in the thirteenth century we read of barbarity and cruelty which would shock even us; we may, I think, admit that our moral level, our general humanity is decidedly higher today, but the level of our imaginative life is incomparably lower; we are satisfied there with a grossness, a sheer barbarity and squalor which would have shocked the thirteenth century profoundly. Let us admit the moral gain gladly, but do we not also feel a loss; do we not feel that the average businessman would be in every way a more admirable, more respectable being if his imaginative life were not so squalid and incoherent? And, if we admit any loss then, there is some function in human nature other than a purely ethical one, which is worthy of exercise.

Now the imaginative life has its own history both in the race and in the individual. In the individual life one of the first effects of freeing experience from the necessities of appropriate responsive action is to indulge recklessly the emotion of self-aggrandisement. The day-dreams of a child are filled with extravagant romances in which he is always the invincible hero. [. . .] But with the teaching of experience and the growth of character the imaginative life comes to respond to other instincts and to satisfy other desires, until, indeed, it reflects the highest aspirations and the deepest aversions of which human nature is capable.

In dreams and when under the influence of drugs the imaginative life passes out of our own control, and in such cases its experiences may be highly undesirable, but whenever it remains under our own control it must always be on the whole a desirable life. That is not to say that it is always pleasant, for it is pretty clear that mankind is so constituted as to desire much besides pleasure, and we shall meet among the great artists, the great exponents, that is, of the imaginative life, many to whom the merely pleasant is very rarely a part of what is desirable. But this desirability of the imaginative life does distinguish it very sharply from actual life, and this is the direct result of that first fundamental difference, its freedom from necessary external conditions. Art, then, is, if I am right, the chief organ of the imaginative life; it is by art that it is stimulated and controlled within us, and, as we have seen, the imaginative life is distinguished by the greater clearness of its perception, and the greater purity and freedom of its emotion.

First with regard to the greater clearness of perception. The needs of our actual life are so imperative, that the sense of vision becomes highly specialized in their service. With an admirable economy we learn to see only so much as is needful for our purposes; but this is in fact very little, just enough to recognize and identify each object or person; that done, they go into an entry in our mental catalogue and are no more really seen. In actual life the normal person really only reads the labels as it were on the objects around him and troubles no further. Almost all the things which are useful in any way put on more or less this cap of invisibility. It is only when an object exists in our lives for no other purpose than to be seen that we really look at it, as for instance at a china ornament or a precious stone, and towards such even the most normal person adopts to some extent the artistic attitude of pure vision abstracted from necessity.

Now this specialization of vision goes so far that ordinary people have almost no idea of what things really look like, so that oddly enough the one standard that popular criticism applies to painting, namely, whether it is like nature or not, is one which most people are, by the whole tenor of their lives, prevented from applying properly. The only things they have ever really *looked* at being other pictures; the moment an artist who has looked at nature brings to them a clear report of something definitely seen by him, they are wildly indignant at its untruth to nature. This has happened so constantly in our own time that there is no need to prove it. One instance will suffice. Monet is an artist whose chief claim to recognition lies in the fact of his astonishing power of faithfully reproducing certain aspects of nature, but his really naïve innocence and sincerity were taken by the public to be the most audacious humbug, and it required the teaching of men like Bastien-Lepage, who cleverly compromised between the truth and an accepted convention of what things looked like, to bring the world gradually round to admitting truths which a single walk in the country with purely unbiased vision would have established beyond doubt.

But though this clarified sense perception which we discover in the imaginative life is of great interest, and although it plays a larger part in the graphic arts than in any other, it might perhaps be doubted whether, interesting, curious, fascinating as it is, this aspect of the imaginative life would ever by itself make art of profound importance to mankind. But it is different, I think, with the emotional aspect. We have admitted that the emotions of the imaginative are generally weaker than those of actual life. The picture of a saint being slowly flayed alive, revolting as it is, will not produce the same physical sensations of sickening disgust that a modern man would feel if he could assist at the actual event; but they have a compensating clearness of presentment to the consciousness. The more poignant emotions of actual life have, I think, a kind of numbing effect analogous to the paralysing influence of fear in some animals; but even if this experience be not generally admitted, all will admit that the need for responsive action hurries us along and prevents us from ever realizing fully what the emotion is that we feel, from coordinating it perfectly with other states. In short, the motives we actually experience are too close to us to enable us to feel them clearly. They are in a sense unintelligible. In the imaginative life, on the contrary, we can both feel the emotion and watch it. When we are really moved at the theatre we are always both on the stage and in the auditorium.

Yet another point about the emotions of the imaginative life – since they require no responsive action we can give them a new valuation. In real life we must to some extent cultivate those emotions which lead to useful action, and we are bound to appraise emotions according to the resultant action. So that, for instance, the feelings of rivalry and emulation do get an encouragement which perhaps they scarcely deserve, whereas certain feelings which appear to have a high intrinsic value get almost no stimulus in actual life. For instance, those feelings to which the name of the cosmic emotion has been somewhat unhappily given find almost no place in life, but, since they seem to belong to certain very deep springs of our nature, do become of great importance in the arts.

Morality, then, appreciates emotion by the standard of resultant action. Art appreciates emotion in and for itself.

This view of the essential importance in art of the expression of the emotions is the basis of Tolstoy's marvellously original and yet perverse and even exasperating book, *What is Art?*, and I willingly confess, while disagreeing with almost all his results, how much I owe to him.

He gives an example of what he means by calling art the means of communicating emotions. He says, let us suppose a boy to have been pursued in the forest by a bear. If he returns to the village and merely states that he was pursued by a bear and escaped, that is ordinary language, the means of communicating facts or ideas; but if he describes his state first of heedlessness, then of sudden alarm and terror as the bear appears, and finally of relief when he gets away, and describes this so that his hearers share his emotions, then his description is a work of art.

Now in so far as the boy does this in order to urge the villagers to go out and kill the bear, though he may be using artistic methods, his speech is not a pure work of art; but if of a winter evening the boy relates his experience for the sake of the enjoyment of his adventure in retrospect, or better still, if he makes up the whole story for the sake of the imagined emotions, then his speech becomes a pure work of art. But Tolstoy takes the other view, and values the emotions aroused by art entirely for their reaction upon actual life, a view which he courageously maintains even when it leads him to condemn the whole of Michelangelo, Raphael and Titian, and most of Beethoven, not to mention nearly everything he himself has written, as bad or false art.

Such a view would, I think, give pause to any less heroic spirit. He would wonder whether mankind could have always been so radically wrong about a function that, whatever its value be, is almost universal. And in point of fact he will have to find some other word to denote what we now call art. Nor does Tolstoy's theory even carry him safely through his own book, since, in his examples of morally desirable and therefore good art, he has to admit that these are to be found, for the most part, among works of inferior quality. Here, then, is at once the tacit admission that another standard than morality is applicable. We must therefore give up the attempt to judge the work of art by its reaction on life, and consider it as an expression of emotions regarded as ends in themselves. And this brings us back to the idea we had already arrived at, of art as the expression of the imaginative life.

If, then, an object of any kind is created by man not for use, for its fitness to actual life, but as an object of art, an object subserving the imaginative life, what will its qualities be? It must in the first place be adapted to that disinterested intensity of contemplation, which we have found to be the effect of cutting off the responsive action. It must be suited to that heightened power of perception which we found to result therefrom.

And the first quality that we demand in our sensations will be order, without which our sensations will be troubled and perplexed, and the other quality will be variety, without which they will not be fully stimulated.

It may be objected that many things in nature, such as flowers, possess these two qualities of order and variety in a high degree, and these objects do undoubtedly stimulate and satisfy that clear disinterested contemplation which is characteristic of the aesthetic attitude. But in our reaction to a work of art there is something more – there is the consciousness of purpose, the consciousness of a peculiar relation of sympathy with the man who made this thing in order to arouse precisely the sensations we experience. And when we come to the higher works of art, where sensations are so arranged that they arouse in us deep emotions, this feeling of a special tie with the man who expressed them becomes very strong. We feel that he has expressed something which was latent in us all the time, but which we never realized, that he has revealed us to ourselves in revealing himself. And this recognition of purpose is, I believe, an essential part of the aesthetic judgement proper.

The perception of purposeful order and variety in an object gives us the feeling which we express by saying that it is beautiful, but when by means of sensations our emotions are aroused we demand purposeful order and variety in them also, and if this can only be brought about by the sacrifice of sensual beauty we willingly overlook its absence.

Thus, there is no excuse for a china pot being ugly, there is every reason why Rembrandt's and Degas' pictures should be, from the purely sensual point of view, supremely and magnificently ugly.

This, I think, will explain the apparent contradiction between two distinct uses of the word 'beauty', one for that which has sensuous charm, and one for the aesthetic approval of works of imaginative art where the objects presented to us are often of extreme ugliness. Beauty in the former sense belongs to works of art where only the perceptual aspect of the imaginative life is exercised, beauty in the second sense becomes as it were supersensual, and is concerned with the appropriateness and intensity of the emotions aroused. When these emotions are aroused in a way that satisfies fully the needs of the imaginative life we approve and delight in the sensations through which we enjoy that heightened experience because they possess purposeful order and variety in relation to those emotions.

One chief aspect of order in a work of art is unity; unity of some kind is necessary for our restful contemplation of the work of art as a whole, since if it lacks unity we cannot contemplate it in its entirety, but we shall pass outside it to other things necessary to complete its unity.

In a picture this unity is due to a balancing of the attractions of the eye about the central line of the picture. The result of this balance of attractions is that the eye rests willingly within the bounds of the picture. [. . .]

The moment representation is introduced forms have an entirely new set of values. Thus a line which indicated the sudden bend of a head in a certain direction would have far more than its mere value as line in the composition because of the attraction which a marked gesture has for the eye. In almost all paintings this disturbance of the purely decorative values by reason of the representative effect takes place, and the problem becomes too complex for geometrical proof.

This merely decorative unity is, moreover, of very different degrees of intensity in different artists and in different periods. The necessity for a closely woven geometrical texture in the composition is much greater in heroic and monumental design than in genre pieces on a small scale. [. . .]

Let us now see how the artist passes from the stage of merely gratifying our demand for sensuous order and variety to that where he arouses our emotions. I will call the various methods by which this is effected the emotional elements of design.

The first element is that of the rhythm of the line with which the forms are delineated.

The drawn line is the record of a gesture, and that gesture is modified by the artist's feeling which is thus communicated to us directly.

The second element is mass. When an object is so represented that we recognize it as having inertia, we feel its power of resisting movement, or communicating its own movement to other bodies, and our imaginative reaction to such an image is governed by our experience of mass in actual life.

The third element is space. The same-sized square on two pieces of paper can be made by very simple means to appear to represent either a cube two or three inches high, or a cube of hundreds of feet, and our reaction to it is proportionately changed.

The fourth element is that of light and shade. Our feelings towards the same object become totally different according as we see it strongly illuminated against a black background or dark against light.

A fifth element is that of colour. That this has a direct emotional effect is evident from such words as gay, dull, melancholy in relation to colour.

I would suggest the possibility of another element, though perhaps it is only a compound of mass and space: it is that of the inclination to the eye of a plane, whether it is impending over or leaning away from us.

Now it will be noticed that nearly all these emotional elements of design are connected with essential conditions of our physical existence: rhythm appeals to all the sensations which accompany muscular activity; mass to all the infinite adaptations to the force of gravity which we are forced to make; the spatial judgement is equally profound and universal in its application to life; our feeling about inclined planes is connected with our necessary judgements about the conformation of the earth itself; light, again, is so necessary a condition of our existence that we become intensely sensitive to changes in its intensity. Colour is the only one of our elements which is not of critical or universal importance to life, and its emotional effect is neither so deep nor so clearly determined as the others. It will be seen, then, that the graphic arts arouse emotions in us by playing upon what one may call the overtones of some of our primary physical needs. They have, indeed, this great advantage over poetry, that they can appeal more directly and immediately to the emotional accompaniments of our bare physical existence.

If we represent these various elements in simple diagrammatic terms, this effect upon the emotions is, it must be confessed, very weak. Rhythm of line, for instance, is incomparably weaker in its stimulus of the muscular sense than is rhythm addressed to the ear in music, and such diagrams can at best arouse only faint ghost-like echoes of emotions of differing qualities; but when these emotional elements are combined with the presentation of natural appearances, above all with the appearance of the human body, we find that this effect is indefinitely heightened. [. . .]

At this point the adversary (as Leonardo da Vinci calls him) is likely to retort, 'You have abstracted from natural forms a number of so-called emotional elements which you yourself admit are very weak when stated with diagrammatic purity; you then put them back, with the help of Michelangelo, into the natural forms whence they were derived, and at once they have value, so that after all it appears that the natural forms contain these emotional elements ready made up for us, and all that art need do is to imitate Nature.'

But alas! Nature is heartlessly indifferent to the needs of the imaginative life; [. . .] Assuredly we have no guarantee that in nature the emotional elements will be combined appropriately with the demands of the imaginative life, and it is, I think, the great occupation of the graphic arts to give us first of all order and variety in the sensuous plane, and then so to arrange the sensuous presentment of objects that the emotional elements are elicited with an order and appropriateness altogether beyond what Nature herself provides.

Let me sum up for a moment what I have said about the relation of art to Nature, which is, perhaps, the greatest stumbling-block to the understanding of the graphic arts.

I have admitted that there is beauty in Nature, that is to say, that certain objects constantly do, and perhaps any object may, compel us to regard it with that intense disinterested contemplation that belongs to the imaginative life, and which is impossible to the actual life of necessity and action; but that in objects created to arouse the aesthetic feeling we have an added consciousness of purpose on the part of the creator, that he made it on purpose not to be used but to be regarded and enjoyed; and that this feeling is characteristic of the aesthetic judgement proper.

When the artist passes from pure sensations to emotions aroused by means of sensations, he uses natural forms which, in themselves, are calculated to move our emotions, and he presents these in such a manner that the forms themselves generate in us emotional states, based upon the fundamental necessities of our physical and physiological nature. The artist's attitude to natural form is, therefore, infinitely various according to the emotions he wishes to arouse. He may require for his purpose the most complete representation of a figure, he may be intensely realistic, provided that his presentment, in spite of its closeness to natural appearance, disengages clearly for us the appropriate emotional elements. Or he may give us the merest suggestion of natural forms, and rely almost entirely upon the force and intensity of the emotional elements involved in his presentment.

We may, then, dispense once for all with the idea of likeness to Nature, of correctness or incorrectness as a test, and consider only whether the emotional elements inherent in natural form are adequately discovered, unless, indeed, the emotional idea depends at any point upon likeness, or completeness of representation.

14   The French Post-Impressionists

Roger Fry

When the first Post-Impressionist Exhibition was held in these Galleries two years ago the English public became for the first time fully aware of the existence of a new movement in art, a movement which was the more disconcerting in that it was no mere variation upon accepted themes but implied a reconsideration of the very purpose and aim as well as the methods of pictorial and plastic art. It was not surprising, therefore, that a public which had come to admire above everything in a picture the skill with which the artist produced illusion should have resented an art in which such skill was completely subordinated to the direct expression of feeling. Accusations of clumsiness and incapacity were freely made, even against so singularly accomplished an artist as Cézanne. Such darts, however, fall wide of the mark, since it is not the object of these artists to exhibit their skill or proclaim their knowledge, but only to attempt to express by pictorial and plastic form certain spiritual experiences; and in conveying these, ostentation of skill is likely to be even more fatal than downright incapacity.

Indeed, one may fairly admit that the accusation of want of skill and knowledge, while ridiculous in the case of Cézanne, is perfectly justified as regards one artist represented – for the first time in England – in the present Exhibition, namely, Rousseau. Rousseau was a custom-house officer who painted without any training in the art. His pretensions to paint made him the butt of a great deal of ironic wit, but scarcely anyone now would deny the authentic quality of his inspiration or the certainty of his imaginative conviction. Here then is one case where want of skill and knowledge do not completely obscure, though they may mar, expression. And this is true of all perfectly naïve and primitive art. But most of the art here seen is neither naïve nor primitive. It is the work of highly civilized and modern men trying to find a pictorial language appropriate to the sensibilities of the modern outlook.

Another charge that is frequently made against these artists is that they allow what is merely capricious, or even what is extravagant and eccentric, in their work – that it is not serious, but an attempt to impose on the good-natured tolerance of the public. This charge of insincerity and extravagance is invariably made against any new manifestation of creative art. It does not of course follow that it is always wrong. The desire to impose by such means certainly occurs, and is sometimes temporarily successful. But the feeling on the part of the public may, and I think in this case does, arise from a simple misunderstanding of what these artists set out to do. The difficulty springs from a deep-rooted conviction due to long-established custom, that the aim of painting is the descriptive imitation of natural forms. Now, these

Source: Roger Fry, *Vision and Design* (Pelican, 1961), pp. 188–193. 'The French Post-Impressionists' first published in Preface to the Catalogue of the Second Post-Impressionist Exhibition, Grafton Galleries, 1912. *Vision and Design* first published in 1920 by Chatto and Windus. This is an edited extract and footnotes have been omitted. Reprinted by permission of Mrs Pamela Diamand and Chatto and Windus Ltd. Copyright © Mrs Pamela Diamand 1920. *Vision and Design* was re-issued in 1981 by Oxford University Press.

artists do not seek to give what can, after all, be but a pale reflex of actual appearance, but to arouse the conviction of a new and definite reality. They do not seek to imitate form, but to create form; not to imitate life, but to find an equivalent for life. By that I mean that they wish to make images which by the clearness of their logical structure, and by their closely knit unity of texture, shall appeal to our disinterested and contemplative imagination with something of the same vividness as the things of actual life appeal to our practical activities. In fact, they aim not at illusion, but at reality.

The logical extreme of such a method would undoubtedly be the attempt to give up all resemblance to natural form, and to create a purely abstract language of form – a visual music; and the later works of Picasso show this clearly enough. They may or may not be successful in their attempt. It is too early to be dogmatic on the point, which can only be decided when our sensibilities to such abstract forms have been more practised than they are at present. But I would suggest that there is nothing ridiculous in the attempt to do this. Such a picture as Picasso's *Head of a Man* would undoubtedly be ridiculous if, having set out to make a direct imitation of the actual model, he had been incapable of getting a better likeness. But Picasso did nothing of the sort. He has shown in his *Portrait of Mlle L.B.* that he could so do at least as well as anyone if he wished, but he is here attempting to do something quite different.

No such extreme abstraction marks the work of Matisse. The actual objects which stimulated his creative invention are recognizable enough. But here, too, it is an equivalence, not a likeness, of nature that is sought. In opposition to Picasso, who is pre-eminently plastic, Matisse aims at convincing us of the reality of his forms by the continuity and flow of his rhythmic line, by the logic of his space relations and, above all, by an entirely new use of colour. In this, as in his markedly rhythmic design, he approaches more than any other European to the ideals of Chinese art. His work has to an extraordinary degree that decorative unity of design which disting- uishes all the artists of this school.

Between these two extremes we may find ranged almost all the remaining artists. On the whole the influence of Picasso on the younger men is more evident than that of Matisse. With the exception of Braque none of them push their attempts at abstraction of form so far as Picasso, but simplification along these lines is apparent in the work of Derain, Herbin, Marchand and Lhote. Other artists, such as Doucet and Asselin, are content with the ideas of simplification of form as existing in the general tradition of the Post-Impressionist movement, and instead of feeling for new methods of expression devote themselves to expressing what is most poignant and moving in contemporary life. But however various the directions in which different groups are exploring the newly formed regions of expressive form, they all alike derive in some measure from the great originator of the whole idea, Cézanne. [. . .]

Finally, I should like to call attention to a distinguishing characteristic of the French artists seen here, namely, the markedly Classic spirit of their work. This will be noted as distinguishing them to some extent from the English, even more perhaps from the Russians, and most of all from the great mass of modern painting in every country. I do not mean by Classic, dull, pedantic, traditional, reserved or any of those similar things which the word is often made to imply. Still less do I mean by calling them Classic that they paint *Visits to Aesculapius* or *Nero at the Colosseum*. I mean that they do not rely for their effect upon associated ideas, as I believe Romantic and Realistic artists invariably do.

   All art depends upon cutting off the practical responses to sensations of ordinary life, thereby setting free a pure and as it were disembodied functioning of the spirit; but in so far as the artist relies on the associated ideas of the objects which he represents, his work is not completely free and pure, since Romantic associations imply at least an imagined practical activity. The disadvantage of such an art of associated ideas is that its effect really depends on what we bring with us: it adds no entirely new factor to our experience. Consequently, when the first shock of wonder or delight is exhausted the work produces an ever-lessening reaction. Classic art, on the other hand, records a positive and disinterestedly passionate state of mind. It communicates a new and otherwise unattainable experience. Its effect, therefore, is likely to increase with familiarity. Such a classic spirit is common to the best French work of all periods from the twelfth century onwards, and though no one could find direct reminiscences of a Nicholas Poussin here, his spirit seems to revive in the work of artists like Derain. It is natural enough that the intensity and singleness of aim with which these artists yield themselves to certain experiences in the face of nature may make their work appear odd to those who have not the habit of contemplative vision, but it would be rash for us, who as a nation are in the habit of treating our emotions, especially our aesthetic emotions, with a certain levity, to accuse them of caprice or insincerity. It is because of this classic concentration of feeling (which by no means implies abandonment) that the French merit our serious attention. It is this that makes their art so difficult on a first approach but gives it its lasting hold on the imagination.

15   'American-Type' Painting

Clement Greenberg

The latest abstract painting offends many people, among whom are more than a few
who accept the abstract in art in principle. New painting (sculpture is a different
question) still provokes scandal when little that is new in literature or even music
appears to do so any longer. This may be explained by the very slowness of painting's
evolution as a modernist art. Though it started on its 'modernization' earlier perhaps
than the other arts, it has turned out to have a greater number of *expendable*
conventions imbedded in it, or these at least have proven harder to isolate and
detach. As long as such conventions survive and can be isolated they continue to be
attacked, in all the arts that intend to survive in modern society. This process has
come to a stop in literature because literature has fewer conventions to expend before
it begins to deny its own essence, which lies in the communication of conceptual
meanings. The expendable conventions in music, on the other hand, would seem to
have been isolated much sooner, which is why the process of modernization has
slowed down, if not stopped, there. (I simplify drastically. And it is understood, I
hope, that tradition is not dismantled by the avant-garde for sheer revolutionary
effect, but in order to maintain the level and vitality of art under the steadily
changing circumstances of the last hundred years – and that the dismantling has its
own continuity and tradition.)

That is, the avant-garde survives in painting because painting has not yet reached
the point of modernization where its discarding of inherited convention must stop
lest it cease to be viable as art. Nowhere do these conventions seem to go on being
attacked as they are today in this country, and the commotion about a certain kind of
American abstract art is a sign of that. It is practiced by a group of painters who came
to notice in New York about a dozen years ago, and have since become known as the
'abstract expressionists', or less widely, as 'action' painters. (I think Robert Coates of
the *New Yorker* coined the first term, which is not altogether accurate. Harold
Rosenberg, in *Art News*, concocted the second, but restricted it by implication to but
three or four of the artists the public knows under the first term. In London, the kind
of art in question is sometimes called 'American-type painting'.) Abstract expressionism is the first phenomenon in American art to draw a standing protest, and the
first to be deplored seriously, and frequently, abroad. But it is also the first on its
scale to win the serious attention, then the respect, and finally the emulation of a
considerable section of the Parisian avant-garde, which admires in abstract expressionism precisely what causes it to be deplored elsewhere. Paris, whatever else it may
have lost, is still quick to sense the genuinely 'advanced' – though most of the
abstract expressionists did not set out to be 'advanced'; they set out to paint good
pictures, and they 'advance' in pursuit of qualities analogous to those they admire in
the art of the past.

Source: Partisan Review Vol. XXII, no. 2, spring 1955, pp. 179–196. A revised version appears in
Clement Greenberg, *Art and Culture: Critical Essays*. Copyright © 1961 by Clement Greenberg. Used by
permission of the author and Beacon Press.

Their paintings startle because, to the uninitiated eye, they appear to rely so much on accident, whim and haphazard effects. An ungoverned spontaneity seems to be at play, intent only on registering immediate impulse, and the result seems to be nothing more than a welter of blurs, blotches and scrawls – 'oleaginous' and 'amorphous', as one British critic described it. All this is seeming. There is good and bad in abstract expressionism, and once one can tell the difference he discovers that the good owes its realization to a severer discipline than can be found elsewhere in contemporary painting; only it makes factors explicit that previous disciplines left implicit, and leaves implicit many that they did not.

To produce important art it is necessary as a rule to digest the major art of the preceding period, or periods. This is as true today as ever. One great advantage the American abstract expressionists enjoyed in the beginning was that they had already digested Klee and Miró – this, ten years before either master became a serious influence in Paris. Another was that the example of Matisse was kept alive in New York by Hans Hofmann and Milton Avery at a time when young painters abroad tended to overlook him. Picasso, Léger and Mondrian were much in the foreground then, especially Picasso, but they did not block either the way or the view. Of particular importance was the fact that a large number of Kandinsky's early abstract paintings could be seen in New York in what is now the Solomon Guggenheim Museum. As a result of all this, a generation of American artists could start their careers fully abreast of their times and with an artistic culture that was not provincial. Perhaps it was the first time that this happened.

But I doubt whether it would have been possible without the opportunities for unconstrained work that the WPA Art Project gave most of them in the late '30s. Nor do I think any one of them could have gotten off the ground as well as he did without the small but relatively sophisticated audience for adventurous art provided by the students of Hans Hofmann. What turned out to be another advantage was this country's distance from the war and, as immediately important as anything else, the presence in it during the war years of European artists like Mondrian, Masson, Léger, Chagall, Ernst and Lipchitz, along with a number of European critics, dealers and collectors. Their proximity and attention gave the young abstract expressionist painters self-confidence and a sense of being in the centre of art. And in New York they could measure themselves against Europe with more benefit to themselves than they ever could have done as expatriates in Paris.

The justification for the term 'abstract expressionist' lies in the fact that most of the painters covered by it took their lead from German, Russian or Jewish expressionism in breaking away from late Cubist abstract art. But they all started from French painting, got their fundamental sense of style from it, and still maintain some sort of continuity with it. Not least of all, they got from it their most vivid notion of an ambitious, major art, and of the general direction in which it had to go in their time.

Picasso was very much on their minds, especially the Picasso of the early and middle '30s, and the first problem they had to face, if they were going to say what they had to say, was how to loosen up the rather strictly demarcated illusion of shallow depth he had been working within, in his more ambitious pictures, since he closed his 'synthetic' Cubist period. With this went that canon of drawing in faired, more or less simple lines and curves that Cubism imposed and which had dominated almost all abstract art since 1920. They had to free themselves from this too. Such problems were not attacked by program (there has been very little that is programmatic about abstract expressionism) but rather run up against simultaneously by a number of young painters most of whom had their first shows at Peggy Guggenheim's gallery in 1943 or 1944. The Picasso of the '30s – whom they followed in reproductions in the *Cahiers d'Art* even more than in flesh-and-blood paintings – challenged and incited as well as taught them. Not fully abstract itself, his art in that period suggested to them new possibilities of expression for abstract and quasi-abstract painting as nothing else did, not even Klee's enormously inventive and fertile but equally unrealized 1930–1940 phase. I say equally unrealized, because Picasso caught so few of the hares he started in the '30s – which may have served, however, to make his effect on certain younger artists even more stimulating.

To break away from an overpowering precedent, the young artist usually looks for an alternative one. The late Arshile Gorky submitted himself to Miró in order to break free of Picasso, and in the process did a number of pictures we now see have independent virtues, although at the time – the late '30s – they seemed too derivative. But the 1910–1918 Kandinsky was even more of a liberator and during the first war years stimulated Gorky to a greater originality. A short while later André Breton's personal encouragement began to inspire him with a confidence he had hitherto lacked, but again he submitted his art to an influence, this time that of Matta y Echaurren, a Chilean painter much younger than himself. Matta was, and perhaps still is, an inventive draughtsman, and in some ways a daring painter, but an inveterately flashy and superficial one. It took Gorky's more solid craft, profounder culture as a painter, and more selfless devotion to art to make many of Matta's ideas look substantial. In the last four or five years of his life he so transmuted these ideas, and discovered so much more in himself in the way of feeling to add to them, that their derivation became conspicuously beside the point. Gorky found his own way to ease the pressure of Picassoid space, and learned to float flat shapes on a melting, indeterminate ground with a difficult stability quite unlike anything in Miró. Yet he remained a late Cubist to the end, a votary of French taste, an orthodox easel painter, a virtuoso of line, and a tinter, not a colorist. He is, I think, one of the greatest artists we have had in this country. His art was largely unappreciated in his lifetime, but a few years after his tragic death in 1948, at the age of forty-four, it was invoked and imitated by younger painters in New York who wanted to save elegance and traditional draughtsmanship for abstract painting. However, Gorky finished rather than began something, and finished it so well that anybody who follows him is condemned to academicism.

Willem de Kooning was a mature artist long before his first show in 1948. His culture is similar to Gorky's (to whom he was close) and he, too, is a draughtsman before anything else, perhaps an even more gifted one than Gorky and certainly more inventive. Ambition is as much a problem for him as it was for his dead friend, but in the inverse sense, for he has both the advantages and the liabilities – which may be greater – of an aspiration larger and more sophisticated, up to a certain point, than that of any other living artist I know of except Picasso. On the face of it, de Kooning proposes a synthesis of modernism and tradition, and a larger control over the means of abstract painting that would render it capable of statements in a grand style equivalent to that of the past. The disembodied contours of Michelangelo's and

Rubens' nude figure compositions haunt his abstract pictures, yet the dragged off-whites, grays and blacks by which they are inserted in a shallow illusion of depth – which de Kooning, no more than any other painter of the time, can deepen without risk of second-hand effect – bring the Picasso of the early '30s persistently to mind. But there are even more essential resemblances, though they have little to do with imitation on de Kooning's part. He, too, hankers after *terribilità*, prompted by a similar kind of culture and by a similar nostalgia for tradition. No more than Picasso can he tear himself away from the human figure, and from the modelling of it for which his gifts for line and shading so richly equip him. And it would seem that there was even more Luciferian pride behind de Kooning's ambition: were he to realize it, all other ambitious painting would have to stop for a while because he would have set its forward as well as backward limits for a generation to come.

If de Kooning's art has found a readier acceptance than most other forms of abstract expressionism, it is because his need to include the past as well as forestall the future reassures most of us. And in any case, he remains a late Cubist. And then there is his powerful, sinuous Ingresque line. When he left outright abstraction several years ago to attack the female form with a fury greater than Picasso's in the late '30s and the '40s, the results baffled and shocked collectors, yet the methods by which these savage dissections were carried out were patently Cubist. De Kooning is, in fact, the only painter I am aware of at this moment who continues Cubism without repeating it. In certain of his latest *Women*, which are smaller than the preceding ones, the brilliance of the success achieved demonstrates what resources that tradition has left when used by an artist of genius. But de Kooning has still to spread the full measure of that genius on canvas.

Hans Hofmann is the most remarkable phenomenon in the abstract expressionist 'school' (it is not really a school) and one of its few members who can already be referred to as a 'master'. Known as a teacher here and abroad, he did not begin showing until 1943, when he was in his early sixties, and only shortly after his painting had become definitely abstract. Since then he has developed as one of a group whose next oldest member is at least twenty years younger. It was only natural that he should have been the maturest from the start. But his prematureness rather than matureness has obscured the fact that by 1947 he stated and won successful pictures from ideas whose later and more single-minded exploitation by others was to constitute their main claim to originality. When I myself not so long ago complained in print that Hofmann was failing to realize his true potentialities, it was because I had not caught up with him. Renewed acquaintance with some of his earlier work and his own increasing frequency and sureness of success have enlightened me as to that.

Hofmann's pictures in many instances strain to pass beyond the easel convention even as they cling to it, doing many things which that convention resists. By tradition, convention and habit we expect pictorial structure to be presented in contrasts of dark and light, or *value*. Hofmann, who started from Matisse, the Fauves and Kandinsky as much as from Picasso, will juxtapose high, shrill colors whose uniform warmth and brightness do not so much obscure value contrasts as render them dissonant. Or when they are made more obvious, it will be by jarring color contrasts that are equally dissonant. It is much the same with his design and drawing: a sudden razor-edged line will upset all our notions of the permissible, or else thick gobs of paint, without support of edge or shape, will cry out against pictorial sense. When Hofmann fails it is either by forcing such things, or by striving for too obvious and pat a unity, as if to reassure the spectator. Like Klee, he works in a variety of manners without seeming to consolidate his art in any one of them. He is willing, moreover, to accept his bad pictures in order to get in position for the good ones, which speaks for his self-confidence. Many people are put off by the difficulty of his art – especially museum directors and curators – without realizing it is the difficulty of it that puts them off, not what they think is its bad taste. The difficult in art usually announces itself with less sprightliness. Looked at longer, however, the sprightliness gives way to calm and to a noble and impassive intensity. Hofmann's art is very much easel painting in the end, with the concentration and the relative abundance of incident and relation that belong classically to that genre. [. . .]

Jackson Pollock was at first almost as much a late Cubist and a hard and fast easel-painter as any of the abstract expressionists I have mentioned. He compounded hints from Picasso's calligraphy in the early '30s with suggestions from Hofmann, Masson and Mexican painting, especially Siqueiros, and began with a kind of picture in murky, sulphurous colors that startled people less by the novelty of its means than by the force and originality of the feeling behind it. Within a notion of shallow space generalized from the practice of Miró and Masson as well as of Picasso, and with some guidance from the early Kandinsky, he devised a language of baroque shapes and calligraphy that twisted this space to its own measure and vehemence. Pollock remained close to Cubism until at least 1946, and the early greatness of his art can be taken as a fulfilment of things that Picasso had not brought beyond a state of promise in his 1932–1940 period. Though he cannot build with color, Pollock has an instinct for bold oppositions of dark and light, and the capacity to bind the canvas rectangle and assert its ambiguous flatness and quite unambiguous shape as a single and whole image concentrating into one the several images distributed over it. Going further in this direction, he went beyond late Cubism in the end.

Mark Tobey is credited, especially in Paris, with being the first painter to arrive at 'all-over' design, covering the picture surface with an even, largely undifferentiated system of uniform motifs that cause the result to look as though it could be continued indefinitely beyond the frame like a wallpaper pattern. Tobey had shown the first examples of his 'white writing' in New York in 1944, but Pollock had not seen any of these, even in reproduction, when in the summer of 1946 he did a series of 'all-over' paintings executed with dabs of buttery paint. Several of these were masterpieces of clarity. A short while later he began working with skeins of enamel paint and blotches that he opened up and laced, interlaced and unlaced with a breadth and power remote from anything suggested by Tobey's rather limited cabinet art. One of the unconscious motives for Pollock's 'all-over' departure was the desire to achieve a more immediate, denser and more decorative impact than his late Cubist manner had permitted. At the same time, however, he wanted to control the oscillation between an emphatic physical surface and the suggestion of depth beneath it as lucidly and tensely and evenly as Picasso and Braque had controlled a somewhat similar movement with the open facets and pointillist flecks of color of their 1909–1913 Cubist pictures. ('Analytical' Cubism is always somewhere in the back of Pollock's mind.) Having achieved this kind of control, he found himself straddled between the easel picture and something else hard to define, and in the last two or three years he has pulled back.

Tobey's 'all-over' pictures never aroused the protest that Pollock's did. Along with Barnett Newman's paintings, they are still considered the *reductio ad absurdum* of abstract expressionism and modern art in general. Though Pollock is a famous name now, his art has not been fundamentally accepted where one would expect it to be. Few of his fellow artists can yet tell the difference between his good and his bad work – or at least not in New York. His most recent show, in 1954, was the first to contain pictures that were forced, pumped, dressed up, but it got more acceptance than any of his previous exhibitions had – for one thing, because it made clear what an accomplished craftsman he had become, and how pleasingly he could use color now that he was not sure of what he wanted to say with it. (Even so, there were still two or three remarkable paintings present.) His second 1950 exhibition, on the other hand, which included four or five huge canvases of monumental perfection and remains the peak of his achievement so far, was the one received most coldly of all.

Many of the abstract expressionists have at times drained the color from their pictures and worked in black, white and gray alone. Gorky was the first of them to do so, in paintings like *The Diary of a Seducer* of 1945 – which happens to be, in my opinion, his masterpiece. But it was left to Franz Kline, whose first show was in 1951, to work with black and white exclusively in a succession of canvases with blank white grounds bearing a single large calligraphic image in black. That these pictures were big was no cause for surprise: the abstract expressionists were being compelled to do huge canvases by the fact that they had increasingly renounced an illusion of depth within which they could develop pictorial incident without crowding; the flattening surfaces of their canvases compelled them to move along the picture plane laterally and seek in its sheer physical size the space necessary for the telling of their kind of pictorial story. [. . .]

The abstract expressionist emphasis on black and white represents one of those exaggerations or apotheoses which betray a fear for their objects. Value contrast, the opposition and modulation of dark and light, has been the basis of Western pictorial art, its chief means, much more important than perspective, to a convincing illusion of depth and volume; and it has also been its chief agent of structure and unity. This is why the old masters almost always laid in their darks and lights – their shading – first. The eye automatically orients itself by the value contrasts in dealing with an object that is presented to it as a picture, and in the absence of such contrasts it tends to feel almost, if not quite as much, at loss as in the absence of a recognizable image. Impressionism's muffling of dark and light contrasts in response to the effect of the glare of the sky caused it to be criticized for that lack of 'form' and 'structure' which Cézanne tried to supply with his substitute contrasts of warm and cool color (these remained nonetheless contrasts of dark and light, as we can see from monochrome photographs of his paintings). Black and white is the extreme statement of value contrast, and to harp on it as many of the abstract expressionists do – and not only abstract expressionists – seems to me to be an effort to preserve by extreme measures a technical resource whose capacity to yield convincing form and unity is nearing exhaustion.

The American abstract expressionists have been given good cause for this feeling by a development in their own midst. It is, I think, the most radical of all developments in the painting of the last two decades, and has no counterpart in Paris (unless in the late work of Masson and Tal Coat), as so many other things in American abstract expressionism have had since 1944. This development involves a more consistent and radical suppression of value contrasts than seen so far in abstract art. We can realize now, from this point of view, how conservative Cubism was in its resumption of Cézanne's effort to save the convention of dark and light. By their parody of the way the old masters shaded, the Cubists may have discredited value contrast as a means to an illusion of depth and volume, but they rescued it from the Impressionists, Gauguin, Van Gogh and the Fauves as a means to structure and form. Mondrian, a Cubist at heart, remained as dependent on contrasts of dark and light as any academic painter until his very last paintings, *Broadway Boogie* and *Victory Boogie* – which happen to be failures. Until quite recently the convention was taken for granted in even the most doctrinaire abstract art, and the later Kandinsky, though he helped ruin his pictures by his insensitivity to the effects of value contrast, never questioned it in principle. Malevich's prophetic venture in 'white on white' was looked on as an experimental quirk (it was very much an *experiment* and, like almost all experiments in art, it failed aesthetically). The late Monet, whose suppression of values had been the most consistently radical to be seen in painting until a short while ago, was pointed to as a warning, and the *fin-de-siècle* muffling of contrasts in much of Bonnard's and Vuillard's art caused it to be deprecated by the avant-garde for many years. The same factor even had a part in the under-rating of Pissarro.

Recently, however, some of the late Monets began to assume a unity and power they had never had before. This expansion of sensibility has coincided with the emergence of Clyfford Still as one of the most important and original painters of our time – perhaps the most original of all painters under fifty-five, if not the best. As the Cubists resumed Cézanne, Still has resumed Monet – and Pissarro. His paintings were the first abstract pictures I ever saw that contained almost no allusion to Cubism. (Kandinsky's relations with it from first to last became very apparent by contrast.) Still's first show, at Peggy Guggenheim's in 1944, was made up predominantly of pictures in the vein of an abstract symbolism with certain 'primitive' and Surrealist overtones that were in the air at that time, and of which Gottlieb's 'pictographs' represented one version. I was put off by slack, wilful silhouettes that seemed to disregard every consideration of plane or frame. Still's second show, in 1948, was in a different manner, that of his maturity, but I was still put off, and even outraged, by what I took to be a profound lack of sensitivity and discipline. The few large vertically divided areas that made up his typical picture seemed arbitrary in shape and edge, and the color too hot and dry, stifled by the lack of value contrasts. It was only two years ago, when I first saw a 1948 painting of Still's in isolation, that I got a first intimation of pleasure from his art; subsequently, as I was able to see still others in isolation, that intimation grew more definite. (Until one became familiar with them his pictures fought each other when side by side.) I was impressed as never before by how estranging and upsetting genuine originality in art can be, and how the greater its pressure on taste, the more stubbornly taste will resist adjusting to it.

Turner was actually the first painter to break with the European tradition of value painting. In the atmospheric pictures of his last phase he bunched value intervals together at the lighter end of the color scale for effects more picturesque than anything else. For the sake of these, the public soon forgave him his dissolution of form – besides, clouds and steam, mist, water and light were not expected to have definite shape or form as long as they retained depth, which they did in Turner's pictures; what we today take for a daring abstractness on Turner's part was accepted then as another feat of naturalism. That Monet's close-valued painting won a similar acceptance strikes me as not being accidental. Of course, iridescent colors appeal to popular taste, which is often willing to take them in exchange for verisimilitude, but those of Monet's pictures in which he muddied – and flattened – form with dark color, as in some of his *Lily Pads*, were almost as popular. Can it be suggested that the public's appetite for close-valued painting as manifested in both Turner's and Monet's cases, and in that of late Impressionism in general, meant the emergence of a new kind of taste which, though running counter to the high traditions of our art and possessed by people with little grasp of these, yet expressed a genuine underground change in European sensibility? If so, it would clear up the paradox that lies in the fact that an art like the late Monet's, which in its time pleased banal taste and still makes most of the avant-garde shudder, should suddenly stand forth as more advanced in some respects than Cubism.

I don't know how much conscious attention Still has paid to Monet or Impressionism, but his independent and uncompromising art likewise has an affiliation with popular taste, though not by any means enough to make it acceptable to it. Still's is the first really Whitmanesque kind of painting we have had, not only because it makes large, loose gestures, or because it breaks the hold of value contrast as Whitman's verse line broke the equally traditional hold of metre; but just as much because, as Whitman's poetry assimilated, with varying success, large quantities of stale journalistic and oratorical prose, so Still's painting is infused with that stale, prosaic kind of painting to which Barnett Newman has given the name of 'buckeye'. Though little attention has been paid to it in print, 'buckeye' is probably the most widely practiced and homogeneous kind of painting seen in the Western world today. I seem to detect its beginnings in Old Crome's oils and the Barbizon School, but it has spread only since the popularization of Impressionism. 'Buckeye' painting is not 'primitive', nor is it the same thing as 'Sunday painting'. Its practitioners can draw with a certain amount of academic correctness, but their command of shading, and of dark and light values in general, is not sufficient to control their color – either because they are simply inept in this department, or because they are naively intent on a more vivid naturalism of color than the studio-born principles of value contrast will allow. 'Buckeye' painters, as far as I am aware, do landscapes exclusively and work more or less directly from nature. By piling dry paint – though not exactly in impasto – they try to capture the brilliance of daylight, and the process of painting becomes a race between hot shadows and hot lights whose invariable outcome is a livid, dry, sour picture with a warm, brittle surface that intensifies the acid fire of the generally predominating reds, browns, greens and yellows. [. . .]

Still, at any rate, is the first to have put 'buckeye' effects into serious art. These are visible in the frayed dead-leaf edges that wander down the margins or across the middle of so many of his canvases, in the uniformly dark heat of his color, and in a dry, crusty paint surface (like any 'buckeye' painter, Still seems to have no faith in diluted or thin pigment). Such things can spoil his pictures, or make them weird in an unrefreshing way, but when he is able to succeed with, or in spite of them, it represents the conquest by high art of one more area of experience, and its liberation from *kitsch*.

Still's art has a special importance at this time because it shows abstract painting a way out of its own academicism. An indirect sign of this importance is the fact that he is almost the only abstract expressionist to 'make' a school; by this I mean that a few of the many artists he has stimulated or influenced have not been condemned by that to imitate him, but have been able to establish strong and independent styles of their own.

Barnett Newman, who is one of these artists, has replaced Pollock as the *enfant terrible* of abstract expressionism. He rules vertical bands of dimly contrasting color or value on warm flat backgrounds – and that's all. But he is not in the least related to Mondrian or anyone else in the geometrical abstract school. Though Still led the way in opening the picture down the middle and in bringing large, uninterrupted areas of uniform color into subtle and yet spectacular opposition, Newman studied late Impressionism for himself, and has drawn its consequences more radically. The powers of color he employs to make a picture are conceived with an ultimate strictness: color is to function as hue and nothing else, and contrasts are to be sought with the least possible help of differences in value, saturation or warmth.

The easel picture will hardly survive such an approach, and Newman's huge, calmly and evenly burning canvases amount to the most direct attack upon it so far. And it is all the more effective an attack because the art behind it is deep and honest, and carries a feeling for color without its like in recent painting. Mark Rothko's art is a little less aggressive in this respect. He, too, was stimulated by Still's example. The three or four massive, horizontal strata of flat color that compose his typical picture allow the spectator to think of landscape – which may be why his decorative simplicity seems to meet less resistance. Within a range predominantly warm like Newman's and Still's, he too is a brilliant, original colorist; like Newman, he soaks his pigment into the canvas, getting a dyer's effect, and does not apply it as a discrete covering layer in Still's manner. Of the three painters – all of whom started, incidentally, as 'symbolists' – Rothko is the only one who seems to relate to any part of French art since Impressionism, and his ability to insinuate contrasts of value and warmth into oppositions of pure color makes me think of Matisse, who held on to value contrasts in something of the same way. This, too, may account for the public's readier acceptance of his art, but takes nothing away from it. Rothko's big vertical pictures, with their incandescent color and their bold and simple sensuousness – or rather than *firm* sensuousness – are among the largest gems of abstract expressionism.

A concomitant of the fact that Still, Newman and Rothko suppress value contrasts and favor warm hues is the more emphatic flatness of their paintings. Because it is not broken by sharp differences of value or by more than a few incidents of drawing or design, color breathes from the canvas with an enveloping effect, which is intensified by the largeness itself of the picture. The spectator tends to react to this more in terms of décor or environment than in those usually associated with a picture hung upon a wall. The crucial issue raised by the work of these three artists is where the pictorial stops and decoration begins. In effect, their art asserts decorative elements and ideas in a pictorial context. (Whether this has anything to do with the artiness that afflicts all three of them at times, I don't know. But artiness is the great liability of the Still school.)

Rothko and especially Newman are more exposed than Still to the charge of being decorators by their preference for rectilinear drawing. This sets them apart from Still in another way, too. By liberating abstract painting from value contrasts, Still also liberated it, as Pollock had not, from the quasi-geometrical, faired drawing which Cubism had found to be the surest way to prevent the edges of forms from breaking through a picture surface that had been tautened, and therefore made exceedingly sensitive, by the shrinking of the illusion of depth underneath it. As Cézanne was the first to discover, the safest way to proceed in the face of this liability was to echo the rectangular shape of the surface itself with vertical and horizontal lines and with curves whose chords were definitely vertical or horizontal. After the Cubists, and Klee, Mondrian, Miró and others had exploited this insight it became a cliché, however, and led to the kind of late Cubist academicism that used to fill the exhibitions of the American Abstract Artists group, and which can still be seen in much of recent French abstract painting. Still's service was to show us how the contours of a shape could be made less conspicuous, and therefore less dangerous to the 'integrity' of the flat surface, by narrowing the value contrast its color made with that of the shapes or areas adjacent to it. Not only does this keep colors from 'jumping', as the old masters well knew, but it gives the artist greater liberty in drawing – liberty almost to the point of insensitivity, as in Still's own case. The early Kandinsky was the one abstract painter before Still to have some glimpse of this, but it was only a glimpse. Pollock has had more of a glimpse, independently of Still or Kandinsky, but has not set his course by it. In some of the huge 'sprinkled' pictures he did in 1950 and showed in 1951, value contrasts are pulverized as it were, spread over the canvas like dusty vapour (the result was two of the best pictures he ever painted). But the next year, as if in violent repentance, he did a set of paintings in black line alone on unprimed canvas.

It is his insights that help explain why a relatively unpopular painter like Still has so many followers today, both in New York and California (where he has taught); and why William Scott, the English painter, could say that Still's was the only completely and originally American art he had yet seen. This was not necessarily a compliment – Pollock, who may be less 'American', and Hofmann, who is German-born, both have a wider range of power than Still – but Scott meant it as one.

The abstract expressionists started out in the '40s with a diffidence they could not help feeling as American artists. They were very much aware of the provincial fate around them. This country had had good painters in the past, but none with enough sustained originality or power to enter the mainstream of Western art. The aims of the abstract expressionists were diverse within a certain range, and they did not feel, and still do not feel, that they constitute a school or movement with enough unity to be covered by a single term – like 'abstract expressionist', for instance. But aside from their culture as painters and the fact that their art was all more or less abstract, what they had in common from the first was an ambition – or rather the will to it – to break out of provinciality. I think most of them have done so by now, whether in success or failure. If they should all miss – which I do not think at all likely, since some of them have already conclusively arrived! – it will be at least with more resonance than that with which such eminent predecessors of theirs as Maurer, Hartley, Dove and Demuth did not miss. And by comparison with such of their present competitors for the attention of the American art public as Shahn, Graves, Bloom, Stuart Davis (a good painter), Levine, Wyeth, etc., etc., their success as well as their resonance and 'centrality' is assured.

If I say that such a galaxy of powerfully talented and original painters as the abstract expressionists form has not been seen since the days of Cubism, I shall be accused of chauvinist exaggeration, not to mention a lack of a sense of proportion. But can I suggest it? I do not make allowances for American art that I do not make for any other kind. At the Biennale in Venice this year, I saw how de Kooning's exhibition put to shame, not only that of his neighbor in the American pavilion, Ben Shahn, but that of every other painter present in his generation or under. The general impression still is that an art of high distinction has as much chance of coming out of America as a great wine. Literature – yes: we now know that we have produced some great writing because the English and French have told us so. They have even exaggerated, at least about Whitman and Poe. What I hope for is a just appreciation abroad, not an exaggeration, of the merits of 'American-type' painting. Only then, I suspect, will American collectors begin to take it seriously. In the meantime they will go on buying the pallid French equivalent of it they find in the art of Riopelle, De Stael, Soulages, and their like. The imported article is handsomer, no doubt, but the handsomeness is too obvious to have staying power. . . .

'Advanced' art – which is the same thing as ambitious art today – persists insofar as it tests society's capacity for high art. This it does by testing the limits of the inherited forms and genres, and of the medium itself, and it is what the Impressionists, the post-Impressionists, the Fauves, the Cubists and Mondrian did in their time. If the testing seems more radical in the case of the new American abstract painting, it is because it comes at a later stage. The limits of the easel picture are in greater danger of being destroyed because several generations of great artists have already worked to expand them. But if they are destroyed this will not necessarily mean the extinction of pictorial art as such. Painting may be on its way towards a new kind of genre, but perhaps not an unprecedented one – since we are now able to look at, and enjoy, Persian carpets as pictures – and what we now consider to be merely decorative may become capable of holding our eyes and moving us much as the easel picture does.

Meanwhile there is no such thing as an aberration in art: there is just the good and the bad, the realized and the unrealized. Often there is but the distance of a hair's breadth between the two – at first glance. And sometimes there seems – at first glance – to be no more distance than that between a great work of art and one which is not art at all. This is one of the points made by modern art.

16   Collage

Clement Greenberg

Collage played a pivotal role in the evolution of Cubism, and Cubism had, of course, a pivotal role in the evolution of modern painting and sculpture. As far as I know, Braque has never explained quite clearly what induced him, in 1912, to glue a piece of imitation wood-grain paper to the surface of a drawing. Nevertheless, his motive, and Picasso's in following him (assuming that Picasso did follow him in this), seems quite apparent by now – so apparent that one wonders why those who write on collage continue to find its origin in nothing more than the Cubists' need for renewed contact with 'reality'.

By the end of 1911 both masters had pretty well turned traditional illusionist paintings inside out. The fictive depths of the picture had been drained to a level very close to the actual paint surface. Shading and even perspective of a sort, in being applied to the depiction of volumetric surfaces as sequences of small facet-planes, had had the effect of tautening instead of hollowing the picture plane. It had become necessary to discriminate more explicitly between the resistant reality of the flat surface and the forms shown upon it in yielding, ideated depth. Otherwise they would become too immediately one with the surface and survive solely as surface pattern. In 1910 Braque had already inserted a very graphic nail with a sharp cast shadow in a picture otherwise devoid of graphic definitions and cast shadows, *Still-life with Violin and Palette*, in order to interpose a kind of photographic space between the surface and the dimmer, fragile illusoriness of the Cubist space which the still-life itself – shown as a picture within a picture – inhabited. And something similar was obtained by the sculptural delineation of a loop of rope in the upper left margin of the Museum of Modern Art's *Man with a Guitar* of 1911. In that same year Braque introduced capital letters and numbers stencilled in *trompe-l'oeil* in paintings whose motifs offered no realistic excuse for their presence. These intrusions, by their self-evident, extraneous and abrupt flatness, stopped the eye at the literal, physical surface of the canvas in the same way that the artist's signature did; here it was no longer a question of interposing a more vivid illusion of depth between surface and Cubist space, but one of specifying the very real flatness of the picture plane so that everything else shown on it would be pushed into illusioned space by force of contrast. The surface was now *explicitly* instead of implicitly indicated as a tangible but transparent plane.

It was towards the same end that Picasso and Braque began, in 1912, to mix sand

Source: First published as 'The pasted-paper revolution' in *Art News* **LVII**, September 1958, pp. 46–49 and p. 60. Illustrations have been omitted. As the original title was not Clement Greenberg's, but that of the editor of *Art News*, we have used the author's revised title as in Clement Greenberg, *Art and Culture: Critical Essays*. Copyright © 1961 by Clement Greenberg. Used by permission of the author and Beacon Press, Boston.

and other foreign substances with their paint; the granular surface achieved thereby called direct attention to the tactile reality of the picture. In that year too, Georges Braque 'introduced bits of green or gray marbleized surfaces into some of his pictures and also rectangular strips painted in imitation of wood grain' (I quote from Henry R. Hope's catalogue for the Braque retrospective at the Museum of Modern Art in 1949). A little later he made his first collage, *Fruit Bowl*, by pasting three strips of imitation wood-grain wallpaper to a sheet of drawing paper on which he then charcoaled a rather simplified Cubist still-life and some *trompe-l'oeil* letters. Cubist space had by this time become even shallower, and the actual picture surface had to be identified more emphatically than before if the illusion was to be detached from it. Now the corporeal presence of the wallpaper pushed the lettering itself into illusioned depth by force of contrast. But at this point the declaration of the surface became so vehement and so extensive as to endow its flatness with far greater power of attraction. The *trompe-l'oeil* lettering, simply because it was inconceivable on anything but a flat plane, continued to suggest and return to it. And its tendency to do so was further encouraged by the placing of the letters in terms of the illusion, and by the fact that the artist had inserted the wallpaper strips themselves partly inside the illusion of depth by drawing upon and shading them. The strips, the lettering, the charcoaled lines and the white paper begin to change places in depth with one another, and a process is set up in which every part of the picture takes its turn at occupying every plane, whether real or imagined, in it. The imaginary planes are all parallel to one another; their effective connection lies in their common relation to the surface; wherever a form on one plane slants or extends into another it immediately springs forward. The flatness of the surface permeates the illusion, and the illusion itself reasserts the flatness. The effect is to fuse the illusion with the picture plane without derogation of either – in principle.

The fusion soon became even more intimate. Picasso and Braque began to use pasted paper and cloth of different hues, textures and patterns, as well as a variety of *trompe-l'oeil* elements, within one and the same work. Shallow planes, half in and half out of illusioned depth, were pressed still closer together, and the picture as a whole brought still closer to the physical surface. Further devices are employed to expedite the shuffling and shuttling between surface and depth. The area around one corner of a swatch of pasted paper will be shaded to make it look as though it were peeling away from the surface into real space, while something will be drawn or pasted over another corner to thrust it back into depth and make the superimposed form itself seem to poke out beyond the surface. Depicted surfaces will be shown as parallel with the picture plane and at the same time cutting through it, as if to establish the assumption of an illusion of depth far greater than that actually indicated. Pictorial illusion begins to give way to what could be more properly called optical illusion.

The paper or cloth had to be cut out, or simulated, in relatively large and simple shapes, and wherever they were inserted the little facet-planes of Analytical Cubism merged perforce into larger shapes. For the sake of harmony and unity this merging process was extended to the rest of the picture. Images began to re-acquire definite and even more recognizable contours, and Synthetic Cubism was on the way. With the reappearance, however, of definite and linear contours, shading was largely suppressed. This made it even more difficult to achieve depth or volumetric form, and there seemed no direction left in which to escape from the literal flatness of the surface – except into the non-pictorial, real space in front of the picture. This, exactly, was the way Picasso chose for a moment, before he went on to solve the terms of Synthetic Cubism by contrasts of bright color and bright color patterns, and by incisive silhouettes whose recognizability and placing called up an association at least, if not a representation, of three-dimensional space.

Some time in 1912 he cut out and folded a piece of paper in the shape of a guitar and glued and fitted other pieces of paper and four taut strings to it. A sequence of flat surfaces on different planes in actual space was created to which there adhered only the hint of a pictorial surface. The originally affixed elements of a collage had, in effect, been extruded from the picture plane – the sheet of drawing paper or the canvas – to make a bas-relief. But it was a 'constructed', not a sculpted, bas-relief, and it founded a new genre of sculpture. Construction sculpture was freed long ago from its bas-relief frontality and every other suggestion of the picture plane, but has continued to this day to be marked by its pictorial origins. Not for nothing did the sculptor-constructor Gonzalez call it the new art of 'drawing in space'. But with equal and more descriptive justice it could be called, harking back more specifically to its birth in the collage: the new art of joining two-dimensional forms in three-dimensional space.

After classical Cubism the development of collage was largely oriented to shock value. Arp, Schwitters and Miró grasped its plastic meaning enough to make collages whose value transcends the piquant, but the genre otherwise declined into montage and stunts of illustration, or into decoration pure and simple. The traps of collage (and of Cubism in general) in this last respect are well demonstrated by Gris's case.

Cubism, in the hands of its inventors – and in those of Léger too – achieved a new, exalted and transfigured kind of decoration by reconstructing the flat picture surface with the very means of its denial. They started with the illusion and arrived at a quasi-abstract literalness. With Gris it was the reverse. As he himself explained, he started with flat and abstract shapes to which he then fitted recognizable three-dimensional images. Whereas Braque's and Picasso's images were dissected in three dimensions in the course of being transposed in two, Gris's tended, especially in the beginning, to be broken up in two-dimensional terms alone, in accordance with rhythms originating on the surface. Later on Gris became more aware of the fact that Cubism was not just a question of decorative overlay and that its surface resonance derived directly from an underlying illusion which, however schematic, was fully felt; and in his collages we can see him struggling with this problem. But his collages also make it clear how unstable his solution was. Precisely because he continued to take the picture surface as given and not needing to be re-created, he became over-solicitous about the illusion. He used his pasted papers and *trompe-l'oeil* textures and lettering to assert flatness all right; but he almost always sealed the flatness inside the illusion of depth by placing images rendered with sculptural vividness on the nearest plane of the picture, and often on the rearmost plane too. At the same time he used more positive color in his collages than Picasso or Braque did, and more light and dark shading. Because their affixed material and their *trompe-l'oeil* seldom declare the surface even ambiguously, Gris's collages lack the immediacy of presence of Braque's and Picasso's. They have about them something of the closed-off presence of the traditional easel picture. And yet, because their decorative elements tend to function solely as decoration – as decoration of the illusion – they also seem more conventionally decorative. Instead of that seamless fusion of the decorative with the spatial structure of the illusion which we get in the collages of the other two masters, there is an alternation, a collocation, of the decorative and the illusioned. And if their relation ever goes beyond that, it is more liable to be one of confusion than of fusion. Gris's collages have their merits, but they have been over-praised. Certainly, they do not confirm the point of Cubism as a renovation of pictorial style.

That point, as I see it, was to restore and exalt decoration by building it, by endowing self-confessedly flat configurations with a pictorial content, an autonomy like that hitherto obtained through illusion alone. Elements essentially decorative in themselves were used not to adorn but to identify, locate, construct; and in being so used, to create works of art in which decorativeness was transcended or transfigured in a monumental unity. Monumental is, in fact, the one word I choose to describe Cubism's pre-eminent quality.

17   Master Léger

Clement Greenberg

Léger was overlooked for a while. The conscious preoccupations of the younger painters in New York during the '40s lay in a different quarter; and so few of his 1910–1913 pictures were known. He was over here during most of the war, and what he showed us then was not impressive. Nor – but let this be said to his credit – did he try to impress us with his personality. Now we have begun to know better. His large retrospective at the Museum of Modern Art (where it came from the Chicago Art Institute, which organized it) makes it quite clear that, besides being a major fountainhead of contemporary style, Léger belongs with Matisse, Picasso and Mondrian among the very greatest painters of the century.

The sequence of promise, fulfillment and decline his exhibition revealed was much like that in the previous Matisse, Picasso and Braque retrospectives, and its dates site the chronological contour lines of School of Paris painting over the last forty or fifty years. For Matisse fulfillment came between 1910 and 1920; for Braque, between 1910 and 1914; for both Picasso and Léger between 1910 and 1925. None of the four was ever, before or after these dates, as consistent in quality, and very seldom as high.

Michel Seuphor refers to 1912 as 'perhaps the most beautiful date in the whole history of painting in France'. That year Cubism reached fullest flower, and Léger was one of the three artists mainly responsible, even though he did not paint with 'cubes'. 1913 was another beautiful year, perhaps more so for him if not for Picasso and Braque. In 1914 he had, like Braque, to go to war, and the few paintings he finished while in the army are rather weak. But he recovered his level as soon as he had the chance to work regularly again, and the pictures he did from 1917 until at least 1922 are just as original and perhaps even more seminal. Yet they do not quite come up to the pure, the utter finality, the poised strength of his 1911–1913 work – just as Picasso's art between 1914 and 1925, while manifesting its own kind of perfection, rarely attains the transcendent perfection it knew before. The same is doubly, triply true in Braque's case, though he did experience a partial – very partial – recovery between 1928 and 1931 or 1932.

The four years from the middle of 1910 to the middle of 1914 were the special ones, then. But just what made them so exceptionally favorable to painting? A trio of geniuses, born within a year of one another, were in their early thirties – but Matisse, who was approaching his peak during the same period, was then in his forties. More of the answer may be given by something that extends far beyond the individual circumstances of the artists involved. In France, and elsewhere, the generation of the avant-garde that came of age after 1900 was the first to accept the modern, industrializing world with any enthusiasm. Even poets – thus Apollinaire – saw, at least for a moment, aesthetic possibilities in a streamlined future, a vaulting modernity; and a

Source: *Partisan Review* Vol. XXI, Jan.–Feb. 1954, pp. 90–97. A revised version appears in Clement Greenberg, *Art and Culture: Critical Essays*. Copyright © 1961 by Clement Greenberg. Used by permission of the author and Beacon Press.

mood of secular optimism replaced the secular pessimism of the Symbolist generation. This mood was not confined to the avant-garde; here, for once, the latter had
been anticipated by the philistines; but the avant-garde was drawing the aesthetic
conclusions at which the philistines balked. Nor was painting – and sculpture – the
only department of culture to benefit by this. Yeats, Joyce, Eliot, Proust, Mann,
Valéry, Rilke, George, Hofmannsthal, Kafka, Stravinsky, Schoenberg, Freud,
Dewey, Wittgenstein, Husserl, Einstein all developed or matured in the years of that
same mood, which underpinned even those who rejected it. But professional tradition in painting, having long been distinctively secular (what great painter since El
Greco was fundamentally a religious man?), now received new and, perhaps, special
confirmation from its public, and felt itself to be more in the truth than ever before.

Whatever the reason, it came about that one of the greatest of all moments in
painting arrived on the crest of a mood of 'materialistic' optimism. And of all the
optimists, materialists and yea-sayers, none was, or has remained, more whole-
heartedly one than Fernand Léger. He has told us about, and we see, his enthusiasm
for machine forms. And we also seem to see in his art all the qualities conventionally
associated with 'materialism'; weight, excessive looseness or else excessive rigidity of
form, crassness, simplicity, cheerfulness, complacency, even a certain obtuseness.
But what a mistake it would be not to see how much else there is in this art, which has
succeeded better, I daresay, than any other in making the rawness of matter wholly
relevant to human feeling.

However, Cubism was more than a response to a certain historical moment and
its mood. It was also the outcome of anterior events within painting, and an
understanding of these opens the way to the understanding of Cubism as an event
itself.

In Renaissance pictorial tradition the represented object always stood, in Aristotelian distinction from everything not itself, in front of or behind something else.
Cézanne was one of the first to worry consciously about how to pass from the
contours of an object to what lay behind or next to it without violating either the
integrity of the picture surface as a flat continuum, or the represented three-
dimensionality of the object itself, which Impressionism had inadvertently
threatened. The Cubists inherited the problem, and solved it, but – as Marx would
say – only by destroying it: willingly or unwillingly, they sacrificed the integrity of
the object almost entirely to that of the surface. This – which had, however, nothing
intrinsic to do with aesthetic value – is why Cubism constituted a turning point in the
history of painting.

Picasso and Braque began as Cubists by modeling the object in little facet-planes,
borrowed from Cézanne, in order to define its volume more vividly. But the
threatened outcome of this was to leave the object standing away from its background like a piece of illustrated sculpture; so, eliminating broad color contrasts and
confining themselves almost entirely to shades of brown, gray and black, they began
to model the background, too, in facet-planes, as Cézanne in his last years had
modeled cloudless skies. These facet planes became increasingly frontal – that is,
parallel to the plane of the canvas – and soon, to make the transition from object to
background even less abrupt, and expedite the transition from plane to plane within

the object itself, the facets were almost all left open; whence the truncated rectangles and triangles and the semi-circles which remained the characteristic vocabulary of Picasso and Braque's Cubism until 1913. Amid all this, contours and silhouetting lines were lost (especially when the object was spread apart so as to show its surface from more than one point of view): the space inside the object now faulted through into surrounding space, and the latter could be conceived of as, in return, penetrating the object. All space became one, neither 'positive' nor 'negative', insofar as occupied space was no longer clearly differentiated from unoccupied. And the object was not so much *formed*, as exhibited by precipitation in groups or clusters of facet-planes out of an indeterminate background of similar planes, which latter could also be seen as vibrating echoes of the object. Either way, the Cubists ended up by doing with form what the Impressionists, when they precipitated their objects out of a mist of paint flecks, had only begun to do with color – they erased the old distinction between object-in-front-of-background and background-behind-and-around-object, erased it at least as something felt rather than merely read. . . .

Picasso and Braque started Cubism; Léger joined it. He, too, was influenced by Cézanne after 1906, but he had used him at first for ends closer to those of Futurism, analyzing the object to show how it could move rather than how it managed to present a closed surface to eye or finger. But by 1912 the main thing for him, as for Picasso and Braque, became to assert the difference between pictorial and three-dimensional space. Though Léger's vocabulary remained different and its units larger in scale, his grammar became a similar one of straight lines and faired curves. The curves predominated with him, but the sketchy black lines that traced them left his forms just as open in effect; and the way he modeled his roundnesses – with primary blues, reds or greens swatched around highlighted axes of crusty white pigment laid on so dry and summarily that the canvas showed through here and there – caused these roundnesses to be felt simultaneously as both curved and flattened planes. The different directions in which the cylindrical or conical forms slanted, the interspersed cubes and rectangles, the equivalence of the different colors none of which advanced or receded more than any other, the sense of volumes compressed in ambiguous space and always presenting their broadest surfaces – all this likewise erased the distinction between object and background, object and ambiance. The objects, or their parts, seemed to well into visibility out of a background of similar, interchangeable elements; or it was as if the surface were repeating itself in endless depth. The first and decisive effect was of a welter of overlapping planes. To sort these into cones, cylinders and cubes was easy enough, but to assemble them into recognizable objects required almost as deliberate an effort on the part of the spectator as to read Picasso's and Braque's 'analytical' Cubism. – And need I say that the deliberate effort contributes least in the experience of art?

The logic of Léger's analysis is nevertheless simpler than Picasso's or Braque's. He dissects broadly, articulating objects into their anatomical units of volume, which remain larger, and more obvious in their references, than the little planes into which the other two artists chip the surfaces of volumes. Perhaps this simplicity is what induced him, in 1913, to abandon recognizable objects altogether and paint several definitely abstract pictures with planes defining cylinders and cones that signify nothing else, and flat rectangles that define not even volume. (These works, of which there is no example in the Chicago Museum of Modern Art show, all have the same title, *Contrast of Forms*.) Only a short while previously, Picasso and Braque had invented the collage, which, for them, turned out to be a way of saving the recognizable object from dissolution in abstract art. The object may have become for a moment even less recognizable than before, but a searching eye could still decipher it. It was Léger alone of the three master Cubists who drove analytical Cubism to its conclusion. Not that he arrived at the flat picture, as Mondrian, drawing the very ultimate consequences of Cubism, was to do, or that he even approached the flatness of Picasso's and Braque's collages: the priority analytical Cubism gave the picture plane was never absolute, and Léger always held on to some sort of illusion of depth. But he did accept, as Picasso and Braque did not, the full implication of the method of analytical Cubism: namely, that once objects are broken up into more or less interchangeable units they themselves are no longer necessary as entities – no longer necessary to the decisive effect – and the artist is free to work with the units alone, since these alone retain aesthetic pertinence. As it happened, the units into which Cubism resolved the object were planear units, but they could conceivably have been the chromatic units of the Impressionists and Neo-Impressionists.

However, Léger's evolution towards abstract art should also be seen in terms more personal to himself: his predilection for weight and decorative balance, and a *horror vacui* [fear of empty space] greater even than Picasso's, led him, again in 1913, to begin packing the picture towards margins formerly left vague, and he found himself mustering his planear units towards a density and compactness for which there were not enough hints in Nature. What Nature could not supply, the planear units did by multiplying themselves in complete independence of the laws under which surfaces and their planes materialize in non-pictorial reality. Léger did not create abstract art for more than a brief period; later on, after the war, he would do a few more abstract pictures, but only intermittently, not as settled practice. In the final reckoning he was no more willing than Picasso or Braque to abandon Nature altogether. The reason for this reluctance on the part of all three, and of Matisse too, is one of the most interesting of topics in contemporary art criticism, but not one to be broached here. Suffice it to say that the personal rejection of abstract art by the artists who did the most to clear the way for it calls for no value judgments.

The realization, original with Cézanne, that the eye, by following the direction of surfaces closely, could resolve all visual substance into a tight continuum of frontal planes, had given the painter a new incentive in the exploration of both nature and his medium – and a rule, at the same time, to guarantee the aesthetic coherence of what was discovered. Picasso, Braque and Léger, it could be said, were the only ones intrepid enough to carry the exploration to its end, and able by genius to apply the rule fully and yet in terms of their own temperaments. (This is to subordinate, but not to dismiss, the work of the other Cubists, who were all their followers to some extent.) Thus these three could for three or four years execute a well-nigh unbroken series of works that were flawless in unity and abundant in matter, works achieving that optimum which consists in a fusion of elegance and power that abates neither. Then the matter, for them, was exhausted, and the rule lapsed. Henceforth neither they nor any other artist could expand taste by these means, and to cling to them any longer would mean to depend on taste instead of creating it.

By 1912 or 1913 'synthesis', as I have indicated, began to replace 'analysis' in Picasso's and Braque's collages. At those points where the picture was nailed to its physical surface by pieces of pasted newspaper or *trompe-l'oeil* textures, the facet-planes fused into larger shapes, and gradually the object or its part re-emerged in flat, distorted profile, to be locked into the equally flat profile of background, or 'negative', space. The result was a tight picture-object in which the illusion of depth was given by overlapping and up-and-down placing but never by shading (which had played an important part in analytical Cubism) or anything else. Bright color came back, but it was almost absolutely flat color. Now the priority of the picture plane was asserted in a different and more radical way: the object was not disintegrated by the pressure of shallow space, but rolled flat in flat space – or at least space that was felt, if not read, as flat. Here Picasso found a new rule of coherence almost, if not quite, as efficacious as the previous one, and it took him ten years to exhaust its application.

Léger entered upon his own variety of synthetic Cubism as soon as he got out of the army, in 1917. In the large *City*, finished in 1919, foreground and background, object and ambiance, are alike cut up into vertical strips and discs and squares that are recombined on the surface as well as in shallow depth in a grandiose montage. He had not had to practice collage in order to learn from it. He still shades, in dark and light now, not in primary colors, but it is more for decorative and architectural effect than to produce the illusion of volume as such, and the contrast of the shaded forms with large and small areas of flat color achieves the effect of a façade, but a façade that transcends architecture by its complexity and intensity. The rhythm counts above all now, and will continue to as the artist veers away from a course parallel to Picasso's and takes hints from the Matisse of the large canvases of 1916 with their discontinuities of imagined space and abrupt but cadenced juxtapositions of broad vertical bands of color. Such concerns remain, and will remain, largely alien to Picasso, whose unrivalled capacity as a composer-designer is tied to a certain traditionalism which makes him reject large, insistent, emphatically decorative rhythms in his easel paintings.

Léger's last complete masterpiece, as far as this writer knows, is the huge *Three Women* (also called *Le Grand Déjeuner*) of 1921, in the Museum of Modern Art's permanent collection, a picture that improves steadily with the passage of time. Later on, Léger will be able to secure unity only by elimination and drastic simplification, but here he achieves it by adding, varying and complicating elements simple in themselves. First, staccato stripings, checkerings, dottings, curvings, anglings – then a massive calm, the calm that always supervenes in great painting. The great tubular, nude forms, so limpid in color, so evenly turgid, yet with their relief so firmly locked in place between busy foreground and even busier background, and their contours so expertly adjusted to still the clamour around them – these own the taut canvas as no projection of a more earnestly meant illusion could.

For Léger, as for Picasso, the impetus of Cubism gave out during the last half of the '20s. Nothing after that – and I say *nothing* advisedly – equals the breadth or finality of the pictures done between 1910 and 1925. We still get the general flavor of a great artist, but not – measured by the standards he himself instanced – great art. The firm, heavy, simplifying hand now reveals its liabilities as well as assets; what it addresses crumbles under the pressure, and machined contours and rawly decorative color schemes freeze it into but a mechanical coherence. Color, which is Léger's secret weapon, never goes quite dead – or never, at any rate, as dead as for Picasso and Braque in these later years – but that is not enough. The color may be justly felt in some of the heraldic clusters of objects and fragments, suspended in mid-air, of which Léger produced so monotonously many in the '30s and '40s, but these hang almost as limp as the others, limp past redemption – unless translated into tapestry, as one was, to its benefit, in 1950. Color, among other things, has a pleasing, old-fashioned, lithographic, popular-print sort of picturesqueness in the *Leisure* of 1949, but the composition wobbles and flutters underneath, and the result is no more than an uncertainly nice picture. And the large, bright *Builders* of 1950 is not even nice.

Despite some appearances to the contrary, Léger remains a very accomplished painter; moreover, he is still able to execute things whose virtues are more than those of plausibility. I have in mind certain small still-lifes done within the past twenty years, but of which there is no example in the present show. On the other hand, there are the showpieces, which are in the show. The large *Three Musicians* of 1944 is solid and compact, but lacks tension and intensity, as does also the large *Adam and Eve* of 1939, whose undulating chiaroscuro, for all its presence, over-unifies the picture and renders it too bland. Yet, as is obvious, only a master – a master who has, or had, greatness in him – could have turned out either of these two paintings. I should have liked to see the final, largest version of the *Bicyclist* series of 1944–1945 in the exhibition; it does much the same thing as *Leisure* but, as I remember it, much better. Certainly, that series did not deserve to be represented by *The Great Julie*, also in the Museum of Modern Art's permanent collection, with its forced, arty color, a middle-sized picture that is still far too large for its content. Perhaps the evidence in general could have been better chosen to make a case for the post-1925 Léger, but even so, I do not think it could have altered the conclusion much.

The decline that overtook Léger after 1925, as it did so many other estimable members of the School of Paris, was made all the more marked in his, as in Picasso's, case by the refusal to sit with past triumphs and repeat himself. Léger having created taste and still seeking to create it, but in vain, taste now revenges itself on him all the more, as it also does on Picasso – and as it seems to have done on other great artists at one time or another in their careers. This, however, is not all there is to it.

And far be it from anyone to write *finis* to a great artist's career before he dies. Matisse surprised us by painting a picture in 1948 that can stand up to anything he did in the past – the *Red Interior*. And Léger is not yet as old as Matisse was then.

18   Three American Painters

Michael Fried

I

For twenty years or more almost all the best new painting and sculpture has been done in America; notably the work of artists such as de Kooning, Frankenthaler, Gorky, Gottlieb, Hofmann, Kline, Louis, Motherwell, Newman, Pollock, Rothko, Smith and Still – apart from those in the present exhibition – to name only some of the best. [. . .]

It is one of the most important facts about the contemporary situation in the visual arts that the fundamental character of the new art has not been adequately understood. This is not altogether surprising. Unlike poets, painters and sculptors rarely practice criticism; and perhaps partly as a consequence of this, the job of writing about art has tended to pass by default to men and women who are in no way qualified for their profession. [. . .] But if the inadequacy of almost all contemporary art criticism is not surprising, it is undeniably ironic, because the visual arts – painting especially – have never been more explicitly self-critical than during the past twenty years.

The first section of this essay attempts an exposition of what, to my mind, are some of the most important characteristics of the new art. At the same time it tries to show why formal criticism, such as that practiced by Roger Fry or, more to the point, by Clement Greenberg, is better able to throw light upon the new art than any other approach. To do this, the development over the past hundred years of what Greenberg calls 'Modernist' painting must be considered, because the work of the artists mentioned above represents, in an important sense, the extension in this country of a kind of painting that began in France with the work of Edouard Manet. [. . .]

Roughly speaking, the history of painting from Manet through Synthetic Cubism and Matisse may be characterized in terms of the gradual withdrawal of painting from the task of representing reality – or of reality from the power of painting to represent it[1] – in favour of an increasing preoccupation with problems intrinsic to painting itself. One may deplore the fact that critics such as Fry and Greenberg concentrate their attention upon the formal characteristics of the works they discuss; but the painters whose work they most esteem on formal grounds – e.g., Manet, the Impressionists, Seurat, Cézanne, Picasso, Braque, Matisse, Léger, Mondrian, Kandinsky, Miró – are among the finest painters of the past hundred years. This is not to imply that only the formal aspect of their paintings is worthy of interest. On the contrary, because recognizable objects, persons and places are often not entirely

Source: Three American Painters: Kenneth Noland, Jules Olitski, Frank Stella, Fogg Art Museum, Harvard University, 1965, pp. 4–10. Footnotes have been omitted.

expunged from their work, criticism which deals with the ostensible subject of a given painting can be highly informative; and in general, criticism concerned with aspects of the situation in which it was made other than its formal context can add significantly to our understanding of the artist's achievement. But criticism of this kind has shown itself largely unable to make convincing discriminations of value among the works of a particular artist; and in this century it often happens that those paintings that are most full of explicit human content can be faulted on formal grounds – Picasso's *Guernica* is perhaps the most conspicuous example – in comparison with others virtually devoid of such content. (It must be granted that this says something about the limitations of formal criticism as well as about its strengths. Though precisely *what* it is taken to say will depend on one's feelings about *Guernica*, etc.)

It is worth adding that there is nothing binding in the value judgments of formal criticism. All judgments of value begin and end in experience, or ought to, and if someone does not feel that Manet's *Déjeuner sur l'Herbe*, Matisse's *Piano Lesson* or Pollock's *Autumn Rhythm* are superb paintings, no critical arguments can take the place of feeling it. On the other hand, one's experiences of works of art are always informed by what one has come to understand about them; and it is the burden of the formal critic both to objectify his intuitions with all the intellectual rigor at his command, and to be on his guard against enlisting a formalist rhetoric in defense of what he fears may be merely private enthusiasms.

It is also imperative that the formal critic bear in mind at all times that the objectivity he aspires towards can be no more than relative. But his detractors would do well to bear in mind themselves that his aspirations towards objectivity are given force and relevance by the tendency of the most important current in painting since Manet to concern itself increasingly, and with growing self-awareness, with formal problems and issues. When Hilton Kramer, in perhaps the most intelligent and serious review of Greenberg's *Art and Culture* that has appeared, complains that:

> In Mr. Greenberg's criticism, the impersonal process of history appears in the guise of an inner artistic logic, which has its own immutable laws of development and to which works of art must conform if they are not to end up on the historical ash heap. This inner artistic logic is purely a matter of the relations that obtain among abstract forms arranged in a decorative pattern . . .

it is not entirely clear whether he is objecting more to a style of argument or to the modernist painting that Greenberg admires. In any case, his characterizations of both seem mistaken at several crucial points.

Nowhere in *Art and Culture* does its author appear to have forgotten that history, works of art and essays in art criticism are all made by men who live at a particular moment in history and whose perceptions and values are, therefore, no more than relative. There is, in a sense, 'an inner artistic logic' in Greenberg's view of the history of modernist painting in France and America; but it is a 'logic' that has come about as the result of decisions made by individual artists to engage with formal problems thrown up by the art of the recent past – decisions and formal problems that Greenberg has done more than any other critic to elucidate. Moreover, the element of internal 'logic' in the development of modernist painting can be perceived only in retrospect. It is hard to think of a single passage in *Art and Culture* that so much as hints at the existence of 'immutable laws' that govern its unfolding. If a critic thought such laws existed, he would surely use them to predict what the modernist art of the future is going to look like. But there are no predictions in Greenberg's book, only repeated attempts to objectify his experience of painting and sculpture in terms that derive from these media alone.

Elsewhere in his review Kramer maintains that Greenberg has employed 'a principle of historical development drawn from Marx' to defend 'a point of view which is completely hostage to the New York School'. My own impression is rather that, starting from his experience of the works of Pollock, de Kooning, Newman and others, Greenberg has come increasingly to perceive their relation to the modernist painting that preceded them. But there is an insight in Kramer's reference to Marx which deserves some discussion.

Ever since the publication in 1888 of Heinrich Wölfflin's first book, *Renaissance und Barock*, many critics of style have tended to rely on a fundamentally Hegelian conception of art history, in which styles are described as succeeding one another in accord with an internal dynamic or dialectic, rather than in response to social, economic and political developments in society at large. One of the stock objections, in fact, to exclusively stylistic or formal criticism of the art of the past – for example, of the High Renaissance – is that it fails to deal with the influence of non-artistic factors upon the art of the time, and as a result is unable both to elucidate the full meaning of individual works and to put forward a convincing account of stylistic change. Such an objection, however, derives the real but limited validity it possesses from the fact that painting and sculpture during the Renaissance were deeply involved, as regards patronage and iconography, with both the Church and State. But by the late nineteenth and early twentieth century, the relation of art – as well as of the Church and State – to society appears to have undergone a radical change. And although the change in question cannot be understood apart from a consideration of economic and other non-artistic factors, by far the most important single characteristic of the new *modus vivendi* between the arts and bourgeois society gradually arrived at during the first decades of the present century has been the tendency of ambitious art to become more and more concerned with problems and issues intrinsic to itself.

All this has, of course, been recounted before. But what has not been sufficiently recognized is that in the face of these developments the same objections that are effective when directed against exclusively formal criticism of High Renaissance painting lose almost all their force and relevance. In comparison with what may be said in precise detail about the relations between High Renaissance art and the society in which it arose, only the most general statements – such as this one – may be made about the relation between modernist painting and modern society. In a sense, modernist art in this century finished what society in the nineteenth began: the alienation of the artist from the general preoccupations of the culture in which he is embedded, and the prizing loose of art itself from the concerns, aims and ideals of that culture. With the achievements of Cubism in the first and second decades of this century, if not before, painting and sculpture became free to pursue concerns intrinsic to themselves. This meant that it was now possible to conceive of stylistic change in terms of the decisions of individual artists to engage with particular formal problems thrown up by the art of the recent past; and in fact the fundamentally Hegelian conception of art history at work in the writings of Wölfflin and Greenberg, whatever its limitations when applied to the art of the more distant past, seems particularly well suited to the actual development of modernism in the visual arts, painting especially.

I am arguing, then, that something like a dialectic of modernism has in effect been at work in the visual arts for roughly a century now; and by dialectic I mean what is essential in Hegel's conception of historical progression, as well as that of the young Marx, as expounded in this century by the Marxist philosopher Georg Lukàcs in his great work, *History and Class Consciousness*, and by the late Maurice Merleau-Ponty in numerous books and essays. More than anything else, the dialectic in the thought of these men is an ideal of action as radical criticism of itself founded upon as objective an understanding of one's present situation as one is able to achieve. There is nothing teleological about such an ideal: it does not aim towards a predetermined end, unless its complete incarnation in action can be called such an end. But this would amount to nothing less than the establishment of a perpetual revolution – perpetual because bent on unceasing radical criticism of itself. It is no wonder such an ideal has not been realized in the realm of politics; but it seems to me that the development of modernist painting over the past century has led to a situation that may be described in these terms. That is, while the development of modernist painting has not been directed towards any particular style of painting, at any moment – including the present one – the work of a relatively few painters appears more advanced, more radical in its criticism of the modernist art of the recent past, than any other contemporary work. The chief function of the dialectic of modernism in the visual arts has been to provide a principle by which painting can change, transform and renew itself, and by which it is enabled to perpetuate virtually intact, and sometimes even enriched, through each epoch of self-renewal, those of its traditional values that do not pertain directly to representation. Thus modernist painting preserves what it can of its history, not as an act of piety towards the past but as a source of value in the present and future.

For this reason, if for no other, it is ironic that modernist painting is often described as nihilistic and its practitioners characterized as irresponsible charlatans. In point of fact, the strains under which they work are enormous, and it is not surprising that, in one way or another, many of the finest modernist painters have cracked up under them. This tendency towards breakdown has been intensified in the past twenty years by the quickening that has taken place in the rate of self-transformation within modernism itself – a quickening that, in turn, has been the result of an increase in formal and historical self-awareness on the part of modernist painters. The work of such painters as Noland, Olitski and Stella not only arises largely out of their personal interpretations of the particular situations in which advanced painting found itself at crucial moments in their respective developments; their work also aspires to be adjudged, in retrospect, to have been necessary to the finest modernist painting of the future. 'History, according to Hegel, is the maturation of a future in the present, not the sacrifice of the present to an unknown future, and the rule of action according to him is not to be effective at any price, but above all to be fecund,' Merleau-Ponty has written. In this sense the ultimate criterion of the legitimacy of a putative advance in modernist painting is its fecundity. But if one seeks to test this criterion against the art of the recent past, one must bear in mind that the finest contemporary painting testifies to the fecundity not only of the art of

Barnett Newman around 1950, but to that of de Kooning as well; and that this is so because of, not in spite of, the fact that Newman's art amounts to the most radical criticism of de Kooning's one can imagine. [. . .]

Once a painter who accepts the basic premises of modernism becomes aware of a particular problem thrown up by the art of the recent past, his action is no longer gratuitous but imposed. He may be mistaken in his assessment of the situation. But as long as he believes such a problem exists and is important, he is confronted by a situation he cannot pass by, but must, in some way or other, pass through; and the result of this forced passage will be his art. This means that while modernist painting has increasingly divorced itself from the concerns of the society in which it precariously flourishes, the actual dialectic by which it is made has taken on more and more of the denseness, structure and complexity of moral experience – that is, of life itself, but life lived as few are inclined to live it: in a state of continuous intellectual and moral alertness.

The formal critic of modernist painting, then, is also a moral critic: not because all art is at bottom a criticism of life, but because modernist painting is at least a criticism of itself. And because this is so, criticism that shares the basic premises of modernist painting finds itself compelled to play a role in its development closely akin to, and potentially only somewhat less important than, that of new paintings themselves. Not only will such a critic expound the significance of new painting that strikes him as being genuinely exploratory, and distinguish between this and work that does not attempt to challenge or to go beyond the achievements of prior modernists; but in discussing the work of painters he admires he will have occasion to point out what seem to him flaws in putative solutions to particular formal problems; and, more rarely, he may even presume to call the attention of modernist painters to formal issues that, in his opinion, demand to be grappled with. Finally, just as a modernist painter may be mistaken in his assessment of a particular situation, or having grasped the situation may fail to cope with it successfully, the formal critic who shares the basic premises of modernist painting runs the analogous risk of being wrong. And in fact it is inconceivable that he will *not* be wrong a fair amount of the time. But being wrong is preferable to being irrelevant; and the recognition that everyone involved with contemporary art must work without certainty can only be beneficial in its effects. For example, it points up the difficulty of trying to decide whose opinions on the subject among the many put forward deserve to be taken seriously – a decision about as hard to make as value-judgments in front of specific paintings.

It may be argued that this is an intolerably arrogant conception of the critic's job of work, and perhaps it is. But it has the virtue of forcing the critic who takes it up to run the same risks as the artist whose work he criticizes. In view of this last point it is not surprising that so few critics have chosen to assume its burdens.

Reference

1. [. . .] This is more than just a figure of speech: it is a capsule description of what may be seen to take place in Manet's paintings. Manet's ambitions are fundamentally realistic. He starts out aspiring to the objective transcription of reality, a world to

which one wholly belongs, such as he finds in the work of Velazquez and Hals. But where Velazquez and Hals took for granted their relation to the worlds they belonged to and observed and painted, Manet is sharply conscious that his own relation to reality is far more problematic. And to paint his world with the same fullness of response, the same passion for truth, that he finds in the work of Velazquez and Hals, means that he is forced to paint not merely his world but his problematic relation to it; his own awareness of himself as *in* and yet *not of* the world. In this sense Manet is the first post-Kantian painter: the first painter whose awareness of himself raises problems of extreme difficulty that cannot be ignored: the first painter for whom consciousness itself is the great subject of his art.

Almost from the first – surely as early as the *Déjeuner sur l'Herbe* – Manet seems to have striven hard to make this awareness function as an essential part of his paintings, an essential aspect of their content. This accounts for the *situational* character of Manet's paintings of the 1860s: the painting itself is conceived as a kind of *tableau vivant* (in this respect Manet relates back to David), but a *tableau vivant* constructed so as to dramatize not a particular event so much as the beholder's alienation from that event. Moreover, in paintings like the *Déjeuner* and the *Olympia*, for example, the inhibiting, estranging quality of self-awareness is literally depicted within the painting: in the *Déjeuner* by the unintelligible gesture of the man on the right and the bird frozen in flight at the top of the painting; in the *Olympia* above all by the hostile, almost schematic cat; and in both by the distancing calm stare of Victorine Meurend.

But Manet's desire to make the estranging quality of self-awareness an essential part of the content of his work – a desire which, as we have seen, is at bottom realistic – has an important consequence: namely, that self-awareness in *this* particular situation necessarily entails the awareness that what one is looking at is, after all, merely a painting. And this awareness *too* must be made an essential part of the work itself. That is, there must be no question but that the painter *intended* it to be felt; and if necessary the spectator must be *compelled* to feel it. Otherwise the self-awareness (and the alienation) Manet is after would remain incomplete and equivocal.

For this reason Manet emphasizes certain characteristics which have nothing to do with verisimilitude but which assert that the painting in question is exactly that: a painting. For example, Manet emphasizes the flatness of the picture surface by eschewing modelling and (as in the *Déjeuner*) refusing to depict depth convincingly, calls attention to the limits of the canvas by truncating extended forms with the framing edge, and underscores the rectangular shape of the picture support by aligning with it, more or less conspicuously, various elements within the painting. (The notions of emphasis and assertion are important here. David and Ingres rely on rectangular composition far more than Manet; and some of Ingres' forms have as little modelling as Manet's. But David and Ingres are not concerned to emphasize the rectangularity or the flatness of the canvas, but rather they make use of these to insure the stability of their compositions and the rightness of their drawing.)

No wonder Manet's art has always been open to contradictory interpretations: the contradictions reside in the conflict between his ambitions and his actual situation. (What one takes to be the salient features of his situation is open to argument; an uncharacteristically subtle Marxist could, I think, make a good case for focusing on the economic and political situation in France after 1848. In this note, however, I have stressed Manet's recognition of consciousness as a problem

for art, as well as the estranging quality of his own consciousness of himself.)
Manet's art represents the last attempt in Western painting to achieve a full equivalent to the great realistic painting of the past: an attempt which led, in quick
inexorable steps, to the founding of modernism through the emphasis on pictorial
qualities and problems in their own right. This is why Manet was so easily thrown
off stride by the advent of Impressionism around 1870: because his pictorial and
formal innovations of the preceding decade had not been made for their own sakes,
but in the service of a phenomenology that had already been worked out in
philosophy, and had been objectified in some poetry (e.g., Blake), but which had
not yet made itself felt in the visual arts. It was only at the end of his life that Manet
at last succeeded in using what he had learned from Impressionism to objectify his
own much more profound phenomenology, in the *Bar aux Folies-Bergère*.

19   What is Revolutionary Art?

Herbert Read

[. . .] Revolutionary art should be revolutionary. That surely is a simple statement from which we can begin the discussion. We can at once dismiss the feeble interpretation of such a statement as an injunction to paint pictures of red flags, hammers and sickles, factories and machines, or revolutionary subjects in general [. . .] But such a feeble interpretation does actually persist among Communists, and was in fact responsible for the failure of the first exhibition organised by the Artists' International.

We can best approach the question from the angle of an abstract art like architecture. [. . .] Architecture is a necessary art, and it is intimately bound up with the social reconstruction which must take place under a Communist régime. How do we, as Englishmen, conceive a Communist architecture? As a reversion to Tudor rusticity, or Georgian stateliness, or the bourgeois pomp of the neo-classical style? Surely none of these styles can for a moment be considered in relation to the city of the future. Must we not rather confidently look forward to a development of the new architecture of which Walter Gropius is the foremost exponent; of that architecture which, in his own words, 'bodies itself forth, not in stylistic imitation or ornamental frippery, but in those simple and sharply modelled designs in which every part merges naturally into the comprehensive volume of the whole'. Only in this manner, by following the path clearly indicated by Gropius in his work and writings, can we find 'a concrete expression of the life of our epoch'. [. . .]

Corresponding to the new architecture, to a large extent arising from the same fertile ground of the Bauhaus experiment founded and directed by Gropius, is the art generally known as 'abstract'. The name is admittedly a makeshift, and between an abstract artist like Mondrian or Ben Nicholson at one end of the scale, and an equally so-called 'abstract' artist like Miró or Henry Moore, there is only a remote connection. But for the moment these differences do not matter. Such names represent the modern school in painting and sculpture in its widest and most typical aspect, and these artists, I wish to claim, are the true revolutionary artists, whom every Communist should learn to respect and encourage.

Such an opinion will be met by a formidable opposition, precisely among Communists who are interested in art. Communist artists from Germany will tell you that they have 'been through all that'; that abstract art is dead, and that in any case it is incomprehensible to the proletariat and of no use to the revolutionary movement. Like the simple bourgeois of another generation, they ask for something they can understand, a 'realistic' art above all, something they can use as propaganda.

Actually, I believe that such artists are confessing their failure – as artists. The abstract movement in art is not dead, and not likely to be for many years to come. That it will gradually be transformed not only the dialectical conception of history,

Source: B. Rea (ed.), *Five on Revolutionary Art* (Artists International Association, London, 1935), pp. 11–22.

but the slightest acquaintance with the history of art, compels us to admit. But how it will be transformed is more than we can tell. The facts we have to recognise are: that all the artists of any intellectual force belong to this movement; that this movement is contemporary and revolutionary; and that only the apparent independence and isolation of the abstract artist – his refusal to toe the line and become an emotional propagandist – only this fact hinders the Communist from accepting the abstract movement in art as the contemporary revolutionary movement in art.

To describe this attitude in the abstract artist as formalistic, as mere decorative dilettantism, not only betrays a lack of aesthetic sensibility, but an ignorance of the actual ideals and personalities of the artists themselves. Most of the artists in question are more or less openly in sympathy with the Communist movement. Why, then, do they adopt in all its integrity what is called the formalist attitude?

The question cannot be answered without a short digression on the nature of art. Any considerable work of art has two distinct elements: a formal element appealing to our sensibility for reasons which cannot be stated with any clarity, but which are certainly psychological in origin; and an arbitrary or accidental element of more complex appeal which is the outer clothing given to these underlying forms. It is at least arguable that the purely formal element in art does not change; that the same canons of harmony and proportion are present in primitive art, in Greek art, in Gothic art, in Renaissance art and in the art of the present day. Such forms, we may say, are archetypal; due to the physical structure of the world and the psychological structure of man. And it is for this reason that the artist, with some show of reason, can take up an attitude of detachment. It is his sense of the importance of the archetypal which makes him relatively indifferent to the phenomenal. The recognition of such universal formal qualities in art is consistently materialistic. It no more contradicts the materialistic interpretation of the history of art than does a recognition of the relative permanency of the human form, or of the forms of crystals in geology. Certain factors in life are constant; but to that extent they are not a part of history. History is concerned with that part of life which is subject to change; and the Marxian dialectic is an interpretation of history, not a theory of the structure or morphology of life.

Another consideration which mitigates the objection to the formalistic attitude is that, granted the existence of permanent and unchanging elements in art, there is, admittedly, at various periods, a different valuation of such elements. In fact, what is the difference between classical and romantic epochs but a difference in the emphasis given to the formal basis of works of art? We cannot say that a romantic painter like Delacroix lacks form – or that a classical painter like Poussin has too much of it. If we could in any way measure the degree of form in these two artists we should probably find that it was equal. But in the classical artist the form is so important that the subject-matter is almost irrelevant; whilst in the romantic artist the subject-matter is so important that it completely overwhelms the form. It is merely, we might say, a difference of accent. But it is in precisely such a way that a reasonable Marxian would expect art to be inflected. We can, therefore, in any broad historical generalisations, dismiss the underlying formal structure of art, to concentrate on style and mannerism. For it is in style and mannerism that the prevailing ideology of a period is expressed.

If we admit so much, it follows that it is a mere illusion for the artist to imagine that he can for ever maintain an attitude of detachment. I can only see one logical exception – the artist who can so deprive his work of temporary and accidental qualities that what he achieves is in effect *pure form*. And significantly enough that is the claim of one extreme of the abstract movement, an extreme which includes some of the most talented artists now living. Having no sympathy with any existing ideology, they attempt to escape into a world without ideologies. They shut themselves within the Ivory Tower, and it is just possible that, *for the time being* (the very special time in which we live) their tactics may be of some advantage to the art of the future. Their position will become clearer as we proceed.

Apart from such a desperate retreat, we have to admit that the artist cannot in any effective way avoid the economic conditions of his time; he cannot ignore them, for they will not ignore him. Reality, in one guise or another, forces the artist along a determined course, and if the artist does not realise this, it is only because he is in the middle of the stream, where the water is deep and the current strong.

As I have said elsewhere, this question of the relation of the individual to the collective society of which he is a member is the fundamental issue, in art as well as in politics. [. . .] Philosophically it is the issue between materialism and idealism. But the relation between mind and reality, between the individual and the community, is not one of precedence; it is more one of action and reaction, a process of tacking against the wind. The current of reality is strong, and troubles the mind; but the mind embraces this contrary force, and is lifted higher, and carried farther, by the very opposition. And so with the individual and the community: complete freedom means inevitable decadence. The mind must feel an opposition – must be tamped with hard realities if it is to have any blasting power.

That by no means exhausts the problem of the relation of the individual to society. [. . .] Actually, I believe the real justification for intellectual freedom will be found on psychological grounds; the psychology of the individual is correlated dialectically with the psychology of the group, and for that reason the old conception of individuality will not serve for the new order of society.

Let us return to the actualities of modern art. Excluding the great mass of academic bourgeois art, and within the general category of revolutionary art, we have two distinct movements, both professing to be modern, both *intentionally* revolutionary.

The first of these has no very descriptive label, but it is essentially formalist, in the sense already mentioned. It is sometimes called abstract, sometimes non-figurative, sometimes constructivist, sometimes geometric. It is most typically represented by painters like Mondrian, Hélion, Ben Nicholson, Moholy-Nagy; and by sculptors like Brancusi, Gabo and Barbara Hepworth.

The second movement has a distinctive name – *Surréalisme* or Superrealism, and is represented by painters like Max Ernst, Salvador Dali, Miró, Tanguy, and by a sculptor like Arp.

The first movement is plastic, objective and ostensibly non-political.

The second group is literary (even in paint), subjective and actively Communist.

Those distinctions are obvious, on the surface. But I want to suggest that we cannot be satisfied with such superficial distinctions. We cannot accept the *sur-*

réalistes at their own valuation, and welcome them as the only true revolutionary artists. Nevertheless, they are performing a very important revolutionary function, and it must be said on their behalf that they realise the importance of their function with far more clarity than the official Marxians, who have shown them no favour. For official Marxians, concentrating on their economic problems, do not see the relevance of the cultural problem, more particularly the artistic problem. The mind of the artist, they complacently assume, that too will, in Trotsky's phrase, limp after the reality they are creating.

But everywhere the greatest obstacle to the creation of this new social reality is the existence of the cultural heritage of the past – the religion, the philosophy, the literature and the art which makes up the whole complex ideology of the bourgeois mind. The logic of the facts – the economic facts: war, poverty amidst plenty, social injustice – that logic cannot be denied. But so long as the bourgeois mind has its bourgeois ideology, it will deny the facts; it will construct an elaborate rationalisation which effectively ignores them.

The superrealists, who possess very forceful expositors of their point of view – writers like André Breton – realise this very clearly, and the object of their movement is therefore to discredit the bourgeois ideology in art, to destroy the academic conception of art. Their whole tendency is negative and destructive. The particular method they adopt, in so far as they have a common method, consists in breaking down the barriers between the conscious reality of life and the unconscious reality of the dream-world – to so mingle fact and fancy that the normal concept of reality no longer has existence. It is a similar tendency which Carl Einstein found in the later work of Braque, and to some extent Braque may be considered as a *surréaliste* – Picasso too. *Surréalistes* like Ernst and Dali complete the disintegration of the academic concept of reality begun by Picasso and Braque.

We can see, therefore, the place of *surréalisme* in the revolutionary movement. What of this other kind of modern art – the art of pure form immured in its Ivory Tower?

That art too, I wish to contend, has its revolutionary function, and in the end it is the most important function of all. Superrealism is a negative art, as I have said, a destructive art; it follows that it has only a temporary role; it is the art of a transitional period. It may lead to a new romanticism, especially in literature, but that lies beyond its immediate function.

But abstract art has a positive function. It keeps inviolate, until such time as society will once more be ready to make use of them, the universal qualities of art – those elements which survive all changes and revolutions. It may be said that as such it is merely art in pickle – an activity divorced from reality, of no immediate interest to the revolutionary. But that, I maintain, is a very short view of the situation. And actually such art is not so much in pickle as might be supposed. For in one sphere, in architecture and to some extent in industrial arts, it is already in social action. There we find the essential link between the abstract movement in modern painting and the most advanced movement in modern architecture. It is not merely a similarity of form and intention, but an actual and intimate association of personalities.

This single link points the way to the art of the future – the art of the new classless society. It is impossible to predict all the forms of this art, and it will be many years before it reaches its maturity. But you cannot build a new society – and you must *build* such a society, with bricks and mortar, steel and glass – you cannot build such a society without artists. The artists are waiting for their opportunity: abstract artists who are, in this time of transition, perfecting their formal sensibility, and who will be ready, when the time comes, to apply their talents to the great work of reconstruction. That is not a work for romanticists and literary sentimentalists. Communism is realist, scientific, essentially classical. But let us realise that we have romanticists in our midst – tender-minded idealists who would like to blur the precise outlines of our vision with democratic ideals of egalitarianism, Tolstoyan simplicity and naivety, community singing and boy-scoutism. Such people imagine that revolutionary art is a kind of folk-art, peasant pottery, madrigals and ballads. Surely that is not a conception of art worthy of the true Communist. We want something tougher, something more intellectual and 'difficult', something that we can without falsity and self-deception put beside the great epochs of art in the past.

REVOLUTIONARY ART IS CONSTRUCTIVE
REVOLUTIONARY ART IS INTERNATIONAL
REVOLUTIONARY ART IS REVOLUTIONARY

Donald Judd

Barnett Newman's paintings are some of the best done in the United States in the last fifteen years. At the moment, despite the difficulties of comparisons and the excellence of the work of Rothko, Noland and Stella,[1] it's not so rash to say that Newman is the best painter in this country. Also, the work of these four artists and that by Reinhardt and Lichtenstein, is considerably better than the European painting evident in the magazines and that shown in New York, except for Yves Klein's blue paintings. These evaluations only involve painting and since painting now shares art equally with sculpture and three-dimensional work more comparisons are possible. But these still leave Newman one of the world's best artists and the best make a short list.

Newman was born in New York City in 1905 and has lived there ever since. He studied art at the Art Students' League. Before 1950 his paintings were shown infrequently in group shows, notably one in 1947 of Abstract Surrealism at the Chicago Art Institute which, for the first time, included all of the artists, Pollock, Still and Rothko for example, who were on the verge of radically changing American art and art as a whole. The term 'Abstract Surrealism' is more or less descriptive of Newman's work then. In 1948 he painted the first painting like his work since, a small one with a stripe down the middle. Late in 1949 or early in 1950 he did a painting with two stripes. Newman's first one-man show was at the Betty Parsons Gallery in 1950. There was a second show there a year later. Since then, other than single paintings in group shows, he has shown three times. In 1959, at the impermanent but important gallery directed by Clement Greenberg for French and Co., there was a large and magnificent show of paintings done between 1946 and 1952, including *Vir Heroicus Sublimis* and *Cathedra*, two large ones. In 1958 this work had been shown at Bennington College. Some of Newman's recent paintings, as well as a few earlier ones, including *The Wild* of 1950, an eight-foot vertical an inch and a half wide, were shown in 1962 with De Kooning's work at the Allan Stone Gallery.

Shining Forth (To George), done in 1961, was shown in New York this year. It's nine and a half feet high and fourteen and a half long. The rectangle is unprimed cotton canvas except for two stripes and the edges of a third. Slightly to the left of the centre there is a vertical black stripe three inches wide. All of the stripes run to the upper and lower edges. Slightly less than a foot in from the left edge there is a black stripe an inch wide. This hasn't been painted directly and evenly like the central stripe, but has been laid in between two stripes of masking tape. The paint has run under the tape some, making the stripe a little rough. A foot in from the right edge there is another stripe an inch wide, but this is one of reserved canvas, made by scraping black paint across a strip of masking tape and then removing it. There isn't much paint on either side of the white stripe; the two edges are sharp just against the

Source: Studio International Feb. 1970, pp. 67–69. The article was written in November 1964. Illustrations have been omitted.

stripe and break into sharp palette knife marks just away from it. Some of the marks have been lightly brushed. The three stripes are fairly sharp but none are perfectly even and straight. It's a complex painting.

Many of Newman's recent paintings are black and white. *Noon-light* is another great one shown recently. It's nine and a half feet high and seven wide. There is a stripe of black about four inches wide along the left edge and there is a black stripe a quarter of an inch wide four inches in from the right edge. The rest is unprimed canvas.

Vir Heroicus Sublimis was done in 1950 and the colour of one stripe was changed in 1951. It's eight feet high and eighteen long. Except for five stripes it's a red near cadmium red medium. From the left, a few feet in, there is an inch stripe of a red close in colour but different in tone; a few feet further there is an inch of white; across the widest area there is an inch and a half of a dark, slightly maroon brown that looks black in the red; a few feet further there is a stripe like the first one on the left; a foot or so before the right edge there is a dark yellow, almost raw sienna stripe, the colour that was changed. These stripes are described in sequence but of course are seen at once, and with the areas.

Shining Forth is symmetrical, but obviously isn't thoroughly symmetrical: the widest black stripe runs down the centre; two large, nearly equal halves lie left and right, each including a large area of canvas, a narrow stripe and a narrow area of canvas. The two halves and their parts are very different. The central line is not simply a dividing line. Like all the areas and lines it can be discrete and it can also be part of the lines and areas to either side. The two narrow stripes are symmetrical, but one is black, thin paint on canvas, and one is white, bare canvas bounded by marks on the canvas; the black stripe is symmetrical to the same surface it's on. The white stripe needs and supports larger areas, on either side, than the black stripe; the right half extends furthest from the central stripe; it's cantilevered but still matches the left half. Both outlying stripes are surprisingly far from the centre and the right one is even further. The narrow black stripe and the wider one are on the canvas surface but the white stripe is that surface. The marks along the white stripe are even more intimately on the canvas than the black stripes. The position of the white stripe is highly ambiguous. It is, approximately, a negative area that comes forward. Since it is the same surface as the rectangle of the painting, that is forced forward. The white stripe is like the rest of the white but it's underneath it and yet forward of it. The whole surface has to come forward. If this didn't occur the black lines would lie slightly in front of the canvas, as most marks do, and the areas would stand back slightly. The areas are as forward and as definite as the stripes. This description may have been dry reading but that is what's there.

It is important that Newman's paintings are large, but it's even more important that they are large scaled. His first painting with a stripe, a small one, is large scaled. The single stripe allowed this and the scale allowed the prominence and assertion of the stripe and the two areas. This scale is one of the most important developments in the twentieth-century art. Pollock seems to have been involved in the problem of this scale first. Newman shared attitudes which were leading to the scale and developed it on his own in 1950. A few others, a little later, recognized its importance. All of the best American art, to this moment, has this scale. The form and qualities of the work couldn't exist otherwise. The major division in contemporary art is between that involving the smaller, older scale. There is a lot of uninteresting art in the United

States based on the smaller scale and a little that is interesting. The most interesting European art, except for Klein's which is broad, is relatively small scaled, judging of course by what has been seen in New York.

The large scale is involved with several important qualities, each of which forces the existence of the others. Obviously Newman's paintings are open, as is much recent work, though not all in the same way. The areas are very broad and are not tightly delimited by either the stripes or the edges of the canvas, both of which are similar. The stripes are not dominant, thoroughly discrete, stopped before the edge or opposed against an area. Newman's openness and freedom are credible now; the earlier closed and somewhat naturalistic form is not. Ordinary abstract painting and expressionistic painting are bound in the rectangle by their composition. Their space and colour are recessed by a residual naturalism. They are still pictures. If forms run off the edges to imply a continuum, the painting is a segment of that continuum, which isn't true of Newman's paintings. They are whole and aren't part of another whole. There is no implication that the parts extend beyond the edges, just as there is none that they occur within the edges. Everything is specifically where it is. This wholeness is also new and important. It is why the stripes and the edges correspond. Mondrian's work, taking it as representative of his generation, if greater, clearly has traditional and naturalistic aspects. The lines are dominant and the white is secondary, volume and space once removed. The white is both comparatively frontal, only recessed a few inches, and infinitely recessive. The lines form a bound structure and one that is very ordered. Newman's work is not geometric in this sense, just as neither his nor Pollock's is expressionistic. Mondrian's fixed platonic order is no longer credible. 'Hard-edge painting', primarily defined by Ellsworth Kelly's work, is mainly old abstraction.[2] It employs, though somewhat abridged, the new scale and simplicity and has some of the new specificity of colour but also uses the old abstract space, composition and colour. The openness of Newman's work is concomitant with chance and one person's knowledge; the work doesn't suggest a great scheme of knowledge; it doesn't claim more than anyone can know; it doesn't imply a social order. Newman is asserting his concerns and knowledge. He couldn't do this without the openness, wholeness and scale that he has developed. The colour, areas and stripes are not obscured or diluted by a hierarchy of composition and a range of associations. The few parts, all equally primary, comprise the quality of a painting.

'We are reasserting man's natural desire for the exalted, for a concern with our relationship to the absolute emotions. We do not need the obsolete props of an outmoded and antiquated legend. We are creating images whose reality is self-evident and which are devoid of the props and crutches that evoke associations with outmoded images, both sublime and beautiful. We are freeing ourselves of the impediments of memory, association, nostalgia, legend, myth, or what have you, that have been the devices of Western European painting. Instead of making *cathedrals* out of Christ, man, or "life", we are making it out of ourselves, out of our own feelings. The image we produce is the self-evident one of revelation, real and concrete, that can be understood by anyone who will look at it without the nostalgic glasses of history.'[3]

We are making it out of ourselves.

The colour or bare canvas of Newman's paintings is very frontal and is necessarily spreading, lateral. The doubled frontality of *Shining Forth* is an example. The colour is usually applied flatly and thinly. Infrequently it is thin enough to show brushmarks and becomes a little illusionistic. Newman's colour is itself a major and influential achievement. It is full, rich and somewhat austere; for example, a lot of maroon and a little orange or a full blue and a whitened cerulean blue. *Vir Heroicus Sublimis* is a good example of the colour. The black and white is also colour. Obviously neither this colour nor the handling of the paint is pure and geometric. As with the canvas, there is much that is specific about what Newman does with the paint, much that is particular to it, such as the way it bled under the masking tape along the narrow black stripe in *Shining Forth* or the effect of stencilling in the white stripe. Similarly, Newman sometimes leaves brushstrokes along an area, since that is the way the paint was applied. A good deal more could be said about Newman's work, but there isn't space. *Shining Forth, Noon-light* and *Vir Heroicus Sublimis* are great paintings.

References

1   Frank Stella has done a lot of good paintings since 1964 and he shouldn't be second even to Newman. [Don Judd, 1969]
2   I haven't changed my mind about the paintings I was writing about, the Arpish ones, but Kelly's later rectangular paintings are another case. At the time I had seen one early sectional rectangular painting in a Green Gallery Show but didn't know there were more like it and took it for a fluke. [Don Judd, 1969]
3   Extract from 'The sublime is now', by Barnett Newman, *Tiger's Eye*, vol. 1, Dec. 1948.

SECTION THREE

Abstraction

21   From the Easel to the Machine

Nikolai Tarabukin

I   The diagnosis

The entire artistic life of Europe for the past ten years has proceeded under the sign of 'the crisis of art'. When Manet's canvases first appeared about sixty years ago at Parisian exhibitions and inspired a complete revolution in the artistic world of Paris of the time, the first stone was removed from the foundation of painting. Until recently, we were still inclined to see the whole subsequent development of painterly forms as a progressive process towards the perfection of those forms. In the light of most recent developments, we now perceive this, on the one hand, as a steady destruction of the integrity of the painterly organism into its constituent elements, and on the other, as a gradual degeneration of painting as the typical art form.

II   The emancipation of painting from literariness and illusionism

The French Impressionists were the first revolutionaries in painting, liberating it from the paralysing paths of naturalistic trends and giving it new directions. They were the first to give pre-eminence, among the artist's skills, to work on form. At the same time, their work was directed towards freeing painting from a content dependent upon ideology or subject matter, and from the 'literary story' which usually prevailed over form in traditional canvases. For modern painters, the still-life, which is devoid of this 'literariness' in its subject matter, replaced the complex ideology of the Classicists and the alluring anecdote of the naturalists. It is possible to say that the concentration on painterly content in a canvas was in reverse proportion to the presence of a subject matter.

This trend is not only characteristic of the visual arts, but it is also true for other forms of contemporary artistic creativity. Thus, poetry, moving from the word as meaning to the word as sound, has replaced ideology and mood with an emphasis on the external structure of the poem, beginning first with Symbolism, then Futurism, Acmeism and Imaginism. The theatre has abandoned attempts at realistic and psychological interpretations of real life and concentrates its experiments on the formal laws of the stage. Music, which has essentially never been completely enthralled by naturalism and the predominance of a subject matter (programme), goes further in the exploration of the laws of rhythm and composition.

But the formal tasks, henceforth undertaken by art, were only partially intended to liberate the work of art from a subject matter. They were directed towards the purely professional exploration of the material elements integral to the forms of every artistic genre, in which the contemporary artist saw the only incontestable basis for the work of art, subject to the creative design. As well as the gradual

Source: Nikolai Tarabukin, *Ot mol'berta k mashine* (Moscow, 1923), ch. 1–12, edited and translated by Dr Christina Lodder.

disappearance of a subject matter and all attendant elements in painting which do not arise from the material structure of the work of art, there was already clearly manifest the painter's struggle against every type of illusionistic element in the construction of the planar forms. Even during the flowering of Impressionism, which was mainly an illusionistic trend, a reaction to it formed from within itself in the person of Cézanne, who gave more importance to colouring than to light illusionism, which was the basic aim of Impressionism. With Cézanne the painter already begins to concentrate his attention on the material and real structure of the canvas, i.e., on colour, texture, construction and on the material itself.

And so in the canvases of contemporary young artists, who have broken away from naturalistic, symbolic, eclectic and similar trends, and who are working primarily on the professional and technical aspect of painting, illusionistic elements such as light, perspective, movement and space begin to disappear or are treated in a completely new way. Thus, for example, the problem of space which in naturalistic painting the artist solved by means of perspectival and light illusion, for the modern artist leads to material and real problems of colour, line, composition and volume, resolved not illusionistically but by means of the planar structure of the surfaces of large and small bodies.

III   The path towards realism

Moving from illusionistic representation towards realistic constructiveness and gradually liberating itself from all external elements, not conditioned by the particularities of the plane as the point of departure for the form of a painterly object, Russian painting has gone through a whole series of stages which have been entirely original and, frequently, completely independent of Western European influences. Passing quickly from Cézanne to objective Cubism, Russian painting split into a number of trends, united by a common direction. Amongst these, abstract Cubism, Suprematism and Constructivism should be mentioned. The basic stimulus for the creative aspirations of these trends was realism, which in the period of an upsurge in creative life has always been a healthy kernel which has fertilised artistic life and obstructed eclectic tendencies.

I use the concept of realism in its widest sense and do not by any means identify it with naturalism, which is one of the forms of realism and, at that, one of the most primitive and naïve. Contemporary aesthetic consciousness has transferred the idea of realism from the subject to the form of a work of art. Henceforth the motive of realistic strivings was not the copying of reality (as it had been for the naturalists) but, on the contrary, actuality in whatever respect ceased to be the stimulus for creative work. In the forms of his art the artist creates its actuality, and for him realism is the creation of a genuine object which is self-contained in form and content, an object which does not reproduce the objects of the real world, but which is constructed by the artist from beginning to end, outside any projected lines extending towards it from reality. If we look at the works of contemporary abstract artists from the point of view of this genuine realism, then we will see that in form and material they are just as remote from utilitarian objects as are the works of traditional art. In these works, the materials (the pigments) and the form (the two-dimensional plane of the canvas) inevitably create convention and artificiality, i.e., not authenticity, but only the projectional quality of the forms of a work of art.

Therefore the painter's move from the plane of the canvas to the contre-relief was quite logically based on the search for realistic forms in art.

IV   Leaving the plane

The artist rejects the brush and palette of artificial colours and begins to work with genuine materials (glass, wood, metals). As far as I know the contre-relief, as an artistic form, first appeared in Russian art. Although Braque and Picasso were the first to use labels, papers, letters as well as sawdust and plaster, etc., as a means of varying texture and intensifying its expressivity, Tatlin went further and created his contre-reliefs from genuine materials. But in the contre-reliefs the artist was not freed from conventional form and the artificiality of composition. In the corner contre-reliefs, which also like painting can only be viewed from one position, i.e., frontally, the composition is structured basically according to the same principles as it would be on the plane of the canvas. In this way, the problem of space is not *really* solved because the forms in it are not three-dimensional in volume.

The next step in this direction of the evolution of artistic forms was the central contre-relief, which was also created by Tatlin and which broke not only with the plane but also with the wall to which the corner contre-relief had been attached. Works of this type include the spatially constructive works by the OBMOKhU, the volumetric, non-planar constructions of Rodchenko and the 'spatial paintings' of Miturich. The term 'spatial painting' can hardly be called suitable or expressive; I would have used the term 'volumetric' because a painting on a flat surface is as spatial as any other form.

If traditional visual art was sharply differentiated into three typical forms: painting, sculpture and architecture, then in the central contre-relief, the volumetric constructions and the 'spatial paintings', we have an attempt to synthesise these forms. In these the artist combines the architectonics of the construction of material masses (architecture) with the volumetric constructiveness of these masses (sculpture) and their colour, textural and compositional expressivity (painting). In these constructions it seemed as though the artist considered himself completely liberated from the illusionism of representation, because he is not reproducing reality but affirming the object as a completely self-contained value. In the spatial and volumetric constructions the artist, using wood, iron, glass, etc., is working with genuine and not artificial materials. In these the problem of space is given a three-dimensional construction and consequently a real and not a conventional solution as on the two-dimensional plane. In a word, in its forms, as in its construction and material, the artist creates a *genuinely real object*.

V   The crisis of 'pure' form

But here the most bitter disillusionment and the most hopeless impasse awaited the artist and that fatal word for modern art, 'crisis', has never perhaps sounded so tragically as it does now. If contemporary aesthetic consciousness is not profoundly satisfied by naturalism with its anecdotes in paint, Impressionism with its attempts to create through colour the illusion of an airy atmosphere, light and shade, Futurism with its fruitless striving, a *contradictio in adjecto*, to convey a cinematic impression of life's dynamic forms on the static canvas, then not more satisfying for that consciousness are the Suprematists with their impenetrable black square on a white background, the non-figurative texturists with their endless laboratory experiments on the surface of the canvas, the Constructivists naïvely imitating technical constructions without that utilitarian expediency which justifies them, and finally all those working on materials for the sake of the material itself, creating aimless forms divorced from the life of creation. Contemporary art, in its extreme 'leftist' expression, has reached an impasse. The artist working on pure form and on form alone has ultimately deprived his creation of all meaning because an unadorned, empty form can never satisfy us, who seek always for a content in it. A work created by a traditional artist had its meaning in its aesthetic effect, on which its author counted. A construction made by a contemporary artist has lost this last meaning because the 'aesthetic' was consciously rejected from the very first step which determined the path of the new art.

VI   The contradictions of Constructivism

Shunning aesthetics, the Constructivists should have given themselves a new aim which logically arose from the very idea of Constructivism, i.e., a utilitarian aim. By construction we normally understand a definite type of structure having some sort of utilitarian character deprived of which it loses its meaning.

But consciously ignoring themselves as painters, the Russian Constructivists have declared their approach 'against art' in its typical museum forms and have collaborated with technology, engineering and industry without, however, possessing any specialised knowledge for this and remaining artists *par excellence* in all their essential characteristics. This idea of Constructivism and the form of imitating technical and engineering structures which they adopted is dilettante and naïve, inspired only by our age's increasingly pious attitude towards industrialism.

Such types of construction should never have been called models because they do not represent projects for buildings – they are only self-contained objects, tolerant only of artistic criteria. Their creators are quintessentially aesthetes and champions of pure art, however fastidiously they wriggle away from such epithets.

Talking of Constructivism in this case, I mean constructions which are made from materials and are three-dimensional in volume. The planar solutions of the ideas of Constructivism are a still more absurd form. Having fought against representation, the Constructivists have remained figurative artists to a far greater degree than their predecessors – the Suprematists – because their structure of a construction on the plane of the canvas was nothing other than the representation of a constructive system or building that could be really built. Every painterly form is essentially figurative whether it is objective, as for the naturalists and the Impressionists, or non-objective, as for the Cubists and Futurists. Consequently, when we draw a decisive distinction between 'old' and 'new' art, it is not representation which is the defining feature but the non-objectivity or the objectivity of this representation. In this respect, the Suprematists, who mainly posed and solved colour problems, went further away from representation than all other artistic movements because the basic element with which they were working – colour – by itself is not enclosed in any representational form and like a sound is formless. The structures of sound and colour (light) have much in common.

VII   The last 'picture'

And so the Constructivists working with the surface plane, despite themselves, confirmed the representational, of which their constructions were an element. And when the artist really wanted to get rid of representation, he achieved this only at the cost of destroying painting and only at the cost of destroying himself as a painter. I am referring to the canvas which Rodchenko offered to the attention of an astonished public at one of this season's exhibitions [5 × 5 = 25, 1921]. This was a smallish, almost square canvas painted entirely in a single red colour. This canvas is extremely significant for the evolution of artistic forms which art has undergone in the last ten years. It is not merely a stage which can be followed by new ones but it represents the last and final step of a long journey, the last word, after which painting must become silent, the last 'picture' made by an artist. This canvas eloquently demonstrates that painting as a figurative art – which it has always been – is outdated. If Malevich's *Black Square on a White Background*, despite the poverty of its artistic meaning, did contain some painterly idea which the author called 'economy', 'the fifth dimension', then Rodchenko's canvas, which is devoid of any content, is a meaningless, dumb and blind wall. However, as a link in the chain of development, viewed not as a self-contained value (which it isn't) but as a stage in evolution, it is historically significant and 'marks an epoch'.

This, once again, confirms that usually the works which acquire historical importance are those which, at the same time, do not possess any great 'specific weight' artistically; and it is precisely on these that art historians base their conclusions. The objection which could be raised by a zealous adherent of historical chronology (for which art historians have a weakness), that Malevich had exhibited a similar canvas several years before, is not, I consider, vital to my argument, because my task is to establish not the historical and chronological landmarks of Russian art but the theoretical basis of a logically developing process. And if Malevich's canvas is chronologically the earlier work, Rodchenko's similar canvas is logically more symptomatic and historically more opportune. The Tretyakov Gallery, which jealously takes care that there should be no gap in the historical course of painterly trends displayed on its walls, must certainly acquire this canvas. And it will acquire it (or a similar work: this is not so important) when, 'through the pressure of events', the aesthetic critics see it as occupying a definite place in the 'historical perspective'. Similarly, 'with time' (when they were recognised by the newspapers) the gallery acquired canvases by Larionov, Tatlin and others, about whom 'at the time' they did not want to hear, considering these canvases to be 'profanations of art'. Suffering from a sight defect which could be described as 'historicity' in their approach to art, these eclectics in charge of the gallery (and those who aren't) are completely unable to gain an understanding of the phenomena of current artistic life and its immediate influence. They only begin to see, and even then weakly, when a definite 'touch of time', 'a patina', appears on the work of art (it is not insignificant that the eclectics so adore green mould). The 'historical perspective' and a more or less prolonged period of time are the invariable concomitants of their aesthetic appreciation and 'recognition'.

This example of Rodchenko's canvas convinces us that painting was, and remains, a representational art and that it cannot escape from these limits of the representational. In traditional art the representation was its content. Ceasing to be representational, painting lost its inner meaning. Laboratory work on bare form enclosed art in a narrow circle, stopped its progress and led it to become impoverished.

VIII   The painterly meaning of the concept of construction

But in surface plane and in spatial and volumetric painting the idea of Constructivism found a solution which arose from the precise meaning of the very idea, understood not technically but in a painterly way, as it has to be understood in painting. The painter could only adopt the general structure of the concept from technology, and not by any means all its elements. The concept of construction in painting is composed of entirely different elements from the same concept in technology. By the general concept of construction, independent of its form and purpose, we mean the whole complex of elements which are united into one whole by a certain kind of principle and which, in its unity, represents a system. Applying this general definition to painting, we should consider the elements of the painterly construction to be the material and real elements of the canvas, i.e., the pigments or other material, the surface texture, the structure of the colour, the technique for working the material, etc., united by the composition (the principle) and, as a whole, forming the work of art (the system).

Clearly, these elements are not dependent on the representational aspect of the work of art but constitute a category *sui generis* inherent in the artistic object, as the product of a definite kind of professional skill.

Cézanne was the first consciously to represent the problem of Constructivism as a purely painterly concept in his works. Cézanne was a prophetic master in many respects and in this instance, as in many others, anticipated an idea which he realized empirically and then threw out to the future. In Cézanne's canvases we see the well-knit surface, the paint applied with a firm hand, the beautifully worked surface texture, the strict structuring of the coloured whole, the absence of dilettantism and, on the contrary, the highest professional skill, behind which we perceive a substantial culture. All these indications provide a basis for considering his canvases to be painterly and constructive, i.e., they are well structured from the point of view of the organisation of the material elements in them.

In their textured canvases the Russian Cubists, Suprematists, Objectivists and Constructivists whom I have already mentioned worked in the same elements which I have included as the constituents of painterly construction. Consequently, they worked, and worked a lot, on the constructive aspect of painting in the sense in which I have tried to clarify this concept. Their working on this professional and technical aspect of painting represents the great service which Russian artists have rendered to art. We can assert with confidence that in the statement and solution of many artistic problems we have, in our purely professional approach, outstripped Western European art both in theory and in practice [. . .]

IX   The social basis of the crisis of art

But the problem of the crisis of art which I have presented in this essay does not lie only in this professional and narrowly technical painterly aspect of the question. It has wider horizons and roots not only of a formal character but also of an ideological and social nature.

Abstracted from all content, the pure form around which art has evolved during the last decade has ultimately revealed its insubstantiality; it has exposed the fruitlessness of an art divorced from life and the inability of the typical forms of creativity, suitable only for the graveyard of the museum, to survive in contemporary conditions. In the past, 'the picture' was figurative and had its aesthetic and meaning in the milieu of a particular class or social group, as an individualistic expression of the aesthetic consciousness of a class or group. Now, when class and related divisions lose their foundation in all essential characteristics, making aesthetic epicurism fruitless, the 'picture' as the typical form of visual art also loses its meaning as a social phenomenon. The confirmation of this idea can be found in facts which cannot be denied. Despite the calm of the last four to five years, the exhibitions of the last winter seasons (1919–1921) were not what could be called successful. They went by completely unnoticed. From being 'events' in artistic life they are becoming phenomena which no longer arouse any interest, are not visited, are not talked about and to which people are indifferent.

The democratisation of the social structure and social relationships in Russia has fatally affected the forms of creativity and the masses appreciating art. In our eyes the psychology of aesthetic perception is radically changing its structure. In the period of class groups, the form of easel painting naturally permits endless variation, fragmentation and individualisation, responding to those varied requirements of a differentiated social milieu. In contrast, during a period of social democratisation, the mass viewer who demands from art forms which will express the idea of the mass, of society and the people as a whole, replaces the class consumer and patron of aesthetic values. Influenced by the requirements of this new mass consumer, art has adopted a democratic form.

X   Easel painting is inevitably a museum art form

Whether the figurativeness of easel painting and sculpture is naturalistic as in Courbet and Repin, allegorical and symbolic as in Böcklin, Stück and Rerikh, or breaking with the objectivity of the concrete image and acquiring a non-objective character as in the majority of contemporary young Russian artists, it is, all the same, museum art and the museum remains the formative influence dictating the form, the reason and the special purpose of the creation. I also relate spatial painting and the contre-relief to the category of museum objects which have no living or practical purpose. All contemporary art created by the 'left' wing finds its justification only on museum walls, and all the revolutionary storm they stirred up finds its final repose in the quiet of the museum graveyard.

Museum workers are confronted with the task of sorting this material which was revolutionary in its time into an historical order and to bury it 'beneath numbers' on inventory lists of the 'artistic storehouses'. And for the art historians, those inexhaustible, dry as dust archaeologists, there awaits a new work in the writing of explanatory texts for this sepulchral crypt so that the descendant, if only he doesn't forget the way to them, can worthily evaluate the past and not confuse the landmarks of 'historical perspectives'. Despite their Futurism these artists do not forget to occupy their proper place in the cemeteries of the past.

XI   The account presented to contemporaneity

Contemporaneity makes completely new demands on the artist. It wants not museum 'pictures' and 'sculptures' from him but objects which are socially justified in form and purpose. The museums are sufficiently full not to require new variations on the old themes. Life no longer justifies art objects which are solely dependent on their form and content. The new democratic art is social in essence, just as individualistic art is anarchic and finds its justification among separate individuals or groups. If the teleological art of the past found its meaning in recognition by the individual, then the art of the future will find such meaning in recognition by society. In a democratic art all form must be socially justified. So, looking at contemporary art from a sociological standpoint, we have arrived at the conclusion that easel painting as a museum art form is outdated socially as well as creatively. Both analyses led to one and the same result.

XII   The rejection of easel painting and the orientation towards production

[. . .] But the death of painting, the death of easel painting as a form, does not yet mean the death of art in general. Art continues to live not as a definite form but as a creative substance. Moreover, at the very moment of the burial of its typical forms, the funeral of which we have attended in the course of the preceding account, unusually wide horizons are now opening out in front of visual art [. . .] presenting art with new forms and a new content. These new forms are called 'production skills'.

In 'production skill', 'the content' is the utility and expediency of the object, its tectonism which conditions its form and construction, and which justifies its social purpose and function.

22   On Non-Objective Painting

Bertolt Brecht

I see that you have removed the motifs from your paintings. No recognizable objects appear there anymore. You reproduce the sweeping curve of a chair – not the chair; the red of the sky, not the burning house. You reproduce the combination of lines and colors, not the combination of things. I must say that I wonder about it, and especially because you say that you are Communists, going out to reconstruct a world which is not habitable. If you were not Communists but subject spirits of the ruling classes, I would not wonder about your painting. It would seem to me then not inappropriate, even logical. Because things as they now are (people are among them, too) arouse for the most part feelings of repugnance – mixed with thoughts that criticism applies to them which would have them other than they are. Painting, reproducing them as recognizable, would fall into this conflict of feelings and thoughts; and if you were subject spirits of the Establishment, it would be cunning of you to make things unrecognizable, since it is things after all which are vexing, and since your patrons would be blamed for it. If you were subject spirits of the Establishment, you would do well to fulfil the wish of your patrons by representations rather opaque, general, uncommitted. It is the ruling classes who enjoy hearing such expressions as: 'One must enjoy one's work, irrespective of what it accomplishes, of how it is to be done, or why': or: 'One can enjoy a forest, even if one doesn't own it'. It is only those who are ruled who cannot enjoy themselves even in the most beautiful landscapes, if, as road workers, they have to pound stones into it – and among whom such strong emotions as love are lost if their living conditions are too bad. As painters and subject spirits of the Establishment, you could proclaim that the most beautiful and important perceptions are composed of lines and colors (so that anyone can enjoy them, even the most costly things, since lines and colors can be obtained *gratis*). And as court painters, you could drag all objects out of the world of perception, everything that is of value, all needs, anything substantial. You would require as painters for the ruling classes no specific perceptions, like anger in the face of injustice, or desire for certain things which are wanting, no perceptions bound to knowledge which call up other perceptions of a changing world – but just quite general, vague, unidentifiable perceptions, available to everyone, to the thieves and to their victims, to the oppressors and to the oppressed. You paint, for example, an indeterminate red; and some cry at the sight of this indeterminate red because they think of a rose, and others, because they think of a child lacerated by bombs and streaming with blood. Your task is then completed: you have composed a perceptual object of lines and colours. It is clear that motifs, recognizable objects in painting, must, in our world of class conflict, redeem the most diverse perceptions. If the profiteer laughs, the man from whom he made the profit cries. The poor man who

Source: B. Lang and F. Williams, Marxism and Art: *Writings in aesthetics and criticism* (McKay, 1972), pp. 423–425. Translated from 'Über gegenstandslose Malerei' in *Schriften zur Literatur und Kunst*. © Stefan S. Brecht 1967. *Gesammelte Werke* © Suhrkamp Verlag, Frankfurt 1967. Reprinted by permission of Methuen Limited. The article was probably written between 1935 and 1939.

lacks a kitchen chair does not lack color and form. The wealthy man who has a beautiful old chair does not regard it as something to sit on, but as form and color. We Communists see things differently than do the profiteers and their lackeys. The difference in our seeing validates things; it is concerned with things not with eyes. If we wish to teach that things should be seen differently, we must teach it to the things. And we want not only that things should simply be seen 'differently', but that they should be seen in a certain way; not just differently from every other way, but correctly – that is, as fits the things. We want to master things in politics and in art; we do not wish simply to 'master'. Assume that someone comes up and says, 'I am mastering.' Would not everyone ask, 'What?' I hear you say: 'With our tubes of oils and our pencils, we can only reproduce the colors and lines of the things, nothing more.' This sounds as if you were modest men, honest men, without pretences. But it sounds better than it is. A thousand examples prove that one can say more about things with tubes of oils and pencils, that one can communicate and expound more than simple solids with lines and colors. Breughel, too, had only tubes of oil and pencils; he, too, reproduced the colors and lines of things – but not only that. The perceptual objects which he composes emerge from his relations to the objects which he reproduced; it is specific objects of perception which may alter the relation of the viewer of his paintings to the objects represented in them. Nor should you say: 'There is much good in art which is not understood in its own time.' It doesn't follow from this that something must be good *if* it is not understood in its own time. You would do better to show in your paintings how man in our times has been a wolf to other men, and to say then: 'This will not be bought in our time.' Because only the wolves have money to buy paintings in our times. But it will not always be this way; and our paintings will contribute to seeing that it will not be.

23   The Beauty of Non-Objectivity

Hilla Rebay

[. . .] There is no representation of objects, nor any meaning of subjects in these paintings of free invention called non-objective art. They represent a unique world of their own, as creations with a lawful organization of colors, variation of forms, and rhythm of motif. These combinations when invented by a genius can bring the same joy, relaxation, elevation and animation of spiritual life as music. Knowledge of point and counterpoint never was necessary for anyone to enjoy the beauty of music. Nor is it necessary in painting to realize the constructional law to feel pleasure in non-objective masterpieces. Everyone reacts differently to melodies and keys in music. The general response to the themes and keys of color in different non-objective paintings is of similar variety. Upon further acquaintance the appeal of a masterpiece attracts concentration which grows into animated enjoyment.

Painting, like music, has nothing to do with reproduction of nature, nor interpretation of intellectual meanings. Whoever is able to feel the beauty of colors and forms has understood non-objective painting.

Beauty of appearance takes its way to the heart through the medium of intuitive intelligence called spirit. Intellect prevents spontaneous reaction to this most elevating joy which sound or vision can give. To be able to penetrate further into the singular worlds of these paintings is to realize their lawfulness, their cosmic inner order, which, if understood, may increase the faculty to enjoy them. But this experience and knowledge is necessary only to those who want to use the fundamentals of creation to become creators of art themselves. Non-objectivity has beauty and spirit combined. Everyone who gives time to it is able to get its blessing, which is refreshment of the soul and elevation into the beyond.

Spirit begins where materialism ends. The clear statement of absolute painting and pure creation in a cosmic sense shatters the illusion of worldly realism in representative painting. Viewpoints have changed as creators discovered world visions and turned away from contemplation of earth. Materialistic inspiration can never start creation, but intuition leads to it.

Non-objective art need not be understood or judged. It must be felt and it will influence those who have eyes for the loveliness of forms and colors. Though we all enjoy sunshine, neither this joy nor the sun's shine have a meaning unless our intellect invents one. Neither a flower nor the moon can be criticized. They would never change themselves. The seed of the flower will continue to produce exactly the same kind despite criticism. It follows the intuitive order of creation. So does the non-objective masterpiece of art. It can be liked or disliked, but its existence is final and its perfection is beautiful.

The positive order in a non-objective picture is no accident. The first accord defines the key of color and form, which has to be followed to solution. The

Source: Solomon R. Guggenheim collection of non-objective paintings, exhibition catalogue, 8–28 February 1937, Philadelphia, pp. 4–13. One illustration has been omitted.

enjoyment, animation and constantly growing appeal which they offer is why it is 'worth the trouble' to get acquainted with them. That is why a man like Mr Guggenheim, who once collected the choicest paintings of past centuries, now prefers to live with non-objective masterpieces because they offer him more from year to year, and satisfy his love for spiritual animation with their unending appeal of beauty and purity of ideal. Such a result cannot be obtained from even the finest representations of earthly objects, because once known, they have nothing new to say. [. . .]

An unchangingly static reproductive picture gets tiresome because it lacks the greatest charm and wealth of nature, its constant change in movement and form, which makes it so elusive and dear to our hearts though familiar to our memory.

A new ideal was needed, something infinitely more alive, vital and valuable to those longing for elevation. If advance of technique on the materialistic side of painting was taken for cultural development – which it was not, because culture is beyond such earthly holdings – even this technique was not of great interest to most people. Humanity resents change so much that technical improvement ended even a Rembrandt in the poorhouse. The laziness of the average mind prefers stagnation to development.

Geniuses do not wait for consent. Their cosmic power has no patience for mediocrity. They induce progress and development in spite of indifference. Stagecoaches no longer fulfil the requirements of our day of aeroplane, radio and television. Why should our need for creation in the art of painting be subversive to traditions of those who can only follow the familiarity of objects? That alone appeals to their eyes, bound by materialism. Apparent safety of intellect hinders enjoyment through real elevation. Of course, many people are unable to get accustomed to a higher viewpoint in the art of painting. They do not feel the inner need for this visionary joy of absolute beauty or else they have been misled and disappointed by the mediocrity of many such paintings. [. . .]

A masterpiece withstands time. Its importance grows on those who feel attracted by its unending life. It creates enthusiasm which spreads from soul to soul, finally bringing the masterpiece world renown for its superiority in an unostentatious way. To those born with rare sense for artistic supremacy, there is no handicap in the lack of an historical background of a yet undiscovered masterpiece. Their conviction needs only such courage as is needed to fight the inexperience of aggressors. [. . .]

Abstraction is merely a forerunner of the achievement of pure art and entire freedom of creation in painting. Objective inspiration can go no further than abstraction. Objective themes here are combined and dissolved almost to the point of free creation, yet as these pictures are still inspired by earth, they are merely abstractions; objects alone can be abstracted; absolute forms like circles, squares and triangles, if abstracted, would lose their identity.

To feel the beauty of art, the layman does not have to know the different classifications of painting which paved the way to non-objectivity. In 1911, the Russian, Vasilly Kandinsky, was the first painter with such intuitive and spiritual freedom as to eliminate entirely the unnecessary hindrance of intellect for the art of vision. Earthly objects and intellectual subjects with titles and meanings, he left to photographers and poets. By entirely giving up the help of earthly inspiration, Kandinsky was the first to accomplish the infinitely more difficult but gratifying task of painting unforeseen beauty with the sole use of spirit and the intuitive sense for cosmic order. By inventing color, form and space combinations without intellectual meanings, he was the first to achieve non-objectivity. He created absolute forms for the realization of spiritual joy and the sole purpose of elating the sense of beauty.

Seeing a circle does not imply sensation nor memory for any known or unknown happening. It is no symbol and has no sense. It is a perfect form with beauty of shape. The three basic forms – square, triangle, circle – offer manifold possibilities for interrelation. The circle is a concentrated continuity in itself, isolated and floating in its own importance, not influenced by what is within or without. The square has eight sides, four within and four without. It gives and receives space, and also points with its corners in further directions. The square, it seems, is a more spiritual form in relationship to space. The triangle, perhaps, less spiritual, emphasizes by pointing from an indifferent base. These are perfected absolute forms of purity and beauty.

They have no meaning unless geometry lends these forms to demonstrate visually the relation of figures to each other, but in geometry the proportion of the number is all that is of importance. So no beauty is accomplished and no spiritual life created. Non-objective forms are accidental tools of science. In art there is no accident in the use or shape of forms.It may seem simple to make a composition with primary forms, yet the artistic value of a creation lies in the combination and is brought to spiritual life only by rhythm and space relationship.

Non-objective pictures, being worlds of their own, have no meaning, and represent nothing. They are lovely or unpleasant to our eyes as music is lovely or disagreeable to our ears. People react differently to the appeal of motifs and melodies. It is as difficult to get acquainted with many non-objective paintings at one time, as it would be, to hear all Beethoven's nine symphonies in succession for the first time. But to a connoisseur, this treat would bring new enjoyment by comparing details and different variations of motives in different keys. [. . .]

The non-objective picture is of world importance due to its educational faculty. This importance does not derive from the quality of beauty in such a painting, but from its beneficial effect on the human race through the welfare of its educational power to elevate up to the immaterialistic plane and to strengthen and develop the creative gift. It has the importance of world vision; compared to the irrelevance of early viewpoints. It influences human improvement of balance, stimulates the sense for intuitive guidance and fortifies the highest intelligence.

Due to nature's everlasting change of light, color, movement and form the painter who tries to catch its charm gets anxious in his restless hunt for original motifs. Not at any time does he relax in order to get the benefit of nature's powerful influence of serenity, which would strengthen and increase the benefit of his intuitive capacity. The painter of non-objectivity does receive this benefit as he is freed of this constantly erratic strife for new patterns from nature in the hope that some may have been overlooked in the reproductive urge.

Objective painters desperately hope for singularity, despite the previous efforts of untold thousands of painters. Even Van Gogh, with his vital technique, could not stir interest for his shoes or pipe by painting them. The pitiful impressions that mass exhibitions with unnecessary quantities of mediocre paintings produce, are full of tokens of this ridiculous search for originality. Objects cannot offer originality since Nature offers the superior pattern. What 428,000 people paint cannot be art! Art is unique and only few geniuses are born. Art and Nature are two worlds as different as eternity and transitoriness. [. . .]

An artist with creative experience and fundamental feeling for art's laws can recognize a genius before others. In realizing the spiritual limitations which handicap himself he is conscious of the advance of genius. His struggle to gain the same perfection rarely succeeds because masters are born. The vocation of a born genius is to lead to new visions of beauty. He seems to have a longer breath with which to achieve, in apparent ease, further climaxes of power, and still has lots to say where others fall silent.

The genius follows his conscience to his pre-ordained destination, and does not need sensation. He develops his masterfulness to stronger power, greater simplicity and superiority of technical experience. His whole life is dedicated to the endless task of increasing and perfecting his faculties. By increasing accomplishments, the vision of further possibilities is enlarged. With cruel self-discipline a born master responds to a sensitive conscience by his unending devotion to the goal of perfection and beauty. All of his existence consists of hard work to reach beauty and increase spiritual wealth on earth. He foresees the necessity of new demands which humanity develops, and usually fulfills this demand long before it is made. Yet often for this reason dies in obscure poverty.

Capacity for creative power, technical quality and honest deference to the unending possibilities of progress, sense of climax, wisdom for elimination and diligence combined with the unsophistication of a child, are the makeup of genius, the prophet of the spirit.

Though the masses proudly enjoy a nation's fame for culture, they usually are the last to deserve it. Culture is always created by great personalities; they are usually neither helped nor understood by the masses, who merely benefit from culture as an attractor of international admirers who bring trade to a center of fame. [. . .]

It is indeed cruelty to offer some people real art, because the lack of title, meaning and intellectual entertainment confuses them beyond words. It angers their imaginary righteous demand for the easy satisfaction to which they have become accustomed. The positiveness of their point of view can hardly be shaken. It is very hard for them to overcome this handicap, as they give their intuitive feeling no opportunity to develop. Because it is so simple to sense the diverting display on earth in realistic painting, their eyes are misled and spiritual joy through vision becomes delayed.

Today demands go further. Already many people use their eyes for spiritual elevation and enjoy forms because they are beautiful in themselves or in their interrelationship of space. Intuitive concentration through great art ought to be taught in schools; there, intellect, memory and knowledge alone are stressed as important, while intuition is not developed, thus accounting for many catastrophies. The wish for intellectual inspiration is of secondary importance considering the poor results it brings about. Spiritual development is of primary importance to the real goal of humanity. [. . .]

Creation in painting is far more concerned with religion than is generally recognized. Like all great ages, ours is a religious one. Non-objectivity will be the religion of the future. Very soon the nations on earth will turn to it in thought and feeling and develop such intuitive powers which lead them to harmony.

Non-objective paintings are prophets of spiritual life. Those who have experienced the joy they can give possess such inner wealth as can never be lost. This is what these masterpieces in their quiet absolute purity can bring to all those who learn to feel their unearthly donation of rest, elevation, rhythm, balance and beauty.

24   Illusion and Visual Deadlock

E. H. Gombrich

None of Molière's immortal witticisms is surer to get a laugh from a modern audience than the surprise of his *Bourgeois Gentilhomme* when he is told that he has been 'talking prose' all his life. But was poor M. Jourdain all that silly? What he had discovered in his frantic efforts to climb into the class of noblemen was, of course, not prose, but verse. The notion of prose as a special kind of speech could never have been thought of without the poet's truly surprising ways with language, so well described by the author of *Alice in Wonderland:*

> For first you write a sentence,
> And then you chop it small;
> Then mix the bits, and sort them out
> Just as they chance to fall:
> The order of the phrases makes
> No difference at all.

The corresponding ways with images practised by twentieth-century artists have turned us all into M. Jourdains. They have shocked us into a fresh awareness of the prose of pictorial representation.

If we had told an art lover of former days that a picture needed deciphering, he would have thought of symbols and emblems with some cryptic 'hieroglyphic' content. Take the still-life by the Dutch seventeenth-century painter Torrentius (*Fig. A*). It seems clear enough as a representation, and for good reasons: We know that the artist used an optical device, the camera obscura, to project the image of the motifs onto the canvas where he traced it as one might trace a projected photograph. What wonder that it seemed just as easy to recognize the objects in the picture as it would be to recognize them on the table. If deciphering came in at all, it applied to a second level of meaning, as it were – to the question of what these objects might signify. To the learned *gentilhomme* they would suggest more than a jug, a glass and a yoke, for he would recognize in this curious assemblage the emblems or 'attributes' of the personification of Temperance, a lady with the laudable habit of pouring water into her wine and a corresponding disposition meekly to accept the bridle and the yoke.[1]

It was only when learned allusions of this kind went out of fashion, and when everybody could reproduce the image of objects by means of his own photographic camera, that artists began to question the simple assumptions underlying the still-life painter's craft. No sooner had they done so than the public questioned their competence. What impudence of the Impressionists to demand that we decipher their blots and splashes! But this is easy, retorted the painter's champion. Just step back and half-close your eyes, and the blots will fall into place. The magic worked,

Source: Professor Sir E. H. Gombrich, *Meditations on a Hobby Horse* (Phaidon, 1971), pp. 151–161
Originally published as 'How to read a painting', *Adventures of the Mind* series in *Saturday Evening Post*, 1961.

and the outcry subsided. What remained was the conviction that the artist knew more about seeing than the layman. Surprising as it may sound, some concluded that the blots must be all we really see of a motif on the table. If we recognize things more easily in life than on Impressionist pictures, it is because we can touch and handle objects and thus acquire knowledge of properties which we have no right to ask the artist to paint.

No right? Why not? Should we not demand of the artist precisely for this reason that he must somehow include in his pictures that indispensable information gained from touch, those tactile values we need for recognition and participation in his world? If so, where should he stop? It is not only touch that gives us information. It is movement, looking at objects from several sides. Without such movement we would never learn to sort out the impressions received by our eyes.

So the debate went on, and representation became self-conscious. The Cubist revolution some fifty years ago established the painter's rights to present his own commentaries to the conundrum of vision. Instead of tracing the image of a camera obscura, the artist superimposes and telescopes fragments of representations which follow a mysterious order of their own (*Fig. D*). No longer will a simple trick suffice to recover the object on the table. Like the ghost of Hamlet's father ' 'Tis here! 'Tis here! 'Tis gone!'

There were and still are critics who claim that this tantalizing method represents some higher order of reality than does the photographic picture. It may well be that Picasso and Braque, who invented the style, were inspired by echoes of similar mystic beliefs. But the continent they found on their voyage of discovery was not the never-never land of the fourth dimension, but the fascinating reality of visual ambiguity. We are in danger of missing this fascination through sheer familiarity with Cubist methods which have long since penetrated into commercial art. The shock has worn off, and we no longer attempt to decipher the images that play hide-and-seek among the facets of ambiguous patterns. And thus we are apt to miss the real problem posed by the first of the 'modern' styles that broke resolutely with the 'photographic' rendering of reality: How should each individual form be read? How are the shapes related to each other? Where is the key to the code?

> For first you paint an object,
> And then you chop it small;
> Then mix the bits, and sort them out
> Just as they chance to fall:
> The order of the aspects makes
> No difference at all.

This strange and fascinating way of jumbling the elements of representation is perhaps a novel kind of verse that makes us aware of the existence of prose. For how are the elements ordered in naturalistic pictures, that we should find it so easy, by contrast, to read into them images of tangible things? The formulation may cause some shaking of heads. Surely we do not read the shape of a jug and a glass *into* the Dutch still-life; we simply recognize it. Of course we do, but where exactly is the borderline here between reading into and reading? We are all familiar with the clouds, rocks or ink blots into which the fanciful can read pictures of monsters or masks. Some vague similarity to a face or body engages our attention, and we proceed, as far as we can, to transform the remaining shapes into an appropriate continuation.

Psychologists and psychiatrists have become interested in this game of the imagination, and ink-blot reading tests, such as the Rorschach, are supposed to tell them much of the working of a person's mind. They are interested, in other words, in the different interpretations that are given of the same blot. It is these differences we have in mind when we speak of 'reading into'. Where people normally see the same image, we call it reading. We all read the jug correctly because it looks like a jug. But this simple formulation begs a good many questions and hides the mystery of reading from us.

We come a little closer to its core with some of the trick pictures in which surrealist artists conjured up the ambiguities of dreams. Tchelitchew, for instance, turns a tree into the image of a hand growing out of a foot (*Fig. F*). He guides our projection by assimilating the shape of the tree to other recognizable forms. But such visual punning is still comparatively simple. For here (not in his other pictures) the artist has taken care that we should know where to look for the meaning. We cannot always take this for granted. Indeed, our tendency to jump to conclusions here has been used by the devisers of puzzle pictures and even by propagandists to catch us off our guard. *Figure E* looks for all the world like the representation of a classic urn set amidst willows. It was circulated during the French Revolution as a clandestine tribute to the royal family. For if we don't focus on the urn, but on the background, we discover the profiles, facing each other, of Louis XVI and Marie Antoinette and, guided by these cues, two further heads, presumably of the Dauphin and some other victim, made by the outline of branches and twigs.

The principle here exploited by a humble draughtsman has played a great role in the discussions of twentieth-century psychologists – it is the relation between 'figure' and 'ground'. As long as we regard the urn as the figure we are not aware of the shape of the ground. Here, therefore, is the simplest case of all where our reading depends on our initial interpretation. We tend to regard the enclosed and articulated shape as the figure and to ignore the background against which it stands. But this interpretation itself is based on an assumption which the artist may choose to knock away. It is then that we discover that there really is something logically prior to the identification of the jug or the urn and so implied by it – the decision on our part which to regard as figure and which as ground.

This is the moment to introduce a contemporary artist whose prints are meditations on image reading. His name is M. C. Escher, and he lives in his native Holland, keeping more contact with mathematicians than with artists and critics.[2] It is indeed doubtful how much the critics would approve of his ingenious exercises in applied geometry and psychology. But to the explorer of the prose of representation, his nightmarish conundrums are invaluable. His double image of *Day and Night* (*Fig. G*) demands an imperceptible switch from figure to ground. The white birds flying across the dark towards the black river come from another side of the world where there is still daylight and where black birds go the other way. And as we search for the dividing line between the two halves, we notice that there is none. It is the interstices between the white birds – the ground – that gradually assume the shape of the black birds, and these checkered patterns merge downwards into the fields of the countryside. Easy as it is to discover this transformation, it is impossible to keep both readings stable in one's mind. The day reading drives out the night from the middle of the sheet, the night reading turns the black birds of the same area into neutral ground. Which forms we isolate for identification depends on where we arrive from.

Reading becomes an alternating 'reading into'; representation merges with guided projection.

But Escher has more tricks in his bag to undermine our confidence in the simplicity of representation. His print *Solid and Hollow* (*Fig. H*) makes use of other forms of ambiguity which had been known to artists and psychologists for a long time, but had never been explored and exploited with such single-mindedness.

Here it is not the relationship between figure and ground that is reversed on the opposite side of the picture, but the very shape and direction of any part of the architecture. Start on the left with the black woman walking over a curved bridge towards some stairs. As long as you stay on her side of the picture you are presented with a weird but plausible view of an old town. Start with the man climbing a ladder on the opposite side and you will read the shapes as equally coherent forms representing an unfinished courtyard with a bridge vaulting over it. But once again either reading is contradicted when you read on towards the central axis. For what looks like a pavilion seen from the outside if you approach it from the side of the black woman on the bridge, is switched into a vaulted corner when seen from the other side. The switch is all the more puzzling as the identical shape nearby must surely be read as a solid pavilion. But soon we discover the same punning with inside and outside all over the print. The floor on which a boy has fallen asleep is a ceiling nearby from which a lamp dangles. Everywhere corresponding shapes must be read as hollow in one context and solid in another and, every time, the meeting of both readings creates a stalemate. The assumption with which we have started breaks down, and we have to begin all over again, only to discover that here too we are led into perplexity.

But even this probing of the mechanisms of image reading is not the most disconcerting of Escher's exercises. The *Belvedere* (*Fig. I*), completed in 1958, may not be very pleasing as a print, but as a demonstration piece it trumps the others. For what looks at first like a rather crude historical illustration is, in fact, a brain teaser of no mean ingenuity. It would make an excellent test of the powers of observation to time the moment when it dawns on the beholder that he is confronted with a self-contradictory structure.[3] Look at the ladder and try to locate it in space. You will find that it leads from a first-floor terrace to a second at right angles to it. The man with the plumed hat on the lower terrace looks out into the landscape behind, the woman under the corresponding arch of the floor above looks sideways. Small wonder, for the arcades of the lower terrace are not composed of columns carrying the vault above them; they are interlaced, as it were, shifting from back to front as we trace their course.

Who can blame the poor imprisoned man in the cellar who looks with amazement at the designer on the bench, for the object he holds in his hands is as unrealizable as the building itself: a cube with interweaving sides.

Whatever we may think of Escher's artistic taste, his prints are worth a whole course in the psychology of perception and its relation to art. Their complexity is far from whimsical. It reveals the hidden complexity of all picture reading. What all these prints have in common is that they compel us to adopt an initial assumption that cannot be sustained as we try to follow it through. The perplexity that ensues suggests that this is an unusual experience.

When we look at a normal representation, there is nothing to prevent us from forming a hypothesis about the figure–ground relationship or about the way the shapes add up to pictures of objects. We therefore believe that we take in the picture more or less at one glance and recognize the motif. Our experience with Escher's contradiction shows that this account is inadequate. We read a picture, as we read a printed line, by picking up letters or cues and fitting them together till we feel that we look across the signs on the page at the meaning behind them. And just as in reading the eye does not travel along at an even pace gathering up the meaning letter by letter and word by word, so our glance sweeps across a picture scanning it for information.

Critics like to tell us how the artist 'leads the eye' along the main lines of his composition. But our roving eyes will not be thus led. The critic's phrase should have become obsolete when eye movements could be filmed and fixation points plotted on pictures.[4] These records confirm what Escher made us suspect: reading a picture is a piecemeal affair that starts with random shots and these are followed by the search for a coherent whole. If that sounds a little abstract let us remember what we would do if we had to 'read' a statue blindfolded. Our first groping for information would be quite hit and miss. We would just try to find contact with the object and moving up and down we would try to seize on an identifiable feature, the nose, the arms or the breast. From that moment our movements would become more purposeful; if that is the nose, the eyes must be somewhere there and they will guide us towards the ears, etc. Sometimes our expectation would be confirmed, often we might have to revise it; our first guess, for instance, may be that the head will be directly over the feet but we may quickly discover that the statue is not standing but sitting or striding. What may take many minutes in this predicament may take less than seconds with the help of the eyes. But however unlike the two processes may be in our experience, their logic is similar. The eye, like the groping hand, scans the page, and the cues or messages it elicits are used by the questioning mind to narrow down our uncertainties. Every piece of information that reaches us through the senses can be thus used to answer a further question and remove a further doubt.

The first truth, which Escher's visual paradoxes illuminate, is this piecemeal character of picture reading. There is a clear limit to the visual information we can assimilate in any given glance. This fits in well with the results of scientists who have studied this limit in the severely practical context of how many pointers a pilot can read at a glance on an instrument panel. His capacity will, of course, vary according to training and experience but the basic fact remains that the eye can take in much less at one glance than the layman imagines. But what about the musician who can read an orchestral score with surprising ease and at amazing speed? Does he not have to take in information at an uncanny rate? Certainly the feat is admirable, but it is only possible because the notes of the score, unlike the pointer readings, are not unconnected signs. Music is an art that follows certain laws or rules which enable the musician to scan the score with certain expectations. Though he cannot know what to expect in the next bar, he knows at least that many possibilities are ruled out. Indeed, if any of those occurred he would probably disregard it as a misprint.

In reading a familiar language, of course, we proceed in a similar way, looking ahead for cues to confirm our expectations and filling in the remainder more or less from experience. The reading of pictures must follow a similar pattern. But once we set out to discover how we read the 'score', in particular how we have to revise our expectations, we become aware of the part which assumptions play in the reading of images.

What, more precisely, are these assumptions? Take any isolated part of Escher's *Belvedere*, the outside terrace, for instance, with its checkerboard floor and the low walls surrounding it. This is quite a normal realistic representation of an architectural feature and does not differ much from a photograph or picture post card of such a motif. How is it that we take in such a situation with such speed and ease? Surely because we are in no doubt about how to supplement the information with which the picture supplies us. We assume that a pavement will most probably be level and a wall upright, that the slabs of the floor will be square and the seat of the bench rectangular. If the shapes representing these objects are tapering and unequal in size, this will obviously be due to foreshortening and perspective.

Assumptions of this kind are so ingrained in us that it needs quite a jolt to prevent our interpretation from running along these convenient grooves. Yet, after all, there could be such things as sloping floors with irregularly sized slabs, tapering walls or rhomboid benches. Such odd shapes might serve a very good purpose in the theatre, near the back of an illusionist stage to give the impression of greater depth (*Figs. B, C*). Once we admit this possibility, our assurance in reading the image collapses. We discover the hidden ambiguity in all representations of solid objects in the flat. If the reader enjoys a whirling head he can now return to a fresh scrutiny of all the three Escher prints (*Figs. G, H, I*) to discover that these teasing images are 'ambiguous' only on the assumption that floors or ceilings are horizontal, columns upright or the water of rivers reasonably level so that the bridge across it cannot lead uphill. Drop these hypotheses, and the neat ambiguity of a mere double meaning sinks into chaos.

We return from this giddy switchback ride with one tormenting question in mind. If the prose of ordinary representations hides such unsuspected ambiguities, what about the reliability of our eyes for telling us about the real world? We need not worry too much, for here the answer is more reassuring. To put the matter briefly, pictures are infinitely ambiguous because they present a flat two-dimensional geometrical projection of a three-dimensional reality. To say of such a projection that it 'looks like reality' begs the question. It may, but it also looks like an infinite number of possible, if improbable, configurations. But this type of ambiguity will rarely trouble us in real life. After all, we experience the real world by moving about it, and our eyes are eminently suited to guide us.

The eyes alone can quickly resolve the question of the real shape of a terrace, for we have a built-in predictor that tells us how any given shape will change when seen from different angles. If one moves straight towards a door, its shape will remain constant, but its size will increase at a predictable rate. The object near the fringe of our vision, on the other hand, will be transformed in shape in a regular and predictable sequence that we can study if we move a film camera in the same direction. It is this melody of transformation that would be entirely different if we moved towards a flat or shallow perspective stage.

The decisive part that movement must play in our visual orientation has only recently been fully brought out by psychologists, notably by James J. Gibson.[5] Here, too, a fresh alternative shocked us into awareness of an old truth we had lazily taken for granted. The problems of vision in rapid flight or even in motoring rendered the old idea of static vision obsolete. Moreover, our engineers had meanwhile learned to simulate the function of sense organs with the uncanny gadgets of homing devices, used in the deadly game of missile development. Cybernetics has taught us to look even at the senses not as passive registration devices but rather as receptors geared to the receipt of a flow of information, which the nervous system is somehow programmed to compare with expectations. Some psychologists think that the simplicity hypothesis, the idea that the floor is 'probably' level, may be built into our receptor organ. But whether they are inborn or acquired, it is now clear that every message sets up a set of expectations with which the incoming flow can be matched to confirm correct assessments or to modify and knock out false guesses.

In looking at a picture we are deprived of this dynamic aid for the weeding out of false interpretations. All we have is a consistency test that compares the messages from various parts of the picture for compatibility. Having done so, our mind makes ready for further tests through movement, but here it is frustrated. This frustration has a curious side-effect that can paradoxically increase the illusion and will never cease to tease our reason. It is the illusion that objects pointing towards us from paintings will follow us as we shift our position.

The most bored and footsore tourist will spring to attention when the guide demonstrates the ancestral portrait that follows him with its eyes or the pointed gun that always aims at him wherever he stands in the hall. It is easy to dismiss this surprise as naïve, but less easy to exhaust the implications of this little mystery. One thing is sure: the mystery does not rest in any particular skill on the part of the painter. The effect is quite frequent and indeed inevitable. The only reason why we need the guide's patter to enlist our attention is that we are but rarely interested in what happens to the appearance of a painting while we shift our position in this way. If we were, we would see that the principal condition for the effect is a sense of depth combined with an unforeshortened portion of an object that appears to lie quite close to the frontal plane.

The woodcut by the German Renaissance artist Hans Baldung Grien (*Fig. 7*), for instance, fulfills these conditions admirably. It is known under the title *The Bewitched Stableboy* and it shows the victim of some evil spell lying on his back, the soles of his feet turned towards us. Critics have wondered what the picture signifies, but surely it is meant to tease us with this magic trick. When we have it in front of us, it works like any picture using perspective. The strong foreshortening is 'read' as depth, and we feel the three-dimensional character of the representation as a compelling illusion. It is consistent with this reading that we should look straight at the soles of the man's shoes and that they should hide from us his feet and ankles which we imagine to be there. But the more firmly we project the image of the whole figure into these marks on the paper, the more will we instinctively expect it to respond to our usual reality tests. A real figure would present different aspects to us if we move sideways. But since what we have in front of us is not a three-dimensional figure but only a flat piece of paper, the expected melody of transformation fails to materialize.

What makes this experience remarkable in our context is the confirmation it provides for our argument that the picture becomes a picture only if the marks on the paper are sorted out by the mind into a consistent and coherent message. Once this consistency is perceived and an interpretation emerges, it takes a great effort to dislodge it. Easy though it is to know intellectually that our poor stableboy's head lies objectively in the same plane as do his feet, we still do not quite see it that way.

It is here, at last, that these investigations of the prose of representation lead back to the problems of artistic poetry. For it is the strength of the forces of illusion that alone accounts for the violent reactions against these forces in twentieth-century art. At all times, of course, the aesthetics of picture-making had more to do with composition than with illusion. Artists have always been poets, striving to achieve a fine balance of shapes and colours and to devise a beautiful pattern to fill the painting surface in a pleasing way. But these efforts could easily be destroyed by the reading mind that rearranged these shapes in an imaginary depth.

Critics wrote and still write as if we could see both the surface and the representation, but artists knew better. Their rebellion against illusion came into the open more than fifty years ago in those conundrums of Cubism which lead our eye a frustrating chase after guitars and bottles, teasing us with false clues only to entrap us in contradictions. It was by exploring these paradoxes that artists wanted to discover new modes of organization.

It is not only Escher who shows us their success. Even abstract art owes some of its most interesting possibilities to the fascination of unresolved ambiguities as in many of the ingenious designs by Albers.[6] By presenting us with these scrambled codes the artist shocks us into realizing how much more there is in pictures than meets the eye.

References

1   B. W. F. van Riemsdijk 'Een schilderstuk van Johannes Torrentius'. *Feest-Bundel, Dr Abraham Bredius aangeboden*, Amsterdam, 1915.
2   *The Graphic Work of M. C. Escher*, Oldbourne Press, London, 1960.
3   L. S. Penrose and R. Penrose, 'Impossible Objects: a special type of visual illusion'. *British Journal of Psychology* vol. **49**, part I, February 1958.
4   J.J. Gibson, *The Perception of the Visual World*, Cambridge (Mass.), 1950, pp. 155 f.
5   J. J. Gibson, loc. cit. For other references see my *Art and Illusion*, New York and London, 1960.
6   François Bucher, *J. Albers: Despite Straight Lines*, Yale University Press, London and New Haven, 1961.

SECTION FOUR

Expressionism

25   Abstraction and Empathy

Wilhelm Worringer

[. . .] Our investigations proceed from the presupposition that the work of art, as an autonomous organism, stands beside nature on equal terms and, in its deepest and innermost essence, devoid of any connection with it, in so far as by nature is understood the visible surface of things. Natural beauty is on no account to be regarded as a condition of the work of art, despite the fact that in the course of evolution it seems to have become a valuable element in the work of art, and to some extent indeed positively identical with it.

This presupposition includes within it the inference that the specific laws of art have, in principle, nothing to do with the aesthetics of natural beauty. It is therefore not a matter of, for example, analysing the conditions under which a landscape appears beautiful, but of an analysis of the conditions under which the representation of this landscape becomes a work of art.

Modern aesthetics, which has taken the decisive step from aesthetic objectivism to aesthetic subjectivism, i.e., which no longer takes the aesthetic as the starting-point of its investigations, but proceeds from the behaviour of the contemplating subject, culminates in a doctrine that may be characterised by the broad general name of 'the theory of empathy'. This theory has been clearly and comprehensively formulated in the writings of Theodor Lipps. For this reason his aesthetic system will serve, as *pars pro toto*, as the foil to the following treatise.

For the basic purpose of my essay is to show that this modern aesthetics, which proceeds from the concept of empathy, is inapplicable to wide tracts of art history. Its Archimedian point is situated at *one* pole of human artistic feeling alone. It will only assume the shape of a comprehensive aesthetic system when it has united with the lines that lead from the opposite pole.

We regard as this counter-pole an aesthetics which proceeds not from man's urge to empathy, but from his urge to abstraction. Just as the urge to empathy as a pre-assumption of aesthetic experience finds its gratification in the beauty of the organic, so the urge to abstraction finds its beauty in the life-denying inorganic, in the crystalline or, in general terms, in all abstract law and necessity.

We shall endeavour to cast light upon the antithetic relation of empathy and abstraction, by first characterising the concept of empathy in a few broad strokes.

The simplest formula that expresses this kind of aesthetic experience runs: aesthetic enjoyment is objectified self-enjoyment. To enjoy aesthetically means to enjoy myself in a sensuous object diverse from myself, to empathise myself into it. 'What I empathise into it is quite generally life. And life is energy, inner working, striving and accomplishing. In a word, life is activity. But activity is that in which I experience an expenditure of energy. By its nature, this activity is an activity of the will. It is endeavour or volition in motion.'

Source: Wilhelm Worringer, *Abstraction and Empathy*, translated by M. Bullock (Routledge and Kegan Paul, 1963), pp. 3–25. Originally published as *Abstraktion und Einfühlung*, Munich, 1908.

Whereas the earlier aesthetics operated with pleasure and unpleasure, Lipps gives to both these sensations the value of tones of sensation only, in the sense that the lighter or darker tone of a colour is not the colour itself, but precisely a tone of the colour. The crucial factor is, therefore, rather the sensation itself, i.e., the inner motion, the inner life, the inner self-activation. [. . .]

This is not the place to follow the system into its wider ramifications. It is sufficient for our purpose to note the point of departure of this kind of aesthetic experience, its psychic presuppositions. For we thereby reach an understanding of the formula which is important to us, which is to serve as a foil to the ensuing treatise, and which we shall therefore repeat here: 'Aesthetic enjoyment is objectified self-enjoyment.'

The aim of the ensuing treatise is to demonstrate that the assumption that this process of empathy has at all times and at all places been the presupposition of artistic creation, cannot be upheld. On the contrary, this theory of empathy leaves us helpless in the face of the artistic creations of many ages and peoples. It is of no assistance to us, for instance, in the understanding of that vast complex of works of art that pass beyond the narrow framework of Graeco-Roman and modern Occidental art. Here we are forced to recognise that quite a different psychic process is involved, which explains the peculiar, and in our assessment purely negative, quality of that style. [. . .]

The need for empathy can be looked upon as a presupposition of artistic volition only where this artistic volition inclines towards the truths of organic life, that is towards naturalism in the higher sense. The sensation of happiness that is released in us by the reproduction of organically beautiful vitality, what modern man designates beauty, is a gratification of that inner need for self-activation in which Lipps sees the presupposition of the process of empathy. In the forms of the work of art we enjoy ourselves. Aesthetic enjoyment is objectified self-enjoyment. The value of a line, of a form consists for us in the value of the life that it holds for us. It holds its beauty only through our own vital feeling, which, in some mysterious manner, we project into it.

Recollection of the lifeless form of a pyramid or of the suppression of life that is manifested, for instance, in Byzantine mosaics tells us at once that here the need for empathy, which for obvious reasons always tends towards the organic, cannot possibly have determined artistic volition. Indeed, the idea forces itself upon us that here we have an impulse directly opposed to the empathy impulse, which seeks to suppress precisely that in which the need for empathy finds its satisfaction.

This counter-pole to the need for empathy appears to us to be the urge to abstraction. My primary concern in this essay is to analyse this urge and to substantiate the importance it assumes within the evolution of art.

The extent to which the urge to abstraction has determined artistic volition we can gather from actual works of art, on the basis of the arguments put forward in the ensuing pages. We shall then find that the artistic volition of savage peoples, in so far as they possess any at all, then the artistic volition of all primitive epochs of art and, finally, the artistic volition of certain culturally developed Oriental peoples, exhibit this abstract tendency. Thus the urge to abstraction stands at the beginning of every art and in the case of certain peoples at a high level of culture remains the dominant tendency, whereas with the Greeks and other Occidental peoples, for example, it slowly recedes, making way for the urge to empathy. This provisional statement is substantiated in the practical section of the essay.

Now what are the psychic presuppositions for the urge to abstraction? We must seek them in these peoples' feeling about the world, in their psychic attitude towards the cosmos. Whereas the precondition for the urge to empathy is a happy pantheistic relationship of confidence between man and the phenomena of the external world, the urge to abstraction is the outcome of a great inner unrest inspired in man by the phenomena of the outside world; in a religious respect it corresponds to a strongly transcendental tinge to all notions. We might describe this state as an immense spiritual dread of space. When Tibullus says: *primum in mundo fecit deus timor*, this same sensation of fear may also be assumed as the root of artistic creation.

Comparison with the physical dread of open places, a pathological condition to which certain people are prone, will perhaps better explain what we mean by this spiritual dread of space. In popular terms, this physical dread of open places may be explained as a residue from a normal phase of man's development, at which he was not yet able to trust entirely to visual impression as a means of becoming familiar with a space extended before him, but was still dependent upon the assurances of his sense of touch. As soon as man became a biped, and as such solely dependent upon his eyes, a slight feeling of insecurity was inevitably left behind. In the further course of his evolution, however, man freed himself from this primitive fear of extended space by habituation and intellectual reflection.

The situation is similar as regards the spiritual dread of space in relation to the extended, disconnected, bewildering world of phenomena. The rationalistic development of mankind pressed back this instinctive fear conditioned by man's feeling of being lost in the universe. The civilised peoples of the East, whose more profound world-instinct opposed development in a rationalistic direction and who saw in the world nothing but the shimmering veil of Maya, they alone remained conscious of the unfathomable entanglement of all the phenomena of life, and all the intellectual mastery of the world-picture could not deceive them as to this. Their spiritual dread of space, their instinct for the relativity of all that is, did not stand, as with primitive peoples, *before* cognition, but *above* cognition.

Tormented by the entangled inter-relationship and flux of the phenomena of the outer world, such peoples were dominated by an immense need for tranquillity. The happiness they sought from art did not consist in the possibility of projecting themselves into the things of the outer world, of enjoying themselves in them, but in the possibility of taking the individual thing of the external world out of its arbitrariness and seeming fortuitousness, of eternalising it by approximation to abstract forms and, in this manner, of finding a point of tranquillity and a refuge from appearances. Their most powerful urge was, so to speak, to wrest the object of the external world out of its natural context, out of the unending flux of being, to purify it of all its dependence upon life, i.e., of everything about it that was arbitrary, to render it necessary and irrefragable, to approximate it to its *absolute* value. Where they were successful in this, they experienced that happiness and satisfaction which the beauty of organic vital form affords *us*; indeed, they knew no other beauty, and therefore we may term it their beauty.

In his *Stilfragen* Riegl writes: 'From the standpoint of regularity the geometric style, which is built up strictly according to the supreme laws of symmetry and rhythm, is the most perfect. In our scale of values, however, it occupies the lowest position, and the history of the evolution of the arts also shows this style to have been peculiar to peoples still at a low level of cultural development.'

If we accept this proposition, which admittedly suppresses the role which the geometric style has played amongst peoples of highly developed culture, we are confronted by the following fact: The style most perfect in its regularity, the style of the highest abstraction, most strict in its exclusion of life, is peculiar to the peoples at their most primitive cultural level. A causal connection must therefore exist between primitive culture and the highest, purest regular art form. And the further proposition may be stated: The less mankind has succeeded, by virtue of its spiritual cognition, in entering into a relation of friendly confidence with the appearance of the outer world, the more forceful is the dynamic that leads to the striving after this highest abstract beauty.

Not that primitive man sought more urgently for regularity in nature, or experienced regularity in it more intensely; just the reverse: it is because he stands so lost and spiritually helpless amidst the things of the external world, because he experiences only obscurity and caprice in the interconnection and flux of the phenomena of the external world, that the urge is so strong in him to divest the things of the external world of their caprice and obscurity in the world-picture and to impart to them a value of necessity and a value of regularity. To employ an audacious comparison: it is as though the instinct for the 'thing in itself' were most powerful in primitive man. Increasing spiritual mastery of the outside world and habituation to it mean a blunting and dimming of this instinct. Only after the human spirit has passed, in thousands of years of its evolution, along the whole course of rationalistic cognition, does the feeling for the 'thing in itself' re-awaken in it as the final resignation of knowledge. That which was previously instinct is now the ultimate product of cognition. Having slipped down from the pride of knowledge, man is now just as lost and helpless *vis-à-vis* the world-picture as primitive man, once he has recognised that 'this visible world in which we are is the work of Maya, brought forth by magic, a transitory and in itself unsubstantial semblance, comparable to the optical illusion and the dream, of which it is equally false and equally true to say that it is, as that it is not'.[1] [. . .]

It would be a misconstruction of the psychological preconditions for the genesis of this abstract art form, to say that a craving for regularity led men to reach out for geometric regularity, for that would presuppose a spiritual–intellectual penetration of abstract form, would make it appear the product of reflection and calculation. We have more justification for assuming that what we see here is a purely instinctive creation, that the urge to abstraction created this form for itself with elemental necessity and without the intervention of the intellect. Precisely because intellect had not yet dimmed instinct, the disposition to regularity, which after all is already present in the germ-cell, was able to find the appropriate abstract expression.

These regular abstract forms are, therefore, the only ones and the highest, in which man can rest in the face of the vast confusion of the world-picture. We frequently find the, at first sight, astonishing idea put forward by modern art theoreticians that mathematics is the highest art form; indeed it is significant that it is precisely Romantic theory which, in its artistic programmes, has come to this seemingly paradoxical verdict, which is in such contradiction to the customary nebulous feeling for art. Yet no one will venture to assert that, for instance, Novalis, the foremost champion of this lofty view of mathematics and the originator of the dicta, 'The life of the gods is mathematics', 'Pure mathematics is religion', was not an artist through and through. Only between this verdict and the elemental instinct of primitive man, there lies the same essential difference that we have just seen to exist between primitive humanity's feeling for the 'thing in itself' and philosophic speculation concerning the 'thing in itself'.

Riegl speaks of crystalline beauty, 'which constitutes the first and most eternal law of form in inanimate matter, and comes closest to absolute beauty (material individuality)'.

Now, as I have said, we cannot suppose man to have picked up these laws, namely the laws of abstract regularity, from inanimate matter; it is, rather, an intellectual necessity for us to assume that these laws are also implicitly contained in our own human organisation – though all attempts to advance our knowledge on this point stop short at logical conjectures, such as are touched on in the second chapter of the present work.

We therefore put forward the proposition: the simple line and its development in purely geometrical regularity was bound to offer the greatest possibility of happiness to the man disquieted by the obscurity and entanglement of phenomena. For here the last trace of connection with, and dependence on, life has been effaced, here the highest absolute form, the purest abstraction has been achieved; here is law, here is necessity, while everywhere else the caprice of the organic prevails. But such abstraction does not make use of any natural object as a model. 'The geometric line is distinguished from the natural object precisely by the fact that it does not stand in any natural context. That which constitutes its essence does, of course, pertain to nature. Mechanical forces are natural forces. In the geometric line, however, and in geometrical forms as a whole, they have been taken out of the natural context and the ceaseless flux of the forces of nature, and have become visible on their own.'[2]

Naturally, this pure abstraction could never be attained once a factual natural model underlay it. The question is therefore: How did the urge to abstraction behave towards the things of the external world? We have already stressed the fact that it was not the imitation impulse – the history of the imitation impulse is a different thing from the history of art – that compelled the reproduction in art of a natural model. We see therein rather the endeavour to redeem the individual object of the outer world, in so far as it particularly arouses interest, from its combination with, and dependence upon, other things, to tear it away from the course of happening, to render it absolute.

Riegl saw this urge to abstraction as the basis of the artistic volition of the early civilisations: 'The civilised peoples of antiquity descried in external things, on the analogy of what they deemed to be their own human nature (anthropism), material individuals of various sizes, but each one joined together into firmly cohering parts, into an indivisible unity. Their sense perception showed them things as confused and obscurely intermingled; through the medium of plastic art they picked out single individuals and set them down in their clearly enclosed unity. Thus the plastic art of the whole of antiquity sought as its ultimate goal to render external things in their clear material individuality, and in so doing to respect the sensible appearance of the outward things of nature and to avoid and suppress anything that might cloud and vitiate the directly convincing expression of material individuality.'[3]

A crucial consequence of this artistic volition was, on the one hand, the approximation of the representation to a plane, and on the other, strict suppression of the representation of space and exclusive rendering of the single form.

The artist was forced to approximate the representation to a plane because three-dimensionality, more than anything else, contradicted the apprehension of the object as a closed material individuality, since perception of three-dimensionality calls for a succession of perceptual elements that have to be combined; in this succession of elements the individuality of the object melts away. On the other hand, dimensions of depth are disclosed only through foreshortening and shadow, so that a vigorous participation of the combinative understanding and of habituation is required for their apprehension. In both cases, therefore, the outcome is a subjective clouding of the objective fact, which the ancient cultural peoples were at pains to avoid.

Suppression of representation of space was dictated by the urge to abstraction through the mere fact that it is precisely space which links things to one another, which imparts to them their relativity in the world-picture, and because space is the one thing it is impossible to individualise. In so far, therefore, as a sensuous object is still dependent upon space, it is unable to appear to us in its closed material individuality. All endeavour was therefore directed towards the single form set free from space. [. . .]

References

1   Schopenhauer A., *Kritik der Kantischen Philosophie.*
2   Lipps T., *Aesthetik*, 249.
3   Riegl A., *Spätrömische Kunstindustrie.*

26   Expressionism

Hermann Bahr

Without precedent

The various sayings and proclamations of Expressionism only tell us that what the Expressionist is looking for is without parallel in the past. A new form of Art is dawning. And he who beholds an Expressionist picture by Matisse or Picasso, by Pechstein or Kokoschka, by Kandinsky or Marc, or by Italian or Bohemian Futurists, agrees; he finds them quite unprecedented. The newest school of painting consists of small sects and groups that vituperate each other, yet one thing they all have in common. They agree only on this point, that they all turn away from Impressionism, turn even against it: hence I class all of them together under the name of Expressionists, although it is a name usually assumed only by one of the sects, while the others protest at being classed in the same category. Whenever Impressionism tries to simulate reality, striving for illusion, they all agree in despising this procedure. They also share in common the passionate denial of every demand that we make of a picture before we can accept it as a picture at all. Although we may not be able to understand a single one of their pictures, of one thing we may be certain, they all do violence to the sensible world. This is the true reason of the universal indignation they arouse; all that has hitherto been the aim of painting, since painting first began, is now denied, and something is striven for which has never yet been attempted. At least so the beholder is likely to think, and the Expressionist will fully agree with him. Only the beholder maintains that whatever nature does not sanction, but that on the contrary deliberately goes against nature, can never be true Art, while the Expressionist insists that just this *is* Art, is *his* Art. And if the beholder retorts vehemently that the painter should express nothing but what he sees, the Expressionists assure him that they too paint only what they see. And on this point there is a continual misunderstanding. Each of them when he speaks of 'seeing' means something totally different. What is meant by 'seeing'?

Seeing

The history of painting is nothing but the history of vision – or seeing. Technique changes only when the mode of seeing has changed; it only changes because the method of seeing has changed. It changes so as to keep pace with changes of vision as they occur. And the eye changes its method of seeing according to the relation man assumes towards the world. A man views the world according to his attitude towards it. All the history of painting is therefore in a sense also a history of philosophy, especially of unwritten philosophy.

The act of seeing in a man is both passive and active. The picture changes according to whether he is more passive or more active, more submissive or more

Source: Hermann Bahr, *Expressionism*, translated by R. T. Gribble (London, 1920), pp. 35–51, 83–88. First published as *Expressionismus*, Munich, 1916.

assertive; according to whether he desires more to receive with greater purity, or to respond with greater force, so does his method of viewing a picture change. Seeing consists of two activities, an outer and an inner one: one which is done to man, and the other which is performed by man subsequently, in response to it. To be able to see at all, something must first have happened outside us; this must impinge on us, a stimulus must reach us. But no sooner does this stimulus from without reach us than we respond instantly, we respond by the action of the eye. It not only submits to the stimulus, it not only receives it, it not only lets it happen, but it acts instantly upon it; it takes it up, it announces it to us, it hands it on to our mind. The stimulus becomes sensation; the sensation becomes conscious and inserts itself into our thought. [. . .] By the time we become conscious of the stimulus, the eye has already transformed it, it bears our impress, is already half our own. And no sooner is it perceived than our thought is busy with it. Goethe says that 'in every attentive glance at the world we theorise', for as long as we don't *think* about the object we behold, we really do not see it at all. To see is always to recognise. Only the stimulus handed by the eye to the mind, and taken up by it and fused into thought, receives form. It is we that have given it form. We see a tree through our power of thought, without that it would only have been a sensation of colour. It is but a green patch which the eye itself might even have produced without any outer occasion, until I give the attention of my thoughts to its consideration. I have to think before I can be certain that the green colour is produced by an extraneous stimulus. I have first to turn upon it man's 'original conception' of cause; I must classify it, I must supplement it from my past experience: only then can I know what the green patch is, and knowing this, I am enabled to see not only a green patch, but from long experience to recognise it as a tree – even more, as an oak, a beech, a fir.

[. . .] As soon as a man realises that his seeing is always the result of some external influence, as well as of his own inner influence, it depends on whether he trusts the outer world more – or himself. Every human relation finally depends on this: once he has arrived at the stage where he can differentiate between himself and the rest of the world, when he can say 'I' and 'you', when he can separate outer from inner, he has no alternative but that of flight from the world into himself, or from himself into the world – or a third choice is possible, that of halting on the boundary line between the two. These are the three attitudes man can assume towards the phenomena of appearance.

When at the dawn of time man first awakened, he was startled by the world. To recover himself, to 'come to', he had to sever himself from Nature; in his later memory this event is echoed and repeated in the impulse to break away from Nature. He hates her; he fears her; she is stronger than he; he can only save himself from her by flight, or she will again seize and devour him. He escapes from her into himself. The fact of having the courage to separate from her, and to defy her, shows him that there must be a secret power in himself, and to this power he entrusts himself. From its depths he draws his own God and sets him up against Nature. He requires a stronger power than himself, but stronger also than the world; enthroned above him, and above her, it can destroy him, but it can likewise protect him against her. Should his offering find favour, his God will banish the terrors of Nature. And thus primeval man draws a magic circle of worship round himself and pricks it out with the signs of his God: Art begins, an attempt of man to break the grip of appearance by making his 'innermost' appear also; within the outer world, he has created another world which belongs to him and obeys him. If the former frightens him into mad flight, alarming and confusing all his senses – the eye, the ear, the groping hand, the moving foot – the latter pacifies and encourages him by its calm, by the rhythm and consonance of its rigid, unreal and unceasing repetition of form. In primitive ornament change is conquered by rest, the appearance to the eye by the picture in the mind, the outer world by the inner man, and when the reality of Nature perplexes and disturbs him because he can never fathom her depths, because she always extends further than he can reach, so that beyond the uttermost limit there stretches something beyond, and beyond this extends the threat of yet further vastness – Art frees him by drawing appearance from the depths and by flattening it out on a plane surface. Primeval man sees lines, circles, squares, and he sees them all flat, and he does so owing to the inner need of turning the threat of Nature away from himself. His vision is in constant fear of being overpowered and so it is always on the defensive, it offers resistance, is ready to hit back. Every fresh outer stimulus alarms the inner perception, which is always armed and ready, never concedes entrance to Nature, but out of the flux of experience he tears her bit by bit – banishing her from the depth to the surface – makes her unreal and human till her chaos has been conquered by his order.

It is not only primeval man who shows us this determined reaction of repulsion to every stimulus experienced. We recognise this attitude again in one of the highest phases of human development, in the East. There too man, now mature and civilised, has overcome Nature. Appearance has been seen through and recognised as illusion, and should the deceiving eye try to entice him into this folly, he is taught by knowledge to withstand. In the East all beholding is tempered by an element of comprehending pity, and wherever the wise man gazes, he sees only that which he knows: the eye takes in the outer stimulus, but only to unmask it instantly. All seeing, for him, is a looking away from Nature. [. . .]

The Impressionist, in visualising, endeavours as much as possible to rule out every inner response to the outer stimulus. Impressionism is an attempt to leave nothing to man but his retina. One is apt to say of Impressionists that they do not 'carry out' a picture; it were better to say, they do not 'carry out' visualisation. The Impressionist leaves out man's participation in appearance, for fear of falsifying it. Every intelligent look 'theorises' at once; it no longer contains only the pure stimulus, it contains also a human addition, and the Impressionist mistrusts Nature. Therefore, the Impressionist wants to surprise Nature before she has become humanised, he goes back to the first moment of sight, he wants to trap the impression at the instant of its first contact with us, at the very moment it first impresses us, while it is in process of turning into a sensation. [. . .]

It is the act of seeing during a period in which man trusts in his senses alone, and mistrusts any manifestation of other powers within him: he clings to Goethe's words: 'The senses do not deceive, the mind does.' To Impressionism man and the world have become completely one; to Impressionism only sense-impressions exist. [. . .]

Artistic vision depends on an inner resolve: the eye of the body conflicts (to speak like Goethe) with the eye of the spirit, and only by the way in which a man decides the issue of opposing forces does he truly become an artist. But how many have ever endured fully? Endured and gone on painting; for only when the strife had been outlasted could their best work really begin. This was, perhaps, what the Japanese painter meant when he said that before a man is ninety he is not able to guess even how much he can do. [. . .]

Expressionism

This is the vital point – that man should find himself again. Schiller asks: 'Can man have been destined, for any purpose whatever, to lose himself?' It is the inhuman attempt of our time to force this loss upon him against his own nature. We would turn him into a mere instrument; he has become the tool of his own work, and he has no more sense, since he serves the machine. It has stolen him away from his soul. And now the soul demands his return. This is the vital point. All that we experience is but the strenuous battle between the soul and the machine for the possession of man. We no longer live, we are lived; we have no freedom left, we may not decide for ourselves, we are finished, man is unsouled, Nature is unmanned. [. . .] Never yet has any period been so shaken by horror, by such a fear of death. Never has the world been so silent, silent as the grave. Never has man been more insignificant. Never has he felt so nervous. Never was happiness so unattainable and freedom so dead. Distress cries aloud; man cries out for his soul; this whole pregnant time is one great cry of anguish. Art too joins in, into the great darkness she too calls for help, she cries to the spirit: this is Expressionism.

Never has any period found a clearer, a stronger mode of self-expression than did the period of bourgeois dominance in Impressionistic art. This bourgeois rule was incapable of producing original music or poetry; all the music or poetry of its day is invariably either a mere echoing of the past, or a presentiment of the future; but in Impressionistic painting it has made for itself such a perfect symbol of its nature, of its disorder, that perhaps some day when humanity is quite freed from its trammels and has attained the serene perspective of historic contemplation, it may be forgiven, because of these shining tokens. Impressionism is the falling away of man from spirit. Impressionism is man lowered to the position of a gramophone record of the outer world. Impressionists have been taken to task for not 'carrying out' their pictures; they do not even carry out their 'seeing', for man of the bourgeois period never 'carries out', never fulfils life. He halts, breaks off midway in the process of seeing, midway in the process of life at the very point where man's participation in life begins. Half-way in the act of seeing these Impressionists stop, just where the eye, having been challenged, should make its reply: 'The ear is dumb, the mouth deaf,' says Goethe; 'but the eye both perceives and speaks.'[1] The eye of the Impressionist only beholds, it does not speak; it hears the question, but makes no response. Instead of eyes, Impressionists have another set of ears, but no mouth, for a man of the bourgeois period is nothing but an ear, he listens to the world, but does not breathe upon it. He has no mouth, he is incapable of expressing himself, incapable of pronouncing judgment upon the world, of uttering the law of the spirit. The Expressionist, on the contrary, tears open the mouth of humanity; the time of its silence, the time of its listening is over – once more it seeks to give the spirit's reply.

Expressionism is as yet but a gesture. It is not a question of this or that Expressionist, much less of any particular work of his. Nietzsche says: 'The first and foremost duty of Art should be to beautify life . . . Thereupon she must conceal or transmute all ugliness – and only after this gigantic task has been achieved can she turn to the special so-called Art of Art-production, which is but the appendage. A man who is conscious of possessing a superfluity of these beautifying and concealing and transmuting powers, will finally seek to disburden himself of this superabundance in works of Art; the same under special conditions applies to a whole nation.

But at present we generally start at the wrong end of Art, we cling to her tail and reiterate the tag, that works of Art contain the whole of Art, and that by these we may repair and transform life . . . simpletons that we are!'[2] Under this bourgeois rule the whole of man has become an appendage. Impressionism makes a splendid tail! The Expressionist, however, does not throw out a peacock's wheel, he does not consider the single production, but seeks to restore man to his rightful position; only we have outgone Nietzsche – or, rather, we have retraced our steps and gone further back beyond him and have arrived at Goethe: art is no longer only to 'beautify' life for us and to 'conceal or transmute ugliness', but art must bring life, produce life from within, must fulfil the function of life as man's most proper deed and action. Goethe says, 'Painting sets before us that which a man could and should see, and which usually he does not see.' If Expressionism at the moment behaves in an ungainly, violent manner, its excuse lies in the prevailing conditions it finds. These really are almost the conditions of crude and primitive humanity. People little know how near the truth they are when they jeer at these pictures and say they might be painted by savages. The bourgeois rule has turned us into savages. Barbarians, other than those feared by Rodbertus, threaten; we ourselves have to become barbarians to save the future of humanity from mankind as it now is. As primitive man, driven by fear of Nature, sought refuge within himself, so we too have to adopt flight from a 'civilisation' which is out to devour our souls. The savage discovered in himself the courage to become greater than the threat of Nature, and in honour of this mysterious inner redeeming power of his, which, through all the alarms and terrors of storm and of ravening beasts and of unknown dangers, never deserted him, never let him give in – in honour of this he drew a circle of guardian signs around him, signs of defiance against the threat of Nature, obstinate signs of demarcation to protect his possessions against the intrusion of Nature and to safeguard his belief in spirit. So, brought very near the edge of destruction by 'civilisation', we discover in ourselves powers which cannot be destroyed. With the fear of death upon us, we muster these and use them as spells against 'civilisation'. Expressionism is the symbol of the unknown in us in which we confide, hoping that it will save us. It is the token of the imprisoned spirit that endeavours to break out of the dungeon – a tocsin of alarm given out by all panic-stricken souls. This is what Expressionism is.

References

1   Goethe J.W. von, *Naturwissenschaftliche Schriften*, Vol. V, p. 12.
2   Nietzsche F.W., *Menschliches, Allzumenschliches*, Vol. II, p. 80.

27   Abstraction and Mysticism

Sheldon Cheney

Continually in earlier chapters the implication has been that subject matter drawn from surface nature had, in Expressionism, receded in importance, as mastery of ordered plastic design increased and the 'hidden' elements of expression became intensified. It was even suggested that, where creative art is concerned, distortion of objective nature might be 'natural'; even to a point where the recognizable visual aspect disappears, in total abstraction.

If the values of photographic or selective imitation of nature – of Naturalism and Realism – are thus discounted, one may ask, what is it that enters as the primary value of painting? If depiction is dropped for expression, what is it that is expressed?

The answer 'Form' is not enough, if we continue to consider form merely as a capitalization of the instrumental means: as a plastic achievement, a mechanical–dynamic order fixed in the canvas. Where does the instinct come from that impels the artist to formal creation? What is the *feeling* inseparable from form-conception and image-fixing? Form is revelation – of what?

It is revelation not merely of a plastic organism, but *through* the plastic of something that might be termed universal or cosmic truth, and, commonly, of human emotion.

Leaving out of consideration here the human or 'subject' aspect, we are seeking clues to the reality of the cosmic or universal value that lies between the mastered means of expression and the human-feeling content.

In truth there is no separating the values, in either creation or appreciation. When the Expressionist claims that the attainment of a structural order, a plastic unity, is basically important, he doubtless is thinking of the order or synthesis both in the mechanical, measurable aspect (which can to a certain extent be diagrammed mathematically) and in an abstract–mystical aspect. That is, he creates a little world with a living order and vitality of its own; and at the same time an image of the macrocosm, echoing the relatedness and order of all that is. We have explored the nature of the immediate pictorial order. Now we are asking to what extent the universal enters in.

There are those who see all abstraction as merely a mathematical and mechanical thing, explainable by its surface aspect of geometrical relationships. There are others – the majority now, I think – who link the abstract with the mystic: who consider it an expression at once of the mathematical and of the spiritual or cosmic. Whether the painter feels that he is, in 'turning abstract', instinctively expressing what is only a mechanical–physical order, or is proceeding in accord with a mystical aesthetic philosophy – apperceiving a deeper meaning in objects and relations than those explainable mechanically through senses and intellect – in either case, he is furthering a main advance of modern art: the march *towards abstraction*. Whether one grants

Source: Sheldon Cheney, *Expressionism in Art* (New York, 1934), pp. 313–335. Illustrations have been omitted. Reprinted by permission of Liveright Publishing Corporation, New York. Copyright 1934, 1948 by Liveright Publishing Corporation. Copyright renewed 1962 by Sheldon Cheney.

or not that *pure* abstraction in painting is possible or desirable, there can be no doubt that the world of art has recently moved in the direction of intenser capitalization of non-objective values.

It is my belief that the greatest art compasses form in the three aspects: as plastic–mechanical, as abstract–universal, and as expression of human feeling.

I believe that the increasing abstract significance in art is one phase of mankind's contemporary advance in spiritual apprehension. In other words, I take the mystic's view of the artist as creator, and count the mystic artist the true modern.

If I am right, we shall see, in the twentieth century, a phenomenal increase in abstract art. I might put it better by saying that there will be both an increase in the amount of totally abstract art, and enlarged emphasis upon the abstract element in art which, in 'content', still deals frankly with the objective world, with symbols, with events. In the Expressionist advance so far, there have been two easily marked divisions: a small but challenging group of artists abandoning objective reality, to seek expression in the absolute abstract, and a larger group who inform their 'more natural' work with an abstract 'structure' or design. When I speak of abstraction in painting, I include both those pictures in which abstract 'meaning' is the central content, and those in which the human subject values lie over a support or core of the abstract. In the latter case, it is the support or core that gives most significance, aesthetically, to the picture. [. . .]

But for those who cannot experience abstraction except mechanically, it may be illuminating to inquire about the balance of objectivity and abstraction in the other arts.

Music is widely considered to be cheapened when the actuality of nature is introduced: as in programme pieces wherein one can hear the babbling stream, the lion's roar, the storm, etc. Hardly less contemned is the subject piece, built not around actual sounds but limited to emotional–interpretive equivalents of living: as too often in the works of Tchaikovsky or the Impressionists. But take a composition of Bach, that we all might admit as great, and immediately it is clear that creation has been arbitrarily divorced from anything heard in nature: is primarily an exercise in the abstract. (It is not, as so many Victorian commentators averred, *intellectual* music, but richly abstract–expressive – or as I would say, abstract–spiritual and cosmic–expressive.) In other words, it is almost universally accepted that music is essentially an abstract art; that it departs from abstraction only at cost to its highest aims and potentialities.

The Expressionist inquires, then, why the materials that are detected by sight cannot be utilized to afford stirring aesthetic experience as readily and purely as the materials addressed to the sense of hearing. Sight and sound afford many parallels: why should the one be bound, as art, to portrayal of objective nature, the other freed for absolute creation? It may be answered that a picture *can* reproduce a view in detail, or tell a story circumstantially. But that is no conclusive argument against there being a department of painting aiming at a degree of abstraction as advanced as that normal to music. [. . .]

In all this I am trying to ease the way for those who are still afraid of abstraction. To me, as appreciator, the question is beside the point. I derive a real and direct enjoyment out of certain purely abstract painting; though that is but one small division of the range of pictures from which I gain aesthetic pleasure. [. . .]

I honestly believe that man's aesthetic appreciative faculty grows with individual use, and, in the mass, with the evolution of the race. It is no assumption of a special sense of superiority when one who has lived intimately with manifestations of the arts claims to experience the values of abstract pictorial form. It is merely an earlier arrival at a sort of sensitivity that will be universal – as the present generations outgrow their false education to Realism, and as the opportunity increases for living with varied sorts of art. At the present stage of comprehension – retarded by education – a few people but an increasing group are sensitive to absolute abstraction, which they may or may not consider a sort of mystic revelation of harmonious cosmic order; and a larger group turn to partially objective painting in which the abstract skeleton or core is richly dominant. They will detect the quality in greater purity as understanding and sensitivity grow; perhaps the individual will march on till he commonly demands abstraction washed of the last remnants of objectivity. In any case I ask the reader to grant me the possibility that this is not mere self-delusion: to go on with me, probationally, to an examination of the mystic significance attributed to abstract pictorial form by many Expressionists.

The commonest explanation put forward by the Expressionists, regarding the mystic element, is that the abstract form fixed in the picture is a direct revelation of cosmic architecture, of the rhythmic order of the continuing universe. That is, the plastic organism, or coiled and poised movement in the spatial field, is not merely of the sort that geometrically pleases the eye – as an old armchair fits the body – but carries with it cosmic and spiritual implications. The order created by the artists is an echo – rather, an implicit part – of first creation, a manifestation proceeding from the center of all that is, a pulsation in little of the rhythm self-perpetuated at life's source.

Formal expression, at its intensest and most significant, embraces, in this view, cosmic and spiritual revelation: the artist touches upon final unknowable truth about life, crystallizes a fragment of the beauty and order that lie beyond the field of sense knowing and intellectual explanation.

The Expressionist's business, then, in creating the plastic synthesis, is to reveal through it the ultimate hidden principle, the all-relating harmony, the sense of cosmic unity. In Realistic art the surface of nature is reproduced or portrayed, and neither the hidden universal value in the object nor the cosmic emotion of the artist enters into the product. But in Expressionist art the two sorts of hidden value primarily determine the excellence of the work. The painting partakes more of the reality of the spirit than of the commonly accepted reality of outward nature.

The picture, with a vitality of its own sort, determined physically by the nature of its materials and means – flat field, spatial sense, voluminous organization, dynamic colors – is in itself a universe in little, yet exhibiting the laws of original creation, and the rhythm and poise of celestial movement. In its finite way, it echoes, in one more manifestation, in one further push of evolutionary achievement, the harmonious order of the infinite. A bit of the equilibrium, of the utter clearness, of intuitively divined perfect order, is fixed, beyond any incidental copying of disordered outward nature.

We have been talking here in terms common to mysticism – a word demanding definition wherever it is used, so great are the differences between one man's and another's interpretations of it.

The mysticism which enters into the conception of Expressionist art is not the playing with veils that too often cheapens the word, and confuses the uninformed public. It is a philosophy of life and a release into richer living.

The mystic believes that the world as known to senses and intellect is only one phase or manifestation of the universe and experience: that there is a world of the spirit, more directly connected with, or expressive of, first principle or divinity. Each man is potentially divine, and through his consciousness maintains a link with original spirit. The individual can purposely develop his consciousness of related- ness to creative spirit, and can illumine every object and event on the immediate material plane of living, by bringing light and understanding to bear from the deeper plane. He may even withdraw occasionally from the surrounding disorder of human physical life, into blissful self-identification with the divine spirit, experiencing the rapture of perfect realization of harmony and order. Whether one prefers to term this identification with God – in the Christian mystic's words – or merely elevation into a region of harmonious accord of spiritual and physical living, there is presupposed a realm beyond the comprehension of the senses, but open nonetheless to human experience: where there is total release from the bondage of material and worldly things, where the individual partakes of the life of the spirit.

The Expressionist in art believes that he brings material or 'meaning' from that realm beyond, when he endows the picture with form affording experience of an unexplainable harmonious order; and that he does this by means of the abstract elements, not the objective, with which he works.

The 'scientific' materialists of the late nineteenth century – when the spirit, and love, and art, were all in line for explanation by test tube and chart – denied reality to everything unexplainable by sense experience and reasoning. They rejected the idea of divinity, denied the spirit, and ridiculed the mystic. They set up sense reality as the only truth, and reason as the only guide to living. A later generation of scientists have helped to discredit materialistic philosophy; but mankind had already descended into that excess of animalism, cupidity and will to power that brought the earth to its present disordered state. The pendulum swings back; the interrupted continuity of spiritual–material expansion is re-affirmed – and the world of man will inevitably resume the march towards order and perfect understanding. But there are artists and critics still who would interpret Modernism from the crassest materialist- ic viewpoint. There have even been books on twentieth century painting that belittle the mystic implication, that make out Expressionism as largely a by-product of scientific–mechanical discovery, and material – even fleshly – living. [. . .]

Far from limiting expression, identification with spirit affords the artist at once the inspiration of universality, of inexhaustible harmonious forms, and absolute freedom of creation on his immediate plane, up to the limits of his mastery of his chosen artistic medium. The artist's creative faculty both lives in the originating spirit or power at the center of all-related life, and continually becomes a fresh center of creative manifestation.

The intellect is but a tool along the way, as the technique of one's art is a tool. Sense knowledge and mastery of one's instruments are necessary; but the greater understanding and power must be from the spiritual center, if one is to illumine life movingly.

In short, the artist is God and man, Creator and creator, drawing from the center of all life and creating new life. For the work of art is itself a living thing, manifesting vitality, order, growth, rest. The greatest art is that which expresses the apprehension of source, spirit, cosmos, and at the same time expresses the creating, feeling self of the artist. Form in art is at once the expression of this dual power or origination, and expression of the potentialities of the particular medium employed: as manifested in the living plastic organism in painting or the typically theatric flow of the stage art. [. . .]

Kandinsky speaks of the artist as having 'a secret power of vision' and of art as 'belonging to the spiritual life'. He avers that 'that which has no material existence cannot be subjected to a material classification. That which belongs to the spirit of the future can only be realized in feeling, and to this feeling the talent of the artist is the only road. . . . In dancing as in painting we are on the threshold of the art of the future. The same rules must be applied in both cases. Conventional beauty must go by the board and the literary element of "story-telling" or "anecdote" must be abandoned as useless. Both arts must learn from music that every harmony and every discord which springs from the inner spirit is beautiful, but that it is essential that they should spring from the inner spirit and from that alone.' [. . .]

If there is a sufficiently general and unified advance towards abstraction to warrant the claims that this is a main path of Expressionism, there is still a very great variety of approach. [. . .]

Kandinsky, of course, is the type exhibit of the mystics who state flatly that creative painting comes from the soul. In most of his mature work the objective element has been so slight that there can be no doubt that his aim is to crystallize some other-worldly order. And yet there is the point that seldom does his work lack, somewhere, a minor link with recognizable objectivity. Kandinsky is an avowed mystic, seeking to bring the light of the spiritual realm to the illumination of earthly life. There was a time when he studied painting by the analogy of music. But he seems to many to have arrived at a point as near pure creation in the terms of his medium, without dragging along suggestions of the other art, as any living painter.

28   Expression and Communication

E. H. Gombrich

The Romantic idea that art is the language of the emotions has a long and complex history reaching back to the belief in spells and incantations. Frequently attacked and questioned, particularly by the upholders of formalist aesthetics, it still maintains its hold; indeed, it may be more firmly entrenched today than in earlier periods. The purpose of this paper is to ask how a language of the emotions might be conceived to function and where the main misconceptions may lie that have laid this theory open to justified attack.

I believe that these misconceptions are conveniently exemplified in the following passage from a lecture by Roger Fry:[1]

> If we take an analogy from the wireless – the artist is the transmitter, the work of art the medium and the spectator the receiver . . . for the message to come through, the receiver must be more or less in tune with the transmitter . . . herein lies the difficulty, for the message of a work of art is generally immensely complex, summarising as I believe a whole mass of experience hidden in the artist's subconsciousness. And this complexity renders it probable that each receiver only picks up a part of the total message . . . many people possess only very imperfect receiving instruments, instruments that can only respond to extremely violent emissions of a crude and elementary kind.

It is never fair to take an analogy literally and there are passages in the same lecture which show that Roger Fry did not want quite to sustain this comparison. If anybody had a right, moreover, to think of his mind as of a sensitive instrument it was this great critic. But Fry's strength lay in the intensity and subtlety of his response rather than in the clarity of his analysis, and the champion of the idea of 'significant form' certainly held some theory of natural resonance. For this is what the analogy from wireless transmissions would seem to imply. It suggests that the artist broadcasts his message in the hope of reaching a mind that will vibrate in unison with his own, and that his medium (the work of art) is only the means to achieve this end. Any failure on our part to respond must ultimately be due to an incapacity for picking up the vibrations that reach us through the medium.

The idea that art effects some kind of emotional contagion has been at the basis of all expressionist aesthetics ever since Horace wrote his famous line:

> *si vis me flere, dolendum est primum ipsi tibi (Ad Pisones*, 103/4) [if you wish me to weep, you must first grieve yourself].

But whatever the value of such injunctions as a technical device for the poet, it is clear, as Susanne Langer has been at pains to point out, that no theory of art could be built on the assumption that, writing a symphony, a composer would have to wait for

Source: Opening paper to a symposium with Professor Ruth Saw on *Art and the Language of the Emotions*, joint session of the Aristotelian Society and Mind Association, 1962. Reprinted in Professor Sir E. H. Gombrich, *Meditations on a Hobby Horse* (Phaidon Press, 1971), pp. 56–69.

a gay moment to put down the *Scherzo* and for a melancholy experience to invent the *Adagio*. Susanne Langer, however, holds fast to the expressionist assumption that forms or tones are analogues of feelings and will therefore convey a specific emotional experience.[2] The transmitter can be operated by an engineer who wants to 'present' a 'pattern of sentience', but the beholder is still a mere receiver who will undergo the same 'progress of excitation' if he tunes in and responds as well as the mechanism of his mind allows.

Indeed, if I understand the assumption of the expressionist theory correctly, it is that expression is somehow rooted in the nature of our minds, and that it therefore stands in no need of conventional signs. The following table may make this pretended opposition clear:

Expression	Communication
Emotion	Information
Symptom	Code
Natural	Conventional

The expression of emotion works through symptoms (such as blushing or laughter) which are natural and unlearned, the communication of information through signs or codes (such as language or writing) which rest on conventions. It is clear from the outset that both sides of this table represent extremes, while most means of communication and expression in our daily lives lie somewhere on a spectrum between these poles. Our speech makes use of conventional symbols which have to be learned, but the tone of voice and speed of utterance serve as an outlet for some symptoms of emotions which can even be picked up by small children or animals. On the other side of the scale, our gestures and expressions which we believe to be 'natural' are still filtered through the conventions of our culture; the smile of the hostess is less a symptom of joy than a conventional sign of welcome and, reading Victorian novels, one may suspect that even the maiden's blush can be somewhat stylized.

If we want to look at art from the point of view of communication and expression, we must also first place it somewhere between these extremes. The traditional symbols and emblems we find in religious painting would belong to one aspect, the symptoms of emotion we believe to detect in the painter's brush strokes to the other. It is true that expressionists tend to regard the conventional aspect as less essential, less artistic than the other. Be that as it may, I should like to argue here that we are certainly more likely to make progress in the discussion of this whole area if we analyse the two extremes in artificial isolation before we look at their possible interdependence.

It is clear that the 'resonance' theory can only apply, if at all, to the extremes of 'natural' symbols. Yawns may produce yawns and symptoms of panic may be contagious in an excited crowd. But not even the most extreme expressionist would want to confine the effects of art to such biological reactions. His case has always rested on the belief that there are such things as natural responses beyond those immediate symptoms of emotions. He points to the 'effects' of forms, tones and colours on man and beast which suggest that the colour red is exciting and slow music soothing. The baby, he would rightly say, does not have to learn the meaning of the lullaby in order to fall asleep and the young child need not be told that bright colours are more cheerful than drab ones.

There are some, I know, who worry about the exact meaning of the statement that a colour is gloomy or a tune sad. I shall assume that we know what is meant. Doubters are recommended to study those cruel anecdotes in which a stammerer, overcome by excitement, is asked to sing his message and blurts out a tale of woe and disaster to the tune of some cheerful 'hit'. We know very well why such a performance makes us laugh. There *is* such a thing as a gay melody and a cheerful colour.

I have discussed this natural equivalence between emotional states and sounds, colours and shapes in various contexts, and have drawn attention, in this connexion, to the experimental tool which C. E. Osgood has developed for their exploration. In Osgood's investigations,[3] the subject is confronted with the question whether, say, black is more sad than gay, more heavy than light, more powerful than weak or more old than young. However irrational these alternatives may sound, answers would appear not to be random. There is some inborn disposition in all of us to equate certain sensations with certain feeling tones.[4] Osgood has arranged these scales in three dimensions to plot what he calls our 'semantic space'. Though this method may well involve an oversimplification, I propose to simplify it in turn and present it for the sake of my argument in a two-dimensional form:

Sensation	Sights	Sounds
		High
		Loud
		Fast
	Red	
	Bright	
Light		
Warm		
Friendly Gay		
Hostile Sad		
Cold		
Heavy		
	Dark	
	Blue	
		Slow
		Soft
		Low

What this diagram suggests is a natural code of equivalences that represents, I think, the core of the expressionist argument. Every colour, sound or shape has a natural feeling tone just as every feeling has an equivalence in the world of sight and sound.

Imagining our basic reactions to be grounded in the biological urge for survival you may say that what is experienced as hostile will make us sad, what strikes us as friendly is gay in mood. Further out on the scale of sensory experiences, we come to the body feeling of change of temperature, where friendliness is experienced as warm and warmth as friendly, hostility as cold and cold as hostile. Along the line of visual sensations, darkness is gloomy and hostile, light warm and friendly. Among colours, red, being brighter than blue, will easily be experienced as the equivalent of warmth and cheerfulness, blue of cold and sadness. And so we come to the gamut of sounds, ranged according to pitch, speed and volume, where the slow, low and soft is more suitable for the funeral march and the fast, tinkling and loud for the triumphal dance.

I am aware of the extreme crudity of this model and would not dream of saddling anyone with the theory in this form. It is clear, for instance, that our Western music has other dimensions than those entered into the diagram, the most important being that between tension and resolution based on the distance from the tonic.[5] But refinements of this kind, however interesting, would not upset my basic contention: they would only add another gamut, this time the gamut of intervals or chords, from the 'warm' and relaxed to the 'cold' and tense ones – an attempt which has actually been made by Deryck Cooke in his recent book *The Language of Music*.[6] The same could be shown for gamuts of lines or shapes, where angular configurations would go to the cold and tense end of the spectrum, round and undulating ones to the friendly and warm pole.

If this doctrine of equivalence contained the truth and nothing but the truth, it would allow us to account for the theory of natural resonance. A painter would be a person naturally disposed to project his feelings on to the gamut of sights, a musician would do the same with scales of sound. Feeling sad in a hostile world, either would select from his medium the exactly equivalent shade and the recipient of his message would experience the identical emotion, since he would share the artist's natural code of equivalence. But it is precisely because this theory has proved so persuasive that we must probe its weakness. From the critic's point of view, surely, its principal weakness lies in its total inability to account for structure. It is no wonder, in fact, that its popularity led to an abandonment of structure and to the increasing cult of the spontaneous 'natural' symptom in abstract expressionism and, beyond, to the uniformly blue canvas that expresses the artist's 'blues'.

Roger Fry would have been the last to be satisfied with this state of affairs. We remember that he criticized people who 'only react to extremely violent emissions of a crude and elementary kind', and he would not have excluded artists from this stricture. But is not this crudeness inherent in the theory? The artist with his blue canvas forgets that whatever message unstructured blue may convey to the applauding critic is not inherent in the blue paint like a fluid or essence, but derives its meaning from its shock effect, its unexpectedness. His very longing to be 'unconventional' draws attention to the importance of convention in this process. We are forced, in other words, to switch our attention to the other side of the diagram, that of communication through conventional signs. And here, of course, the resonance theory lets us down immediately.

I confess that I have selected Roger Fry's formulation of this theory precisely because the analogy from wireless makes it especially easy to show up this weakness. For the conditions of wireless transmissions have been analysed together with other devices of telecommunication by communication engineers who have developed the mathematical theory of information.[7] What this theory has taught us unmathematical laymen to see with greater clarity is the process of interpretation that is bound up with the reception of any signal. It is human beings who communicate, not channels. Hence it is by no means the case that it needs a very sensitive instrument to pick up a complex message. Any channel that can be 'off' and 'on' can transmit a series of messages interpretable as instructions to select one of two alternatives, and this can be done sequentially much as in the game 'Twenty Questions'.

Technicians, I know, look with some misgivings at the uncritical use which is sometimes being made of their concepts outside the area for which they were intended. Intellectual fashions always carry such dangers. We certainly should not take a method of description for a new aesthetic prescription. One of the most interesting devices of information theory, for instance, is the possibility of measuring the information content of any message as inverse in ratio to the prior probability of its occurrence. The entirely anticipated obviously brings no fresh information; it is the unexpected that is news. This way of looking at signals in terms of their expectedness or unexpectedness has proved fruitful in the analysis of style in music and language. [8,9] But it may also have its share in the present cult of the 'random' in art and music which considers creativity entirely in the trivial terms of the invention of the unexpected.

The use I propose to make of the analysis of communication is a much more modest and, I hope, a safer one. It is not to explain art, but to criticize certain assumptions about art. For just as I think that the critic can learn from Osgood's psychological method of questionnaires, despite the fact that art is more than an exploration of 'semantic space', so I will try to show that the new approach of the engineer has yielded some helpful tools for the probing of the 'language of the emotions'. In my present context the most important reminder is perhaps the obvious fact that (in the words of Professor Colin Cherry):

> signals do not convey information as railway trucks carry coal. Rather we should say: signals have an information content by virtue of *their potential for making selections*. Signals operate upon the alternatives forming the recipient's doubt. They give power to discriminate amongst or select from these alternatives.

It is not my intention to apply this technical passage to a discussion of *Hamlet* or of Rembrandt's *Night Watch*. I should rather show its bearing on our problem with a famous story from antiquity which is closer to communication than it is to art. When Theseus' father, Aegeus, scanned the sea for the returning expedition against the Minotaur, he thought of the pre-arranged code according to which a white sail would mean success, a black one defeat. Theseus having lost Ariadne on Naxos, forgot to hoist the white sail and his father drowned himself. Of course, the code could have been enriched to include other possibilities, but nothing Theseus could have done at that distance could have conveyed to his father his state of mind which was indeed plunged in gloom, but for entirely unforeseen reasons. The sail could only function as a signal 'operating on the alternatives forming the recipient's doubt'.

The example is not quite uninstructive in our context because here, too, we have a case where a conventional code interacts with something felt to be 'natural'. Surely it was no accident that black rather than white was the sign agreed upon for failure. Black seems to us a more 'natural' sign for grief, and white for a 'brighter' mood: and even though we know that cultural conventions also play their part (and that black is not everywhere the colour of mourning), the correlation makes sense in terms of expressiveness. But clearly, black is infinitely more likely to be thus interpreted as an expression of gloom where we know, as we know in this case, that there is a choice between alternatives, one of which is to be taken as expressive of gloom. There are plenty of contexts where we are not aware of any possible alternatives and where black, therefore, is of no expressive significance: for instance, ordinary printer's ink ordinarily used.

It may be a little easier now to show up the theoretical fallacies of our hypothetical blue canvas 'charged', as the jargon has it, with the artist's blues; for we are certainly forced to reconsider the expressionist diagram of synaesthetic equivalences in the light of the theory of communication. If there is anything in this doctrine of natural signs, it only applies to the relationship of alternatives. Where there is a choice between red and blue, the move towards blue is more likely to be felt as equivalent to a move towards the sad end of the spectrum. I need not labour this point, for I have made it in the chapter on 'Expression' in my book on *Art and Illusion*, where I tried to show that all kinds of relationships or transitions can be equated in our half-dreaming mind with the transition from 'ping' to 'pong'. There may be a layer deep down in our mind (if I may speak in metaphors) for which these sensory categories are only different aspects of the same experience. But maybe it is precisely because they all converge in one point that even the directions seem extraordinarily unstable. That same scale from low pitch to high pitch that looks, in one aspect, equivalent to that from sadness to gaiety, can also be seen as going from warm to cool. Often it is a mere matter of nuance that effects a complete reversal. Tinkling is gay, but a shrill sound is like a shriek and chills you to the marrow. Our culture and our education, moreover, have effectively interfered with our primitive reactions. That all-important contrast between relaxation and tension can also become the opposition between indulgence and restraint; and in contrast with tension, restraint is surely a value, equated in aesthetics with the heroic, the chaste and the pure. These acquired scales turn out to be especially unstable. The sign of indulgence that moves one person to tears may disgust another – not because he has failed 'to pick up the message' but because he understands it all too well. One of the weakest points in the theory of natural resonance is this tendency to equate any failure to respond with a failure to understand.

For those of us who reject the resonance theory, understanding the language of the emotions is much more like any other understanding. It presupposes a knowledge of the language and therefore a grasp of alternatives open to the artist, but it also presupposes what the Romantic would describe as natural sympathy. Without acquaintance with the potentialities of the artist's medium and the tradition within which he works those natural equivalences which interest the expressionist could not come into play. What strikes us as a dissonance in Haydn might pass unnoticed in a post-Wagnerian context and even the *fortissimo* of a string quartet may have fewer decibels than the *pianissimo* of a large symphony orchestra. Our ability to interpret the emotional impact of one or the other depends on our understanding that this is the most dissonant or the loudest end of the scale within which the composer operated.

This is one of the reasons why concentration on the physiognomic properties of sights and sounds will never yield a theory of artistic expression unless it is coupled with a clear awareness of the structural conditions of communication. Granted that colours, shapes or harmonies can be experienced as expressive, the artist can only use these qualities with some confidence within a limited choice situation. The critics who worry how a chord can possibly be described as 'sad' are justified in one respect: it is not the chord, but the choice of the chord within an organized medium to which we so respond. The artist who wants to express or convey an emotion does not simply find its God-given natural equivalent in terms of tones or shapes. Rather, he proceeds as he proceeds in the portrayal of reality – he will select from his palette the pigment from among those available that to his mind is most like the emotion he wishes to represent. The more we know of his palette, the more likely we are to appreciate his choice.

It is clear from this point of view that the traditional media of art may have come into existence by accident. In theory, there is no reason why other media or gamuts should not be created which serve a similar function. The experiments of contemporary painters with textures are a case in point. I have little doubt that it is possible to build up a response to such novel scales. What I doubt, here and in all similar cases, is only that this response can be an immediate resonance. We would again have to learn, first of all, to regard the degree of smoothness or roughness as part of the message and become familiar with the scale within which the artist operates.

As soon as we look at the artist's ideal public less in terms of minds mysteriously attuned to one another than in terms of people ready to appreciate each other's choice of alternatives, we can ask once more how far such decisions can be interpreted as communicating emotions.

Returning to our highly simplified model, it might be worth examining how far the simplest form of equiprobable alternatives might still take us. In the arts that unfold in time, this principle is easily found; for here we have the example of the engineer's methods. All we would need is to adopt some convention according to which every message presents a binary choice articulated by a subsequent message. If we are sick of 'ping' and 'pong', we can take the contrast between bright and dark (*b* and non-*b*). The first message would tell us to look at the brighter side of the scale, the subsequent, if it happened to be non-*b*, on the darker half of that brighter side and the next, perhaps, on the brighter eighth. Since the original dimensions of the scale are indeterminate, the process would lack a quantitative precision, but as a relational progression it could be imagined to move to increasingly finer distinctions. Let us go back to our example of Theseus: a white sail was to announce success, a black failure. Had he foreseen the possibility of failure in success, he could first have hoisted the white sail and only then the black to indicate that he was victorious but sad, or better still, he could have retained the white sail but modified its message by a black pennant. Crude as the example may be, it may still illustrate the possibility of more subtle methods of articulation which must play their part in the arts of time, such as the rich language of Western music. What else is modulation but the modification in progression of the tonality first established? Of course, in music the black pennant that modifies the white sail can by a sort of magic become itself the principal message when the key relations change. The language of music would certainly not permit any mechanical application of the principle of progressive subdivision and modification, *ad infinitum*.

But then, neither music nor any other art ever worked with one binary code. Western music, as we have seen, combines the gamuts of rhythm, pitch and volume with those of tension (to recapitulate, only those we have mentioned already): Western painting makes use of shapes, colours, texture – not to speak of subject matter. Even if we imagined for argument's sake that each of these allowed only of one choice of alternatives, the number of possible combinations and permutations would rapidly increase. Given the many gamuts at our disposal, the complexity that can be achieved with this simple vocabulary is quite respectable. For each of these parallel gamuts can be used to support or, if necessary, enforce or enfeeble the message sent on the other channel. Even the painter of our monochrome canvas, after all, which he feels to be 'pong', can reinforce the effect by using the expressive effect of a heavy, downward brushstroke as a further symptom of his blues, or alternatively, he can dab the paint on with such a light 'ping' touch that he counteracts the impression of melancholy.

Much of traditional aesthetics is concerned with the doctrine of mutual reinforcement of various sense modalities and scales, often treated under the rather misleading name of 'decorum' (or fittingness):

'Whatever the general character of the story is, the picture must discover it throughout, whether it be joyous, melancholy, grave, terrible, etc. The nativity, resurrection, and ascension ought to have the general colouring, the ornaments, back-ground, and everything in them riant and joyous, and the contrary in a crucifixion, internment, or *pietà*', says Jonathan Richardson[10] in the eighteenth century. Criticism often consists in pointing out the observance or non-observance of these rules of 'mutual reinforcement' – how the vowels of a poem or its rhythms vary in tune with its mood,[11] or how a composer enhances a text by the choice of harmonies, dynamics and even orchestration. In the chilling language of engineers, such duplication of messages would probably fall under the heading of 'redundancies'.[7] Even engineers, however, know the importance of redundancies to defeat what they call 'noise'. Their practice of repeating important messages is only the simplest instance. Our speech, as is well known, uses the device of redundancy freely to aid our interpretations, useful where we have failed to attend to every part of a message. It seems to me quite possible that what we call form in art, symmetries and simplicities of structure, might well be connected with the ease and pleasure of apprehension that goes with well-placed redundancies.

The psychological instability of our individual gamuts must make this possibility of mutual reinforcement and anchorage of obvious importance for our model. But given such anchorage, the opposite possibility of mutual modification is even more interesting. A glance at the spectra of sound may illustrate my point. It suggests that the dimensions of louder, of faster and of higher may tend to be experienced as parallel. There are memorable passages in music, such as the climax of Beethoven's *Leonora* No. 3 in which these dimensions are used to reinforce each other and volume, speed and pitch rise to tremendous tension. Practising musicians know that these three dimensions do indeed tend to fuse, that there is a natural temptation for the 'expressive' player to turn a *crescendo* also into an *accelerando* and to press on a high note. But music would not be the subtle instrument of expression it has become in the hands of our masters if this link were, in fact, always observed. The *crescendo* that remains disciplined within the tempo of the movement is often the more impressive because of its sense of control. No artist is worth his salt who cannot keep the various dimensions of his language apart and use them for different articulations. After all, if an increase along all these dimensions is the 'expected' and the 'obvious' thing, his discipline will earn him the reward of doing the improbable and all the more convincing. We can catch a glimpse here of the direction in which our model could easily be enriched if we abandoned the primitive ping-pong structure and allowed for differences in probability. However, such an attempt would soon take us out of the possibilities that can be sketched out in words. Nor do I think we have as yet exhausted the potentialities even of our crude binary model.

Even in this model such possibilities of mutual modification would increase the artist's range and subtlety considerably. Let us imagine, for argument's sake, that our 'ping' 'pong' is played in print with two types of lettering, normal and **bold**. According to the theory of 'decorum', '**pong**' would obviously have to be printed in heavy type and 'ping' normal, but our modulator would be free to inverse the order to achieve a 'pong' modified by lighter print and a '**ping**' charged with some heaviness. We are free, if we like, to add other possibilities such as 𝔤𝔬𝔱𝔥𝔦𝔠 and latin script. Again, our tendency might be to use a bold gothic for '𝔭𝔬𝔫𝔤', but it is precisely for this reason that a normal gothic '𝔭𝔬𝔫𝔤' might strike you as unexpected and subtle. Perhaps the effect of such mutual modification is no more predictable than it is in cookery, but its possibilities must increase enormously with every new dimension added to the artists' gamuts.

But it is also clear, at least intuitively, that an increase in gamuts or media will not necessarily be a gain for this kind of 'language'. There must come a moment when the message is muffled because of the many signals that we are supposed to attend to. We no longer know which of them is intended to modify what, and thus ambiguity and obscurity increase. The only way out of this impasse would be the establishment of some hierarchy comparable to the temporal hierarchy of subsequent messages. If we knew which was the dominant scale, as it were, and which the subsequent modifications, we could still attend to them one by one in their intended rank. In our example of Theseus, the first message with the sail might be called the classifier, indicating the class of message to which we now shall have to attend, while the pennant might be described as the modifier. Clearly, in larger hierarchies these would become relational terms, every modifier could be a classifier for a subsequent modification.

I realize that this proposal sounds abstruse, but I believe that it really matters a good deal which of two distinctions is seen as the dominant one. That this is so with the distinctions of speech is easily shown. Take the momentous question which Tovey asked, whether good bad music was better or worse than bad good music. Looking at the example, we see that the English language makes sure of this distinction by making the adjective nearer the noun the dominant classifier, the one further removed the subordinate modifier. It is not uninstructive to look for similar examples, such as the difference between a left-wing Right-wing politician and his right-wing Left-wing rival, or, more simply, that between a reddish blue and a bluish red.

Perplexing as these distinctions are, the psychology of perception suggests that in the field of vision, at least, we are all marvellously adept at playing the game of 'classifiers and modifiers'. Our ability to separate what is called the local colour of things from the colour of illumination is based on this skill. We easily recognize the difference between a white wall in the shade and a grey wall in sunlight; more than that, even where the light reaching our retinas from both may be identical the two will 'look' quite different to our interpreting mind. And so with all sense modalities. The same scent or taste is known to affect us very differently according to our interpretation of its source. It is not a question so much of how a dish tastes as what dish is modified by this particular flavour. Plutarch remarks somewhere that that fish looks and tastes best that appears to be meat, and that meat that looks and tastes like fish. I have not tested this idea, nor would I like to. But everybody has experienced how closely related the 'what' and the 'how' are to our minds. The *haut goût* of venison would repel us in beef.

The point of this digression was to give one more reason for the importance of context and structure in our interpretation of expression. For if hierarchies could be shown to play their part in the language of the emotions, they would allow us to distinguish between degrees of understanding and misunderstanding. It is an experience common to all of us that great works of art are inexhaustible. Contrary to our crude models, their texture of relationships is so rich that we can never get tired of exploring them. But there is a difference, I would contend, between this feeling of understanding a work better and better, without changing one's basic interpretation, and another, more disconcerting experience when we discover, or believe we discover, that we have misunderstood it altogether and have to start from scratch because we had got the hierarchies of meaning upside down. To give a simple example: *Don Quixote* is (probably) rightly understood as a comic novel with tragic overtones which, of course, have their comic aspects and so on, *ad infinitum*. To take it the other way round and read it as a tragic work with comic touches is the kind of misunderstanding I would distinguish from incomplete understanding. It may be more intense, but it is also more wrong-headed than a superficial reading that only takes in the crude first pointers.

We have thus come a little closer, after all, to the traditional problems posed by *Hamlet* or Rembrandt's *Night Watch*. We can see why it makes a difference whether *Hamlet* is primarily to be understood as a tragedy of revenge or as a study of neurotic indecision, or whether the *Night Watch* is primarily a group portrait or a history piece.

Dilemmas of this kind only throw into relief the firm guidance which tradition and experience usually give us. In traditional art forms, the category or *genre* provides the first pointer. The grim *scherzo*, the melancholy waltz, even the senseless shaggy dog story, could not deliver their 'message' without this firm context. In painting, of course, the traditions of subject matter used to establish the dominant classifier even where they were modified beyond recognition. Courbet's *Stonebreakers* presented the public with a figure from 'low life' on a heroic scale. Turner's late landscapes modified the traditional Academy picture in the direction of the sketch. Each of these achieved some of their 'expressive' force by what, in a strictly technical sense, should be called a breach of decorum. If the history of an art is of any relevance to aesthetics, it is precisely because it will help us in these first rough and ready classifications on which all our subsequent understanding may hinge. Granted that a great work of art is so rich in structure that it remains potent even when misunderstood: if we are really out to receive its 'message', we cannot do without all the contextual aids the historian can unearth.

One example must suffice here. Its bearing on our argument is all the greater as it concerns a work by an Expressionist painter which has recently been used with much success to elucidate the expressionist theory of art. In his Charlton Lecture on Kandinsky's painting *At Rest (Ruhe) (Fig. M)*, Professor Ettlinger has shown convincingly[12] how Kandinsky used unstructured colours and geometrical shapes in the belief that these were inherently charged with emotive power. The artist's theoretical writings testify to his interest in all ideas of spiritual resonance, from those of the Romantics to those of Theosophists and Anthroposophists. He also appears to have interpreted the investigations of Gestalt psychology in the light of these preoccupations. Professor Ettlinger makes it clear that Kandinsky wanted the shapes themselves to suggest and convey the feeling of calm or repose. He mentions the similarity of the configuration with a 'harbour with sailing boats and a steamer', but he is convinced, in the light of Kandinsky's declared aims, that such an interpretation is as wide of the mark as are the notorious diagrams transposing Raphael's paintings into systems of triangles and squares. In the terminology of this paper, we could say that Raphael may have painted Madonnas modified into triangles but Kandinsky, at most, triangles modified into a harbour scene. Professor Ettlinger makes no secret of his opinion that Kandinsky's experiment did not quite come off. I certainly doubt that even the most sensitive beholder would feel 'at rest' in front of this picture.

It so happens, however, that we can restore a clear expressive meaning to Kandinsky's composition by placing it in its historical context. During the 'twenties, the artist worked side by side with Paul Klee at the *Bauhaus*, and the two were friends. In a humorous snapshot of 1929 they posed together as the famous twin monument to Goethe and Schiller.[13] Now, in 1927 Klee, who never shunned representation, had experimented with the suggestion of movement in ships, first in a drawing of slightly swaying sailing boats and then in a larger harbour scene which he called *Activity of the Port (Aktivität der Seestadt) (Fig. L)*. It is a witty experiment in conveying the bustle and restlessness of the harbour by novel graphic means. What is relevant to our context is only how much Kandinsky's work, painted a year later, gains in intelligibility when placed side by side with Klee's. Suddenly the massive rectangular forms acquire indeed the dimensions of heaviness and calm, they are the 'pong' to Klee's 'ping'. The artist may well have thought all the same that his picture speaks for itself. Whether we are writers, critics or painters, we are all apt to forget that not everyone shares our knowledge and our past experience. But without such sharing, messages will die on the way from transmitter to receiver, not because we fail to be 'attuned', but simply because there is nothing to relate them to. Neither communication nor expression can function in a void.

But this refutation of the resonance theory would hardly have warranted our effort if the results only applied to the receiving end of the transmission. I believe that the examples studied must also have their bearing on the understanding of the role of language of emotions for the artist himself. Surely Kandinsky's starting point can hardly have been a feeling of calm which he wanted to 'code' in terms of shapes. Whether he knew it or not, his imagination was kindled by Klee's experiments. The discovery of how much could be conveyed by lines and shapes must have stimulated him to explore how far such means could be simplified and still be used for varying expressions. It was the challenge of modifying an existing configuration. In playing these games, the artist becomes his own public, as it were. He is fascinated by the possibilities of choice and of variation within a restricted medium not only, as the formalists would have it, because of the fascination of structure as such, but also as we have seen, because it is this restriction alone which enables him to equate his choice with the 'ping' and 'pong' of feeling tones. No emotion, however strong or however complex, can be transposed into an unstructured medium. Both the transmitter and the receiver need the right degree of guidance by an array of alternatives within which the choice can become expressive.

Having been so much concerned with games and models, I should like to conclude with a suggestion of how to replace Roger Fry's analogy while remaining in the area of communication. Instead of his simile of transmitters, let us think of a correspondent who regularly writes letters overseas at the present postage rate of sixpence. One day, in a receptive state of mind, he is struck by the prosy purple colour of the sixpenny stamp and, being in a playful mood, he casts around for other combinations that would express his feelings more adequately. Needless to say, the recipient might never notice his deviation from the norm if he were not told of the birth of a new art form. But once the stage is set, our players could start the game. Their medium consists of ten denominations of stamps – ½d., orange; 1d., blue; 1½d., green; 2d., brown; 2½d., red; 3d., purple; 4d., light blue; 4½d., light red; 5d., light brown; 6d., light purple. Both financial prudence and a sense of form impose the rule of affixing the right amount. Even within this limiting rule, however, there are no less than six choices of uniform colours (12 orange, 6 blue, 4 green, 3 brown, 2 purple, 1 light purple) which may reflect quite a variety of moods – 'reflect', that is, for the partner who would appreciate the message of three brown stamps as about the drabbest that could be selected. Given such a partner, he would surely and rightly expect a splendid piece of news when he saw the envelope decorated with the maximum of variety, one orange, say, one blue, one red, one green, then another orange, keeping the contrasts throughout at the widest. Combine the two oranges and go thence to red and then from blue to green, and the tension has subsided although the mood is still very bright. Of course, the two can also agree on the direction of reading, making the left-hand stamp the 'classifier' that stands for the dominant mood, while the others articulate it in succession. Perhaps great anger and some sadness would lead to two red, and one blue stamp. Only a fit of reckless fury, however, would break through the rules altogether and affix three red stamps at the gratuitous expense of 1½d. But in such a fit of extreme expressionist abandon, our correspondent would be in danger of spoiling his medium for good. Once the rule is broken, there is no valid reason why he should not plaster the whole envelope with colours. Moreover, going back to the rules will be increasingly difficult, for it would now imply that his emotions have cooled more than he would like to indicate. As a true artist, therefore, our correspondent will not yield to this temptation of 'breaking the form', at least till he has exhausted all its possibilities. What challenges his imagination is rather the game itself, the wealth of combinations adding up to sixpence which the reader is invited to explore. Perhaps those who get really absorbed in the game will try to fit their moods to interesting combinations rather than make the message fit the mood. Only those who do, I believe, may have the true artistic temperament – but that is a different story.

References

1   Roger Fry, 'Art History as an Academic Discipline.' *Last Lectures*, Cambridge, 1933.
2   S.K. Langer, *Philosophy in a New Key*, Cambridge (Mass.), 1942, chap. VIII; *Feeling and Form*, London, 1953, chap. XX.
3   Charles E. Osgood, George J. Suci and Percy H. Tennenbaum, *The Measurement of Meaning*, Urbana, 1957.
4   Glenn O'Malley, 'Literary synesthesia', *Journal of Aesthetics and Art Criticism* **XV**, 1957.
5   R. Frances, *La Perception de la Musique* (Études de Psychologie et de Philosophie, publiées sous la direction de P. Guillaume et I. Meyerson, **XIV**), Paris, 1958.
6   Deryck Cooke, *The Language of Music*, London, 1959.

7   Colin Cherry, *On Human Communication*, New York, 1957.
8   Leonard B. Meyer, 'Meaning in music and information theory', *Journal of Aesthetics and Art Criticism* **XV**, 1957.
9   David Kraehenbuehl and Edgar Coons, 'Information as a measure of the experience of music', *Journal of Aesthetics and Art Criticism* **XVII**, 1958–1959.
10 Jonathan Richardson, *The Theory of Painting (The Works of Jonathan Richardson)*, London, 1792, p. 39.
11 William T. Moynihan, 'The auditory correlative', *Journal of Aesthetics and Art Criticism* **XVII**, 1958.
12 L.D. Ettlinger, *Kandinsky's 'At Rest'*, Oxford, 1961.
13 Carola Giedion-Welcker, *Paul Klee in Selbstzeugnissen und Bilddokumenten*, 1962, p. 84.

29 Art and Inquiry

Nelson Goodman

A persistent tradition pictures the aesthetic attitude as passive contemplation of the immediately given, direct apprehension of what is presented, uncontaminated by any conceptualization, isolated from all echoes of the past and from all threats and promises of the future, exempt from all enterprise. By purification rites of disengagement and disinterpretation we are to seek a pristine, unsullied vision of the world. The philosophic faults and aesthetic absurdities of such a view need hardly be recounted until someone seriously goes so far as to maintain that the appropriate aesthetic attitude towards a poem amounts to gazing at the printed page without reading it.

I maintain, on the contrary, that we have to read the painting as well as the poem, and that aesthetic experience is dynamic rather than static. It involves making delicate discriminations and discerning subtle relationships, identifying symbol systems and characters within these systems and what these characters denote and exemplify, interpreting works and reorganizing the world in terms of works and works in terms of the world. Much of our experience and many of our skills are brought to bear and may be transformed by the encounter. The aesthetic 'attitude' is restless, searching, testing – is less attitude than action: creation and re-creation.

What, though, distinguishes such aesthetic activity from other intelligent behavior such as perception, ordinary conduct and scientific inquiry? One instant answer is that the aesthetic is directed to no practical end, is unconcerned with self-defense or conquest, with acquisition of necessities or luxuries, with prediction and control of nature. But if the aesthetic attitude disowns practical aims, still aimlessness is hardly enough. The aesthetic attitude is inquisitive as contrasted with the acquisitive and self-preservative, but not all non-practical inquiry is aesthetic. To think of science as motivated ultimately by practical goals, as judged or justified by bridges and bombs and the control of nature, is to confuse science with technology. Science seeks knowledge without regard to practical consequences, and is concerned with prediction not as a guide for behavior but as a test of truth. Disinterested inquiry embraces both scientific and aesthetic experience.

Attempts are often made to distinguish the aesthetic in terms of immediate pleasure, but troubles arise and multiply here. Obviously, sheer quantity or intensity of pleasure cannot be the criterion. That a picture or poem provides more pleasure than does a proof is by no means clear; and some human activities unrelated to any of these provide enough more pleasure to render insignificant any differences in amount or degree among various types of inquiry. The claim that aesthetic pleasure is of a different and superior *quality* is by now too transparent a dodge to be taken seriously.

Source: Nelson Goodman, *Problems and Projects*, (Hackett Publishing Company, 1972), pp. 103–119. Reprinted by permission of Nelson Goodman and Hackett Publishing Company Inc., Indianapolis, Indiana.

The inevitable next suggestion – that aesthetic experience is distinguished not by pleasure at all but by a special aesthetic emotion – can be dropped on the waste-pile of 'dormitive virtue' explanations.

This clears the way for the sophisticated theory that what counts is not pleasure yielded but pleasure 'objectified', pleasure read into the object as a property thereof. Apart from images of some grotesque process of transfusion, what can this mean? To consider the pleasure as possessed rather than occasioned by the object – to say in effect that the object is pleased – may amount to saying that the object expresses the pleasure. But since some aesthetic objects are sad – express sadness rather than pleasure – this comes nowhere near distinguishing in general between aesthetic and non-aesthetic objects or experience.

Some of these difficulties are diminished and others obscured if we speak of satisfaction rather than pleasure. 'Satisfaction' is colorless enough to pass in contexts where 'pleasure' is ludicrous, hazy enough to blur counter-instances, and flexible enough to tolerate convenient vacillation in interpretation. Thus we may hope to lessen the temptation to conjure up a special quality or kind of feeling or to indulge in mumbo-jumbo about objectification. Nevertheless, satisfaction pretty plainly fails to distinguish aesthetic from non-aesthetic objects and experiences. Not only does some scientific inquiry yield much satisfaction, but some aesthetic objects and experiences yield none. Music and our listening, pictures and our looking, do not fluctuate between aesthetic and non-aesthetic as the playing or painting varies from exalted to excruciating. Being aesthetic does not exclude being unsatisfactory or being aesthetically bad.

The distinguishing feature, some say, is not satisfaction secured but satisfaction sought: in science, satisfaction is a mere by-product of inquiry; in art, inquiry is a mere means for obtaining satisfaction. The difference is held to be neither in process performed nor in satisfaction enjoyed but in attitude maintained. On this view the scientific *aim* is knowledge, the aesthetic *aim* satisfaction.

But how cleanly can these aims be separated? Does the scholar seek knowledge or the satisfaction of knowing? Obtaining knowledge and satisfying curiosity are so much the same that trying to do either without trying to do the other surely demands a precarious poise. And anyone who does manage to seek the satisfaction without seeking the knowledge will pretty surely get neither, while on the other hand abstention from all anticipation of satisfaction is unlikely to stimulate research. One may indeed be so absorbed in working on a problem as never to think of the satisfaction to be had from solving it; or one may dwell so fondly on the delights of finding a solution as to take no steps towards arriving at one. But if the latter attitude is aesthetic, aesthetic understanding of anything is foredoomed. And I cannot see that these tenuous, ephemeral and idiosyncratic states of mind mark any significant difference between the aesthetic and the scientific.

Failure to arrive at an acceptable formulation in terms of pleasure or satisfaction, yielded or 'objectified' or anticipated, will hardly dislodge the conviction that the distinction between the scientific and the aesthetic is somehow rooted in the difference between knowing and feeling, between the cognitive and the emotive. This latter deeply entrenched dichotomy is in itself dubious on many grounds, and its application here becomes especially puzzling when aesthetic and scientific experience alike are seen to be fundamentally cognitive in character. But we do not easily part with the idea that art is in some way or other more emotive than is science.

The shift from pleasure or satisfaction to emotion-in-general softens some of the crudities of the hedonistic formulas but leaves us with trouble enough. Paintings and concerts, and the viewing and hearing of them, need not arouse emotion, any more than they need give satisfaction, to be aesthetic; and anticipated emotion is no better criterion than anticipated satisfaction. If the aesthetic is characteristically emotive in some way, we have yet to say in what way.

Any picture of aesthetic experience as a sort of emotional bath or orgy is plainly preposterous. The emotions involved tend to be muted and oblique as compared, for example, with the fear or sorrow or depression or exultation that arises from actual battle or bereavement or defeat or victory, and are not in general keener than the excitement or despair or elation that accompanies scientific exploration and discovery. What the inert spectator feels falls far short of what the characters portrayed on the stage feel, and even of what he himself would feel on witnessing real-life events. And if he leaps on the stage to participate, his response can no longer be called aesthetic. That art is concerned with simulated emotions suggests, as does the copy theory of representation, that art is a poor substitute for reality; that art is imitation, and aesthetic experience a pacifier that only partly compensates for lack of direct acquaintance and contact with the Real.

Often the emotions involved in aesthetic experience are not only somewhat tempered but also reversed in polarity. We welcome some works that arouse emotions we normally shun. Negative emotions of fear, hatred, disgust may become positive when occasioned by a play or painting. The problem of tragedy and the paradox of ugliness are made to order for ancient and modern Freudians, and the opportunity has not been neglected. Tragedy is said to have the effect of purging us of pent-up and hidden negative emotions, or of injecting measured doses of the killed virus to prevent or mitigate the ravages of an actual attack. Art becomes not only palliative but therapeutic, providing both a substitute for good reality and a safeguard against bad reality. Theatres and museums function as adjuncts to Departments of Public Health.

Again, even among works of art and aesthetic experiences of evident excellence, the emotive component varies widely – from, say, a late Rembrandt to a late Mondrian, or from a Brahms to a Webern quartet. The Mondrian and the Webern are not obviously more emotive than Newton's or Einstein's laws; and a line between emotive and cognitive is less likely to mark off the aesthetic neatly from the scientific than to mark off some aesthetic objects and experiences from others.

All these troubles revive the temptation to posit a special aesthetic emotion or feeling or a special coloration of other emotions occurring in aesthetic experience. This special emotion or coloring may be intense when other emotions are feeble, may be positive when they are negative, and may occur in experience of the most intellectual art and yet be lacking in the most stirring scientific study. All difficulties are resolved – by begging the question. No doubt aesthetic emotions have the property that makes them aesthetic. No doubt things that burn are combustible. The theory of aesthetic phlogiston explains everything and nothing.

Thus two stubborn problems still confront us. First, despite our conviction that aesthetic experience is *some*how emotive rather than cognitive, the failure of formulae in terms of either yielded or anticipated emotions has left us with no way of saying *how*. Second, despite our recognition that emotion in aesthetic experience tends to be denatured and often even inverted, the obvious futility of explanations in terms of a special secretion of the aesthetic glands leaves us without any way of saying *why*. Perhaps the answer to the second question will be found in the answer to the first; perhaps emotion in aesthetic experience behaves as it does because of the role it plays.

Most of the troubles that have been plaguing us can, I have suggested, be blamed on the domineering dichotomy between the cognitive and the emotive. On the one side, we put sensation, perception, inference, conjecture, all nerveless inspection and investigation, fact and truth; on the other, pleasure, pain, interest, satisfaction, disappointment, all brainless affective response, liking and loathing. This pretty effectively keeps us from seeing that in aesthetic experience the *emotions function cognitively*. The work of art is apprehended through the feelings as well as through the senses. Emotional numbness disables here as definitely if not as completely as blindness or deafness. Nor are the feelings used exclusively for exploring the emotional content of a work. To some extent, we may feel how a painting looks as we may see how it feels. The actor or dancer – or the spectator – sometimes notes and remembers the feeling of a movement rather than its pattern, insofar as the two can be distinguished at all. Emotion in aesthetic experience is a means of discerning what properties a work has and expresses.

To say this is to invite hot denunciation for cold over-intellectualization; but rather than aesthetic experience being here deprived of emotions, the understanding is being endowed with them. The fact that emotions participate in cognition no more implies that they are not felt than the fact that vision helps us discover properties of object implies that color sensations do not occur. Indeed, emotions must be felt – that is, must occur, as sensations must – if they are to be used cognitively. Cognitive use involves discriminating and relating them in order to gauge and grasp the work and integrate it with the rest of our experience and the world. If this is the opposite of passive absorption in sensations and emotions, it by no means amounts to cancelling them. Yet it explains the modifications that emotions may undergo in aesthetic experience.

In the first place, a context of inquiry rather than of indulgence or incitement may result in a characteristic displacement of emotion. The psychological, physiological and physical setting is different. A dollar earned, a dollar saved, a dollar spent, is still a dollar; affection eventuating in slavery, in frustration, in illumination, is still affection; but in neither case are all three quite the same. Emotions are not so insular as to be untouched by their environment, but cognitive use neither creates new emotions nor imparts to ordinary emotions some magic additive.

Furthermore the frequent disparity between the emotion felt and the emotive content thereby discovered in the object is now readily understood. Pity on the stage may induce pity in the spectator; but greed may arouse disgust, and courage admiration. So may a white house look white at noon, but red at sunset; and a globe looks round from any angle. Sensory and emotive experiences are related in complex ways to the properties of objects. Also, emotions function cognitively not as separate items but in combination with one another and with other means of knowing. Perception, conception and feeling intermingle and interact; and an alloy often resists analysis into emotive and non-emotive components. The same pain (or is it the same?) tells of ice or fire. Are anger and indignation different feelings or the same feeling under different circumstances? And does awareness of the overall difference arise from or lead to awareness of the difference in circumstances? The answers do not matter here; for I am not resting anything on the distinction between emotion and other elements in knowing but rather insisting that emotion belongs with them. What does matter is that the comparisons, contrasts and organization involved in the cognitive process often affect the participating emotions. Some may be intensified, as colors are against a complementary ground, or pointed up by subtle rhyming; others may be softened, as are sounds in a louder context. And some emotions may emerge as properties of the orchestrated whole, belonging like the shape of an eggshell to none of the lesser parts.

Again, negative emotions obviously function cognitively quite as well as positive ones. The horror and revulsion we may feel at *Macbeth* are not lesser means of understanding than the amusement and delight we may find in *Pygmalion*. We are not called upon to suppose that somehow – say by catharsis – the revulsion is transformed into delight, or to explain why the most forbidding portrait is as legitimately aesthetic as the most appealing one; for pleasantness in an emotion is no more a condition for cognitive functioning than is redness in a color sensation. In aesthetic experience, emotion positive or negative is a mode of sensitivity to a work. The problem of tragedy and the paradox of ugliness evaporate.

Equally plainly, quantity or intensity of emotion is no measure of its cognitive efficacy. A faint emotion may be as informative as an overwhelming one; and finding that a work expresses little or no emotion can be as significant aesthetically as finding that it expresses much. This is overlooked by all attempts to distinguish the aesthetic in terms of amount or degree of emotion.

Although many puzzles are thus resolved and the role of emotion in aesthetic experience clarified, we are still left without a way of distinguishing aesthetic from all other experience. Cognitive employment of the emotions is neither present in every aesthetic, nor absent from every non-aesthetic, experience. We have already noted that some works of art have little or no emotive content, and that even where the emotive content is appreciable, it may sometimes be apprehended by non-emotive means. In daily life, classification of things by feeling is often more vital than classification by other properties: we are likely to be better off if we are skilled in fearing, wanting, braving or distrusting the right things, animate or inanimate, than if we perceive only their shapes, sizes, weights, etc. And the importance of discernment by feeling does not vanish when the motivation becomes theoretic rather than practical. The zoologist, psychologist, sociologist, even when his aims are purely theoretic, legitimately employs emotion in his investigations. Indeed, in any science, while the requisite objectivity forbids wishful thinking, prejudicial reading of evidence, rejection of unwanted results, avoidance of ominous lines of inquiry, it does not forbid the use of feeling in exploration and discovery, the impetus of inspiration and curiosity, or the cues given by excitement over intriguing problems and promising hypotheses. And the more we discuss these matters, the more we come to realize that emotions are not so clearly differentiated or so sharply separable from other elements in cognition that the distinction can provide a firm basis for answering any moot question.

Repeated failure to find a neat formula for sorting experiences into aesthetic and non-aesthetic, in rough conformity with rough usage, suggests the need for a less simple-minded approach. Perhaps no single, simple, significant feature neatly marks off all arts from all sciences and technologies, or all aesthetic from all scientific and practical experience. In some respects, certain arts may be less like others than like some sciences and technologies; and the traditional classification of objects and activities into the aesthetic and the non-aesthetic may be more harmful than helpful.

Aesthetic and scientific activity alike, I have suggested, consist to a large extent of symbol processing: of inventing, applying, interpreting, transforming, manipulating, symbols and symbol systems. Thus what is called for is a grounded and circumstantial investigation of the most important features of likeness and difference among symbol systems in general, both linguistic and non-linguistic – a study of systems of description, representation, mapping, diagramming, exemplification, expression and formal notation. Occasional earlier efforts towards a general theory of symbols have been at best fragmentary and at worst infected with serious fallacies and confusions, such as that so-called iconic signs can be distinguished from others on the basis of resemblance to what they stand for, that languages differ from pictures in being more artificial or conventional, and that the difference between analogue and digital systems has something to do with analogy and digits.

I cannot now undertake to outline a more systematic investigation into the general theory of symbols, or even to make clear some of its results. I can only try to give you some inkling of what I mean. Some of the features that seem to me to constitute important distinctions among types of symbol system are these:

1 *Syntactic density*, depending not upon the internal structure of symbols but on the number of symbols and the nature of their ordering in an entire scheme – a feature that distinguishes representational systems from the articulate systems of languages and notations.

2 *Semantic density*, depending upon the number of reference-classes and the nature of their ordering under a given symbol system – a feature that distinguishes ordinary languages from notational systems such as that of music.

3 *Exemplification*, reference running not from a label to what it denotes but from a sample to a label denoting it – a feature that distinguishes expression from representation and description; and

4 *Relative syntactic repleteness*, depending on the comprehensiveness of the set of features that are constitutive of the characters of the scheme – a feature that distinguishes pictures from graphic diagrams. I list these without any adequate explanation and without any attempt to justify their choice, merely in order to suggest the kind of characteristics of symbol systems that seems to me relevant.

Taken severally, these features are neither necessary nor sufficient for aesthetic experience. Each cuts across the usual boundary between the aesthetic and the non-aesthetic, and effects some interesting new alliances and alienations. Pictorial representation, for example, is like the symbol system involved in gauging weights or temperatures in being both syntactically and semantically dense; literary expression and geological sampling share the property of being syntactically less replete. Yet while any of the four symptoms may be absent from aesthetic or present in non-aesthetic experience, they probably tend to be present, or present in higher degree, in aesthetic experience. If they are *severally* neither sufficient nor necessary for aesthetic experience, they may be *conjunctively* sufficient and *disjunctively* necessary; perhaps, that is, an experience is aesthetic if it has all these attributes and only if it has at least one of them.

I am not claiming that this proposal conforms faithfully to ordinary usage. Presystematic usage of 'aesthetic' and 'non-aesthetic' is even less clearly established by practice, and more seriously infected with inept theorizing, than in the case of most terms. Rather I am suggesting that we have here an appropriate use for some badly abused terms. Density, repleteness and exemplification, then, are earmarks of the aesthetic; articulateness, attenuation and denotation are earmarks of the non-aesthetic. A vague and yet harsh dichotomy of experiences gives way to a sorting of features, elements and processes. Classification of a totality as aesthetic or non-aesthetic counts for less than identification of its aesthetic and non-aesthetic aspects. Phases of a decidedly aesthetic compound may be utterly non-aesthetic; for example, a score and its mere reading may be devoid of all aesthetic aspects. On the other hand, aesthetic features may predominate in the delicate qualitative and quantitative discrimination required in testing some scientific hypotheses. Art and science are not altogether alien.

The distinction here drawn between the aesthetic and the non-aesthetic is independent of all considerations of aesthetic value. That is as it should be. An abominable performance of the *London Symphony* is as aesthetic as a superb one; and Piero's *Risen Christ* is no more aesthetic but only better than a hack's. The symptoms of the aesthetic are not marks of merit; and a characterization of the aesthetic neither requires nor provides a definition of aesthetic excellence.

Folklore has it that the good picture is pretty. At the next higher level, 'pretty' is replaced by 'beautiful', since the best pictures are often obviously not pretty. But again, many of them are in the most obvious sense ugly. If the beautiful excludes the ugly, beauty is no measure of aesthetic merit; but if the beautiful may be ugly, then 'beauty' becomes only an alternative and misleading word for aesthetic merit.

Little more light is shed by the dictum that while science is judged by its truth, art is judged by the satisfaction it gives. Many of the objections urged earlier against satisfaction, yielded or anticipated, as a distinguishing feature of the aesthetic weigh also against satisfaction as a criterion of aesthetic merit: satisfaction cannot be identified with pleasure, and positing a special aesthetic feeling begs the question. We are left with the unhelpful formula that what is aesthetically good is aesthetically satisfactory. The question is what makes a work good or satisfactory.

Being satisfactory is in general relative to function and purpose. A good furnace heats the house to the required temperature evenly, economically, quietly, and safely. A good scientific theory accounts for the relevant facts clearly and simply. We have seen that works of art or their instances perform one or more among certain symbol functions: representation, description, exemplification, expression. The question what constitutes effective symbolization of any of these kinds raises in turn the question what purpose such symbolization serves.

An answer sometimes given is that exercise of the symbolic faculties beyond immediate need has the more remote practical purpose of developing our abilities and techniques to cope with future contingencies. Aesthetic experience becomes a gymnasium work-out, pictures and symphonies the bar-bells and punching bags we use in strengthening our intellectual muscles. Art equips us for survival, conquest and gain. And it channels surplus energy away from destructive outlets. It makes the scientist more acute, the merchant more astute, and clears the streets of juvenile delinquents. Art, long derided as the idle amusement of the guilty leisure class, is acclaimed as a universal servant of mankind. This is a comforting view for those who must reconcile aesthetic inclinations with a conviction that all value reduces to practical utility.

More lighthearted and perhaps more simple-minded is the almost opposite answer: that symbolization is an irresponsible propensity of man, that he goes on symbolizing beyond immediate necessity just for the joy of it or because he cannot stop. In aesthetic experience, he is a puppy cavorting or a well-digger who digs doggedly on after finding enough water. Art is not practical but playful or compulsive. Dogs bark because they are canine, men symbolize because they are human; and dogs go on barking and men go on symbolizing when there is no practical need just because they cannot stop and because it is such fun.

A third answer, bypassing the issue of practicality versus fun, points to communication as the purpose of symbolizing. Man is a social animal, communication is a requisite for social intercourse, and symbols are media of communication. Works of art are messages conveying facts, thoughts and feelings; and their study belongs to the obstreperous and omnivorous new growth called 'communications theory'. Art depends upon and helps sustain society – exists because, and helps insure that, no man is an island.

Each of these explanations – in terms of gymnastics, play or conversation – distends and distorts a partial truth. Exercise of the symbolizing skills may somewhat improve practical proficiency; the cryptographic character of symbol invention and interpretation does give them the fascination of a game; and symbols are indispensable to communication. But the lawyer or admiral improving his professional competence by hours in museums, the cavorting puppy, the neurotic well-digger, and the woman on the telephone do not, separately or together, give the whole picture. What all three miss is that the drive is curiosity and the aim enlightenment. Use of symbols beyond immediate need is for the sake of understanding, not practice; what compels is the urge to know, what delights is discovery, and communication is secondary to the apprehension and formulation of what is to be communicated. The primary purpose is cognition in and for itself; the practicality, pleasure, compulsion and communicative utility all depend upon this.

Symbolization, then, is to be judged fundamentally by how well it serves the cognitive purpose: by the delicacy of its discriminations and the aptness of its allusions; by the way it works in grasping, exploring and informing the world; by how it analyses, sorts, orders and organizes; by how it participates in the making, manipulation, retention and transformation of knowledge. Considerations of simplicity and subtlety, power and precision, scope and selectivity, familiarity and freshness, are all relevant and often contend with one another; their weighting is relative to our interests, our information and our inquiry.

So much for the cognitive efficacy of symbolization in general, but what of aesthetic excellence in particular? Distinguishing between the aesthetic and the meritorious cuts both ways. If excellence is not required of the aesthetic, neither is the excellence appropriate to aesthetic objects confined to them. Rather, the general excellence just sketched becomes aesthetic when exhibited by aesthetic objects; that is, aesthetic merit is such excellence in any symbolic functioning that, by its particular constellation of attributes, qualifies as aesthetic. This subsumption of aesthetic under cognitive excellence calls for one more reminder that the cognitive, while contrasted with both the practical and the passive, does not exclude the sensory or the emotive, that what we know through art is felt in our bones and nerves and muscles as well as grasped by our minds, that all the sensitivity and responsiveness of the organism participates in the invention and interpretation of symbols.

The problem of ugliness dissolves; for pleasure and prettiness neither define nor measure either the aesthetic experience or the work of art. The pleasantness or unpleasantness of a symbol does not determine its general cognitive efficacy or its specifically aesthetic merit. *Macbeth* and the Goya *Witches' Sabbath* no more call for apology than do *Pygmalion* and the Botticelli *Venus*.

The dynamics of taste, often embarrassing to those who seek inflexible standards of immutable excellence, also become readily understandable. After a time and for a time, the finest painting may pall and the greatest music madden. A work may be successively offensive, fascinating, comfortable and boring. These are the vicissitudes of the vehicles and instruments of knowledge. We focus upon frontiers; the peak of interest in a symbol tends to occur at the time of revelation, somewhere midway in the passage from the obscure to the obvious. But there is endurance and renewal, too. Discoveries become available knowledge only when preserved in accessible form; the trenchant and laden symbol does not become worthless when it becomes familiar, but is incorporated in the base for further exploration. And where there is density in the symbol system, familiarity is never complete and final; another look may always disclose significant new subtleties. Moreover, what we read from and learn through a symbol varies with what we bring to it. Not only do we discover the world through our symbols but we understand and reappraise our symbols progressively in the light of our growing experience. Both the dynamics and the durability of aesthetic value are natural consequences of its cognitive character.

Like considerations explain the relevance to aesthetic merit of experience remote from the work. What a Manet or Monet or Cézanne does to our subsequent seeing of the world is as pertinent to their appraisal as is any direct confrontation. How our lookings at pictures and our listenings to music inform what we encounter later and elsewhere is integral to them as cognitive. The absurd and awkward myth of the insularity of aesthetic experience can be scrapped.

The role of theme and variation – common in architecture and other arts as well as in music – also becomes intelligible. Establishment and modification of motifs, abstraction and elaboration of patterns, differentiation and interrelation of modes of transformation, all are processes of constructive search; and the measures applicable are not those of passive enjoyment but those of cognitive efficacy: delicacy of discrimination, power of integration, and justice of proportion between recognition and discovery. Indeed, one typical way of advancing knowledge is by progressive variation upon a theme. Among modern composers, theme and variation along with all recognizable pattern is sometimes scorned, and maximum unpredictability is the declared aim; but as C. I. Lewis pointed out, complete irregularity is inconceivable – if no sequence is ever repeated in a given composition, that fact in itself constitutes a notable regularity.

Aesthetic merit, however, is by no means my main concern, and I am somewhat uncomfortable about having arrived at an incipient definition of what is often confusingly called 'beauty'. Excessive concentration on the question of excellence has been responsible, I think, for constriction and distortion of aesthetic inquiry. To say that a work of art is good or even to say how good it is does not after all provide much information, does not tell us whether the work is evocative, robust, vibrant or exquisitely designed, and still less what are its salient specific qualities of color, shape or sound. Moreover works of art are not racehorses, and picking a winner is not the primary goal. Conceiving of aesthetic experience as a form of understanding results both in resolving and in devaluing the question of aesthetic value.

In saying that aesthetic experience is cognitive experience distinguished by the dominance of certain symbolic characteristics and judged by standards of cognitive efficacy, have I overlooked the sharpest contrast: that in science, unlike art, the ultimate test is truth? Do not the two domains differ most drastically in that truth means all for the one, nothing for the other?

Despite rife doctrine, truth by itself matters very little in science. We can generate volumes of dependable truths at will so long as we are unconcerned with their importance; the multiplication tables are inexhaustible, and empirical truths abound. Scientific hypotheses, however true, are worthless unless they meet minimal demands of scope or specificity imposed by our inquiry, unless they effect some telling analysis or synthesis, unless they raise or answer significant questions. Truth is not enough; it is at most a necessary condition. But even this concedes too much; the noblest scientific laws are seldom quite true. Minor discrepancies are overridden in the interest of breadth or power or simplicity. Science denies its data as the statesman denies his constituents – within the limits of prudence.

Yet neither is truth one among competing criteria involved in the rating of scientific hypotheses. Given any assemblage of evidence, countless alternative hypotheses conform to it. We cannot choose among them on grounds of truth; for we have no direct access to their truth. Rather we judge them by such features as their simplicity and strength. These criteria are not supplemental to truth but applied hopefully as a means for arriving at the nearest approximation to truth that is compatible with our other interests.

Does this leave us with the cardinal residual difference that truth – though not enough, not necessary and not a touchstone for choosing among hypotheses – is nevertheless a consideration relevant in science but not in art? Even so meek a formulation suggests too strong a contrast. Truth of a hypothesis after all is a matter of fit – fit with a body of theory, and fit of hypothesis and theory to the data at hand and the facts to be encountered. And as Philipp Frank liked to remind us, goodness of fit takes a two-way adjustment – of theory to facts and of facts to theory – with the double aim of comfort and a new look. But such fitness, such aptness in conforming to and reforming our knowledge and our world, is equally relevant for the aesthetic symbol. Truth and its aesthetic counterpart amount to appropriateness under different names. If we speak of hypotheses but not of works of art as true, that is because we reserve the terms 'true' and 'false' for symbols in sentential form. I do not say this difference is negligible, but it is specific rather than generic, a difference in field of application rather than in formula, and marks no schism between the scientific and the aesthetic.

None of this is directed towards obliterating the distinction between art and science. Declarations of indissoluble unity – whether of the sciences, the arts, the arts and sciences together or of mankind – tend anyway to focus attention upon the differences. What I am stressing is that the affinities here are deeper, and the significant differentia other, than is often supposed. The difference between art and science is not that between feeling and fact, intuition and inference, delight and deliberation, synthesis and analysis, sensation and cerebration, concreteness and abstraction, passion and action, mediacy and immediacy, or truth and beauty, but rather a difference in domination of certain specific characteristics of symbols.

The implications of this reconception may go beyond philosophy. We hear a good deal about how the aptitudes and training needed for the arts and for the sciences contrast or even conflict with one another. Earnest and elaborate efforts to devise and test means of finding and fostering aesthetic abilities are always being initiated. But none of this talk or these trials can come to much without an adequate conceptual framework for designing crucial experiments and interpreting their results. Once the arts and sciences are seen to involve working with – inventing, applying, reading, transforming, manipulating – symbol systems that agree and differ in certain specific ways, we can perhaps undertake pointed psychological investigation of how the pertinent skills inhibit or enhance one another; and the outcome might well call for changes in educational technology. Our preliminary study suggests, for example, that some processes requisite for a science are less akin to each other than to some requisite for an art. But let us forego foregone conclusions. Firm and usable results are as far off as badly needed; and the time has come in this field for the false truism and the plangent platitude to give way to the elementary experiment and the hesitant hypothesis.

Whatever consequences might eventually be forthcoming for psychology or education would in any case count as by-products of the theoretical inquiry. The prior aim is to take some steps towards a systematic study of symbols and symbol systems and the ways they function in our perceptions and actions and arts and sciences, and thus in the creation and comprehension of our worlds.

SECTION FIVE

Art and Society

30   The Development of Modern Art

Julius Meier-Graefe

The incomprehensibility of painting and sculpture to the general public has been shrouded in a veil of pretentious exposition. The amount of talking and writing about art in our day exceeds that in all other epochs put together. The increase of sociability arising from increase of wealth made it necessary to invent suitable occupations for unproductive energies. Chatter about art became a highly popular form of such amusement; it requires no special preparation, no exertion, is independent of weather and seasons, and can be practised in drawing-rooms! Art has become like caviar – every one wants to have it, whether they like it or not. The immaterial elements of the former give a certain intellectual tone to the sport, which is lacking in a feast of caviar; it is therefore complacently opposed to such material enjoyments. The discussion of art in Germany (the home, par excellence, of such discussion) originated in the dark days of the nation during the first quarter of the nineteenth century, when men were dreaming romantically of the great things they lacked. Nevertheless, it was more fruitful than it is now; it was the sphere of great personalities, and the origin of an idealism, which, though impotent, was sincere. Nothing of all this has survived but a subsidiary function. It is the form of entertainment affected by families who do not give expensive dinner-parties. It has become the feudal cognisance of the aspiring bourgeoisie, as necessary to the well-educated as some indispensable garment.

Love of art, however, especially the kind of love that goes beyond platonic limits, becomes rarer as those who meddle with it multiply in every land. Purchase has become the touchstone of such affection; like marriage, it is a practical token of sentiment, and even to the artist, this evidence is generally more important than the impulse that inspired it.

It can hardly be otherwise now. If art is to be anything, it must not arouse merely that languid attention which people manifest when they politely approve something as 'very interesting'. It is not enough that it should inspire the pens of scribblers, and develop itself alone, and not others. In the form to which it is confined today – that of picture or statue, a marketable commodity – it could only exercise an influence by fulfilling the purpose of other marketable things: that of being purchased. But the popularisation of art is rendered impossible by the extravagant prices commanded by recognised works of art and demanded for those that are not so recognised, by a frantic, absurd and, unhappily, thoroughly dishonest traffic. I can conceive of rich people who would refrain from the purchase of pictures out of sheer disgust at the trade, a desire to keep their hands clean. The purchasing amateur is a personality made up of the most obscure springs of action. The absolutely incalculable fluctuations in prices, the influence of fashion, nowhere so demented as in this

Source: Julius Meier-Graefe, *Modern Art*, translated by F. Simmonds and G. W. Chrystal (Heinemann, 1908), pp. 5–9. First published in German in 1904.

connection, the desire to go on improving his collection, i.e., to bring it up to the fashionable standard of the moment, forces the collector to be always selling, to become the shamefaced dealer, who is, of course, the most shameless, and who introduces additional elements of disorder into a commerce already chaotic. The result is that there are, as a fact, no buyers, but only dealers, people who pile their pictures one above the other, deal exclusively, or almost exclusively, with each other, and have no connection with the real public. Statistics, showing how few are the hands to which the immense artistic wealth of the world is confined, would make a sensation. A great London dealer once told me that he had only three customers! Durand-Ruel, of Paris, has several times had certain famous Impressionist pictures in his possession at progressive prices, rising some 1000 per cent each time, and the purchasers have often been the same persons on several occasions.

Such conditions reduce the aesthetic usefulness of a work to a minimum. Pictures become securities, which can be kept locked up like papers. Even the individual, the owner, ceases to enjoy his possession. Nine-tenths of the most precious French pictures are kept for nine-tenths of the year in magnificent cases, to protect them from dust. Sales are effected as on the Bourse, and speculation plays an important part in the operations. The goods are scarcely seen, even at the sale. A typical, but by no means unique, example is afforded by the late Forbes collection. It consisted of I forget how many hundreds or thousands of pictures. To house them, the owner rented the upper storey of one of the largest London railway stations, vast storehouses, but all too circumscribed to allow of the hanging of the pictures. They stood in huge stacks against the walls, one behind the other: the Israels, Mauves and Marises were to be counted by hundreds, the French masters of 1830 by dozens; there were exquisite examples of Millet, Corot, Daubigny, Courbet, etc., and Whistler. Although the stacks of pictures were held up by muscular servants, the enjoyment of these treasures was a tremendously exhausting physical process. One walked between pictures; one felt capable of walking calmly over them! After five minutes in the musty atmosphere, goaded by the idiotic impulse to see as much as possible, and the irritating consciousness that it was impossible to grasp anything, every better instinct was stifled by an indifference that quenched all power of appreciation. The deathly calm one broke in upon, as one toiled sweating through these bare gigantic rooms where there was no space to turn, the whistling of the engines, the trembling of the floor as the trains ran in and out below, seemed to inspire a kind of strange fury, a silent longing to destroy the whole lot.

Who would be the loser if this were actually done? If anything could justify anarchism, it is the knowledge that the greatest artists toil in poverty, to enable a few dealers to grow rich after their deaths, and a few fanatics to hoard their works in warehouses. The most notorious vices are not so grotesquely irrational as this mania for hoarding, which, owing to its apparent innocuousness, has not yet been recognised as a malady. All the famous collectors of Paris, London and America are more or less tainted with this disease. We enter their houses full of eager anticipation, and quit them with a sigh of relief, half suffocated by the pictures that cover every inch of wall-space, and wholly depressed, not by a feeling of envy, but by the thought that there are people who have voluntarily accepted the torture of spending their lives among all these things.

Even if a wiser economy should improve the conditions we have described, it will never be possible to induce a better appreciation of art by commercial means. Hence all the fine ideas of 'popular art' are doomed to remain mere dreams. It is materially impossible to produce pure works of art at prices that will bring them within the means of the masses. The Fitzroy Society in England, and the publishers of the prints for the Rivière School in Paris made the attempt, and in Germany Thoma was inspired by the same ideal in the production of his lithographs. All these attempts have only served to stimulate the collecting mania. Every speculation that panders to this instinct is successful, whether it deals with postage stamps or pictures. There is no question of aesthetic principle in the matter. I believe that the plebeian would really prove accessible to a revival of artistic influences, if he could possess a picture of his own, to hang up. But a work of art could never be cheap enough for this, for if it cost but tenpence, the poor man will always prefer to save his tenpence, towards the purchase of something necessary to his physical well-being. An artistic propaganda that relies on purchasable and abstract works of art must always fail. It can only succeed by means of industry, by producing things which combine artistic and utilitarian qualities. As long as we neglect these, we need not wonder to find the artistic sense of the lower orders more depraved than at any other period of the world's history.

The social struggle is breaking down class distinction; the intelligent outcast of today is the millionaire of tomorrow. Nothing opposes the rise of the proletarian in the modern state, and he brings his lack of culture with him into his higher sphere. The man who has had no aesthetic stimulus in his period of development will, as a rule, have no lofty requirements when chance has made him an influential member of the community, though he may stimulate these, and so add a new source of error to those already present.

For what then do artists create, pending what is generally the posthumous consummation – that accumulation of their works described above? Some for an unattainable object, every step towards which is marked by tears and blood, an ideal that can only be described in somewhat metaphysical rhetoric: the satisfaction of a conscience that has no relation to extrusive things of a supernal ambition, grandiose and dazzling into conscious determination, in its consistent effort towards the elusive goal, amazing in the unconsciousness with which it achieves results that would seem only possible to the most strenuous toil. Creation for the sake of creation. A far-seeing idealism sustains them, the hope that they will succeed in giving a new form of beauty.

Sometimes that which appears to them in their confident self-knowledge their greatest work, is recognised by the enlightened at last, and becomes an eternal possession, a lasting element in after generations of artists, in whose works it lives in another form, completed by a new achievement it passes into the artistic heritage of the nation and finally plays its part in national culture. Others fail, not that their self-knowledge is at fault, but that their talent or their intelligence falls short. Their numeric preponderance is so great that they completely crowd out the few, and the limited demand of the public for pictures is supplied almost exclusively by them. I suppose that to every thousand painters of one class, there is not more than one of the other. Imagine such a proportion in any other calling!

But the artist can mislead the public more easily than can a man of any other profession, for setting aside the affinity of the herd for all that is superficial, a sort of halo surrounds the painter; he profits by a number of institutions very able to favour mediocrity which gives a certain importance to the metier as such, and are readily turned to account by the adroit.

Foremost among these is the art exhibition, an institution of a thoroughly bourgeois nature, due to the senseless immensity of the artistic output, and the consequent urgency of showing regularly what has been accomplished in the year. This institution may be considered the most important artistic medium of our age.

It would have a certain appositeness as a shop in the grand style, arranged with a luxury befitting the wares. But this purpose, which seems to be included in the general scheme, is quite subsidiary, as may be seen from a glance at the sale statistics.

Artists acquiesce in the system, because if they held aloof their last means of expression would be denied them. This they want at least, to let their work be seen, and see it themselves, even among that of thousands, even for a few months, even under barbaric conditions. What becomes of it after the exhibition is indifferent to them. It is enough if a picture fulfills its purpose at the exhibition, attracts attention, is discussed by the critics, and perhaps, even – this culminating distinction! – receives a medal.

To secure these results in competition with the thousands who are bent on the same ends, it is above all things necessary that a picture should have certain qualities that distinguish it from the rest. If the artist is bold enough he makes it very large, or at all events very insistent, that it may strike the eye even if badly hung.

It is obvious that under such conditions the purpose achieved by competition in other domains – that of promoting the selection of the best – can never be fulfilled. A variety of base impulses, which always urge on the compact majority against the loftier individuality, play their part in the results. Rarely, indeed, has a genius been brought to light through these channels. The greater artist avoids these exchanges and even the amateur does not frequent them, since quantity is not the only thing he craves.

31   Literature and Revolution

Leon Trotsky

The error of the 'Lef', at least of some of its theorists, appears to us in its most generalized form, when they make an ultimatum for the fusion of art with life. It is not to be argued that the separation of art from other aspects of social life was the result of the class structure of society, that the self-sufficient character of art is merely the reverse side of the fact that art became the property of the privileged classes, and that the evolution of art in the future will follow the path of a growing fusion with life, that is, with production, with popular holidays and with the collective group life. It is good that the 'Lef' understands this and explains it. But it is not good when they present a short-time ultimatum on the basis of the present-day art, when they say: leave your 'lathe' and fuse with life. In other words, the poets, the painters, the sculptors, the actors must cease to reflect, to depict, to write poems, to paint pictures, to carve sculptures, to speak before the footlights, but they must carry their art directly into life. But how, and where, and through what gates? Of course, one may hail every attempt to carry as much rhythm and sound and color as is possible into popular holidays and meetings and processions. But one must have a little historic vision, at least, to understand that between our present-day economic and cultural poverty and the time of the fusion of art with life, that is, between the time when life will reach such proportions that it will be entirely formed by art, more than one generation will have come and gone. Whether for good or for bad, the 'lathe-like' art will remain for many years more, and will be the instrument of the artistic and social development of the masses and their aesthetic enjoyment, and this is true not only of the art of painting, but of lyrics, novels, comedies, tragedies, sculpture and symphony. To reject art as a means of picturing and imaging knowledge because of one's opposition to the contemplative and impressionistic bourgeois art of the last few decades, is to strike from the hands of the class which is building a new society its most important weapon. Art, it is said, is not a mirror, but a hammer: it does not reflect, it shapes. But at present even the handling of a hammer is taught with the help of a mirror, a sensitive film which records all the movements. Photography and motion-picture photography, owing to their passive accuracy of depiction, are becoming important educational instruments in the field of labor. If one cannot get along without a mirror, even in shaving oneself, how can one reconstruct oneself or one's life, without seeing oneself in the 'mirror' of literature? Of course no one speaks about an exact mirror. No one even thinks of asking the new literature to have a mirror-like impassivity. The deeper literature is, and the more it is imbued with the desire to shape life, the more significantly and dynamically it will be able to 'picture' life. [. . .]

In reply to criticisms against the 'Lef', which are often more insulting than convincing, the point is emphasized that the 'Lef' is still constantly seeking.

Source: Leon Trotsky, *Literature and Revolution* (The University of Michigan Press, 1968), pp. 136–161. Written in 1923.

Undoubtedly the 'Lef' seeks more than it has found. But this is not a sufficient reason why the Party cannot do that which is persistently recommended, and canonize the 'Lef' or even a definite wing of it, as 'Communist art'. It is as impossible to canonize seekings as it is impossible to arm an army with an unrealized invention.

But does this mean that the 'Lef' stands absolutely on a false road, and that we can have nothing to do with it? No, it does not mean this. The situation is not that the Party has definite and fixed ideas on the question of art in the future, and that a certain group is sabotaging them. This is not the case at all. The Party has not, and cannot have, ready-made decisions on versification, on the evolution of the theater, on the renovation of the literary language, on architectural style, etc., just as in another field the Party has not and cannot have ready-made decisions on the best kind of fertilization, on the most correct organization of transport, and on the most perfect machine guns. But as regards machine guns and transportation and fertilization, the practical decisions are needed immediately. What does the Party do then? It assigns certain Party workers to the task of considering and mastering these problems, and it checks up these Party workers by the practical results of their achievements. In the field of art the question is both simpler and more complex. As far as the political use of art is concerned, or the impossibility of allowing such use by our enemies, the Party has sufficient experience, insight, decision and resource. But the actual development of art, and its struggle for new forms are not part of the Party's tasks, nor are they its concern. The Party does not delegate anyone for such work. At the same time, a certain point of contact exists between the problems of art, politics, technique and economics. It is necessary for the inner interdependence of these problems. This is what the group of the 'Lef' is concerned with. This group plays tricks, plunges to this side and that, and – let them not be offended by this – does a good deal of theoretical bluffing. But did we not, and are we not also bluffing in fields much more vitally important? In the second place, did we try seriously to correct errors of theoretic approach or of partisan enthusiasm in practical work? We have no reason to doubt that the 'Lef' group is striving seriously to work in the interest of Socialism, that it is profoundly interested in the problems of art, and that it wants to be guided by a Marxian criterion. Why, then, do they begin with a rupture, and not with an effort to influence and to assimilate? The question is not at all so imminent. The Party has plenty of time for an examining, for a careful influencing and a selection. Or have we so much skilled strength that we can so light-heartedly be wasteful of it? But the centre of gravity lies, after all, not in the theoretic elaboration of the problems of the new art, but in its poetic expression. What is the situation as regards the artistic expression of Futurism and its gropings and accomplishments? Here there is even less ground for haste and intolerance.

Today, one can hardly deny entirely the Futurist achievements in art, especially in poetry. With very few exceptions, all our present-day poetry has been influenced by Futurism, directly or indirectly. One cannot dispute Mayakovsky's influence on a whole series of proletarian poets. Constructivism has also made significant conquests, though not at all in the direction it had marked out for itself. Articles are continually being published on the complete futility and on the counter-revolutionary character of Futurism between covers made by the hand of the Constructivist. In the most official editions, Futurist poems are published side by side with the most destructive summings up of Futurism. The Proletkult [the organization for proletarian culture] is united to the Futurists by living cords. *Gorn* is edited at present in a quite clear spirit of Futurism. To be sure, there is no use exaggerating the significance of these facts, because they take place, as in the great majority of all our groups of art, in an upper and for the time being quite superficial stratum, and are very feebly connected with the working masses. But it would be stupid to close one's eyes to these facts, and to treat Futurism as a charlatan invention of a decadent intelligentsia. Even if tomorrow the fact will be disclosed that the strength of Futurism is declining – and I do not consider this quite impossible – today, at any rate, the strength of Futurism is greater than all those tendencies at whose expense Futurism is spreading. [. . .]

When one breaks a hand or a leg, the bones, the tendons, the muscles, the arteries, the nerves and the skin do not break and tear in one line, nor afterwards do they grow together and heal at the same time. So, in a revolutionary break in the life of society, there is no simultaneousness and no symmetry of processes either in the ideology of society, or in its economic structure. The ideologic premises which are needed for the revolution are formed before the revolution, and the most important ideologic deductions from the revolution appear only much later. It would be extremely flippant to establish by analogies and comparisons the identity of Futurism and Communism, and so form the deduction that Futurism is the art of the proletariat. Such pretensions must be rejected. But this does not signify a contemptuous attitude towards the work of the Futurists. In our opinion they are the necessary links in the forming of a new and great literature. But they will prove to be only a significant episode in its evolution. To prove this, one has to approach the question more concretely and historically. The Futurists in their way are right when, in answer to the reproach that their works are above the heads of the masses, they say that Marx's *Capital* is also above their heads. Of course the masses are culturally and aesthetically unprepared, and will rise only slowly. But this is only one of the causes of it being above their heads. There is another cause. In its methods and in its forms, Futurism carries within itself clear traces of that world, or rather, of that little world in which it was born, and which – psychologically and not logically – it has not left to this very day. It is just as difficult to strip Futurism of the robe of the intelligentsia as it is to separate form from content. And when this happens, Futurism will undergo such a profound qualitative change that it will cease to be Futurism. This is going to happen, but not tomorrow. But even today one can say with certainty that much in Futurism will be useful and will serve to elevate and to revive art, if Futurism will learn to stand on its own legs, without any attempt to have itself decreed official by the government, as happened in the beginning of the Revolution. The new forms must find for themselves, and independently, an access into the consciousness of the advanced elements of the working class as the latter develop culturally. Art cannot live and cannot develop without a flexible atmosphere of sympathy around it. On this road, and on no other, does the process of complex inter-relation lie ahead. The cultural growth of the working class will help and influence those innovators who really hold something in their bosom. The mannerisms which inevitably crop out in all small groups will fall away, and from the vital sprouts will come fresh forms for the solution of new artistic tasks. This process implies, first of all, an accumulation of material culture, a growth of prosperity and a development of technique. There is no other road. It is impossible to think seriously that history will simply conserve the works of the Futurists, and will serve them up to the masses after many years, when the masses will have become ripe for them. This, of course, would be *passéism* of the purest kind. When that time, which is not immediate, will come, and the cultural and aesthetic education of the working masses will destroy the wide chasm between the creative intelligentsia and the people, art will have a different aspect from what it has today. In the evolution of that art, Futurism will prove to have been a necessary link. And is this so very little?

32   The Author as Producer

Walter Benjamin

The task is to win over the intellectuals to the working class by making them aware of the identity of their enterprises and of their conditions as producers.

Ramon Fernandez

You will remember how Plato, in his model state, deals with poets. He banishes them from it in the public interest. He had a high conception of the power of poetry. But he believed it harmful, superfluous – in a *perfect* community, of course. The question of the poet's right to exist has not often, since then, been posed with the same emphasis; but today it poses itself. Probably it is only seldom posed in this *form*. But it is more or less familiar to you all as the question of the autonomy of the poet: of his freedom to write whatever he pleases. You are not disposed to grant him this autonomy. You believe that the present social situation compels him to decide in whose service he is to place his activity. The bourgeois writer of entertainment literature does not acknowledge this choice. You prove to him that, without admitting it, he is working in the service of certain class interests. A more advanced type of writer does recognize this choice. His decision, taken on the basis of a class struggle, is to side with the proletariat. That puts an end to his autonomy. His activity is now decided by what is useful to the proletariat in the class struggle. Such writing is commonly called *tendentious*.

There you have the catchword around which has long circled a debate familiar to you. Its familiarity tells you how unfruitful it has been. For it has not advanced beyond the monotonous reiteration of arguments for and against: *on one hand*, the correct political line is demanded of the poet; *on the other*, it is justifiable to expect his work to have quality. Such a formulation is of course unsatisfactory as long as the connection between the two factors, political line and quality, has not been *perceived*. Of course, the connection can be asserted dogmatically. You can declare: a work that shows the correct political tendency need show no other quality. You can also declare: a work that exhibits the correct tendency must of necessity have every other quality.

This second formulation is not uninteresting, and further: it is correct. I make it my own. But in doing so I abstain from asserting it dogmatically. It must be *proved*. And it is in order to attempt to prove it that I now claim your attention. This is, you will perhaps object, a very specialized, out-of-the-way theme. And how do I intend to promote the study of fascism with such a proof? That is indeed my intention. For I hope to be able to show you that the concept of political tendency, in the summary form in which it usually occurs in the debate just mentioned, is a perfectly useless instrument of political literary criticism. I should like to show you that the tendency

Source: Walter Benjamin, *The Author as Producer*, address delivered at the Institute for the Study of Fascism, Paris, 27 April, 1934. Reproduced in *Reflections*, translated by Edmund Jephcott, published exclusively in the United States and Canada by Harcourt Brace Jovanovich Inc., and used by permission of Harcourt Brace Jovanovich Inc. An alternative translation appears in *Understanding Brecht*, New Left Books, 1977.

of a literary work can only be politically correct if it is also literarily correct. That is to say that the politically correct tendency includes a literary tendency. And I would add straight away: this literary tendency, which is implicitly or explicitly contained in every *correct* political tendency, alone constitutes the quality of the work. The correct political tendency of a work includes its literary quality *because* it includes its literary *tendency*. [. . .]

Social conditions are, as we know, determined by conditions of production. And when materialist criticism approached a work, it was accustomed to ask how this work stood in relation to the social relations of productions of its time. This is an important question. But also a very difficult one. Its answer is not always unambiguous. And I should like now to propose to you a more immediate question. A question that is somewhat more modest, somewhat less far-reaching, but which has, it seems to me, more chance of receiving an answer. Instead of asking: what is the attitude of a work to the relations of production of its time? does it accept them? is it reactionary – or does it aim at overthrowing them? is it revolutionary? – Instead of this question, or at any rate before this question, I should like to propose another. Rather than asking: what is the *attitude* of a work to the relations of production of its time? I should like to ask: what is its *position* in them? This question directly concerns the function the work has within the literary relations of production of its time. It is concerned, in other words, directly with the literary *technique* of works.

In the concept of technique, I have named that concept which makes literary products directly accessible to a social and therefore a materialist analysis. At the same time, the concept of technique provides the dialectical starting point from which the unfruitful antithesis of form and content can be surpassed. And furthermore, this concept of technique contains an indication of the correct determination of the relation between tendency and quality, the question raised at the outset. If, therefore, we stated earlier that the correct political tendency of a work includes its literary quality, because it includes its literary tendency, we can now formulate this more precisely by saying that this literary tendency can consist either of progress or of regression in literary technique. [. . .]

For the transformation of the forms and instruments of production in the way desired by a progressive intelligentsia – that is, one interested in freeing the means of production and serving the class struggle – Brecht coined the term *Umfunktionierung*. He was the first to make of intellectuals the far-reaching demand: not to supply the apparatus of production without, to the utmost extent possible, changing it in accordance with socialism. 'The publication of the *Versuche*,' the author writes in introducing the series of writings bearing this title, 'occurred at a time when certain works ought no longer to be individual experiences (have the character of works), but should rather concern the use (transformation) of certain institutes and institutions.' It is not spiritual renewal, as fascists proclaim, that is desirable: technical innovations are suggested. I shall come back to these innovations. I should like to content myself here with a reference to the decisive difference between the mere supplying of a productive apparatus and its transformation. And I should like to preface my discussion of the 'New Matter-of-Factness' with the proposition that to supply a productive apparatus without – to the utmost extent possible – changing it would still be a highly censurable course even if the material with which it is supplied seemed to be of a revolutionary nature. For we are faced by the fact – of which the past decade in Germany has furnished an abundance of examples – that the bourgeois apparatus of production and publication can assimilate astonishing qualities of revolutionary themes, indeed, can propagate them without calling its own existence, and the existence of the class which owns it, seriously into question. This remains true at least as long as it is supplied by hack writers, even though they be revolutionary hacks. I define the hack writer as the man who abstains in principle from alienating the productive apparatus from the ruling class by improving it in ways serving the interests of socialism. And I further maintain that a considerable proportion of so-called left-wing literature possessed no other social function than to wring from the political situation a continuous stream of novel effects for the entertainment of the public. This brings me to the New Matter-of-Factness. Its stock-in-trade was reportage. Let us ask ourselves to whom this technique was useful.

For the sake of clarity I shall place its photographic form in the foreground. What is true of this can be applied to the literary form. Both owe the extraordinary increase in their popularity to the technology of publication: the radio and the illustrated press. Let us think back to Dadaism. The revolutionary strength of Dadaism consisted in testing art for its authenticity. Still-lifes put together from tickets, spools of thread, cigarette butts, were linked with artistic elements. They put the whole thing in a frame. And they thereby show the public: look, your picture frame ruptures the age; the tiniest authentic fragment of daily life says more than paintings. Just as the bloody finger print of a murderer on a page of a book says more than the text. Much of this revolutionary content has sought survival in photo-montage. You need only think of the work of John Heartfield, whose technique made the book cover into a political instrument. But now follow the path of photography further. What do you see? It becomes ever more *nuancé*, ever more modern, and the result is that it can no longer photograph a tenement block or a refuse heap without transfiguring it. It goes without saying that it is unable to say anything of a power station or a cable factory other than this: what a beautiful world! *A Beautiful World* – that is a title of the well-known picture anthology by Renger-Patsch, in which we see New Matter-of-Fact photography at its peak. For it has succeeded in making even abject poverty, by recording it in a fashionably perfected manner, into an object of enjoyment. For if it is an economic function of photography to restore to mass consumption, by fashionable adaptation, subjects that had earlier withdrawn themselves from it – springtime, famous people, foreign countries – it is one of its political functions to renew from within – in other words: fashionably – the world as it is.

Here we have a flagrant example of what it means to supply a productive apparatus without changing it. To change it would have meant to overthrow another of the barriers, to transcend another of the antitheses, which fetter the production of intellectuals. In this case, the barrier between writing and image. What we require of the photographer is the ability to give his picture that caption which wrenches it from modish commerce and gives it revolutionary use-value. But we shall make this demand most emphatically when we – the writers – take up photography. Here, too, therefore, technical progress is for the author as producer the foundation of his political progress. In other words: only by transcending the specialization in the process of production which, in the bourgeois view, constitutes its order, is this production made politically valuable; and the limits imposed by specialization must be breached jointly by both the productive forces that they were set up to divide. The author as producer discovers – in discovering his solidarity with the proletariat – that simultaneity with certain other producers who earlier seemed scarcely to concern him. [. . .]

I spoke of the procedure of a certain modish photography whereby poverty is made an object of consumption. In turning to New Matter-of-Factness as a literary movement, I must take a step further and say that it has made the *struggle against poverty* an object of consumption. The political importance of the movement was indeed exhausted in many cases by the conversion of revolutionary reflexes, insofar as they occurred in the bourgeoisie, into objects of amusement which found their way without difficulty into the big-city cabaret business. The transformation of the political struggle from a compulsion to decide into an object of contemplative enjoyment, from a means of production into a consumer article, is the defining characteristic of this literature. A perceptive critic has explained this, using the example of Erich Kästner, as follows: 'With the workers' movement this left-wing radical intelligentsia has nothing in common. [. . .] Their function is to produce, from the political standpoint, not parties but cliques; from the literary standpoint, not schools but fashions; from the economic standpoint, not producers but agents. Agents or hacks who make a great display of their poverty, and a banquet of yawning emptiness. One could not be more totally accommodated in an uncozy situation.'

This school, I said, made a great display of its poverty. It thereby shirked the most urgent task of the present-day writer: to recognize how poor he is and how poor he has to be in order to begin again from the beginning. For that is what is involved. The Soviet state will not, it is true, banish the poet like Plato, but it will assign him tasks which do not permit him to display in new masterpieces the long-since counterfeit wealth of creative personality. To expect a renewal in terms of such personalities and such works is a privilege of fascism.[. . .] [The work of] the author who has reflected deeply on the conditions of present-day production will never be merely work on products but always, at the same time, on the means of production. In other words: his products must have, over and above their character as works, an organizing function, and in no way must their organizational usefulness be confined to their value as propaganda. Their political tendency alone is not enough. The excellent Lichtenberg has said: 'A man's opinions are not what matters, but the kind of man these opinions make of him.' Now it is true that opinions matter greatly, but the best are of no use if they make nothing useful out of those who have them. The best political tendency is wrong if it does not demonstrate the attitude with which it is to be followed. And this attitude the writer can only demonstrate in his particular activity: that is in writing. A political tendency is the necessary, never the sufficient condition of the organizing function of a work. This further requires a directing, instructing stance on the part of the writer. And today this is to be demanded more than ever before. *An author who teaches writers nothing, teaches no one*. What matters therefore is the exemplary character of production, which is able first to induce other producers to produce, and second to put an improved apparatus at their disposal. And this apparatus is better the more consumers it is able to turn into producers, that is, readers or spectators into collaborators. [. . .]

33   The Work of Art in the Age of Mechanical Reproduction

Walter Benjamin

I

In principle a work of art has always been reproducible. Man-made artifacts could always be imitated by men. Replicas were made by pupils in practice of their craft, by masters for diffusing their works, and, finally, by third parties in the pursuit of gain. Mechanical reproduction of a work of art, however, represents something new. Historically, it advanced intermittently and in leaps at long intervals, but with accelerated intensity. The Greeks knew only two procedures of technically reproducing works of art: founding and stamping. Bronzes, terra cottas and coins were the only art works which they could produce in quantity. All others were unique and could not be mechanically reproduced. With the woodcut graphic art became mechanically reproducible for the first time, long before script became reproducible by print. The enormous changes which printing, the mechanical reproduction of writing, has brought about in literature are a familiar story. However, within the phenomenon which we are here examining from the perspective of world history, print is merely a special, though particularly important, case. During the Middle Ages engraving and etching were added to the woodcut; at the beginning of the nineteenth century lithography made its appearance.

With lithography the technique of reproduction reached an essentially new stage. This much more direct process was distinguished by the tracing of the design on a stone rather than its incision on a block of wood or its etching on a copperplate and permitted graphic art for the first time to put its products on the market, not only in large numbers as hitherto, but also in daily changing forms. Lithography enabled graphic art to illustrate everyday life, and it began to keep pace with printing. But only a few decades after its invention, lithography was surpassed by photography. For the first time in the process of pictorial reproduction, photography freed the hand of the most important artistic functions which henceforth devolved only upon the eye looking into a lens. Since the eye perceives more swiftly than the hand can draw, the process of pictorial reproduction was accelerated so enormously that it could keep pace with speech. A film operator shooting a scene in the studio captures the images at the speed of an actor's speech. Just as lithography virtually implied the illustrated newspaper, so did photography foreshadow the sound film. The technical reproduction of sound was tackled at the end of the last

Source: H. Arendt (ed.), *Illuminations* (Cape, 1970), pp. 219–226. Originally published in *Zeitschrift für Sozialforschung* V, 1, 1936. Footnotes have been omitted. Abridged from Walter Benjamin, *Illuminations* © 1955 by Suhrkamp Verlag, Frankfurt. English translation by Harry Zohn, edited by Hannah Arendt, © 1968 by Harcourt Bracc Jovanovich Inc. Reproduced by permission of Harcourt Brace Jovanovich Inc. and Jonathan Cape Limited.

century. [. . .] Around 1900 technical reproduction had reached a standard that not only permitted it to reproduce all transmitted works of art and thus to cause the most profound change in their impact upon the public; it also had captured a place of its own among the artistic processes. For the study of this standard nothing is more revealing than the nature of the repercussions that these two different manifestations – the reproduction of works of art and the art of the film – have had on art in its traditional form.

II

Even the most perfect reproduction of a work of art is lacking in one element: its presence in time and space, its unique existence at the place where it happens to be. This unique existence of the work of art determined the history to which it was subject throughout the time of its existence. This includes the changes which it may have suffered in physical condition over the years as well as the various changes in its ownership. The traces of the first can be revealed only by chemical or physical analyses which it is impossible to perform on a reproduction; changes of ownership are subject to a tradition which must be traced from the situation of the original.

The presence of the original is the prerequisite to the concept of authenticity. Chemical analyses of the patina of a bronze can help to establish this, as does the proof that a given manuscript of the Middle Ages stems from an archive of the fifteenth century. The whole sphere of authenticity is outside technical – and, of course, not only technical – reproducibility. Confronted with its manual reproduction, which was usually branded as a forgery, the original preserved all its authority; not so *vis à vis* technical reproduction. The reason is twofold. First, process reproduction is more independent of the original than manual reproduction. For example, in photography, process reproduction can bring out those aspects of the original that are unattainable to the naked eye yet accessible to the lens, which is adjustable and chooses its angle at will. And photographic reproduction, with the aid of certain processes, such as enlargement or slow motion, can capture images which escape natural vision. Secondly, technical reproduction can put the copy of the original into situations which would be out of reach for the original itself. Above all, it enables the original to meet the beholder halfway, be it in the form of a photograph or a phonograph record. The cathedral leaves its locale to be received in the studio of a lover of art; the choral production, performed in an auditorium or in the open air, resounds in the drawing room.

The situations into which the product of mechanical reproduction can be brought may not touch the actual work of art, yet the quality of its presence is always depreciated. This holds not only for the art work but also, for instance, for a landscape which passes in review before the spectator in a movie. In the case of the art object, a most sensitive nucleus – namely, its authenticity – is interfered with whereas no natural object is vulnerable on that score. The authenticity of a thing is the essence of all that is transmissible from its beginning, ranging from its substantive duration to its testimony to the history which it has experienced. Since the historical testimony rests on the authenticity, the former, too, is jeopardized by reproduction when substantive duration ceases to matter. And what is really jeopardized when the historical testimony is affected is the authority of the object. One might subsume the eliminated element in the term 'aura' and go on to say:

that which withers in the age of mechanical reproduction is the aura of the work of art. This is a symptomatic process whose significance points beyond the realm of art. One might generalize by saying: the technique of reproduction detaches the reproduced object from the domain of tradition. By making many reproductions it substitutes a plurality of copies for a unique existence. And in permitting the reproduction to meet the beholder or listener in his own particular situation, it reactivates the object reproduced. These two processes lead to a tremendous shattering of tradition which is the obverse of the contemporary crisis and renewal of mankind. Both processes are intimately connected with the contemporary mass movements. Their most powerful agent is the film. Its social significance, particularly in its most positive form, is inconceivable without its destructive, cathartic aspect, that is, the liquidation of the traditional value of the cultural heritage. [. . .]

III

During long periods of history, the mode of human sense perception changes with humanity's entire mode of existence. The manner in which human sense perception is organized, the medium in which it is accomplished, is determined not only by nature but by historical circumstances as well. The fifth century, with its great shifts of population, saw the birth of the late Roman art industry and the Vienna Genesis, and there developed not only an art different from that of antiquity but also a new kind of perception. The scholars of the Viennese school, Riegl and Wickhoff, who resisted the weight of classical tradition under which these later art forms had been buried, were the first to draw conclusions from them concerning the organization of perception at the time. However far-reaching their insight, these scholars limited themselves to showing the significant, formal hallmark which characterized perception in late Roman times. They did not attempt – and, perhaps, saw no way – to show the social transformations expressed by these changes of perception. The conditions for an analogous insight are more favorable in the present. And if changes in the medium of contemporary perception can be comprehended as decay of the aura, it is possible to show its social causes.

The concept of aura which was proposed above with reference to historical objects may usefully be illustrated with reference to the aura of natural ones. We define the aura of the latter as the unique phenomenon of a distance, however close it may be. If, while resting on a summer afternoon, you follow with your eyes a mountain range on the horizon or a branch which casts its shadow over you, you experience the aura of those mountains, of that branch. This image makes it easy to comprehend the social bases of the contemporary decay of the aura. It rests on two circumstances, both of which are related to the increasing significance of the masses in contemporary life. Namely, the desire of contemporary masses to bring things 'closer' spatially and humanly, which is just as ardent as their bent towards overcoming the uniqueness of every reality by accepting its reproduction. Every day the urge grows stronger to get hold of an object at very close range by way of its likeness, its reproduction. Unmistakably, reproduction as offered by picture magazines and newsreels differs from the image seen by the unarmed eye. Uniqueness and permanence are as closely linked in the latter as are transitoriness and reproducibility in the former. To pry an object from its shell, to destroy its aura, is the mark of a perception whose 'sense of the universal equality of things' has increased to such a degree that it extracts it even from a unique object by means of reproduction. Thus is manifested in the field of perception what in the theoretical sphere is noticeable in the increasing importance of statistics. The adjustment of reality to the masses and of the masses to reality is a process of unlimited scope, as much for thinking as for perception.

IV

The uniqueness of a work of art is inseparable from its being imbedded in the fabric of tradition. This tradition itself is thoroughly alive and extremely changeable. An ancient statue of Venus, for example, stood in a different traditional context with the Greeks, who made it an object of veneration, than with the clerics of the Middle Ages, who viewed it as an ominous idol. Both of them, however, were equally confronted with its uniqueness, that is, its aura. Originally the contextual integration of art in tradition found its expression in the cult. We know that the earliest art works originated in the service of a ritual – first the magical, then the religious kind. It is significant that the existence of the work of art with reference to its aura is never entirely separated from its ritual function. In other words, the unique value of the 'authentic' work of art has its basis in ritual, the location of its original use value. This ritualistic basis, however remote, is still recognizable as secularized ritual even in the most profane forms of the cult of beauty. The secular cult of beauty, developed during the Renaissance and prevailing for three centuries, clearly showed that ritualistic basis in its decline and the first deep crisis which befell it. With the advent of the first truly revolutionary means of reproduction, photography, simultaneously with the rise of socialism, art sensed the approaching crisis which has become evident a century later. At the time, art reacted with the doctrine of *l'art pour l'art*, that is, with a theology of art. This gave rise to what might be called a negative theology in the form of the idea of 'pure' art, which not only denied any social function of art but also any categorizing by subject matter. (In poetry, Mallarmé was the first to take this position.)

An analysis of art in the age of mechanical reproduction must do justice to these relationships, for they lead us to an all-important insight: for the first time in world history, mechanical reproduction emancipates the work of art from its parasitical dependence on ritual. To an ever greater degree the work of art reproduced becomes the work of art designed for reproducibility. From a photographic negative, for example, one can make any number of prints; to ask for the 'authentic' print makes no sense. But the instant the criterion of authenticity ceases to be applicable to artistic production, the total function of art is reversed. Instead of being based on ritual, it begins to be based on another practice – politics.

34   Poetic Evidence

Paul Eluard

The time has come for poets to proclaim their right and duty to maintain that they are deeply involved in the life of other men, in communal life.

On the high peaks! – yes, I know there have always been a few to try and delude us with that sort of nonsense; but, as they were not there, they have not been able to tell us that it was raining there, that it was dark and bitterly cold, that there one was still aware of man and his misery; that there one was still aware and had to be aware of vile stupidity, and still hear muddy laughter and the words of death. On the high peaks, as elsewhere, more than elsewhere perhaps, for him who sees, for the visionary, misery undoes and remakes incessantly a world, drab, vulgar, unbearable and impossible.

No greatness exists for him that would grow. There is no model for him that seeks what he has never seen. We all belong to the same rank. Let us do away with the others.

Employing contradictions purely as a means to equality, and unwilling to please and be self-satisfied, poetry has always *applied itself*, in spite of all sorts of persecutions, to refusing to serve other than its own ends, an undesirable fame and the various advantages bestowed upon conformity and prudence.

And what of pure poetry? Poetry's absolute power will purify men, all men. 'Poetry must be made by all. Not by one.' So said Lautréamont. All the ivory towers will be demolished, all speech will be holy, and, having at last come into the reality which is his, man will need only to shut his eyes to see the gates of wonder opening.

Bread is more useful than poetry. But love, in the full, human sense of the word, the passion of love is not more useful than poetry. Since man puts himself at the top of the scale of living things, he cannot deny value to his feelings, however non-productive they may be. 'Man,' says Feuerbach, 'has the same senses as the animals, but in man sensation is not relative and subordinated to life's lower needs – it is an absolute being, having its own end and its own enjoyment.' This brings us back to necessity. Man has constantly to be aware of his supremacy over nature in order to guard himself against it and conquer it.

In his adolescence man is obsessed by the nostalgia of his childhood; in his maturity, by the nostalgia of his youth; in old age, by the bitterness of having lived. The poet's images grow out of something to be forgotten and something to be remembered. Wearily he projects his prophecies into the past. Everything he creates vanishes with the man he was yesterday. Tomorrow holds out the promise of novelty. But there is no today in his present.

Imagination lacks the imitative instinct. It is the spring and torrent which we do not re-ascend. Out of this living sleep daylight is ever born and ever dying it returns there. It is a universe without association, a universe which is not a part of a greater

Source: H. Read (ed.), *Surrealism* (Faber, 1936), pp. 171–183. Originally given as a lecture at the New Burlington Galleries, 24 June 1936. Translated by George Reavey. Illustrations have been omitted.

universe, a godless universe, since it never lies, since it never confuses what will be with what has been. It is the truth, the whole truth, the wandering palace of the imagination. Truth is quickly told, unreflectingly, plainly; and for it, sadness, rage, gravity and joy are but changes of the weather and seductions of the skies.

The poet is he who inspires more than he who is inspired. Poems always have great white margins, great margins of silence where eager memory consumes itself in order to re-create an ecstasy without a past. Their principal quality is, I insist again, not to invoke but to inspire. So many love poems without an immediate object will, one fine day, bring lovers together. One ponders over a poem as one does over a human being. Understanding, like desire, like hatred, is composed of the relationship between the thing to be understood and the other things, either understood or not understood.

It is his hope or his despair which will determine for the watchful dreamer – for the poet – the workings of his imagination. Let him formulate this hope or despair and his relationship with the world will immediately change. For the poet everything is the object of sensations and, consequently, of sentiments. Everything concrete becomes food for his imagination, and the motives of hope and despair, together with their sensations and sentiments, are resolved into concrete form.

I have called my contribution to this volume 'Poetic Evidence'. For if words are often the medium of the poetry of which I speak, neither can any other form of expression be denied it. Surrealism is a state of mind.

For a long time degraded to the status of scribes, painters used to copy apples and become virtuosos. Their vanity, which is immense, has almost always urged them to settle down in front of a landscape, an object, an image, a text, as in front of a wall, in order to reproduce it. They did not hunger for themselves. But Surrealist painters, who are poets, always think of something else. The unprecedented is familiar to them, premeditation unknown. They are aware that the relationships between things fade as soon as they are established, to give place to other relationships just as fugitive. They know that no description is adequate, that nothing can be reproduced literally. They are all animated by the same striving to liberate the vision, to unite imagination and nature, to consider all possibilities a reality, to prove to us that no dualism exists between the imagination and reality, that everything the human spirit can conceive and create springs from the same vein, is made of the same matter as his flesh and blood, and the world around him. They know that communication is the only link between that which sees and that which is seen, the striving to understand and to relate – and, sometimes, that of determining and creating. To see is to understand, to judge, to deform, to forget or forget oneself, to be or to cease to be.

Those who come here to laugh or give vent to their indignation, those who, when confronted with Surrealist poesy, either written or painted, talk of snobbism in order to hide their lack of understanding, their fear or their hatred, are like those who tortured Galileo, burned Rousseau's books, defamed William Blake, condemned Baudelaire, Swinburne and Flaubert, declared that Goya or Courbet did not know how to paint, whistled down Wagner and Stravinsky, imprisoned Sade. They claim to be on the side of good sense, wisdom and order, the better to satisfy their ignoble appetites, exploit men, prevent them from liberating themselves – that they may the better degrade and destroy men by means of ignorance, poverty and war.

The genealogical tree painted upon one of the walls of the dining-room of the old house in the north of France, inhabited by the present counts de Sade, has only one blank leaf, that of Donatien Alphonse François de Sade, who was imprisoned in turn by Louis XV, Louis XVI, the Convention and Napoleon. Interned for thirty years, he died in a madhouse, more lucid and pure than any of his contemporaries.

In 1789, he who had indeed deserved the title of the 'Divine Marquis' bestowed upon him in mockery, called upon the people from his cell in the Bastille to come to the rescue of the prisoners: in 1793, though devoted body and soul to the revolution, and a member of the *Section des Piques*, he protested against the death penalty, and reproved the crimes perpetrated without passion: he remained an atheist when Robespierre introduced his new cult of the Supreme Being; he dared to pit his genius against that of the whole people just beginning to feel its new freedom. No sooner out of prison than he sent the First Consul the first copy of a pamphlet attacking him.

Sade wished to give back to civilised man the force of his primitive instincts, he wished to liberate the amorous imagination from its fixations. He believed that in this way, and only in this way, would true equality be born.

Since virtue is its own reward, he strove, in the name of all suffering, to abase and humiliate it; he strove to impose upon it the supreme law of unhappiness, that it might help all those it incites to build a world befitting man's immense stature. Christian morality, which, as we often have to admit to our despair and shame, is not yet done with, is no more than a mockery. All the appetites of the imaginative body revolt against it. How much longer must we clamour, struggle and weep before the figures of love become those of facility and freedom?

Let us now listen to Sade and his profound unhappiness: 'To love and to enjoy are two very different things: the proof is that we love daily without enjoyment, and more often still we enjoy without loving.' And he concludes: 'Moments of isolated enjoyment thus have their charms, they may even possess them to a greater degree than other moments; yes, and if it were not so, how would so many old men, so many dissemblers and people full of blemishes, enjoy themselves? They are sure of not being loved; they are certain that it is impossible to share their experience. But is their pleasure any the less for that?'

And justifying those men who introduce some singularity into the things of love, Sade rises up against those who regard love as proper only to the perpetuation of their miserable race. . . . 'Pedants, executioners, turnkeys, legislators, tonsured rabble, what will become of you when we shall have reached that point? What will become of your laws, of your morality, of your religion, of your gallows, of your paradise, of your gods, of your hell, when it shall be demonstrated that such and such a flow of liquids, such a kind of fibre, such a degree of acidity in the blood or in the animal spirits, is sufficient to make a man the object of your penalties or of your rewards?'

It is his perfect pessimism which gives his words their sober truth. Surrealist poetry, the poetry of always, has never achieved more. These are sombre truths which appear in the works of true poets, but they are truths, and almost all the rest is false. And let us not be accused of contradiction when we say this! Let them not try to bring against us our revolutionary materialism! Let them not tell us that man must live first of all by bread! The maddest and the most solitary of the poets we love have perhaps put food in its proper place, but that place is the highest of all because it is both symbolical and total. For everything is re-absorbed in it.

There is no portrait of the Marquis de Sade in existence. It is significant that there is none of Lautréamont either. The faces of these two fantastic and revolutionary writers, the most desperately audacious that ever were, are lost in the night of the ages.

They both fought fiercely against all artifices, whether vulgar or subtle, against all traps laid for us by that false and importunate reality which degrades man. To the formula: *'You are what you are*,' they have added: *'You can be something else.'*

By their violence Sade and Lautréamont strip solitude of all its adornments. In solitude each being, each object, each convention, each image also, premeditates a return to its own non-becoming reality, to have no longer a secret to reveal, to lie hatching peacefully and uselessly in the atmosphere it creates.

Sade and Lautréamont, who were solitary to the last degree, have revenged themselves by mastering the miserable world imposed upon them. In their hands they held earth, fire and water, the arid enjoyment of privation, and also weapons; and anger was in their eyes. They demolish, they impose, they outrage, they ravish. The doors of love and hate are open to let in violence. Inhuman, it will arouse man, really arouse him, and will not withhold from him, a mere accident on earth, the possibility of an end. Man will emerge from his hiding-places and, faced with the vain array of charms and disenchantments, he will be drunk with the power of his ecstasy.

He will then no longer be a stranger either to himself or to others. Surrealism, which is an instrument of knowledge, and therefore an instrument of conquest as well as of defence, strives to bring to light man's profound consciousness. Surrealism strives to demonstrate that thought is common to all, it strives to reduce the differences existing between men, and, with this end in view, it refuses to serve an absurd order based upon inequality, deceit and cowardice.

Let man discover himself, know himself, and he will at once feel himself capable of mastering all the treasures of which he is almost entirely deprived – all the treasures, material as well as spiritual, which he has accumulated throughout time, at the price of the most terrible sufferings, for the benefit of a small number of privileged persons who are blind and deaf to everything that constitutes human greatness.

Today the solitude of poets is breaking down. They are now men among other men, they have brothers.

There is a word which exalts me, a word I have never heard without a tremor, without feeling a great hope, the greatest of all, that of vanquishing the power of the ruin and death afflicting men – that word is fraternisation.

In February 1917, the Surrealist painter Max Ernst and I were at the front, hardly a mile away from each other. The German gunner, Max Ernst, was bombarding the trenches where I, a French infantryman, was on the look-out. Three years later, we were the best of friends, and ever since we have fought fiercely side by side for one and the same cause, that of the total emancipation of man.

In 1925, at the time of the Moroccan war, Max Ernst upheld with me the watchword of fraternisation of the French Communist Party. I affirm that he was then attending to a matter which concerned him, just as he had been obliged, in my sector in 1917, to attend to a matter which did not concern him. If only it had been possible for us, during the war, to meet and join hands, violently and spontaneously, against our common enemy: THE INTERNATIONAL OF PROFIT.

'O, you who are my brothers because I have enemies!' said Benjamin Péret.

Even in the extremity of discouragement and pessimism, we have never been completely alone. In present-day society everything conspires at every step we take to humiliate us, to constrain us, to enchain us and to make us turn back and retreat. But we do not overlook the fact that that is so because we ourselves are the evil, the evil in the sense in which Engels meant it; that is so because, with our fellow men, we are conspiring in our turn to overthrow the bourgeoisie, and its ideal of goodness and beauty.

That goodness and that beauty are in bondage to the ideas of property, family, religion and country – all of which we repudiate. Poets worthy of the name refuse, like proletarians, to be exploited. True poetry is present in everything that does not conform to that morality which, to uphold its order and prestige, has nothing better to offer us than banks, barracks, prisons, churches, and brothels. True poetry is present in everything that liberates man from that terrible ideal which has the face of death. It is present in the work of Sade, or Marx, or of Picasso, as well as in that of Rimbaud, Lautréamont or of Freud. It is present in the invention of the wireless, in the Tcheliouskin exploit, in the revolt of the Asturias, in the strikes of France and Belgium. It may be present in chill necessity, that of knowing or of eating better, as well as in a predilection for the marvellous. It is over a hundred years since the poets have descended from the peaks upon which they believed themselves to be established. They have gone out into the streets, they have insulted their masters, they have no gods any longer, they have dared to kiss beauty and love on the mouth, they have learned the songs of revolt sung by the unhappy masses and, without being disheartened, they try to teach them their own.

They pay little heed to sarcasms and laughter, they are accustomed to these; but now they have the certainty of speaking in the name of all men. They are masters of their own conscience.

35   Popularity and Realism

Bertolt Brecht

Whoever looks for slogans to apply to contemporary German literature, must bear in mind that anything that aspires to be called literature is printed exclusively abroad and can almost exclusively be read only abroad. The term *popular* as applied to literature thus acquires a curious connotation. The writer in this case is supposed to write for a people among whom he does not live. Yet if one considers the matter more closely, the gap between the writer and the people is not as great as one might think. Today it is not quite as great as it seems, and formerly it was not as small as it seemed. The prevailing aesthetic, the price of books and the police have always ensured that there is a considerable distance between writer and people. Nevertheless it would be wrong, that is to say unrealistic, to view the widening of this distance as a purely 'external' one. Undoubtedly special efforts have to be made today in order to be able to write in a popular style. On the other hand, it has become easier; easier and more urgent. The people have split away more clearly from their upper layers; their oppressors and exploiters have stepped out and joined a bloody battle with them of vast dimensions. It has become easier to take sides. An open battle has so to speak broken out among the 'public'.

The demand for a realistic style of writing can also no longer be so easily dismissed today. It has acquired a certain inevitability. The ruling classes use lies oftener than before – and bigger ones. To tell the truth is clearly an ever more urgent task. Suffering has increased and with it the number of sufferers. In view of the immense suffering of the masses, concern with little difficulties or with difficulties of little groups has come to be felt as ridiculous, contemptible.

There is only one ally against growing barbarism – the people, who suffer so greatly from it. It is only from them that one can expect anything. Therefore it is obvious that one must turn to the people, and now more necessary than ever to speak their language. Thus the terms *popular art* and *realism* become natural allies. It is in the interest of the people, of the broad working masses, to receive a faithful image of life from literature, and faithful images of life are actually of service only to the people, the broad working masses, and must therefore be absolutely comprehensible and profitable to them – in other words, popular. Nevertheless these concepts must first be thoroughly cleansed before propositions are constructed in which they are employed and merged. It would be a mistake to think that these concepts are completely transparent, without history, uncompromised or unequivocal. ('We all know what they mean – don't let's split hairs.') The concept of *popularity* itself is not particularly popular. It is not realistic to believe that it is. There is a whole series of abstract nouns ending in 'ity' which must be viewed with caution. Think of *utility*, *sovereignty*, *sanctity*; and we know that the concept of *nationality* has a quite

Source: 'Against Georg Lukács', translated by S. Hood in R. Taylor (ed.), *Aesthetics and Politics* (New Left Books, 1977), pp. 79–85. First published in *Schriften zur Literatur und Kunst*, Frankfurt, 1967. One footnote has been omitted.

particular, sacramental, pompous and suspicious connotation, which we dare not overlook. We must not ignore this connotation, just because we so urgently need the concept *popular*.

It is precisely in the so-called poetical forms that 'the people' are represented in a superstitious fashion or, better, in a fashion that encourages superstition. They endow the people with unchanging characteristics, hallowed traditions, art forms, habits and customs, religiosity, hereditary enemies, invincible power and so on. A remarkable unity appears between tormenters and tormented, exploiters and exploited, deceivers and deceived; it is by no means a question of the masses of 'little' working people in opposition to those above them.

The history of the many deceptions which have been practised with this concept of the people is a long and complicated one – a history of class struggles. We do not intend to go into it here – we only wish to keep the fact of the deception in sight, when we say that we need popular art and mean thereby art for the broad masses, for the many who are oppressed by the few, 'the people themselves', the mass of producers who were for so long the object of politics and must now become the subject of politics. Let us recall that the people were for long held back from any full development by powerful institutions, artificially and forcefully gagged by conventions, and that the concept *popular* was given an ahistorical, static, undevelopmental stamp. We are not concerned with the concept in this form – or rather, we have to combat it.

Our concept of what is popular refers to a people who not only play a full part in historical development but actively usurp it, force its pace, determine its direction. We have a people in mind who make history, change the world and themselves. We have in mind a fighting people and therefore an aggressive concept of what is *popular*.

Popular means: intelligible to the broad masses, adopting and enriching their forms of expression/assuming their standpoint, confirming and correcting it/representing the most progressive section of the people so that it can assume leadership, and therefore intelligible to other sections of the people as well/relating to traditions and developing them/communicating to that portion of the people which strives for leadership the achievements of the section that at present rules the nation.

Now we come to the concept of *realism*. This concept, too, must first be cleansed before use, for it is an old concept, much used by many people and for many ends. This is necessary because the people can only take over their cultural heritage by an act of expropriation. Literary works cannot be taken over like factories; literary forms of expression cannot be taken over like patents. Even the realistic mode of writing of which literature provides many very different examples, bears the stamp of the way it was employed, when and by which class, down to its smallest details. With the people struggling and changing reality before our eyes, we must not cling to 'tried' rules of narrative, venerable literary models, eternal aesthetic laws. We must not derive realism as such from particular existing works, but we shall use every means, old and new, tried and untried, derived from art and derived from other sources, to render reality to men in a form they can master. We shall take care not to describe one particular, historical form of novel of a particular epoch as realistic – say that of Balzac or Tolstoy – and thereby erect merely formal, literary criteria for realism. We shall not speak of a realistic manner of writing only when, for example, we can smell, taste and feel everything, when there is 'atmosphere' and when plots are so contrived that they lead to psychological analysis of character. Our concept of realism must be wide and political, sovereign over all conventions.

Realistic means: discovering the causal complexes of society/unmasking the prevailing view of things as the view of those who are in power/writing from the standpoint of the class which offers the broadest solutions for the pressing difficulties in which human society is caught up/emphasizing the element of development/making possible the concrete, and making possible abstraction from it.

These are vast precepts and they can be extended. Moreover we shall allow the artist to employ his fantasy, his originality, his humour, his invention, in following them. We shall not stick to too detailed literary models; we shall not bind the artist to too rigidly defined modes of narrative.

We shall establish that the so-called sensuous mode of writing – where one can smell, taste and feel everything – is not automatically to be identified with a realistic mode of writing; we shall acknowledge that there are works which are sensuously written and which are not realistic, and realistic works which are not written in a sensuous style. We shall have to examine carefully the question whether we really develop a plot best when our ultimate objective is to reveal the spiritual life of the characters. Our readers will perhaps find that they have not been given the key to the meaning of the events if, led astray by various artistic devices, they experience only the spiritual agitation of the heroes. By adopting the forms of Balzac and Tolstoy without testing them thoroughly, we might weary our readers – the people – as much as these writers often do themselves. Realism is not a mere question of form. Were we to copy the style of these realists, we would no longer be realists.

For time flows on, and if it did not, it would be a bad prospect for those who do not sit at golden tables. Methods become exhausted; stimuli no longer work. New problems appear and demand new methods. Reality changes; in order to represent it, modes of representation must also change. Nothing comes from nothing; the new comes from the old, but that is why it is new.

The oppressors do not work in the same way in every epoch. They cannot be defined in the same fashion at all times. There are so many means for them to avoid being spotted. They call their military roads motorways; their tanks are painted so that they look like MacDuff's woods. Their agents show blisters on their hands, as if they were workers. No: to turn the hunter into the quarry is something that demands invention. What was popular yesterday is not today, for the people today are not what they were yesterday.

Anyone who is not a victim of formalistic prejudices knows that the truth can be suppressed in many ways and must be expressed in many ways. One can arouse a sense of outrage at inhuman conditions by many methods – by direct description (emotional or objective), by narrative and parable, by jokes, by over- and under-emphasis. In the theatre, reality can be represented both in objective and in imaginative forms. The actors may not use make-up – or hardly any – and claim to be 'absolutely natural' and yet the whole thing can be a swindle; and they can wear masks of a grotesque kind and present the truth. It is hardly open to debate that the means must be questioned about the ends they serve. The people understand this. Piscator's great theatrical experiments in which conventional forms were constantly destroyed, found their greatest support in the most advanced cadres of the working class; so have my own. The workers judged everything according to the truth of its content; they welcomed every innovation which helped the representation of truth, of the real mechanism of society; they rejected everything that seemed theatrical, technical equipment that merely worked for its own sake – that is to say, that did not yet fulfil, or no longer fulfilled, its purpose. The workers' arguments were never literary or stated in terms of theatrical aesthetics. One never heard it said that one can't mix theatre and film. If the film was not inserted properly in the play, then the most that was said was: 'We don't need that film. It's distracting.' Workers' choirs spoke verse-parts with complicated rhythms ('If it was in rhyme it would go down like water and nothing would be left'), and sang difficult (unfamiliar) compositions by Eisler ('That's strong stuff'). But we had to change certain lines whose sense was not clear or which were wrong. In the case of marching-songs, which were rhymed so that they could be learnt more quickly, and had a simpler rhythm so that they sank in better, certain refinements were introduced (irregularities, complications). Then they said: 'There's a little twist there – that's fun.' Anything that was worn out, trivial, or so commonplace that it no longer made one think, they did not like at all ('You get nothing out of it'). If one needed an aesthetic, one could find it here. I shall never forget how a worker looked at me when I replied to his suggestion that I should add something to a chorus about the Soviet Union ('It has to go in – otherwise what's the point?'), that it would destroy the artistic form. He put his head on one side and smiled. A whole area of aesthetics collapsed because of this polite smile. The workers were not afraid to teach us and they were themselves not afraid to learn.

I am speaking from experience when I say that one need not be afraid to produce daring, unusual things for the proletariat so long as they deal with its real situation. There will always be people of culture, connoisseurs of art, who will interject: 'Ordinary people do not understand that.' But the people will push these persons impatiently aside and come to a direct understanding with artists. There is high-flown stuff, made for cliques, and intended to create new cliques – the two-thousandth reblocking of an old felt hat, the spicing of old, rotting meat: this the proletariat rejects ('What a state they must be in!') with an incredulous, yet tolerant shake of the head. It was not the pepper that was rejected, but the decaying meat: not the two-thousandth blocking, but the old felt. When they themselves wrote and produced for the stage they were wonderfully original. So-called agitprop art, at which people, not always the best people, turned up their noses, was a mine of new artistic methods and modes of expression. From it there emerged magnificent, long-forgotten elements from ages of genuine popular art, boldly modified for new social aims: breathtaking contractions and compressions, beautiful simplifications, in which there was often an astonishing elegance and power and a fearless eye for the complex. Much of it might be primitive, but not in that sense in which the spiritual landscapes of bourgeois art, apparently so subtle, are primitive. It is a mistake to reject a style of representation because of a few unsuccessful compositions – a style which strives, frequently with success, to dig down to the essentials and to make abstraction possible. The sharp eyes of the workers penetrated the surface of naturalistic representations of reality. When the workers in *Driver Henschel* said of spiritual analyses, 'We don't want to know all that', they were expressing a desire to receive a more accurate image of the real social forces at work under an immediately visible surface. To cite my own experience, they did not object to the fantastic costumes and the apparently unreal milieu of the *Threepenny Opera*. They were not narrow – they hated narrowness (their homes were narrow and cramped). They did things on a grand scale; the entrepreneurs were mean. They found some things superfluous which the artists declared to be necessary; but then they were generous and not against excess; on the contrary they were against those who were superfluous. They did not put on a muzzle on a willing horse but they saw that it pulled its weight. They did not believe in such things as 'the' method. They knew that many methods were necessary to attain their goal.

The criteria for popular art and realism must therefore be chosen both generously and carefully, and not drawn merely from existing realistic works and existing popular works, as often happens; by so doing, one would arrive at formalistic criteria, and at popular art and realism in form only.

Whether a work is realistic or not cannot be determined merely by checking whether or not it is like existing works which are said to be realistic, or were realistic in their time. In each case, one must compare the depiction of life in a work of art with the life itself that is being depicted, instead of comparing it with another depiction. Where popularity is concerned, there is one extremely formalistic procedure of which one must beware. The intelligibility of a literary work is not guaranteed merely if it is written exactly like other works which were understood in their time. These other works which were understood in their time were also not always written like the works before them. Steps had been taken to make them intelligible. In the same way, we must do something for the intelligibility of new works today. There is not only such a thing as *being popular*, there is also the process of *becoming popular*.

If we wish to have a living and combative literature, which is fully engaged with reality and fully grasps reality, a truly popular literature, we must keep step with the rapid development of reality. The great working masses are already on the move. The industry and brutality of their enemies is proof of it.

The Sociological Approach: The
Concept of Ideology in the History of
Art

Arnold Hauser

[. . .] The problem of ideology takes on a different form in the field of art from that
in the sciences, the concept of truth in art being so strikingly different from that of
theoretical truth. A work of art is not 'correct' or 'incorrect' in the way a scientific
theory is; it cannot properly speaking be termed either true or false. The concept of
changeless, superhistorical validity can be applied to art only with very special
reservations, and here all talk of 'false consciousness', as of correct consciousness, is
out of place. In other words: when truth is not what is aimed at, it is idle to speak of
conformity to it or evasion of it. Art is partisan through and through, and because a
view of reality which did not reflect any particular standpoint would be devoid of all
artistic quality, the problem of relativity simply does not arise in art. Every aspect of
art is a perspective; only one that involves an inner contradiction can rightly be
termed 'false'.

And yet it would be wrong to deny to art all claim of achieving truth, to deny that
it can make a valuable contribution to our knowledge of the world and of man. [. . .]
The sociologist can only feel uneasy about any too radical separation of art and
science. For after all, the world-view of a generation – or, more exactly, of a group
that is historically and socially self-contained – is an indivisible whole. Attempts to
demarcate the different fields in which this world-view manifests itself may be very
promising from the epistemological point of view, but to the sociologist they appear
as violent dissections of the reality he studies. To him, philosophy, science, law,
custom and art are different aspects of one unitary attitude to reality: in all these
forms men are searching for an answer to the same question, for a solution to one and
the same problem of how to live. They are not ultimately concerned with
formulating scientific truths, producing works of art, or even laying down moral
precepts, but with achieving a workable world-view, a reliable guiding principle for
life. [. . .]

Art can express social aims in two different ways. Its social content can be clothed
in the form of explicit avowal – confessions of belief, express doctrines, direct
propaganda – or in that of mere implication, that is, in terms of the outlook tacitly
presupposed in works which seem devoid of social reference. It can be frankly
tendentious or a vehicle of an unconscious and unacknowledged ideology. The social
content of a definite creed or an explicit message is consciously realized by the
speaker and consciously accepted or rejected by the hearer; on the other hand, the
social motive behind a personal manifesto can be unconscious, and can operate

Source: Arnold Hauser, *The Philosophy of Art History* (Routledge and Kegan Paul, 1959), pp. 21–40.
Footnotes have been omitted. Copyright © 1958 by Arnold Hauser. Reprinted by permission of Alfred
A. Knopf Inc. and Routledge and Kegan Paul Limited.

without men being aware of it; it will be the more effective the less it is consciously expressed and the less it is or appears to be consciously aiming to gain approbation. Nakedly tendentious art often repels where veiled ideology encounters no resistance. [. . .] And in art, the indirect, ideological mode of expression is not only the more effective, it is also the more illuminating from a historical point of view, for in truth a social outlook creates a style only when it cannot find expression directly. The open expression of a social outlook is compatible with the most various stylistic forms, as in that case the content of ideas is simply superimposed upon a given formal structure; no transformation of this content into novel forms of expression is required. [. . .] The translation of a social outlook into a style evidently requires quite a different mechanism from that which suffices for its straightforward expression in a political program or a manifesto. The artist as exponent of a style is not merely the mouthpiece of society, and his function as representing a social group cannot be explained in psychological terms alone; it becomes intelligible only through research into the nature of connections that are the theme of historical materialism.

Historical materialism is not a psychological theory; it derives ideologies not from the motives of persons, but from objective conditions that work themselves out often without the consciousness, and not infrequently contrary to the intentions, of the participants. Even to speak of 'interests' in this connection is not altogether appropriate, for the thoughts, feelings and actions of men are by no means always in accord with what, from a psychological point of view, one might designate as their interests. They generally think and act in accord with a class-consciousness for which the maintenance of a certain class is the cardinal, though not always the acknowledged, aim. Men's thinking depends on this consciousness, although the collective unity with which they are at one is not always the social class from which they sprang, and although they are not always aware of their class-situation. The motives, for example, which lead someone to volunteer for a certain war may from a subjective point of view be wholly idealistic; nevertheless, not only can the war be economically conditioned, but also there may be operative, behind the idealistic motives of the volunteer, unconscious factors of a materialistic, interested and class-determined character. Class-consciousness is not a psychological reality; it materializes only to the extent to which individuals do in fact behave in accord with their class-situation. [. . .] Men's thought is much more decisively influenced by their social situation than by their illusions or by their conscious reflections on their situation – although current social conditions presumably work only through psychological motivation, or as Engels has it, 'everything that sets men in motion must go through their minds'. [. . .]

The concept of ideology can be sensibly employed only in relation to a certain social group; to speak of the ideology of a historical epoch, without an attempt to differentiate classes or groups, is sociologically meaningless. Only when we assign ideological phenomena to particular social units do we get beyond a mere registering of historical sequence; only then are we able to work out a concrete, sociologically useful concept of ideology. In a historically advanced period there is no one ideology, but only ideologies – in the same way as there is not just Art, but the various arts, or as there are several relevant artistic trends to be distinguished, corresponding with the various influential social strata. This does not alter the fact that in any historical period one class predominates, but it reminds us that this predominance does not go unchallenged by competitors in the spiritual realm any more than in economics or politics. As a rule, the new forces of production begin to manifest themselves in the form of 'new ideas', giving rise to dialectical tensions in the field of thought which often work themselves out in economic organization only at a later date; but this does not invalidate the contention of Marx and Engels that the new ideas are only a sign 'that within the old society, the elements of a new one have been created'. In fact, we frequently get a situation in which the spiritual tendencies are much more tangled, more pervaded by deep-seated oppositions than the economic; in which, as for example in the age of the enlightenment, the ruling class was already spiritually divided into two hostile camps while economically it still maintained an appearance of unity.

The differing composition of the publics is undoubtedly not the sole explanation of the differing speeds of change found in the different arts. In the various branches of art, the traditional formal rules that prescribe modes of representation and set limits to what may be represented can be more rigorous or less, and so can offer more resistance or less to the influence of contemporary social conditions. [. . .] But for the formation of new ideologies all tradition is a factor of inertia, as both Marx and Engels observe. 'The tradition of all the dead generations weighs down the brains of the living,' says Marx, and Engels, somewhat more favorably, but still with a certain horror, speaks of tradition as a 'great conservative force in all ideological fields'.

Tradition owes its existence to the fact that cultural structures outlast the socio-historical conditions of their origin, and can live on, although, as it were, without roots. There exists a remarkable linkage of transitory and enduring factors, whose problematic character Marx seems to have noticed first when he came to deal with artistic experience. The passage in the Introduction to the *Critique of Political Economy* in which he speaks of the difficulty of accounting for the effect of the Greek epic upon generations living in a world utterly different from that of Homer is well-known. Here Marx stumbled upon the discrepancy between genesis and validity; without, however, being able to formulate the problem accurately. He was scarcely aware that he was concerned with a peculiarity of all forms of spiritual activity, and thus with the central and most difficult problem of the whole doctrine of ideology: the circumstance that the so-called superstructure has a vitality of its own, that spiritual structures have both the capacity and the tendency to cast loose from their origins and go their own way. In other words, they become the origin of new structures that develop according to inner laws of their own, and also come to have a value of their own which enjoys more than ephemeral validity. This phenomenon, by which the cultural structures that were once vital tools and weapons, means for mastering nature and organizing society, gradually become formalized and neutralized, and finally ends in themselves, is no doubt closely akin to the process of 'reification' (*Verdinglichung*) discovered and so vividly described by Marx. The spiritual structures, with their independence, autonomy and immanence, their formal, superhistorical values, confront us as so many 'alien natural forces' – as Marx terms the institutions of capitalist society. Even in art, the most human of all human forms of expression, this alien character is felt whenever art is treated as pure form. A work of art, taken as a purely formal product, a mere play of lines or tones, an embodiment of timeless values without relevance to anything historical or social, loses its vital relationship to the artist and its human significance for the person contemplating it. In art, especially in art, the setting up or postulating of supertemporal and superpersonal values has about it something of 'fetishism', which Marx held was the essence of 'reification'. By the setting up of such abstract values and the marking off of distinct mental faculties which goes with it, that unity of the spiritual world which the romantic philosophy of history discerned in the so-called 'organic' cultures, with their total world-view and their natural growth, is finally destroyed. Marx himself describes in somewhat romantic terms the dissolution of this natural state, which he makes coincide with the beginning of modern capitalism, as 'the end of human innocence'. His messianic gospel, with its dominant theme of the 'absolute sinfulness' of the capitalist era and its promise of classless society, is certainly a romantic legacy. [. . .]

In spite of the process, almost uninterrupted from that time on, of increasing separation of the cultural fields, with the autonomy of art growing more and more assured, still in no phase of art history, not even in times of the most extreme aestheticism and formalism, do we find the development of art completely independent of the current economic and social conditions. Artistic creations are far more intimately linked with their own time than they are with the idea of art in general or the history of art as a unitary process. The works of different artists do not have any common aim or common standard; one does not continue another or supplement another; each begins at the beginning and attains its goal as best it can. There is not really any progress in art; later works are not necessarily more valuable than earlier; works of art are in fact incomparable. That is what makes truth in art so very different from truth in science; it also explains why the value of the knowledge gained and propagated by art is not at all impaired by its ideological character. The fact that the insights gained by art often so quickly go out of currency and never really secure universal acceptance does not trouble us in the least. We regard them as uncommonly, often indeed uniquely, valuable interpretations of life, not as objectively compulsive, demonstrable, or even, properly speaking, arguable propositions. The artist's communications about reality intend to be and ought to be relevant; they do not have to be true or indisputable. We can be completely overwhelmed by a work of art, and yet quite reconciled to the fact that it leaves other men, who are our spiritual neighbours, unmoved. That there is nothing compulsive about judgments of taste is one of the earliest aesthetic insights, *de gustibus non disputandum* being almost a piece of popular proverbial wisdom. The remarkable thing is that judgments of taste do none the less make a claim, and though not claiming universal validity, do have a normative aspect: the person judging believes himself to be recognizing an objective value that is in a way binding, at least for him. This complication deserves to be noted, but does not alter the fact that validity in art is utterly different from validity in science, and that there is no contradiction in art's being ideological and at the same time having objective value.

But the problem of relativity of values, which we thus avoid in considering the actual production and enjoyment of art, confronts us when we turn to art history as a science with difficulties almost as great as are encountered in any other field of study. The development of art history does not even manifest that rather small element of continuous progress which can be detected in other branches of historical writing. In the case of art, the historical interpretations and evaluations of one generation not only are not felt to be binding upon the next, but often have to be positively ignored, even fought against, in order that the new generation may gain its own direct access to the works of the past. We enjoy all this variety and many-sidedness of historical interpretation, feel infinitely enriched and enlivened by such constant shifts in the point of view from which sensitive and ingenious art historians investigate and reflect upon the works of the masters; in the end, the question of the validity of all these different interpretations which successive generations put upon the artistic creations of the past obtrudes itself and demands further investigation. [. . .] Are such interpretations correct or incorrect? Is one more correct than another? Is a later interpretation always more correct than an earlier? Or has the temporal sequence of judgments in this case nothing whatever to do with progress, with any progressive discovery of truth? Is relativism in art history inevitable and unobjectionable? Or have we in the last resort to do with assertions that are not to be distinguished as true or false, but according to some quite different criteria, such as the degree of relevance of the connections pointed out, or the extent of the deepening and enrichment of our aesthetic experience which may result? It certainly seems clear that the course not merely of art, but of art history also – that is, not only of the practice but also of the interpretation of art – is subject to the laws of something like Alfred Weber's 'cultural development', which is not a strictly progressive movement, unlike the continuous process of cumulative achievement which he terms 'civilization'. The judgments of art history can be neither completely objective nor absolutely compelling; for interpretations and evaluations are not so much knowledge, but are ideological desiderata, wishes and ideals that one would like to see realized.

Works or schools of art of the past are interpreted, discovered, appraised, neglected in accord with the point of view and current standards of the present. Each generation judges the artistic endeavors of former ages more or less in the light of its own artistic aims; it regards them with renewed interest and a fresh eye only when they are in line with its own objectives. [. . .]

The evaluations and revaluations of art history, it is plain, are governed by ideology, not by logic. They relate to the same living conditions, are based upon the same social foundations as are the contemporary artistic tendencies and, like these, express and reveal a definite world-view. [. . .]

37　　Léger

John Berger

Our productive, scientific abilities have outstripped our ethical and social conscience. That is platitude and no more than a half-truth, but it is nevertheless a way of summing up at least an aspect of the crisis of our time. Nearly all contemporary artists who have faced up to this crisis at all, have concentrated on the ensuing conflict of conscience. Léger was unique because he seized upon our technical achievements and by concentrating upon their real nature was led on to discover the spirit, the ethics, the attitude of mind, necessary to control and exploit them to our full advantage. It is because of this – because Léger put the facts of our environment first and through them arrived at his attitude to life – that one can claim that he was so boldly a materialist.

As an artist Léger is often accused of being crude, vulgar, impersonal. He is none of these things. It is his buoyant confidence that makes him seem crude to the diffident. It is his admiration of industrial techniques and therefore of the industrial worker that makes him seem vulgar to the privileged; and his belief in human solidarity that makes him seem impersonal to the isolated. His works themselves refute the charge. Look at them. I always feel absurdly pretentious when trying to write about Léger. His works so clearly affirm themselves. In front of a painting by Picasso or Bonnard, one senses such an urgency of conflict that it seems quite appropriate to discuss the debate and plead for all the issues involved. But in front of a Léger one thinks: There it is. Take it or leave it. Or rather, take it when you want it, and leave it when you don't. Scribble moustaches on his girls if you like. Buy a postcard of it and send it home along with a vulgar one. Lean against it, and prompted by the bicycle in it, discuss where you're going next Sunday. Let the dumb-bells in another remind you that you've stopped doing your early morning exercises. Or stand entranced and reflect afterwards that he has probably learned more from Michelangelo than from any other artist. It doesn't matter. Look at his bicycles, and his girls in their sports clothes, and his holiday straw hats, and his cows with their comic camouflage dapples, and his steeplejacks and acrobats each knowing what the other takes, and his trees like the sprigs you put into a jam jar, and his machinery as gay as the youth who plans to paint his motor-bike, and his nudes as familiar as wives – what other modern painter doesn't paint a nude as though she were either a piece of studio furniture or a surreptitious mistress? – and his compasses and keys painted as if they were emblems on flags to celebrate their usefulness – does his work seem mechanical and cold?

Léger's greatest works are those which he painted since the war and those in

Source: John Berger, *Permanent Red* (Methuen, 1960), pp. 121–125. Reprinted by permission of Methuen and Co. Ltd; and Writers and Readers Co-operative Society Ltd., London.

which, dealing with the human figure, he expressed directly the profound humanism of his materialist philosophy. Among these are the studies for his famous large painting of builders working together on scaffolding, and the monumental heads with their striped flags of bright colours superimposed over their contours.

These heads with their strips of bright orange, red and blue, represent the culmination of Léger's art. Léger began with the machine. His cubist pictures were untheoretical. In them he simply used the cube and the cylinder to recreate the energy of machine blocks and pistons. Then he discovered the machine-made object. Unlike most artists, but like the average man of our century, he was not interested in its associations but in how it was made. From this period in his painting he learned how to manage solids – how to manufacture them, how to preserve a surface with paint, how to dazzle with contrasts, how to assemble mass-produced signs with colour. Later, interested by how colour changed the appearance of shapes and vice versa, he began designing abstract murals. Yet, unlike so many others, he always realized that abstract painting meant nothing if separated from architecture. 'It is our duty,' he said, 'to spread light and colour' – and he meant into the mean, grimed city apartments. From this phase he learned to see beyond the single static object: he learned to connect. And with this formal development came a human one. He saw that the machine had made labour collective, that its discipline had created a new class, that it could offer freedom. He suddenly saw machines as tools in the hands of men, no longer as mere objects in themselves. From that moment everything he painted ceased to be a celebration of the mechanical industrial world as it is, and became a celebration of the richer human world to which industrialization would eventually lead. He painted Adam and Eve and made them a French worker and his girl granted leisure. He painted bicycles as a symbol of the machine available to the working class which could convey them to where they wished. And he painted his monumental heads with their waving flags of colour.

Léger was not one to parade his sensibility as though it were his only virtue. The bright dynamic colours reflect what he learned from the machine. The unblinking confidence of the heads, expressed in their faces themselves and in the steady unchanging contours which define them, reflect what he learned from those who work machines. The two then combine. These paintings incorporate all the formal discoveries of modern art and yet are classic, suggest order and yet are full of gaiety. The strips of colour run across many different forms yet are so finely modified and placed that they give to each a solidity and definition which is nothing short of miraculous. I have called these works flags. They are emblems for something permanent and are as full of movement as pennants in the wind.

In fact Léger was the only modern European artist to have created an heroic style. Many factors prove this; that his work has a dignity and a sense of scale which in no way relies upon his literal subject; that on one hand it is as formal and architectural as a Corbusier building, and on the other is as simple in meaning as a ballad; that the nudity of his figures is less private than any painted since Michelangelo. He makes his figures nude to emphasize what they have in common. He calls one picture *Les Trois Soeurs*. The heroic artist cannot by definition be interested in idiosyncrasies.

Léger rejected every implication of 'glamour'. 'Glamour', as it has now come to be understood, stands for everything that separates one person from another, whether it is their 'special' understanding of art or the colour of their lipstick; Léger was only concerned with what we have in common. The current vision of the genius is almost synonymous with that of the mysterious, misunderstood outcast; Léger's vision of the genius was of a man with an imagination so in tune with his time and therefore so easily understandable, that he could become almost anonymous – his works as easy and yet sharp to the eye as popular proverbs to the ear.

He stands beside Picasso. Picasso is the painter of today; his greatness rests on the vitality with which he expresses our present conflicts. Léger is the painter of the future. And by that I do not simply mean that his future as an artist is assured, but that he assures his audience, if they have the courage to accept it, of their future. Yet at the same time Léger was not Utopian. He recognized human vulnerability and allowed for it by the tenderness of gesture and mood of his figures. In a Utopia there might be gaiety and co-operation and happiness but there would be no need for tenderness, for tenderness is the result of understanding human weakness. His *Constructeurs* do not only build together: they also protect one another – as, in practice, men working on high scaffolding must. His portrait of Eluard shows all the doubting that a lyrical poet must undergo. In one of his last canvases, called *Maternité*, the typical bands of bright colour set the drawing flying, as gay as a tricolour, but the daughter's hand touches her mother's cheek with the necessary reassurance that children can give. Such tenderness is not innocent.

38   Art History and Class Struggle

Nicos Hadjinicolaou

Style

[. . .] The first definition of style predominates among those who conceive art history as the history of form or of works of art, and sometimes even among those who take a psychological approach to art.

This is the most widespread definition of style, and encompasses innumerable variants.

> The characteristics of a style do not in fact consist of a repertory of ornamental components which in any case cannot be confined to any one period of art: many of them appear over and over again down the ages. Rather is a style characterised by the manner in which form is interpreted and by the flavour of the interpretation.[1]

This type of definition of style is not only very common but also the most impoverishing since it strips all historical significance from an artistic work. For this reason, the pejorative use of the label 'formalist' for a scholar like Wölfflin is in this case largely justified. In vain one insists on the class character of this conception of style, which repudiates all research into the *raison d'être* of styles and their relationship to social groups.

A second definition takes Riegl's idea of the 'artistic will' and expands it to consider style not just as form but as something deeper which cannot be comprehended simply by studying form: 'What force transforms form? What is it that changes fundamentally when style changes on the surface?' An alteration of the 'artistic will', that is to say in style, corresponds to a transformation of the 'ideals' of the social group which sustains that particular style. A completely different solution is given by the Russian emigré Wladimir Weidlé when he writes:

> Style is not a general notion which arises from classification according to formal features, but is the name given to a true *spiritual force* which is at work in history. . . . And where does this force come from? It can only come from one source, and that is religion. . . . Styles are the pictorial languages of whole religions or of religious variants of the same religion.

Here, under cover of an attempt to deepen the notion of 'art history as the history of styles' which goes much further than Wölfflin's formalism, we arrive at the point of seeing art history as a branch of theology! It is no accident that Weidlé condemns any attempt 'to interpret style as the expression of the spirit of an age, of a feeling or a vision of the world'. This school of thought goes further than formalism, but only in order to replace formalism with a teleological argument. Their use of the notion of style is ambiguous because its religious basis is often concealed beneath harsh criticism of formalism, which could be deceptive as to its real intentions.

Source: Nicos Hadjinicolaou, *Art History and Class Struggle*, translated by L. Asmal (Pluto Press, 1978), pp. 89–148. First published as *Histoire de l'art et lutte des classes*, Librairie Française Maspero, 1973. Footnotes have been omitted. Copyright © Pluto Press 1973, 1978, and reproduced with permission.

The third definition of style is put forward by those who see art history as part of the history of culture, the history of ideas or even the history of societies. Style stems directly from the society which produces it. Art, as already explained, is seen as an integral part of a larger whole, and therefore the elements which go to make up the other parts of this whole must also be reflected in art. [. . .]

The only writer who has reached the heart of the problem is Frederick Antal, when he states:

> The subject-matter of a work of art is of no less importance than its formal elements. Considering each style as a specific combination of the elements of subject and form, the thematic elements offer an immediate transition to the general outlook on life, the philosophy, from which the pictures in question derive. Works of art considered thus are no longer isolated; we have penetrated beyond the formal and are touching upon something deeper, upon the conception of life. The formal elements, for their part, are on final analysis also dependent on the philosophies of the day; but the relationship is less direct and can be clearly discerned only after the primary connection is understood. For the theme, the subject-matter of a picture, shows more clearly than anything else how completely the picture as a whole is but part of the outlook, the ideas, of the public, expressed through the medium of the artist. But the public is by no means unanimous in its outlook on life, and this divergence of outlook among its various sections explains the coexistence of different styles in the same period. Such divergence is, in its turn, due to the fact that what we call the public is not a homogeneous body, but is split up into various often antagonistic groupings. Since the public is merely another word for society in its capacity as recipient of art, what is required next is to examine the structure of society and the relationship between its various sections. To this end, we must ascertain the economic and social causes which have produced these divisions. This should be our first concern, for here alone have we solid ground under our feet. To sum up: we can understand the origins and nature of coexistent styles only if we study the various sections of society, reconstruct their philosophies and thence penetrate to their art.

[. . .] Antal's contribution is of major importance: he is the first art historian who has adequately defined 'style' and showed that style always belongs to a class or a section of a class.

Following the path mapped out by Antal, style can now be defined as the way in which the formal and thematic elements of a picture are combined on each specific occasion. This combination is a particular form of the overall ideology of a social class. [. . .]

Style as visual ideology

I hope to show that a particular style is synonymous to what I shall subsequently call 'visual ideology'.

If we substitute this last term for style in the definition arrived at earlier, it would then read: 'Visual ideology is the way in which the formal and thematic elements of a picture are combined on each specific occasion. This combination is a particular form of the overall ideology of a social class.'

The change is not simply quibbling with words, but should enable us to give a new meaning to the notion of style. The new term ought to be precisely defined, and we should eschew all unhelpful associations arising from current understanding of its separate components. In the Oxford dictionary ideology is defined as 'the science of ideas', whereas here ideology is understood as 'a relatively coherent whole made up of ideas, values and beliefs, by which people express the way they relate their lives to the conditions in which they live'.

The Oxford dictionary gives seven main definitions of the word 'visual', of which the one which most nearly approaches to the sense here is 'perceptible; visible'.

When I speak of visual ideology, I intend the term to be understood in a literal sense: 'a specific combination of the formal and thematic elements of a picture through which people express the way they relate their lives to the conditions of their existence, a combination which constitutes a particular form of the overall ideology of a social class'.

This conception will, I hope, throw new light on our knowledge of style, especially if it is further clarified through historical analysis.

Visual ideology occupies the same place here as style in Antal's writings. However, there is an essential difference in that the concept of visual ideology could lead to the solution of two problems which the notion of style, even as used by Antal, cannot overcome: one is the enormous and delicate problem of relating style to the overall ideology of a social class, and the second is the question of the specificity of the production of pictures as an autonomous process (though highly dependent on other kinds of production), which is not and hence never should be considered as a pure and simple transcription of the political and social ideology of a class into the domain of art.

To the extent that the use of certain words can act as a talisman to ward off error, I would say that the simple use of the term 'visual ideology' impels us to search for the link that connects style with the overall ideology of a social class, and to conceive style as a particular form of ideology.

The search for this link is highly complicated. It takes a great deal of painstaking research to identify different ideological forms as forms of a class ideology and then, while still taking into account the specificity of each form, to see them as parts of a whole. Visual ideology cannot be *deduced* from an overall class ideology, but each presupposes the existence of the other, and any scientific research into the one throws light on the other. To define a visual ideology contributes to the knowledge of a historically specific class ideology; and the definition of an overall class ideology (reached through knowledge of the literary, aesthetic, religious, political, economic and other ideologies of that class) plays an important role in understanding the visual ideology of that same class. This circular situation, characteristic of any scientific research, does not alter the fact that a visual ideology will be ascertained principally through research in the specific field of the production of pictures.

The substitution of the concept of visual ideology for that of style would seem to deprive everyday language of the notion of aesthetic value as automatically attributed to style, and in so doing to discard what is generally considered to be the essence of art, its aesthetic element. However, by no means all bourgeois art historians consider style as an aesthetic category and some even go so far as to say that style has no aesthetic value whatsoever, but is neutral. [. . .]

To sum up, it can be said that the substitution of visual ideology for the notion of style does not disregard the specificity of 'art' since the notion of style itself is value-free, contrary to some of its accepted meanings.

So visual ideology, like style, is not an objective fact, nor can it be identified with a 'fact' such as a visual image, but it is a theorctical concept which allows us a better grasp of the particularities of the production of pictures and its history. This history is none other than the history of visual ideologies. In this sense, we can substitute for the old bourgeois watchword of the 1920s, 'art history is the history of styles', the following: 'the history of the production of pictures is the history of visual ideologies'. It follows that the subject-matter of the discipline of art history is the visual ideologies that have occurred in the course of time.

In using the notion of 'style', people speak of 'individual style' (meaning the style of a particular artist), 'regional style' (which is representative of a geographical region during a historical period), 'national style' and 'the style of an epoch', whereas it must be stressed that the concept of visual ideology corresponds essentially to that of 'the style of a social group'. As already explained, visual ideology considered as a specific combination of the formal and thematic elements of a picture is a type of the overall ideology of a social class; it therefore goes beyond the limits of a picture and, very often, of a region or national territory, while at the same time being in turn limited and determined in space and time by each social formation. [. . .]

As regards the visual ideology of an individual work of art, it is legitimate to speak of it only in the sense that each picture is not just part of a collective visual ideology but is in addition a particular and unique concretisation of it.

To conclude: while admitting that the term 'style' has some use, I doubt the validity of adopting particular terms which are traditionally linked with the idea of style, such as 'an artist's style', 'regional style' or 'national style'. Apart from the use of style to designate a non-individual (collective) phenomenon, only the conception of 'a picture's style' can be retained. In this sense one may speak of the visual ideology of Rubens' *Marie de Medici Landing at Marseilles* (Louvre) and its relation with 'baroque style'. Thus both the style of a particular work and the style prevailing in a region or on a nation-wide scale can only be approached through the study of their relationship with contemporary collective styles. On the other hand, a collective visual ideology (as, for example, 'baroque style') can only be studied seriously by means of an analysis of individual pictures. Here the art historian must again pursue his research within an apparently vicious circle, as he did when investigating the relationship between an overall class ideology and a visual ideology. Research into the style of an individual picture cannot be carried out in isolation from the collective visual ideology to which it belongs, but the collective visual ideology cannot be ascertained without reference to individual pictures.

Visual ideology and social classes

The sense of visual ideology can be further elucidated by linking it with the concept of ideology in general. It will be recalled that 'in ideology the real relation of men to their real conditions of existence is inevitably invested in the imaginary relation, a relation that expresses a will (conservative, conformist, reformist or revolutionary), a hope or a nostalgia, rather than describing a reality' and also that

> every ideological representation is in a way a representation of reality, it somehow makes *allusion* to reality, but equally produces only an *illusion*. We understand too that ideology gives men some kind of *cognition* of their world – or rather, by allowing them to *recognise* themselves in their world, gives them some *recognition* while at the same time leading them to a misappreciation of their world. Ideology, considered from the point of view of its relation to reality, yields only an allusion to reality which is always accompanied by an illusion, a comprehension accompanied by a misapprehension.[2]

This allusion–illusion or comprehension–misapprehension of reality that characterises ideology differs according to social class. The place that a social class occupies
in society enforces a specific view of social reality that no other class possesses.
Dominant classes and dominated classes (even though the latter may, as has been
pointed out earlier, be impregnated with the ideology of the dominant classes)
cannot have the same ideology. Even within each class, there are sections or layers
which have their own individual features at the ideological level.

It would seem therefore that this two-way allusion–illusion feature which
characterises ideology in general is also a feature of visual ideology. Each style makes
allusion to reality, to one particular reality which is the combination of the
consciousness a class has of itself and its view of the world. This allusion to reality
goes together with an illusion about the objective place the class occupies within class
relations in a society. Historical analysis of each visual ideology is needed to reveal
this two-way allusive–illusory process which characterises the production of pictures
in general.

One may therefore conclude that the production of pictures constitutes a sphere
of the ideological level, since every picture belongs to a visual ideology even when it
can in some way be considered as inaugurating a new one. However one must not
forget that this sphere has specific features and some autonomy even though it is not
independent. Its autonomy is shown by the fact that the elements of which it is
composed do not exist as such, or certainly not all of them, in other types of ideology.
Its dependence is shown by the fact that it is always determined by other types or
spheres of the ideological level, according to the mode of production and the social
formation. Thus, to give an example, between the fourth and fourteenth centuries
within the ideological level the sphere of visual ideology was determined by the
sphere of religious ideology.

If the production of pictures is defined as one sphere of the ideological level, it
follows necessarily that what is valid for ideology in general is equally valid for visual
ideology. Thus neither social classes nor different layers or sections of different
classes can have the same visual ideology. From an abstract point of view each class
or layer or section of a class 'ought' to have at each historical 'moment' its own visual
ideology, given the particular vision each has of itself, of other classes and of society
in general. In reality, however, things are a great deal more complex, for in the first
place some classes have never historically had a developed visual ideology of their
own. In some cases they did not produce a certain type of picture, for example
paintings, at all. This comes from the fact that the need to produce some types of
image presupposes a specific ideology, and a particular social position. In the second
place, the visual ideology of the dominant classes strongly permeates the visual
ideologies of the dominated classes, to the point where the latter may be totally
distorted. It has a kind of monopoly over the whole of society. So if I speak of class
struggle in the context of the arts, and say that it appears in this domain through the
existence of styles, and even sometimes through the struggle between styles, it must
be recognised that *this 'struggle' takes place more often between the visual ideologies of
layers or sections of the same class or of the ruling classes than between the visual ideologies
of the ruling classes and the dominated classes*. It is not far from the truth to affirm, even
in this exaggerated form, that in all societies up to our times the history of the
production of pictures is the history of ruling class visual ideologies. Pictures are
often the product in which the ruling classes mirror themselves.

Visual ideology and knowledge

[. . .] What is the relationship between art and knowledge? Should art be conceived as a form of knowledge? Here the concept of visual ideology can be of use. What is the relationship between art and visual ideology? Let us begin by replacing the word 'art' by 'production of pictures'. This empirical term refers back to the simple and concrete fact of the production of certain two- or three-dimensional objects on which lines and colours have been variously placed, and it is preferable to the ambiguous and emotive term 'art'. It is not a precise term, and is retained purely as an indication of the type of production under discussion. On the other hand, visual ideology is to be understood as comprising the *essential* aspect of the objects which belong to the domain of the production of pictures. Every picture, whether considered as a major or minor work of art, belongs to a collective visual ideology while at the same time possessing its own unique features. This is common to all pictures, and is what makes each one different. Thus visual ideologies form the essence of the production of pictures. If this is so, the question as to the relationship between the latter and knowledge should be replaced by the following paradoxical question: what is the relationship between visual ideology and knowledge? At first glance even the existence of such a relationship may seem dubious. In fact, strictly speaking one cannot but assert that such a relationship does not exist. Visual ideology, with its double aspect of comprehension–misapprehension and illusion–allusion to reality, bears no relation to the scientific knowledge of this reality. Visual ideology and scientific knowledge are two distinct realities which do not coincide. [. . .]

In fact, if it is true that the essence of every picture lies in its visual ideology, it is also true that in the course of history one can discern two different kinds of visual ideology manifesting themselves in individual paintings: one which I shall subsequently call 'positive visual ideology' and one which I shall call 'critical visual ideology'. Positive visual ideology implies that there is no apparent contradiction in the relationship between a work's visual ideology and other types of ideology to which some elements of the picture refer. This positive, non-antagonistic relationship can go so far as to glorify other types of ideology through visual ideologies (this is the case with political and religious allegories, for instance).

On the other hand, critical visual ideology implies that a work's visual ideology exerts a critical function in regard to other non-visual kinds of ideologies, some elements of which are to be found in the work. Criticism is carried out through the *treatment* of the work's subject.

So, from the point of view of the relationship between art and knowledge, both positive and critical ideology (in their problematical relationship with other types of ideology) reveal and help us to 'know' their relationship with the overall ideology of a social class, and eventually their relationship with some contemporary non-visual ideologies. However, this kind of knowledge is not scientific but rather is felt or experienced, and requires the art historian's intervention in order to be transformed into scientific knowledge.

References

1 Robert Ducher, *Caractéristique des Styles*, Flammarion, 1944, p. 7.
2 Louis Althusser, 'Théorie et formation théorique – Idéologie et lutte idéologique', *Casa de las Americas*, no. 34, Havana.

39   On the Social History of Art

T. J. Clark

Art – in other words the search for the beautiful and the perfecting of truth, in his own person, in his wife and children, in his ideas, in what he says, does and produces – such is the final evolution of the worker, the phase which is destined to bring the Circle of Nature to a glorious close. Aesthetics and above Aesthetics, Morality, these are the keystones of the economic edifice.
(A passage copied by Baudelaire in 1848 from Proudhon's *Système des contradictions économiques ou Philosophie de la misère* (1846).)

In our oh-so-civilized society it is necessary for me to lead the life of a savage; I must free myself even from governments. My sympathies are with the people, I must speak to them directly, take my science from them, and they must provide me with a living. To do that, I have just set out on the great, independent, vagabond life of the Bohemian.
(Courbet, letter of 1850 to Francis Wey.)

To glorify the worship of images (my great, my only, my primitive passion).
To glorify vagabondage and what one might call Bohemianism, the cult of multiplied sensation, expressing itself through music. Refer here to Liszt.
(Baudelaire, *Mon cœur mis à nu*.)

M. Courbet is the Proudhon of painting. M. Proudhon – M. Courbet, I should say – does democratic and social painting – God knows at what cost.
(The critic L. Enault, reviewing the 1851 Salon in the *Chronique de Paris*.)

Pen in hand, he wasn't a bad fellow; but he was not, and could never have been, even on paper, a *dandy*; and for that I shall never forgive him.
(Baudelaire on Proudhon, letter of 2 January 1866 to Sainte-Beuve.)

These statements conjure up an unfamiliar time, a time when art and politics could not escape each other. For a while, in the mid-nineteenth century, the State, the public and the critics agreed that art had a political sense and intention. And painting was encouraged, repressed, hated and feared on that assumption.

Artists were well aware of the fact. Some, like Courbet and Daumier, exploited and even enjoyed this state of affairs; some, following Théophile Gautier, withdrew inside the notion of *l'Art pour l'Art*, a myth designed to counter the insistent politicization of art. Others, like Millet, accepted the situation with a wry smile – in a letter of 1853 he wondered whether the socks which one of his peasant girls was darning would be taken, by the Government, as giving off too much of a 'popular odour'.

This book sets out to explore this specific moment in French art; to discover the actual, complex links which bind together art and politics in this period; to explain, for example, the strange transitions in the five opening sayings. To call a worker an artist; to call a painting 'democratic and social'; to condemn an anarchist because he failed to be a dandy – these are, to say the least, unfamiliar manœuvres. What kind of an age was it when Baudelaire took notes from Proudhon and three years later

Source: T. J. Clark, *Image of the People: Gustave Courbet and the 1848 Revolution* (Thames and Hudson, 1973), pp. 9–20. Footnotes have been omitted.

dismissed *l'Art pour l'Art* as a 'puerile utopia', saying that art was 'hitherto inseparable from morality and utility'? Why did Courbet believe that art for the people was bound up with a Bohemian life-style? What was it about the *Burial at Ornans* that moved M. Enault to such anger? Such an age needs explaining, perhaps even defending.

It is not simply that the terms are out of fashion (or back in fashion, with a difference). It is the bizarre *certainty* of the arguments; it is the way they suggest an alien situation for art, an alien power. Power – no word could be more inappropriate, more absurd, now, when we talk of art. Which is if anything the reason for this book: it tries to reconstruct the conditions in which art was, for a time, a disputed, even an effective, part of the historical process.

When one writes the social history of art, it is easier to define what methods to avoid than propose a set of methods for systematic use, like a carpenter presenting his bag of tools, or a philosopher his premises. So I begin by naming some taboos. I am not interested in the notion of works of art 'reflecting' ideologies, social relations, or history. Equally, I do not want to talk about history as 'background' to the work of art – as something which is essentially absent from the work of art and its production, but which occasionally puts in an appearance. (The intrusion of history discovered, it seems, by 'common sense': there is a special category of historical references which can be identified in this way.) I want also to reject the idea that the artist's point of reference as a social being is, *a priori*, the artistic community. On this view, history is transmitted to the artist by some fixed route, through some invariable system of mediations: the artist responds to the values and ideas of the artistic community (in our period that means, for the best artists, the ideology of the *avant-garde*), which in turn are altered by changes in the general values and ideas of society, which in turn are determined by historical conditions. For example, Courbet is influenced by Realism which is influenced by Positivism which is the product of Capitalist Materialism. One can sprinkle as much detail on the nouns in that sentence as one likes; it is the verbs which are the matter.

Lastly, I do not want the social history of art to depend on intuitive analogies between form and ideological content – on saying, for example, that the lack of firm compositional focus in Courbet's *Burial at Ornans* is an expression of the painter's egalitarianism, or that Manet's fragmented composition in the extraordinary *View of the Paris World's Fair (1867)* is a visual equivalent of human alienation in industrial society.

Of course analogies between form and content cannot be avoided altogether – for a start, the language of formal analysis itself is full of them. The very word 'composition', let alone formal 'organization', is a concept which includes aspects of form *and* content, and suggests in itself certain kinds of relation between them – all the more persuasively because it never states them out loud. For that reason it is actually a strength of social art history that it makes its analogies specific and overt: however crude the equations I mentioned, they represent some kind of advance on the language of formal analysis, just because they make their prejudices clear. Flirting with hidden analogies is worse than working openly with inelegant ones, precisely because the latter can be criticized directly. In any discourse analogies are useful and treacherous at the same time; they open up the field of study, but may simply have deformed it; they are a kind of hypothesis that must be tested against other evidence. This is as true of art history as any other discipline. Faced with the strange and disturbing construction of the *Burial at Ornans*, it would be sheer cowardice not to give some account of the meaning of that construction; but I shall try to keep that account in contact and conflict with other kinds of historical explanation.

The question is: what in this subject can be studied, once these various comforting structures are set aside? Must we retreat at once to a radically restricted, empirical notion of the social history of art, and focus our attention on the immediate conditions of artistic production and reception: patronage, sales, criticism, public opinion? Clearly these are the important fields of study: they are the concrete means of access to the subject; time and again they are what we start from. But, to put it briefly, the study of any one 'factor' in artistic production leads us very swiftly back to the general problems we hoped to avoid. The study of patronage and sales in the nineteenth century cannot even be conducted without some general theory – admitted or repressed – of the structure of a capitalist economy. Imagine a study of the critical reaction to Courbet which had no notion of the function of art criticism in nineteenth-century Paris, no theory of the critics' own social situation, their commitments, their equivocal relation – half contemptuous, half servile – to the mass public of the Salons. Perhaps I should have said remember, not imagine: the kind of haphazard collage which results, the dreary mixture of 'absurd' and 'sensitive' remarks, is all too familiar to art historians.

Not that I want to ignore the critics and the texture of what they wrote: on the contrary. No less than forty-five writers had their say about Courbet in the Salon of 1851, and that mass of words is crucial evidence for us. It makes up a complex dialogue – between artist and critic, between critic and critic, between critic and public (sometimes that public makes an appearance, in imaginary form, within the criticism itself; for the most part it is an implied presence, a shadow, an occlusion; it is what critic and artist, in their civilized and hypocritical discourse, agree to leave out – but without success). In that weird, monotonous chorus, what matters is the structure of the whole, and the whole as a structure hiding and revealing the relation of the artist to his public. For our purposes, the public is different from the audience: the latter can be examined empirically, and should be. The more we know about the audience – about the social classes of Paris, the consumption habits of the bourgeoisie, how many people went to exhibitions – the more we shall understand that curious transformation in which it is given form, imagined, by the critic and by the artist himself.

As for the public, we could make an analogy with Freudian theory. The unconscious is nothing but its conscious representations, its closure in the faults, silences and caesuras of normal discourse. In the same way, the public is nothing but the *private* representations that are made of it, in this case in the discourse of the critic. Like the analyst listening to his patient, what interests us, if we want to discover the meaning of this mass of criticism, are the points at which the rational monotone of the critic breaks, fails, falters; we are interested in the phenomena of obsessive repetition, repeated irrelevance, anger suddenly discharged – the points where the criticism is incomprehensible are the keys to its comprehension. The public, like the unconscious, is present only where it ceases; yet it determines the structure of private discourse; it is the key to what cannot be said, and no subject is more important.

These are, I think, the only adequate attitudes to patronage and criticism in this period. And they lead us back to the terrain of those earlier theories I rejected – that is, the complex relation of the artist to the total historical situation, and in particular to the traditions of representation available to him. Even if one distrusts the notions of reflection, of historical background, of analogy between artistic form and social ideology, one cannot avoid the problems they suggest.

What I want to explain are the connecting links between artistic form, the available systems of visual representation, the current theories of art, other ideologies, social classes, and more general historical structures and processes. What the discarded theories share is the notion that all artists experience, answer and give form to their environment in roughly the same way – via the usual channels, one might say. That may be a convenient assumption, but it is certainly wrong. If the social history of art has a specific field of study, it is exactly this – the processes of conversion and relation, which so much art history takes for granted. I want to discover what concrete transactions are hidden behind the mechanical image of 'reflection', to know *how* 'background' becomes 'foreground'; instead of analogy between form and content, to discover the network of real, complex relations between the two. These mediations are themselves historically formed and historically altered; in the case of each artist, each work of art, they are historically specific.

What is barren about the methods that I am criticizing is their picture of history as a definite absence from the act of artistic creation: a support, a determination, a background, something never actually *there* when the painter stands in front of the canvas, the sculptor asks his model to stand still. There is a mixture of truth and absurdity here. It is true and important that there is a gap between the artist's social experience and his activity of formal representation. Art is autonomous in relation to other historical events and processes, though the grounds of that autonomy alter. It is true that experience of any kind is given form and acquires meaning – in thought, language, line, colour – through structures which we do not choose freely, which are to an extent imposed upon us. Like it or not, for the artist those structures are specifically aesthetic – as Courbet put it in his 1855 Manifesto, the artistic tradition is the very material of individual expression. 'To know in order to be able to do, that was my idea'; '*Savoir pour pouvoir, telle fut ma pensée*.' Nevertheless, there is a difference between the artist's contact with aesthetic *tradition* and his contact with the artistic world and its aesthetic *ideologies*. Without the first contact there is no art; but when the second contact is deliberately attenuated or bypassed, there is often art at its greatest.

The point is this: the encounter with history and its specific determinations is made by the artist himself. The social history of art sets out to discover the general nature of the structures that he encounters willy-nilly; but it also wants to locate the specific conditions of one such meeting. How, in a particular case, a content of experience becomes a form, an event becomes an image, boredom becomes its representation, despair becomes *spleen*: these are the problems. And they lead us back to the idea that art is sometimes historically effective. The making of a work of art is one historical process among other acts, events and structures – it is a series of actions in but also on history. It may become intelligible only within the context of given and imposed structures of meaning; but in its turn it can alter and at times disrupt these structures. A work of art may have ideology (in other words, those ideas, images and values which are generally accepted, dominant) as its material, but it *works* that material; it gives it a new form and at certain moments that new form is in itself a subversion of ideology. Something like that happened in the Salon of 1851.

I have been arguing for a history of mediations, for an account of their change and ambiguity. What this means in practice may become clearer if I tie it down to some familiar problems of art history. Take, for example, the artist's relation to the artistic world and its shared ideologies. In its usual form this is a question of the artist's membership of one particular 'school' – in particular whether or not he was one of the *avant-garde*. Clearly we want to know how the *avant-garde* was formed, but we equally want to know what it was *for*; in both cases what we need is a sense that the category itself is fundamentally unstable, illusory. To write a history of the *avant-garde* simply in terms of personnel, recruitment, fashion: nothing could be more misguided. It ignores the essential – that the concept of *avant-garde* is itself profoundly ideological; that the aim of the *avant-garde* was to snatch a transitory and essentially false identity from the unity of the Parisian artistic world. It is the unity that is fundamental, not the factions.

The more we look at the artistic world in Paris, the more its schools and dogmas seem an artifice; what really mattered was the ease of transition from attitude to attitude, style to style, posture to imposture. Balzac was the great exponent of such transformations; below him (below his real, hard-won inclusiveness) lesser men traded allegiances, played at metamorphosis for a living. Gautier, the refined Parnassian poet and the agile, time-serving critic, could write a poem to the mummified hand of the poet-murderer Lacenaire (which Maxime du Camp kept in a jar), or could dash off a set of pornographic letters to Madame Sabatier. The same Madame Sabatier, queen of the literary salons in the early 1850s, was portrayed at one time or another by Flaubert, Gautier (in his official role), Clésinger, Baudelaire, even Meissonier. A minor figure like the novelist Duranty could combine aggressive Realism with a projected biography of Baudelaire; Baudelaire himself was reconciled with his Catholic critic Veuillot. These are random examples; the list could go on indefinitely.

In such a world, being *avant-garde* was just an institutionalized variant of everyone's gambit. It was a kind of initiation rite – a trek out into the bush for a while, then a return to privileged status within the world you had left. It was a finishing-school, an unabashed form of social climbing. When we look at Champfleury, Courbet's mentor and parasite, we see that process to perfection.

In this light the real history of the *avant-garde* is the history of those who bypassed, ignored and rejected it; a history of secrecy and isolation; a history of escape from the *avant-garde* and even from Paris itself. The hero of that history is Rimbaud, but it makes sense of many others in the nineteenth century: Stendhal, Géricault, Lautréamont, Van Gogh, Cézanne. It applies precisely, I think, to four of the greatest artists of the mid-nineteenth century: Millet, Daumier, Courbet and Baudelaire. [. . .] Each of them had truck with the *avant-garde* and its ideas; each of them was part of it at certain moments or in certain moods; but in each case the relationship is shifting and ambiguous, a problem rather than a 'given'. We shall not solve the problem by counting heads known, ideas shared, salons visited. Count these by all means, but also measure the distance these men established from Paris and its coteries. We need to search for the conditions of this distance: the reasons for rejection and escape as much as the continuing dependence on the world of art and its values. We need also to distinguish *avant-garde* from Bohemia: they fought, for a start, on different sides of the barricades in June: the Bohemians with the insurrection, and the *avant-garde*, of course, with the forces of order. We need to unearth the real Bohemia from the *avant-garde's* fantasy of it; to rescue Bohemia from Murger's *Scènes de la Vie de Bohème*. These are distinctions with some relevance to the present.

This brings us back to the problem of artist and public. I want to put back ambiguity into that relation: to stop thinking in terms of the public as an identifiable 'thing' whose needs the artist notes, satisfies or rejects. The public is a prescience or a phantasy within the work and within the process of its production. It is something the artist himself invents, in his solitude – though often in spite of himself, and never quite as he would wish. [. . .]

For the artist, inventing, affronting, satisfying, defying his public is an integral part of the act of creation. We can go further – we need to, if we are to understand the strength of mid nineteenth-century art and the desperation of what followed. It is when one of those stances towards the public becomes an autonomous or over-riding consideration (on the one hand, *épater le bourgeois*, on the other, producing specifically for the market), or when the public becomes either too fixed and concrete a presence or too abstract and unreal a concept, that a radical sickness of art begins.

All this is vital because Courbet was an artist for whom the public was very much present, richly, ambiguously defined: subject-matter and spectator, the mainspring of his art. I am talking here of Courbet in his thirties, from 1848 to 1856, the great period of his painting. His decline after 1856 had a lot to do with the disappearance of that public.

Finally, there is the old familiar question of art history. What use did the artist make of pictorial tradition; what forms, what schemata, enabled the painter to see and to depict? It is often seen as the only question. It is certainly a crucial one, but when one writes the social history of art one is bound to see it in a different light; one is concerned with what prevents representation as much as what allows it; one studies blindness as much as vision. [. . .]

When the blindness is breached by extreme circumstances the result is pathos. Listen to Tocqueville, suddenly confronted, when the National Assembly was invaded by the clubs on 15 May 1848, with the arch-revolutionary Louis-Auguste Blanqui:

> It was then I saw appear, in his turn at the rostrum, a man whom I never saw save on that day, but whose memory has always filled me with disgust and horror. His cheeks were pale and faded, his lips white; he looked ill, evil, foul, with a dirty pallor and the appearance of a mouldering corpse; no linen as far as one could see, an old black frock-coat thrown about spindly and emaciated limbs; he might have lived in a sewer and have just emerged from it. I was told that this was Blanqui.

It is not merely that this description of Blanqui is untrue – though we have only to put Tocqueville's paragraph against the drawing by David d'Angers (done eight years earlier) to show that. It is more that we are confronted with prejudice which clearly believes itself to be description: before our eyes depiction changes into ideology. [. . .]

So the problem of schema and pictorial tradition is rather altered. The question becomes: in order to see certain things, what should we believe about them? What enables an artist to make effective use of a certain schema or the formal language of a certain artist of the past? There is nothing unchanging or automatic about this. To take one example, it became quite fashionable in certain circles after 1848 to admire the art of the seventeenth-century brothers Le Nain. Several critics praised them; several artists attempted to imitate them. But your Le Nains and my Le Nains? Courbet's Le Nains and Champfleury's? Worlds apart, we shall discover – indeed, what Champfleury half-laughingly called their weaknesses, Courbet went ahead and used. What we want to know are the reasons for that difference; and we shan't find them by adding up 'influences'.

The same thing applies to popular imagery. When Courbet said, in his 1850 letter to Francis Wey, that he wanted to draw his science from the people, he meant, among other things, pictorial science. All his circle of friends and admirers were interested in popular art; but how many put it to use instead of collecting it? How many realized that they needed its forms and structures if, 'below a certain social plane', they were to see at all? Courbet did; his friend Buchon knew it but could not act upon it; I doubt if Champfleury, the great propagandist for popular imagery, really understood the point. So here too one must integrate the separate art-historical problem into a wider account; one must ask, ultimately, what kind of 'visibility' a certain symbolic system made possible; and in what specific circumstances one artist could take advantage of this, and another fail to. To answer merely in terms of artistic competence is just begging the question.

There is thus a general question which cannot be avoided, though the means of access to it must be particular: whether we can discover in the complex and specific material of a single artist's historical situation and experience the foundation of his unique subject-matter and 'style'.

Let us take the case of Courbet. It is fairly easy to list the various factors to be taken into account when we talk about his art: his situation in rural society and his experience of changes within it; the various representations – verbal and visual – of rural society available to him; the social structure of Paris in the 1840s; the iconography of Bohemia and his use of it; the nature and function of his notorious life-style in the city; the artistic ideas of the period; the aspects of artistic tradition which interested him. We shall have to give flesh to these bare categories of experience; but the list itself, however elaborate, stays this side of explanation. The real problem is to describe the specific constellation of these factors in 1849–1851, and what determined that constellation. In other words, what made Courbet's art distinctive, effective, at a certain moment?

To answer that, we shall have to go far afield, from painting to politics, from a judgment of colour to more general concerns – concerns which touch the State, which move anger and delight because they are the concerns of many. But we shall discover these politics in the particular, in the event, in the work of art. Our starting point is a certain moment of historical coalescence – a gesture, or a painting, which is supercharged with historical meaning, round which significance clusters. The *Burial at Ornans*, the *Stonebreakers* and the *Peasants of Flagey* are paintings like this –

the more we look and enquire, the more facets of social reality they seem to touch and animate.

Take one small but significant gesture to illustrate the point. In May 1850, in Salins in the Jura, a religious procession took place. The *Procureur général*, the political prosecutor of the regime, reported on the matter to the Minister in Paris:

> The situation in the town of Salins, the most degenerate of all the Jura towns, shows signs of improving. The processions for Corpus Christi day were very colourful and went off in a very orderly way; a special procession, ordered in this town by the Bishop of Saint-Claude, *to atone for Proudhon's blasphemies*, did not give rise to any disturbances, even minor ones. We were extremely surprised to see citizen Max Buchon taking part in this procession, candle in hand, and in a state of perfect composure; he is one of the leaders of the Socialist party, a professed advocate of the doctrine of Proudhon, and apparently his intimate friend. Did his presence at this ceremony indicate, as many have supposed, sincere contrition? I see it rather as one of those eccentricities which we have long since been led to expect from this man, who loves above all to strike a pose and make himself a talking-point.

Max Buchon cracks a joke: one which typifies the time. Jokes resemble art, certain Freudians have suggested, in their treatment of unconscious material; perhaps in their treatment of historical material too. Buchon's joke plays on his audience's doubts about history; he puts the unexpected in contact, confuses codes; instead of an argument he uses an act and its ambiguity. In this particular case, the tactic was advisable – it was difficult, even in 1850, to send a man to jail for a joke you did not quite understand, and Buchon wanted to avoid jail (he had been acquitted of revolutionary conspiracy four months earlier at the Jura assizes).

As with the pictures, I shall later have to explain the point of the joke and its material, spoiling it in the process. We shall have to know more about Buchon himself, Courbet's oldest friend, poet and translator, dedicated revolutionary. More also about Salins and the strange politics of 1850; about the radical confusion of religion and politics after 1848; about the nature of this kind of public irony, the whiff of the dandy and Baudelaire in the whole performance (if Proudhon was no dandy, some of his followers were). Knowing about Buchon and Salins (a twenty-five-mile walk from Ornans, and Courbet's point of political reference) will eventually lead us back to the *Burial at Ornans*, the beadles' red noses and Buchon's place in that particular religious procession (he lurks in the background, sixth from the left).

From a wisecrack to a masterpiece; but in both cases it is what is done to the historical material that counts. Joke and picture play with different contexts of meaning in order to constitute an individuality. Discover the codes by all means. Investigate burials, religion, Salins and Ornans; describe the political temper of the Jura, the social significance of a frock-coat and spats. But remember also that Buchon and Courbet juggle with meanings, switch codes, lay false trails and make *one* thing, not many. (A quick pun, not an immense shaggy dog story.) Look at the process of transformation – call it work, call it play – as well as what the work is done to.

Striking that balance is sometimes difficult, especially in the social history of art. Just because it invites us to more contexts than usual – to a material denser than the great tradition – it may lead us far from the 'work itself'. But the work itself may appear in curious, unexpected places; and, once disclosed in a new location, the work may never look the same again.

I have been saying that there can be no art history apart from other kinds of history. But let us restrict ourselves in a rough and ready way to art history 'proper'. Even within the discipline – perhaps especially here, just because its limits are so artificial – there is a problem of choice of perspectives.

So far, nineteenth-century art history has usually been studied under two headings: the history of an heroic *avant-garde*, and the movement away from literary and historical subject-matter towards an art of pure sensation. But what a bore these two histories have become! It is not that they are false in any simple sense – just that they are no more than fragments of the story. And one cannot help feeling that what they miss is precisely the essential. Try to understand, for example, the careers of Cézanne and Van Gogh with their aid! We shall retrieve the meaning of these concepts only if we demote them, uncover the *avant-garde* only if we criticize it, see the point of an art of pure sensation only if we put back the terror into the whole project. In other words, explain Mallarmé's words to Villiers de l'Isle-Adam: 'You will be terrified to learn that I have arrived at the idea of the Universe by sensation alone (and that, for example, to keep firm hold of the notion of pure Nothingness I had to impose on my brain the sensation of the absolute void).' Which leads us straight to Hegel and other disagreeable topics.

What we need, and what a study of any one period or problem in detail suggests, is a multiplicity of perspectives. Let me name a few, more or less in note form.

First, the dominance of classicism in nineteenth-century art – not just the continuing power of academic classicism in the Salon, but the bias of French art towards an introspective, fantastic, deeply literary painting and sculpture which drew on antique form and subject-matter. An art history which sees Chassériau, Moreau, Gérôme, Rodin, Puvis and Maurice Denis as marginal episodes, rather than the most vivid representatives of a vigorous, enduring tradition – that art history will not do. Precisely because it fails to account for the ambivalence of artists whom we call *avant-garde*: the classicism of Corot, of Daumier, of Millet, Degas, Seurat. Realism is an episode against the grain of French art; and therefore its forms have to be extreme, explosive. Hence Courbet's Realism; hence Cubist realism which looked back to Courbet as its extremist founding father; hence, finally, Dada. And hence also the neo-classical reaction against all three.

Second, the progress of individualism in French art – which is something different from the movement towards an art of absolute sensation. It was a doctrine with confusing implications for the arts. Moreau and Rodin thought it meant the reworking of classical form and content. Courbet thought it meant immersion in the physical world, a rediscovery of the self the other side of matter (in this he was the carrier of his friends' Hegelianism). Gautier and the classicists thought it an unworthy ideal. Individualism was the platitude of the age, contradictory, inflated, often absurd; yet somehow or other the idea that art was nothing if not the expression of an individuality, and that its disciplines were all means to this ambiguous end, survived. The Realist movement was shot through with this dogma; why it persisted, and what in practical terms it prescribed, is a central nineteenth-century problem.

Third, whether to sanctify the newly dominant classes or to look for a means to subvert their power. Whether to address your respectful, ironic preface *Aux Bourgeois*; or to climb the barricades, hands black with powder, to dispute their rule. Baudelaire tried both solutions in the space of two years, and then gradually retreated into an icy disdain: 'What does it matter whether the bourgeoisie keeps or loses an illusion?', as he commented in 1859. But it continued to matter for artists; they continued to wonder whether bourgeois existence was heroic, or degraded, or somehow conveniently both. They did so because it was a doubt that touched their own identity. Was one to be, as in Renoir's *Portrait of Alfred Sisley and his Wife*, the artist as bourgeois; or was one to be, in fact or dream, in a thousand evasive self-portraits, the artist as outcast? Or, perhaps, the artist as opponent – Courbet's intention, which also persisted. (In the 1880s and 1890s art and anarchism renewed their contact.)

Fourth, the problem of popular art, which is part of this wider crisis of confidence. In its most acute form – in Courbet, in Manet, in Seurat – the problem was whether to exploit popular forms and iconography to reanimate the culture of the dominant classes, or attempt some kind of provocative fusion of the two, and in so doing destroy the dominance of the latter. On its own, a Utopian project. But one which haunted French art, from Géricault's London lithographs to Van Gogh's Arlesian portraits. Hence, once again, the connection of art with political action.

Fifth and last, the withering-away of art. In a century which 'liberated the forms of creation from art' – the century of the photograph, the Eiffel Tower, the Commune – iconoclasm is not incidental. No theme is more insistent; it is, necessarily, part of the century's Realism: Iconoclasm and *l'Art pour l'Art* are different responses to the same unease. When Proudhon wrote in *Philosophie du progrès* in November 1851, 'For our own most rapid regeneration, I should like to see the museums, cathedrals, palaces, salons, boudoirs, with all their furniture, ancient and modern, thrown to the flames – and artists forbidden to practise their art for fifty years. Once the past was forgotten, we would do something', he was, surprisingly, addressing himself to the same problem that exercised Gautier. His bluster is only the other side of Gautier's irony ('You think me cold and do not see that I am imposing on myself an artificial calm,' as Baudelaire put it later).

Somewhere between irony and bluster lie Courbet's attitudes, or Baudelaire's conviction in 1851 that 'art *had to be* inseparable from . . . utility'. In Baudelaire's case that belief lasted three or four years at the most; afterwards came blackness, despair, the first poetry to celebrate 'the theatrical and joyless futility of everything' (Jacques Vaché). If art was useless, so was life; and that was not an idiosyncratic conclusion. It leads us to Mallarmé's 'horrible vision of a work that is pure' ('*vision horrible d'une œuvre pure*'), to Tzara's 'Rhymes ring with the assonance of the currencies, and the inflexion slips along the line of the belly in profile', and to Miró's 'murder of painting'.

The inheritor of Baudelaire's short-lived belief is Surrealism: in Breton's words, 'We have nothing to do with literature, but we are quite capable, when the need arises, of making use of it like everyone else'. Though by then the implications of that belief were clearer: to quote the Surrealist Declaration of 1925, 'We are not utopians: we conceive of this Revolution only in its social form.'

When Proudhon talked in *Du principe de l'art* of creative activity entering the world and taking it as its material, to be altered directly and not just on canvas, he echoed Hegel but presaged the moderns. Malevich said, 'Let us seize the world from the hands of nature and build a new world belonging to man himself.' And Mondrian: 'One day the time will come when we shall be able to do without all the arts, as we know them now; beauty will have ripened into palpable reality. Humanity will not lose much by missing art.'

40   Preliminaries to a Possible Treatment of *Olympia* in 1865

T. J. Clark

I

Manet was not in the habit of hesitating before trying to put his large-scale works on public exhibition; he most often sent them to the Salon the same year they were painted. But for reasons we can only guess at, he kept the picture entitled *Olympia* in his studio for almost two years, perhaps repainted it, and submitted it to the Jury in 1865. It was accepted for showing, initially hung in a good position, and was the subject of excited public scrutiny and a great deal of writing in the daily newspapers and periodicals of the time. The 1860s were the heyday of the Parisian press, and a review of the Salon was established as a necessary feature of almost any journal. [. . .] The eighty-odd pieces of writing on the Salon in 1865, and the sixty or so which chose to mention Manet, were thoroughly aware of themselves as members of a family, jibing at each other's preferences, borrowing each other's turns of phrase, struggling for room (for 'originality') in a monotonous and constricting discourse.

If Manet's hesitation had to do with anxieties over what the papers would say, then what happened when the Salon opened was to prove his worst fears well-founded. The critical reaction to *Olympia* was decidedly negative. Only four critics out of sixty were favourably disposed to the picture, and that figure disguises the extremity of the situation: if we apply the test not merely of approval, but of some sustained description of the object in hand – some effort at controlled attention to particulars, some ordinary mobilisation of the resources of criticism in 1865 – then a response to *Olympia* simply does not exist, except in a solitary text written by Jean Ravenel. Although there is also, I believe, some real investigation of *Olympia* in three caricatures, each with elaborate captions, by Bertall and Cham. That caricatures can have truck with Manet's picture in a way which art criticism cannot, points to one aspect of the problem. Their success has to do, I suppose, with the possibilities provided by a very different set of discursive conventions – a discourse in which the unmentionable and indescribable, for art criticism, can be readily articulated in comic form. It was not, incidentally, that the art critics failed to try for comic effect at *Olympia*'s expense; they did so interminably; but jokes, in this case, were rarely productive of knowledge.

I believe this mass of disappointing art criticism can provide an opportunity to say more about the relation of a text to its spectators. I shall regularly use the words 'text' and 'spectator' in this article, for all their awkwardness as applied to pictures. In the case of *Olympia* the vocabulary is not especially forced, since an important part of what spectators reacted to in 1865 was textual in the ordinary sense of the word:

Source: Screen vol. **21**, no. 1, Spring 1980, pp. 18–41. Illustrations have been omitted.

the perplexing title, the outlandish five lines of verse provided in the Salon *livret*:

> *Quand, lasse de rêver, Olympia s'éveille,*
> *Le Printemps entre au bras du doux messager noir,*
> *C'est l'esclave á la nuit amoureuse pareille,*
> *Qui vient fleurir le jour délicieux à voir:*
> *L'auguste jeune fille en qui la flamme veille.*

> When, weary of dreaming, Olympia awakes,
> Spring enters in the arms of a gentle black messenger.
> It is the slave who, like the amorous night,
> Comes in and makes the day delicious to see with flowers:
> The august young woman in whom the flame [of passion] burns constantly.

These verses greatly exercised the critics: they figured as one of the grounds for their contemptuous dislike.

A complete study of *Olympia* and its spectators would be cumbersome, and I am not going to present it here. What I intend instead is to sketch the necessary components of such a study, to raise some theoretical questions which relate to *Screen's* recent concerns, and to give, in conclusion, a rather fuller account of the ways in which this exercise might provide

a materialist reading [specifying] articulations within the [picture] on determinate grounds. [1]

II

[. . .] It seems to me that *Olympia* in 1865 provides us with something close to a limiting case of recalcitrance [to critical or public understanding . . .] Recalcitrance is almost too weak a word, and insignificance or unavailability might do better, for what we are dealing with in 1865 are the remains of various failures – a collective failure, minus Ravenel – to pull *Olympia* within the field of any of the discourses available, and restructure it in terms which gave it a sense. There is a danger of exaggeration here, since the disallowed and the unforgivable are in themselves necessary tropes of nineteenth-century art criticism: there had to be occupants of such places in every Salon. But a close and comprehensive reading of the sixty texts of 1865 ought to enable us to distinguish between a rhetoric of incomprehension, produced smoothly as part of the ordinary discourse of criticism, and another rhetoric – a breaking or spoiling of the critical text's consistency – which is produced by something else, a real recalcitrance in the object of study. It is an open question whether what we are studying here is an instance of subversive refusal of the established codes, or of a simple ineffectiveness; and it is an important question, given *Olympia's* canonical (and deserved) status in the history of avant-garde art.

III

I would like to know which set of discourses *Olympia* encountered in 1865, and why the encounter was so unhappy. I think it is clear that two main discourses were in question: a discourse in which the relations and disjunctions of the terms 'woman'/'nude'/'prostitute' were obsessively rehearsed (which I shall call, clumsily, 'The discourse on Woman in the 1860s'), and the complex but deeply repetitive discourse of aesthetic judgment in the Second Empire. These are immediately historical categories, of an elusive and developing kind; they cannot be deduced from the critical texts alone, and it is precisely their absence from the writings on *Olympia* – their appearance there in spasmodic and unlikely form – which concerns us most. So we have to establish, in the familiar manner of the historian, some picture of normal functioning: the regular ways in which these two discourses worked, and their function in the historical circumstances of the 1860s.

Olympia is a picture of a prostitute: various signs declare that unequivocally. The fact was occasionally acknowledged in 1865: several critics called the woman *courtisane*, one described her as 'some redhead from the *quartier Bréda*' (the notorious headquarters of the profession), another referred to her as '*une manolo du bas étage*'. Ravenel tried to specify more precisely, calling her a 'girl of the night from Paul Niquet's' – in other words, a prostitute operating right at the bottom end of the trade, in the all-night bar run by Niquet in Les Halles, doing business with a clientele of market porters, butchers and *chiffonniers*. But by and large this kind of recognition was avoided, and the sense that Olympia's was a sexuality laid out for inspection and sale appeared in the critics' writings in a vocabulary of uncleanness, dirt, death, physical corruption and actual bodily harm. Now this is odd, because both the discourse on Woman in the 1860s, and the established realm of art, had normally no great difficulty in including and accepting the prostitute as one of their possible categories. There is even a sense, as Alain Corbin establishes in his study of *le discours prostitutionnel* in the nineteenth century, in which the prostitute was necessary to the articulation of discourse on woman in general.[2] She was maintained – anxiously and insistently – as a *unity*, which existed as the end-stop to a series of differences which constituted the feminine. The great and absolute difference was that between *fille publique* and *femme honnête*: the two terms were defined by their relation to each other, and therefore it was necessary that the *fille publique* – or at least her *haute bourgeoise* variant, the *courtisane* – should have her representations. The *courtisane* was a category in use in a well-established and ordinary ideology; she articulated various (false) relations between sexual identity, sexual power and social class. Of course at the same time she was declared to be almost unmentionable – at the furthest margin of the categorisable – but that only seemed to reaffirm her importance as a founding signification of Woman.

So it was clearly not the mere fact – the palpable signs – of Olympia being a prostitute that produced the critics' verbal violence. It was some transgression of *le discours prostitutionnel* that was at stake; or rather, since the characterisation of the *courtisane* could not be disentangled from the specification of Woman in general in the 1860s, it was some disturbance in the normal relations between prostitution and femininity.

When I introduced the notion of a discourse on Woman in the 1860s, I included the nude as one of its terms. Certainly it deserves to take its place there, but the very word indicates the artificiality of the limits we have to inscribe – for description's sake – around our various 'discourses'. The nude is indelibly a term of art and art criticism: the fact is that art criticism and sexual discourse intersect at this point, and the one provides the other with crucial representations, forms of knowledge and standards of decorum. One could almost say that the nude is the mid-term of the series which goes from *femme honnête* to *fille publique*: it is the important form (the complex of established forms) in which sexuality is revealed and not revealed, displayed and masked, made out to be unproblematic. It is the frankness of the bourgeoisie: here, after all, is what Woman looks like; and she can be known, in her nakedness, without too much danger of pollution. This too *Olympia* called into question, or at least failed to confirm.

One could put the matter schematically in this way. The critics asked certain questions of *Olympia* in 1865, and did not get an answer. One of them was: what sex is she, or has she? Has she a sex at all? In other words, can we discover in the image a preordained constellation of signifiers which keeps her sexuality in place? Further question: can *Olympia* be included within the discourse on Woman/the nude/the prostitute? Can this particular body, acknowledged as one for sale, be articulated as a term in an artistic tradition? Can it be made a modern example of the nude? Is there not a way in which the terms *nude* and *fille publique* could be mapped on to each other, and shown to belong together? There is no *a priori* reason why not. (Though I think there may be historical reasons why the mapping could not be done effectively in 1865: reasons to do with the special instability of the term 'prostitute' in the 1860s, which was already producing, in the discourse on Woman, a peculiar mythology of invasion, whereby the prostitute was made out to have vacated her place at the edge of society, and be engaged in building a new city, in which everything was edges and no single demarcation was safe.)

It is a matter of tracking down, in the writings on *Olympia*, the appearance of the normal forms of discourse and the points/topics/tropes at which (or around which) they are simply absent, or present in a grossly disturbed state. For instance, the various figures of uncleanness, and the way these figures cannot be maintained as descriptions of sexual or moral status, but always teeter over into figures of death and decay. Or the figures which indicate the ways in which the hand of Olympia – the one spread over her pubic hair – disobeys, crucially, the conventions of the nude. The hand is *shamelessly flexed*, it is *improper*, it is *in the form of a toad*, it is *dirty*, it is in a state of *contraction*. It comes to stand for the way Olympia's whole body is disobedient: the hand is the sign of the unyielding, the unrelaxed, the too definite where indefiniteness is the rule, the non-supine, the concealment which declares itself as such: the 'unfeminine', in short. Or again: the figures of physical violence done to the body, or of hideous constraint:

> a woman on a bed, or rather some form or other, blown up like a grotesque in indiarubber, a skeleton dressed in a tight jacket made of plaster, outlined in black, like the armature of a stained glass window without the glass.[3]

Or the figures which intimate – no more than that – the critics' unease over Olympia's handling of hair and hairlessness: precious *pudeurs*, with which the nude makes clear its moral credentials. One of the easy triumphs of Bertall's caricature is to put the cat and flowers in place of the hand, and let us have the great explosion of foliage, and the black absence at its centre.

IV

Would it be helpful to say, at the conclusion of a reading of the critics, that *Olympia* failed to signify in 1865? I have already indicated some reservations about this:

another would be the sheer neatness of the formula. But I think it possible to say that at its first showing *Olympia* was not given a meaning that was stabilised long enough to provide the framework for any further investigation – for some kind of knowledge, for criticism. It seems reasonable to call that a failure on *Olympia's* part; since the picture, it is clear to us now, certainly attempts – blatantly, even ponderously – to instate within itself a relationship to established, previous forms of representation. The evidence suggests that this relationship was *not* instated, for the spectators in 1865; or that even when it was – in the very few cases when the picture's points of reference were perceived – this did not lead to an articulated and consistent reading (whether one of approval or dissent).

I shall give two examples: one concerning *Olympia's* relation to Titian's so-called *Venus of Urbino*, and the other Ravenel's treatment of the picture's relation to the poetry of Baudelaire. That *Olympia* is arranged in such a way as to invite comparison with the Titian has become a commonplace of criticism in the twentieth century, and a simple charting of the stages of Manet's invention, in preparatory sketches for the work, is sufficient to show how deliberate was the reference back to the prototype.[4] The reference was not obscure in the nineteenth century: the Titian painting was a hallowed and hackneyed example of the nude: when Manet had done an oil copy of it as a student, he would have known he was learning the very alphabet of art. Yet in the mass of commentary on *Olympia* in 1865, only two critics talked at all of this relation to Titian's *Venus*; only twice, in other words, was it allowed that *Olympia* existed 'with reference to' the great tradition of European painting. And the terms in which it was allowed are enough to indicate why the other critics were silent.

'This Olympia,' wrote Amédée Cantaloube in *Le Grand Journal*, 21 May 1865,

> sort of female gorilla, grotesque in indiarubber surrounded by black, apes on a bed, in a complete nudity, the horizontal attitude of the Venus of Titian, the right arm rests on the body in the same way, except for the hand which is flexed in a sort of shameless contraction.

The other, a writer who called himself Pierrot, in a fly-by-night organ called *Les Tablettes de Pierrot*, had this entry:

> a woman on a bed, or rather some form or other blown up like a grotesque in indiarubber; a sort of monkey making fun of the pose and the movement of the arm of Titian's Venus, with a hand shamelessly flexed.

The duplication of phrases is too close, surely, to be a matter of chance, or even of dogged plagiarism. The two texts seem to me to be the work of the same hand – the same hack bashing out a swift paragraph in various places under various names. Which makes it one voice out of sixty, rather than two.

In any case the point is this. For the most part, for almost everyone, the reference back to tradition in *Olympia* was invisible. Or if it could be seen, it could certainly not be said. And if, once, it could be spoken of, it was in these terms: Titian's arrangement of the nude was there, vestigially, but in the form of absolute travesty, a kind of vicious aping which robbed the body of its femininity, its humanity, its very fleshiness, and put in its place *une forme quelconque*, a rubber-covered gorilla flexing her dirty hand about her crotch.

I take Pierrot's entry, and the great silence of the other texts, as licence to say, quite crudely in the end, that the meaning contrived in terms of Titian – *on* and *against* that privileged schema of sex – was *no* meaning, had no meaning, in 1865. (This is a matter which becomes familiar in the later history of the avant garde: the moment at which negation and refutation becomes simply too complete; they erase what they are meant to negate, and therefore no negation takes place; they refute their prototypes too effectively and the old dispositions are – sometimes literally – painted out; they 'no longer apply'.)

The example of Ravenel is more complex. I have already said that Ravenel's text is the only one in 1865 that could possibly be described as articulate, and somehow appropriate to the matter in hand. But it is an odd kind of articulacy. Ravenel's entry on *Olympia* comes at the end of the eleventh long article in an immense series he published in *L'Epoque*, a paper of the far left opposition.[5] It comes in the middle of an alphabetical listing of pictures which he has so far left out of account, and not allotted their proper place in the extended critical narrative of the first ten instalments of the Salon. The entry itself is a peculiar, brilliant, *inadvertent* performance; a text which blurts out the obvious, blurts it out and passes on; ironic, staccato, as if aware of its own uncertainty.

> M. Manet – *Olympia*. The scapegoat of the Salon, the victim of Parisian lynch law. Each passer-by takes a stone and throws it in her face. *Olympia* is a very crazy piece of Spanish madness, which is a thousand times better than the platitude and inertia of so many canvases on show in the Exhibition.
>
> Armed insurrection in the camp of the bourgeois: it is a glass of iced water which each visitor gets full in the face when he sees the BEAUTIFUL courtesan in full bloom.
>
> Painting of the school of Baudelaire, freely executed by a pupil of Goya; the vicious strangeness of the little *faubourienne*, woman of the night out of Paul Niquet, out of the mysteries of Paris and the nightmares of Edgar Poe. Her look has the sourness of someone prematurely aged, her face the disturbing perfume of a *fleur de mal*; the body fatigued, corrupted ['*corrumpu*' also carries the meaning 'tainted', 'putrid'], but painted under a single transparent light, with the shadows light and fine, the bed and the pillows are put down in a velvet modulated grey. Negress and flowers insufficient in execution, but with real harmony to them, the shoulder and arm solidly established in a clean and pure light. The cat arching its back makes the visitor laugh and relax, it is what saves M. Manet from a popular execution.

> *De sa fourrure noire* [sic] *et brune*
> *Sort un parfum si doux, qu'un soir*
> *J'en fus embaumé pour l'avoir*
> *Caressé* [sic] *une fois . . . rien qu'une.*

> From its black and brown fur
> Comes a perfume so sweet, that one evening
> I was embalmed in it, from having
> Caressed it once . . . only once.

> *C'est l'esprit familier du lieu;*
> *Il juge, il préside, il inspire*
> *Toutes choses dans son empire:*
> *Peut-être est-il fée, est-il dieu?*

> It is the familiar spirit of the place;
> It judges, presides, inspires
> All things within its empire;
> Is it perhaps a fairy, or a god?

M. Manet, instead of M. Astruc's verses would perhaps have done well to take as epigraph the quatrain devoted to Goya by the most advanced painter of our epoch:

> *GOYA Cauchemar plein de choses inconnues*
> *De foetus qu'on fait cuire au milieu des sabbats,*
> *De vieilles au miroir et d'enfants toutes nues*
> *Pour tenter les démons ajustant bien leurs bas.*

GOYA – Nightmare full of unknown things
Of foetuses cooked in the middle of witches' sabbaths,
Of old women at the mirror and children quite naked
To tempt demons who are making sure their stockings fit.

Perhaps this *olla podrida de toutes les Castilles* is not flattering for M. Manet, but all the same it is something. You do not make an Olympia simply by wanting.

This is effective criticism, there is no doubt. But let me restrict myself to saying one thing about it. Ravenel – it is the achievement which first impresses us, I suppose – breaks the codes of *Olympia*. He gets the picture right, and ties the picture down to Baudelaire and Goya; he is capable of discussing the image, half playfully and half in earnest, as deliberate provocation, designed to be anti-bourgeois; he can even give Olympia, for a moment, a class identity, and call her a *petite faubourienne* – a girl from the working-class suburbs – or a *fille des nuits de Paul Niquet*. But getting things right does not seem to enable Ravenel to accede to meaning: it is almost as if breaking the codes makes matters worse from that point of view; the more particular signifiers and signifieds are detected, the more perplexing and unstable the totality of signs becomes. What, for instance, does the reference to Baudelaire *connote*, for Ravenel? There are, as it were, four signs of that connotation in the text: the 'school of Baudelaire' leads on (1) to the disturbing perfume of a *fleur du mal*; then (2) to two verses from a short poem from the first book of Baudelaire's collection, entitled *Le Chat*, a poem precise in diction, spare and lucid in rhythm, deliberately decorous in its intimations of sexuality; and then, in passing, (3) to the description of Baudelaire as 'le peintre le plus *avancé* de notre époque', where the ironic underlining of *avancé* does not make the meaning any easier to pin down; and finally (4) to the nightmare ride of the Goya quatrain from *Les Phares*, the fetid stew of cooked foetuses and devil women, the self-consciously Satanic Baudelaire, the translator of *Tales of Mystery and Imagination*.

My point is this: the discovery of Baudelaire does not stabilise meaning. On the contrary, for a reader like Ravenel it destabilises meaning still further, since Baudelaire's meanings are so multiple and refractory, so unfixed, so unmanageable, in 1865. We are face to face with the only text equipped and able to take on the picture's central terms of reference; and this is how it takes them, as guarantee of its own perplexity, its opinion that the picture is a stew of half-digested significations. Perhaps guarantee is too weak a word in this connection: the code, once discovered, compounds the elusiveness; it speeds up the runaway shifts of connotation; it fails, completely, to give them an anchorage in any one pre-eminent, privileged system of signs.

The same is true for the recognition or attribution of class. Once again, we are entitled to draw breath at Ravenel's *petite faubourienne*: it may seem to us close to the mark, that phrase. But what does it signify in the text itself, what system of meanings does it open on to? It means nothing precise, nothing maintainable: it opens on to three phrases, *'fille des nuits de Paul Niquet, des mystères de Paris et des cauchemars d'Edgar Poe'*. A working girl from the *faubourgs*/a woman from the farthest edges of *la prostitution populaire clandestine*, soliciting the favours of *chiffonniers* (one might reasonably ask: With a black maid bringing in a tribute of flowers? Looking like this, with these accessories, this décor, this imperious presentation of self?)/a character out of Eugène Sue's melodramatic novel of the city's lower depths/a creature from Edgar Allen Poe. The shifts are motivated clearly, but it is thoroughly unclear what the motivation *is*: the moves are too rapid and abrupt, they fail to confirm each other's sense – or even to intimate some one thing, too elusive to be caught directly, but to which the various metaphors of the text all tend.

The identification of class is not a *brake* on meaning: it is the trigger, once again, of a sequence of connotations which do not add up, which fail to circle back on themselves, declaring their meaning evident and uniform. It may be that we are too eager, now, to point to the illusory quality of that circling back, that closure against the 'free play of the signifier'. Illusion or not, it seems to me the necessary ground on which meanings can be established and maintained: kept in being long enough, and endowed with enough coherence, for the ensuing work of dispersal and contradiction to be seen to matter – to have matter, in the text, to work against.

V

[. . .] I suppose it will be obvious that *my* reading of *Olympia* will be produced as a function of the analysis of its first readings: I do not claim that this gives it some kind of objectivity, or even some privileged status 'within historical materialism'. But it provides the reading with certain tests of appropriateness, or, to put it another way, it presents the reading with a set of particular questions to answer, which have been produced as part of historical enquiry. (I do not object to the formula 'historian's practice' here, as long as we are free to debate whether there are some practices of knowledge with more articulated notions of evidence, testing and 'matching' than others.)

My reading of *Olympia* would address the question: what is it in the image which produces, or helps produce, the critical silence and uncertainty I have just described? What is it that induces this interminable displacement and conversion of meanings? I would like, ideally, to give the answer to those questions an interleaved, almost a scholiastic form, tying my description back and back to the terms of the critics' perplexity, and its blocked, unwilling insight into its own causes. Clearly, the reading would hinge on *Olympia*'s handling of sexuality, and its relation to the tradition of the nude. (It would also have to deal with its relation to a new and distinctive subset of that tradition: the burlesque and comic refutation of the nude's conventions set in train by Courbet in the 1850s. There is no doubt that the critics in 1865 wanted *Olympia* to be part of that subset, whose terms they approximately understood, if only to abhor them; and there are ways in which the picture does relate to Courbet's Realism. A painting of a prostitute in 1865 inevitably bore comparison with Courbet's *Demoiselles de la Seine* or *Venus Capitonnée*; a comparison of subject-matter, obviously, but also of modes of address to the viewer, forms of disobedience to that 'placing of the spectator in a position of imaginary knowledge' which was the nude's most delicate achievement.) I shall give some element of the reading here.

VI

We might approach the problem by asking, would it do to describe the disposition of signs in *Olympia* as producing some kind (various forms) of *ambiguity*? The things I shall point out in the image may seem at first sight nothing very different from this. And the word would provide us with a familiar critical comfort, since it seems to legitimise the position of the a-historical 'interpreter' and allow the open, endless procession of possible meanings to be the very nature of the text, the way *art* ('literature') works, as opposed to mere practical discourse. I do not agree with that ethic of criticism, or the art practice it subtends. On the contrary, it seems to me that ambiguity is only functional in the text when a certain hierarchy of meanings is established and agreed on between text and reader – whether it be a hierarchy of exoteric and esoteric, or common-sense and 'contrary', or narrative discourse and non-narrative connotation, or whatever. There has to be a structure of dominant and dominated meanings, within which ambiguity occurs as a qualifier, a chorus, a texture of overtone and undertone around a *tone* which the trained ear recognises or invents. [. . .]

It could be argued that *Olympia*'s recalcitrance is different from this. The work of contradiction – to repeat and generalise the point made with reference to Titian – might seem to be so complete in this picture that the reader is left with no primary system of signifieds to refer to, as a test for deviations. *Olympia* could be described as a tissue of loose ends, false starts, unfinished sequences of signification: none of them the main theme, none accompaniment exactly; neither systematic nor floating *semes*.

The picture turns, inevitably, on the signs of sexual identity. I want to argue that, for the critics of 1865, sexual identity was precisely what Olympia did not possess. She failed to occupy a place in the discourse of Woman, and specifically she was neither a nude, nor a prostitute: by that I mean she was not a modification of the nude in ways which made it clear that what was being shown was sexuality on the point of escaping from the constraints of decorum – sexuality proffered and scandalous. There is no scandal in *Olympia*, in spite of the critics' effort to construct one. It was the odd coexistence of decorum and disgrace – the way in which neither set of qualities established its dominance over the other – which was the difficulty of the picture in 1865.

For instance, since the structure is grossly obvious here, the picture's textual support. On the one hand, there is the title itself: classical apparently, and perceived by some critics as a reference to a notorious *courtisane* of the Renaissance; but in 1865, taking its place in the normal repertoire of prostitution, part of the tawdry, mock-classical lexicon of the trade.[6] But that *false* classical does not subsist as the undisputed timbre of *Olympia*: in the Salon *livret*, the reader was confronted by the five lines of 'explanatory' verse I have quoted already. It is bad poetry, but correct. It is a performance in an established mode, Parnassian; restrained in diction, formal, euphemistic. Is the reader to take it seriously? Is it to be Olympia, cynical pseudonym, or '*l'auguste jeune fille en qui*' – preposterous evasion – '*la flamme veille*'? The disparity was obvious, I have said, and the critics could deal with it by simple, calm derision: they regularly did.

Other kinds of unco-operativeness were subtler and more complete, and the critics could only rarely identify what it was that refused their various strategies. I shall deal with three aspects of the matter here: (1) The question of access and address; (2) The 'incorrectness' in the drawing of the body; (3) The handling of hair and hairlessness.

1 One of the primary operations of the nude is, to borrow MacCabe's phrase, 'a placing of the spectator in a position of imaginary knowledge'. The spectator's access to the presented body has to be arranged rather precisely; and this is done first through a certain arrangement of distance, which must be neither too great nor too small; and then through a placing of the naked body at a determinate height, which in turn produces a specific relation to the viewer. The body, again, must not be too high – put up on some fictive pedestal – nor too low, otherwise it may turn into an object of mere scrutiny, or humiliation – laid out on the dissecting table of sight.

In the 1830s, Realism had invented a set of refutations of just these placings; though it should be admitted that the refutations were intermittent and unstable. Perhaps it would be better to say that in certain paintings by Courbet there appeared the first forms, the first suggestions, of ways in which the placings of the nude might be negated. Courbet's *The Bather* of 1853 is the strongest case, since it seems to have been such a deliberate sabotage: a travesty of the normal canons of 'beauty', obviously, and an attempt to make the nude, of all unlikely genres, exemplify the orders of social class. *The Bather* was meant to be read as a *bourgeoise*, not a nude: she was intended to register as the unclothed opposite and opponent of male proletarian nakedness; and so Courbet displayed the painting in the Salon alongside another of roughly equal size, in which a pair of gnarled and exhausted professional wrestlers went through their paces in the *Hippodrome des Champs-Elysées*.

But *The Bather* broke the rules of the nude in other ways which were hardly more subtle, but perhaps more effective. It seemed to be searching for ways to establish the nude in opposition to the spectator, in active refusal of his sight. It did so grossly, clumsily, but not without some measure of success, so that the critic at the time who called the woman 'this heap of matter, powerfully rendered, who turns her back with cynicism on the spectator' had got the matter right. The pose and the scale and the movement of the figure end up being a positive aggression, a resistance to vision in normal terms.

There is no doubt that for Manet and his critics in 1865 these precedents were inescapable: as I have said already, the critics *wanted* Manet to be a Realist in Courbet's terms. But *Olympia*, I would argue, takes up neither the arrangements by which the canonical images of the nude establish access, nor Realism's knock-about refutations. What it contrives is stalemate, a kind of baulked invitation, in which the spectator is given no established place for viewing and identification, nor offered the tokens of exclusion and resistance. This is done most potently, I suppose, by the woman's gaze – the jet-black pupils, the slight asymmetry of the lids, the smudged and broken corner of the mouth, the features half-adhering to the plain oval of the face. It is a gaze which gives nothing away, as the reader attempts to interpret its blatancy; a look direct and yet guarded, poised very precisely between address and resistance. So precisely, so deliberately, that it comes to be read as a *production* of the depicted person herself; there is an inevitable elision between the qualities of precision and contrivance in the image and those qualities as inhering in the fictive subject: it is *her* look, her action on us, her composure, her composition of herself. But the gaze would not function as it does – as the focus of other uncertainties – were it not aided and abetted by the picture's whole composition. Pre-eminently, if it is access that is in question, there is the strange indeterminate scale of the image, neither intimate nor monumental; and there is the disposition of the unclothed body in relation to the spectator's imaginary position: she is put at a certain, deliberate marked height, on the two great mattresses and the flounced-up pillows; in terms of the tradition, she is at a height which is just too high, suggesting the stately, the body *out of relation* to the viewer's body; and yet not stately either, not looking down at us, not hieratic, not imperial: looking directly out and across, with a steadying, dead-level interpellation. The stalemate of 'placings' is impeccable and *typical*, that is my point. If at this primary level – the arrangement within the rectangle, so to speak, the laying-out in illusory depth – the spectator is offered neither access nor exclusion, then the same applies, as I shall try to show, to the picture's whole representation of the body.

2 What the critics indicated by talk of 'incorrectness' in the drawing of Olympia's body, and a wilder circuit of figures of dislocation and physical deformity, is, I would suggest, the way the body is constructed in two inconsistent graphic modes, which once again are allowed to exist in too perfect and unresolved an equilibrium. One aspect of the drawing of Olympia's body is emphatically linear: it was the aspect seized on by the critics, and given a metaphorical force, in phrases like 'cernés de noir', 'dessinée au charbon', 'raies de cirage', 'avec du charbon tout autour', 'le gros matou noir . . . ait déteint sur les contours de cette belle personne, après s'être roulé sur un tas de charbon'.[7] (These are figures which register also a reaction to Manet's elimination of half-tones, and the abruptness of the shadows at the edges of his forms: but this, of course, *is* an aspect of his drawing, taken in its widest sense.) The body is composed of smooth hard edges, deliberate intersections: the lines of the shoulders, singular and sharp; the far nipple breaking the contour of the arm with an artificial exactness; the edge of thigh and knee left flat and unmodulated against the dark green and pink; the central hand marked out on a dark grey ground, *'impudiquement crispée'* – in other words, as Pierrot implies, refusing to fade and elide with the sex beneath, in the metaphoric way of Titian and Giorgione. Yet this is an incomplete account. The critics certainly conceive of Olympia as too definite – full of *'lignes heurtées qui brisent les yeux'*[8] – but at the same time the image was accused of *lacking* definition. It was 'unfinished', and drawing 'does not exist in it'; it was *'impossible'*, elusive, *'informe'*. Olympia was disarticulated, but she was also inarticulate. I believe that this is a reaction on the critics' part to other aspects of the drawing: the suppression of demarcations and definitions of parts: the indefinite contour of Olympia's right breast, the faded bead of the nipple; the sliding, dislocated line of the far forearm as it crosses (touches?) the belly; the elusive logic of the transition from breast to ribcage to stomach to hip to thigh. There is a lack of articulation here. It is not unprecedented, this refusal; and in a sense it tallies well with the conventions of the nude, where the body is regularly offered as a fluid, infinite territory on which spectators are free to impose their imaginary definitions. But the trouble here is the incompatibility of this uncertainty and fullness with the steely precision of the edges which contain it. The body is, so to speak, tied down by drawing, held in place – by the hand, by the black tie around the neck, by the brittle inscription of grey wherever flesh is to be distinguished from flesh, or from the white of a pillow or the colour of a cashmere shawl. The way in which this kind of drawing qualifies, or relates to, the

other is unclear: it does not qualify it, because it does not relate: the two systems coexist: they describe aspects of the body, and point to aspects of that body's sexual identity, but they do not bring those aspects together into some single economy of form.

3 The manipulation of the signs of hair and hairlessness is a delicate matter for a painter of the nude. Peculiar matters of decorum are at stake, since hair let down is decent, but unequivocal: it is some kind of allowed disorder, inviting, unkempt, a sign of Woman's sexuality – a permissible sign, but quite a strong one. Equally, hairlessness is a hallowed convention of the nude: ladies in paintings do not have hair in indecorous places, and that fact is one guarantee that in the nude sexuality will be displayed but contained: nakedness in painting is not like nakedness in the world. There was no question of *Olympia* breaking the rules entirely; pubic hair, for Manet as much as Cabanel and Giacomotti, was indicated by its absence. But *Olympia* offers us various substitutes. The hand itself, which insists so tangibly on what it hides; the trace of hair in the armpit; the grey shadow running up from the navel to the ribs; even, another kind of elementary displacement, the frothing grey, white and yellow fringe of the shawl, falling into the grey folds of pillow and sheet – the one great accent in that open surface of different off-whites.

There are these kinds of displacement, discreetly done; and then there is an odd and fastidious reversal of terms. *Olympia*'s face is framed, mostly, by the brown of a Japanese screen, and the neutrality of that background is one of the things which makes the address and concision of the woman's face all the sharper. But the neutrality is an illusion: to the right of *Olympia*'s head there is a shock of auburn hair, just marked off enough from the brown of the screen to be visible, with effort. Once it is seen, it changes the whole disposition of head and shoulders: the flat, cut-out face is surrounded and rounded by the falling hair, the flower converts from a plain silhouette into an object resting in the hair below; the head is softened, given a more familiar kind of sexuality. The qualification remains, however: once it is seen, this happens: but in 1865 it was not seen, or certainly not seen to do the things I have just described. And even if it is noticed – the connoisseur's small reward for looking closely – it cannot, I would argue, be held in focus. Because, once again, we are dealing with incompatibilities precisely tuned: there are two faces, one produced by a ruthless clarity of edge and a pungent certainty of eyes and mouth, and the other less clearly demarcated, opening out into the surrounding spaces. Neither reading is suppressed by the other, nor can they be made into aspects of the *same* image, the same imaginary shape. [. . .] The face and the hair cannot be fitted together because they do not obey the usual set of equations for sexual consistency, equations which tell us what bodies are like, how the world of bodies is divided, into male and female, resistant and yielding, closed and open, aggressive and vulnerable, repressed and libidinous. [. . .]

Hair, pubic or otherwise, is a detail in *Olympia*, and should not be promoted unduly. But the detail is significant, and it obeys the larger rule I wish to indicate. The signs of sex are there in the picture, in plenty, but drawn up in contradictory order; one that is unfinished, or rather, more than one; *orders* interfering with each other, signs which indicate quite different places for *Olympia* in the taxonomy of Woman; and none of which she occupies.

VII

A word on effectiveness, finally. I can see a way in which most of what I have said about *Olympia* could be reconciled with an enthusiasm for the 'dis-identificatory practices' of art, 'those practices which displace the agent from his or her position of subjective centrality', and, in general, with 'an emphasis on the body and the impossibility of its exhaustion in its representations'. It would be philistine not to take that enthusiasm seriously, but there are all kinds of nagging doubts – above all, about whether 'dis-identificatory practices' *matter*. [. . .]

Is there a difference – a difference with immediate, tactical implications – between an allowed, arbitrary and harmless play of the signifier and a kind of play which contributes to a disruption of the smooth functioning of the dominant ideologies? If so, artistic practice will have to *address itself* to 'the specific positioning of the body in the economic, political and ideological practices'; it cannot take its own disruptions of the various signifying conventions as somehow rooted, automatically, in the struggle to control and position the body in political and ideological terms; it has to articulate the relations between its own minor acts of disobedience and the major struggles – the class struggle – which define the body and dismantle and renew its representations. Otherwise its acts will be insignificant – as Manet's were, I believe, in 1865.

There is a danger of sounding a hectoring, or even a falsely optimistic, note at this point. Only a sense that the burden of modernity in the arts *is* this insignificance will save us from the absurdity of feeling that we are not involved in Manet's failure; it might lead us to make a distinction between those works, like *Olympia*, which succumb to modernity as a fate they do not welcome, and those bland battalions which embrace emptiness and discontinuity as their life's blood, their excuse, their 'medium'. *Olympia* is not like these, its progeny; its failure to mean much is a sign of a certain obdurate strength. It is admirable in 1865 for a picture *not* to situate Woman in the space – the dominated and derealised space – of male fantasy. But this refusal – to sound again the demanding note – is compatible with situating Woman somewhere else: making her part of a fully coded, public and familiar world, to which fantasy has entry only in its real, uncomfortable, dominating and dominated form. One could imagine a different picture of a prostitute, in which there would be depicted the production of the sexual subject (the subject 'subjected', subject to and subject of fantasy). Even, perhaps, the production of the sexual subject in a particular class formation. But to do that – to put it crudely – Manet would have had to put a far less equivocal stress on the signs of social identity in this body and this locale. In fact, as we have seen, the signs of social identity are as unstable as all the rest. Olympia has a maid, which seems to situate her *somewhere* on the social scale; but the maid is black, convenient sign, stock property of any harlot's progress, derealised, telling us little or nothing of social class. She receives elaborate bouquets of flowers, but they are folded up in old newspaper; she is *faubourienne*, Ravenel is right, in her face and her disabused stare, but *courtisane* in her stately pose, her delicate shawl, her precious slippers.

Let me make what I am saying perfectly clear. Olympia refuses to signify – to be read according to the established codings for the nude, and take her place in the imaginary. But if the picture were to do anything more than that, it (she) would have to be given, much more clearly, a place in another classed code – a place in the code of classes. She would have to be given a place in the world which *manufactures* the imaginary, and reproduces the relations of dominator/dominated, fantasiser/fantasised.

The picture would have to construct itself a position – it would be necessarily a complex and elliptical position, but it would have to be readable somehow – within the actual conflict of images and ideologies surrounding the practice of prostitution in 1865. What that conflict consisted in was indicated, darkly, by the critics' own fumbling for words that year – the shift between *petite faubourienne* and *courtisane*. In other words, between the prostitute as proletarian, recognised as such and recognising herself as such, and the other, 'normal' Second Empire situation: the endless exchange of social and sexual meanings, in which the prostitute is alternately – fantastically – recognised as proletarian, as absolutely abject, shameless, seller of her own flesh, and then, in a flash, misrecognised as *dominator*, as *femme fatale*, as imaginary ruler. (This dance of recognition and misrecognition is one in which the prostitute shares, to a certain degree. But she is always able – indeed liable – to flip back to the simple assessment of herself as just another seller of an ordinary form of labour power. She has to be constantly re-engaged in the dance of ideology, and made to collude again in her double role.)

I think I should have to say that in the end *Olympia* lends its peculiar confirmation to the latter structure, the dance of ideology. It erodes the *terms* in which the normal recognitions are enacted, but it leaves the structure itself intact. The prostitute is still double, abject and dominant, equivocal, unfixed. To escape that structure what would be needed would be, exactly, another set of terms – terms which would be discovered, doubtless, in the act of unsettling the old codes and conventions, but which would have themselves to be *settled*, consistent, forming a finished sentence.

It may be that I am asking for too much. Certainly I am asking for the difficult, and equally certainly for something Manet did not do. I am pointing to the fact that there are always *other* meanings in any given social space – counter-meanings, alternative orders of meaning, produced by the culture itself, in the clash of classes, ideologies and forms of control. And I suppose I am saying, ultimately, that any critique of the established, dominant systems of meaning will degenerate into a mere refusal to signify unless it seeks to found its meanings – discover its contrary meaning – not in some magic re-presentation, on the other side of negation and refusal, but in signs which are already present, fighting for room – meanings rooted in actual forms of life; repressed meanings, the meanings of the dominated.

How exactly that is to be done is another matter. It will most assuredly not be achieved in a single painting. (There is no hope for 'Socialism in one Art-work', to borrow a phrase from Art-Language.) A clue to Manet's tactics in 1865, and their limitations, might come if we widened our focus for a moment and looked not just at *Olympia* but its companion painting in the Salon, *Jesus Insulted by the Soldiers*. This picture was also unpopular in 1865: some critics held it to be worse than *Olympia*, even; and many agreed in seeing it as a deliberate caricature of religious art. But the operative word here is *art*: if the *Jesus* is paired with the *Olympia*, the effect of the pairing is to entrench both pictures in the world of painting: they belong together only as contrasting artistic categories, as bizarre versions of the nude and the altarpiece. [. . .] The ambiguities of Manet's strategy are clear. What gives his work in the 1860s its peculiar force, and perhaps its continuing power of example, is that at the same time as his art turns inward on its own means and materials – clinging, with a kind of desperation, to the fragments of tradition left to it – it encounters and engages a whole contrary iconography. Its subjects are vulgar; the fastidious action of paint upon them does not soften, but rather intensifies, their awkwardness; the painting's purpose seems to be to show us the artifice of this familiar repertoire of modern life, and call in question the forms in which the city contrives its own appearance. Doing so, as we have seen, excluded Manet's art from the care and comprehension of almost all his contemporaries; though whether that is matter for praise or blame depends, in the end, on our sense of the possible, now and then.

References

1   C. MacCabe, 'The Discursive and the Ideological in Film'; *Screen*, vol. **19**, no. 4, p. 36.
2   A. Corbin, *Les Filles de noces. Misère sexuelle et prostitution aux 19e et 20e siècles*. Paris, 1978.
3   Pierrot, 'Histoire de la Semaine – Une première visite au Salon', *Les Tablettes de Pierrot*, 14 May 1865, p. 11; A.J. Lorentz, *Dernier Jour de L'Exposition de 1865*, p. 13.
4   See B. Farwell, *Manet and the Nude, A Study in Iconography in the Second Empire*. Unpublished PhD thesis, University of California at Los Angeles, 1973, pp. 199–204.
5   7 June 1865.
6   See B. Farwell, op. cit., p. 233.
7   L. de Laincel, *L'Echo de Provinces*, 25 June 1865, p. 3.
8   P. Gille, *L'International*, 1 June 1865.

41 The Laundress in Late Nineteeth-Century French Culture: Imagery, Ideology and Edgar Degas

Eunice Lipton

When art historians think of laundresses, Daumier and Degas come to mind. Depictions of these women were actually a commonplace in middle-class nineteenth-century French culture. Whether one thumbed through *Le Charivari*, visited the annual painting and sculpture Salons, frequented the theatre, read best-selling novels or coveted pornographic photographs, the laundress was everywhere. Most often she was a washerwoman – robust, hardworking, sometimes a drudge; frequently she was an ironer – pretty, street-elegant, flirtatious (*Fig. N*). [. . .]

In *Femme à Paris* (1894), a popular history of the time, Octave Uzanne wrote the following about ironers:

> [They] . . . are clean, coquettish, and often really pretty. . . . It cannot be said that their souls are as immaculate as the linen they iron. These girls have a shocking reputation for folly and grossness. . . . They haunt the outskirt of the city, are inveterate dancers, descend sometimes to the lowest forms of prostitution, and are also given to drink.

In addition, Uzanne noted, they quarrel ferociously, hurling a most 'remarkable vocabulary' at one another. Georges Montorgueil, a self-educated worker, journalist and popular writer, also commented on the laundresses' love of dancing. He suspected they were even abandoning laundering to become dancers at the neighbouring café-concerts.

The laundresses' moral code (or lack of it) motivated a great deal of Emile Zola's narrative in *L'Assommoir* (1887) as well. For all the attention Zola paid to the mundane details of working-class life and the ravages of alcoholism, it was the sexually titillating content of the novel which drew the critics' wrath and probably also attracted the enormous number of readers. [. . .]

Laundresses were not only popular in literature, but in painting too. Salon exhibits from 1865 to the end of the century showed at least one and sometimes as many as six paintings with titles such as *La reine des blanchisseuses* [The Queen of the Laundresses], *Lavoir dans le parc de Grandbourg* [Washing in the Grandbourg Park], *Au Lavoir* [At the Wash-house], *Soubrette Repassant* [Maid Ironing], and *Blanch-isseuses* [Laundresses]. These depicted both washerwomen and ironers. [. . .] More often than not, real toil was altogether eschewed in the paintings. Among the images of ironers a depiction of hard work is rarely found; virtually all of the ironers directly or indirectly flirt with the spectator. [. . .]

Source: Art History vol. 3, no. 3, Sept. 1980, pp. 295–313. Footnotes and one illustration have been omitted.

What is merely suggested in paintings becomes explicit in newspaper illustrations, popular prints and photographs of the day. When a laundress is depicted in *Le Charivari* (12 April 1859, *Fig. O*), for example, it is her flirtatiousness and easy morals which emerge as characteristic. [. . .] Earlier prints of the 1830s and '40s were the most explicit however. In *La Repasseuse* [The Ironer] (1837), an old woman enters, surprising a younger woman ironer who has just (none too successfully) hidden a suitor under the bed. The young woman, taken aback, attempts to pull her kerchief back into place. Her hot iron lies face-down, unnoticed, on a piece of unfinished work. [. . .] So predictably alluring were the ironers that when the fledgling photography business looked at them, they were seen as erotic objects as well (*Fig. P*).

Both the abundance of laundress images and the emphasis, especially among ironers, on sexuality are striking. One wonders why these particular female workers were so popular. A partial answer lies in their conspicuousness. The laundry industry occupied one-fifth to one-third of the population of Paris and its suburbs. The women were seen picking up and delivering their clients' laundry and laboriously transporting it to and from the washhouses. In addition, the windows and doors of their excessively hot ground-floor shops were thrown open so that any passer-by could easily see them working, semi-undressed in the heat. In most cases, this visibility cut across class lines, because Paris, more than other European capitals, maintained class fluidity through its structure. Despite the increasing ghettoization of the poor in the eastern part of the city and in the industrializing suburbs (accelerated by Haussmann's rebuilding of Paris in the 1850s and '60s), the city remained remarkably integrated. The social structure of many apartment buildings provided that integration: shops and concierges occupied the ground floor; the most prosperous tenants lived on the lower floors; the poorer ones higher up. The building's layout, therefore, schematized and heightened class distinctions, but it also fostered familiarity.

Visibility alone, however, does not explain middle-class cultural fascination with sexually provocative details and narratives. In fact this inclination is all the more striking and disturbing if one studies contemporary labour reports. We learn from them that a commercial laundress' life was a hard one – hours, pay and working conditions were wretched. The laundress worked up to fifteen and even eighteen hours a day, starting at 5 a.m. and continuing until 11 p.m. And she considered herself lucky to work those hours, because she wasn't always able to find employment.

The tasks of the ironers and washerwomen were quite different. Ironers working in small indoor spaces manoeuvred six- to seven-pound irons, often in devastating heat. They spent their time either carrying out demanding precision work on bonnets, blouses and shirt fronts – of which they were quite proud – or doing boring and repetitive work on sheets, table cloths and curtains. The monotony of the latter and most abundant type of work, plus the endless hours, had a stupefying effect.

The enclosed environment of the ironer was in striking contrast to the washerwoman's terrain – the city streets and washhouses. A washerwoman trekked through the city with twenty to thirty pounds of linen at her hip. She arrived at the washhouse only to experience the additional stress of having to compete with other women for space. Of course, another side of that competition was the lively give and take that echoed down the rows of tubs. Alliances shifted but no one could deny the mood of camaraderie that filled washhouses and ironing shops alike.

Sharing the work, however, did not necessarily compensate for the low pay. Ironers earned more than washerwomen, they were the skilled labourers of the trade. In 1881 a Parisian laundress brought home an average of 3.25 fr. a day – 30 centimes purchased about a kilogram of bread, 2.00 fr. about a kilogram of fresh meat. There were of course labourers who earned less. Lacemakers, for example, made approximately 3 fr. a day and ordinary seamstresses earned 2. But a teacher in a Catholic school made about 14, and a well-paid Parisian department store employee earned 70. The owner of a cotton spinning factory could accumulate 5000 in a day.

A woman who earned 3.75 fr. a day and was able to find work 260 days out of the year – which was unusual – would spend her year's income as follows:

Food	670.00 fr.
Rent	150.00
Clothing	110.00
Linen	93.60
Shoes	23.00
Heating and Lighting	12.65
Laundry	66.00
Misc.	50.00
	1175.25

Even living so stringently, her expenses exceeded her earnings by 200.25 fr., and she went into debt.

In addition, laundresses suffered from such physical ailments as inflammation of the abdomen and throat, bronchitis and tuberculosis. Ninety out of a hundred lived in only two rooms, one for ironing, one for sleeping. Quarters were cramped, and in most cases there was no kitchen. The women prepared food and ate in the rooms where they also counted, marked and sorted dirty laundry. The stench was awful. Dust and other particles released during sorting contaminated the air which was constantly heated by the furnace keeping the irons hot – a perfect breeding ground for germs.

Drinking provided laundresses, as it did other workers, with a ready escape from the daily strain. Encouraged by their employers, they began drinking – mostly wine and brandy – at about 11 a.m. and continued all day. So prevalent was this habit among laundresses that wine merchants set up canteens at the door of public washhouses and sometimes inside the washhouses themselves.

Objectively, then, laundresses were overworked, underpaid, sick and frequently alcoholic. What happened to this reality in the cultural images we examined earlier? Why did middle-class culture insist on seeing ironers almost exclusively in sexually alluring terms? There were, after all, other aspects of their lives which could have generated a good story or a lively painting. The answer to this question is embedded in the prevailing ideology of the urban middle classes.

As implied in the preceding paragraph, the concept ideology is being used here in a specifically Marxian sense. It refers to an outlook or set of ideas that is class-determined, that is, a set of ideas which defines and advances the interests of a dominant class: 'In this sense ideology is class domination in the realm of ideas.' Moreover, this conception of ideology assumes the presence of distortion. Ideology is:

an invocation of fictive entities, pseudo-rational constructions and abstract principles which concretely *justify and hide* a social historical practice whose true signification lies elsewhere. (Italics added.)

The discrepancy between prevalent cultural images of laundresses and the actual conditions of their lives is a concrete instance of hiding and justifying 'a social practice whose true signification lies elsewhere'. The harsh reality of the commercial laundress' daily life is concealed; she becomes both a sex object and the butt of class prejudice. Such ideologies, however, are by definition contradictory in that the distortions are not altogether untrue; they are not purely fabrications with no basis in reality; they are, rather, selective redefinitions of given elements of the conditions of life. In the instance of the laundresses' transformation into sex objects, we know, for example, that the women picked up and delivered laundry in what could become the provocative intimacy of a bachelor's rooms. Women who worked in devastating heat did in fact violate middle-class standards of dress and 'lady-like' conduct; as we have seen, they were semi-undressed much of the time. [. . .] It may actually have been the case that the sexual practices of individual laundresses were freer than those prescribed by the bourgeois concept of 'lady-like', although this may well have been true of many middle-class women as well. [. . .] But to what end did prevailing middle-class ideology emphasize the sexuality of working-class women? It can be argued that it accomplished two things: it neutralized middle-class fear and guilt towards workers, and it rationalized exploitation. [. . .]

In the social arena bourgeois fear of workers was often manifested as disdain. Daniel Halévy, a young friend of Edgar Degas, expressed just this prejudice when he said:

> The masses have always been the enemy of society. The aristocratic solution is to conquer them. The democratic (detestable word) is to suppress them while transforming them.

And in 1891 Edmond de Goncourt, another acquaintance of Degas, decried 'the weakness of present-day governments in the face of the working-class scum. . . '.

Another form of bourgeois class disdain was sexualizing the poor. [. . .] As long as laundresses were seen as immoral, they clearly deserved to earn less and to live in squalor. This selective redefinition of the condition of their lives legitimized their exploitation – 'one gets what one deserves'. [. . .]

It may come as something of a surprise that Edgar Degas' place in the history of laundress imagery is nothing less than extraordinary. If he does not escape his culture's ideologies (which no one can), he does positively subvert them. Yet there is not a hint of this in the Degas literature which tends to be formalist, anecdotal or analytical in terms of high culture. No one has even remarked on the anomaly of Degas depicting people working at all. Consider, for example, the extent to which people absolutely do not work in most Impressionist painting and how much Impressionism relentlessly presented a life of leisure and pleasure. From that vantage point alone, Degas' laundresses – and milliners, dancers and café singers – look quite exceptional indeed.

Degas painted and drew ironers and washerwomen over a thirty-three year period (*c.* 1869–*c.* 1902). In all, excluding his notebook sketches, there are twenty-seven works. Unlike his portraits of women of his own class, his images of laundresses are, in general, more genre-like than specific. The women stand in a small variety of poses and settings. The majority are ironers, nine are washerwomen. They are all simply drawn with a minimum of physical and contextual details. All the washerwomen lean away from the baskets of linen balancing at their hips (the most famous of these is the *Two Laundresses*, Sachs Collection, N.Y., 1876–1878). The ironers are similarly uncomplicated. Most of them incline in the direction of their work and have lost or vague profiles like *Woman Ironing* in the Metropolitan Museum of Art (*c*. 1874). The settings are spare, even empty, except for hanging laundry or naked architectural supports (indicative of the commercial locales). Another type of ironer is the double or multiple image (also indicative of a commercial space). These paintings are the most graphically descriptive – ironers stretching, yawning, chatting or merely working together (see, for example, *The Ironers*, The Norton Simon Museum of Art, Pasadena, 1882; *Two Laundresses*, Jeu de Paume, *c*. 1884; and the monotype *Ironers*, Foundation Jacques Doucet, *c*. 1880). The most specifically drawn, and therefore exceptional, among the ironers, are *The Ironer* (Bayerischen Staatsgemäldesammlungen, Munich, *c*. 1869), looking at us full-face, and the painting of the same name and date in the Jeu de Paume, which depicts a woman in three-quarter profile. All the ironers are in a state of semi-undress.

All we know from an initial encounter with these works is that the images are by and large genre-like depictions of lower-class women working in commercial spaces. They are also more abstract, atmospheric and evocative than they are literally descriptive. But nothing much seems to be happening in them. Or is it that we are so inured to looking at these works simply as beautiful objects that we are not capable of seeing the 'events' that are taking place? We now know that Degas' very choice of laundresses, or more particularly, commercial ironers, was itself provocative, since these women were full of sexual meaning for a middle-class spectator. We also know that laundresses had a special meaning for Degas, not merely because he painted and drew them so often, but because he described them in writing – and not disinterestedly.

When Degas visited relatives in New Orleans in 1872, he wrote to his friends in Paris fairly often. The letters were chatty and descriptive, with flashes of witty, sometimes near-passionate, longings for home. It is those longings that interest us, for he wrote to the painter Jacques Joseph Tissot, 'Everything is beautiful in this world of the people. But one Paris laundry girl, with bare arms, is worth it all for such a pronounced Parisian as I am.' And, again, in a letter to Henri Rouart, 'I shall leave it all without regret. Life is too short and the strength one has only just suffices. – Well then, Long live fine laundering in France.' Fresh linen and pretty laundresses evidently unleashed vivid and delicious memories of home for Degas. At the least, the letters evoke images of robust energy. In order to find out what else laundresses meant to Degas we have to take a more circuitous and speculative route through his social milieu.

Although it is difficult to locate, or label Degas socially, he did exhibit many dandyish qualities. He was repulsed, according to Gustave Coquiot, by painters who did not dress or speak well, his manners were cool and superior; he rejected social proprieties in so far as he refused to make polite conversation when he didn't want to; he positively dreaded the vulgar; and he hated the Salon with its mass public. His daily haunts were also the haunts of dandies: opera and theatre foyers, cafés, brothels, racetracks, the boulevards. Dandies were attracted to lower-class, sexually accessible women; that they were also repulsed by these women seemed to make the encounter all the more exciting. Dancers were an obvious choice for such men, laundresses were another. Chroniclers of *la vie élégante*, the dandy life – artists like Eugène Lami, Constantin Guys and Gavarni – in fact depicted laundresses and ballet dancers as well as milliners and café singers.

It is quite likely, then, judging from Degas' letters, his dandyish tastes and the prevailing ideology concerning ironers, that these women had clear sexual implications for Degas, and that those implications in part signified class disdain (see page 278). But, the reader might well protest, the works themselves have nothing to do with sex. Let's look again and this time more closely. In the Munich *Ironer*, for example, a young woman looks out at us immobilized, as if momentarily stunned. Her face is sensual and distinctly drawn with its slightly open, full-lipped mouth, languid eyes and faintly swollen lids. In *The Laundress* (The Norton Simon Museum of Art, Pasadena, Calif., 1873), the ironer's face is flushed as she leans intently into her work; we are startled to notice not only her high colour but her unbuttoned bodice. She is working, but she is tacitly seductive too.

While the above two works are only indirectly sexual in content, one work does exist in which sexual references are more explicit. In a Degas notebook (number 28, 1877) there is a drawing in which a man sits at the corner of a table around which four ironers are standing and sitting. The man is Degas' friend, the composer Ernest Reyer; Degas' inscription at the top left reads '*Reyer proposant pendant longtemps une troisième loge à une blanchisseuse*'. The man holds a piece of paper, perhaps announcing a theatrical or operatic performance to which he is inviting one of the laundresses to share a *loge*, or box. Or perhaps '*troisième loge*' is metaphorical and implies a third place in his amorous life. Whatever the precise meaning, the implication is flirtatious. That Reyer was associated with sex in Degas' mind is supported by another notebook page of about the same date. On it Degas wrote his own signature and copied those of Delacroix, Doré, Ingres and Reyer; around Reyer's is a graffito-like drawing of male genitalia.

Degas could depict his friend Reyer in the laundry shop, but not himself, just as he could not render the laundresses, even the Munich and Norton Simon laundresses, as overtly sexy. In both paintings we regard the ironers at a distance across deep and activated spaces, as well as from discomforting angles. In both works the tables are pushed just far enough away from the picture plane to create an acute angle, subtly warning us to keep our distance. In the Munich painting, a delicately sprawling lace curtain spreads out and falls, close to us, down the picture plane, in the Norton Simon image another curtain, table cloth or sheet ripples restlessly on the table's deep diagonal surface. Distance *and* sexual allure inform these works. We might say that potential class disdain has been mitigated in this instance by Degas' personal shyness.

Indeed, with the unusual exception of the brothel monotypes, Degas almost never deals overtly with sexual content. That is no surprise. His own sex life was shrouded in mystery. One can speculate that he was discomforted by intimate relationships with women (whether of his own class or another), since there is no substantive evidence that he ever had any. In fact his relationships with women in general were unusual. His mother's death when he was only thirteen may have been a decisive factor in his adult behaviour. In any case, the women to whom he attached himself were absolutely unavailable to him sexually. [. . .] Perhaps it was guilt that coloured and inhibited his attachments to women. For his own galaxy of reasons, he may have been mourning, and maintaining a bond with, the mother he had lost. In this context, is it merely coincidental that at precisely the time Degas was close to his aunt – during the last half of 1858 and the early months of 1859 – he was also taking extensive notes and transcribing whole sections of Sophocles' *Oedipus Rex*? Was he not perhaps subtly rehearsing, through Oedipus' tragedy, the tabooed desire for his mother and the horror of exacted retribution?

I think we can assume that guilt and paralysis in the realm of sexual love were probably Degas' unhappy lot. In the 1870s his letters betray a longing for family. By the mid-'80s he had given up and described himself as 'unhappy', 'single, 50 years of age . . ., blocked, impotent'. Such a man might well find some comfort in a sublimated relationship with a lower-class woman like a laundress (or a milliner, dancer or café singer). The sexual inactivity and distancing that sublimation requires may indeed have been translated in Degas' style, and may be a partial explanation of why he regarded laundresses, for example, across obstacle-ridden paths and from oblique angles. More importantly, however, it is because he consistently withheld explicit sexual references in his work that he graced his images with a dignity that was highly unusual given his culture. But the built-in distances in the works have other than psycho-sexual explanations.

At first Degas' images seem far indeed from the women or conditions described in the labour reports. The ironer in *Woman Ironing* (Metropolitan Museum), for example, appears quietly absorbed in her work. Light, colour, brush-strokes, dazzle the spectator's eyes; the distillation of a particular gesture compels us; the ironer's line of vision, as well as the movement of her body, draws us into her task. Far from seeming weak, sickly or alcoholic, she appears confident and decisive. [. . .] The accoutrements of work are there: a spacious worktable, a shirt-front and hanging laundry, but the colourful atmosphere and self-contained absorption scarcely evoke industrial malaise. And even in the Norton Simon *Ironers*, where the yawn and stretch of the bodies might induce empathetic physical responses in the spectator, the light pastel hues, the decorative and composed line of the bodies, the whimsically detailed, almost anthropomorphically alert, starched collars militate against any sense of discomfort. The sheer beauty and decorativeness of these works may well be a gauge of Degas' disinterestedness or even his trivialization of a very harsh work reality, but that aspect constitutes only one layer of the works' meaning, which layer, parenthetically, is integrally related to the choice of subject matter. If we take seriously, however, both some of the literal details and the formal implications of these works and others by Degas, another layer of content emerges.

In the Norton Simon *Ironers* and the Jeu de Paume *Two Laundresses* we find that on the left in both pictures a woman grips a bottle whose function is unclear. Yet another look at the notebook drawing discussed above provides absolute clarity. The bottle contains wine and the laundress is drinking. Degas, the realist, who noted the architectural setting, the irons and water containers, also saw the bottle, but he would no more depict a drunken laundress than a tubercular one. In his hands alcoholism is neither a disease as described by the labour reports nor the degenerate habit denounced by Zola. It is simply a fact.

Slowly but surely the reality of the laundresses' worklife comes into focus. Whether in the Metropolitan Museum image, the National Gallery painting or the

Doucet monotype, the simple repetition of gestures and the relatively uncluttered contexts urge us to focus on the bending form. That silhouette has the flavour of infinitude, as if the figure were locked or sewn into position. Degas distilled the ironer's most suggestive gesture and hypnotizes us with it. Similar gestural expressiveness and simplicity occur in the paintings that show two women, for example the Norton Simon *Ironers* and Jeu de Paume *Laundresses*. In both works the woman to the right tucks in her head and rolls all her strength into her torso and out through her pressing arms and hands. The other woman does the opposite: she unfolds her body, stretches and yawns while firmly gripping a wine bottle. The body language here as in the other works is congealed and pared down, the forms riveted into place.

Through a delimited and explicitly vocational repertory of gestures, Degas captures the ritualistic nature of ironing and forces us to see it. He does not, as the Degas literature would have us believe, merely wrap the women in a hazy glow of palpable light, nor is he simply fascinated with motion. Rather his drawing and spatial constructions reveal the women's solitude, their withdrawal, their fatigue. And when for a moment we are no longer only mesmerized by the magical light and brilliant drawing, we may be shocked to find ourselves face-to-face with the boredom and alienation inherent in such labour.

Degas perceived what very few of his contemporaries could. He 'saw' – unwittingly, I believe – the price exacted for alienated labour. In this way his paintings are penetrated by the class conflict endemic to his times. The discrepancy between his social and political conservatism on the one hand and his radically demystifying vision of these workers on the other, is stunning. One is reminded of no one so much as Balzac who, as Frederick Engels wrote in 1888:

> was politically a legitimist. . . . But for all that, his satire is never keener, his irony never more bitter, than when he sets in motion the very men and women with whom he sympathizes most deeply – the nobles. And the only men of whom he speaks with undisguised admiration are his bitterest political antagonists, . . . the popular masses.
>   That Balzac was thus compelled to go against his own class sympathies and political prejudices . . . that he *saw* the real men of the future . . . that I consider one of the greatest triumphs of realism. . . . (Italics in original.)

One wonders what permitted Degas and Balzac such visions. In the case of Degas, a profound empathy with skilled work is a partial explanation. He was an assiduous and painstaking craftsperson who deeply admired those qualities in others. His young friend Daniel Halévy noted Degas' interest, for example, in artisanal work like canemaking and stonemasonry. Degas' preference for ironers over washerwomen may also be a gauge of his predisposition towards skilled labour. Another explanation for his unique vision, as has been suggested, may well have been his own sexual inhibitions which precluded his sexualizing the women in ways that other men of his background had. An additional reason for Degas' special vision was probably his own ambiguous position in society.

We are speaking of a once rich man, no longer so, who does not identify with the bourgeoisie, the aristocracy, or even with the life of the dandy which had grown, by the 1870s, as passé as the old-fashioned family bank the Degas' once ran. He was brought up well, and attended the Lycée Louis-le-Grand, one of only three lycées in Paris which prepared young men for the École Normale Supérieure (France's élite educational institution). He travelled regularly when young, and had access to the kind of culture only the rich could enjoy. [. . .]

In addition, Degas held opinions shared by the conservative pre-capitalist rich or once rich. He was anti-Republican, nationalistic, militaristic and anti-semitic, the latter probably being a symptom of his anti-capitalism and his regret over bygone days. Degas knew that the old way was passing. He had lived through the rebuilding of Paris, the bloody and terrifying revolutions of 1848 and 1871, and the subsequent population expansion and social differentiation of Paris. And although he tried to maintain his cultivated tastes by going regularly to the opera, by travelling to Dieppe and Ménil-Hubert (in Normandy) to visit friends, by taking the waters at Cauterets (one of the most stylish spas in France), he was also very attracted to the new. He was fascinated by photography, and, as Theodore Reff has pointed out, he incorporated and developed artistic techniques based on modern scientific discovery. And through his friend Henri Rouart, a metallurgist and inventor, he was in constant contact with engineers. He was also so fascinated by the new Paris – Haussmann's Paris – that he regularly travelled its length and breadth by tram.

Degas was a man caught in the social mechanisms of his time. Through personal and social circumstances beyond his control, he was left more and more bereft of his former class position and the power it implied. Not only did he know that the world was changing, he also knew that the social power of people like himself was shrinking. He was in the position shared by a myriad of aristocratic and wealthy people who were displaced by capitalism and its values. *He had irreparably lost status*. [. . .]

No longer rich and powerful, nor even thoroughly committed to the rituals of that life, Degas was a socially marginal person. His anxiety about status was chronic and manifested itself in his nationalism, his anti-semitism, his constant hypochondria, his bitter humour, his nervousness and in the shape and meaning of his paintings. Although a very uncomfortable situation for the artist, admirers of Degas' work have benefited from his dilemma. Because Degas had little at stake in the prejudices of a particular social group, his curiosity could extend beyond the limits set by social commitment. He could see more than most of his contemporaries, in part because he was socially nomadic. He could perceive, for example, some of the realities of working-class women. His location outside conventional social and emotional structures contributed to his profound loneliness, but it also provided him with a unique and subversive vision of society. It propelled him towards undermining at least one prevalent ideology, the ideology which claimed that working-class people are inferior and contemptible, and when they are women, sex objects. Degas' paintings of laundresses are emblems both of one man's deep and prevailing ambivalence and of the increasingly alienated labour of capitalism.

The author would like to thank Nina Fortin and Wanda Corn for their help in preparing this article.

42   Les Données Bretonnantes: La Prairie de la Représentation

Fred Orton and Griselda Pollock

The term 'Post-Impressionism' floats in the clouds of Academe above Portman Square and Central Park, over the Thames and Hudson rivers. It is a signifier in a camouflaging rhetoric of Modernist art history that will not name those concrete historical and social relations, those structures and conditions of art practice which determine and mediate the complex and opaque representations made by some of the painters working in Europe between the mid-1880s and the early years of this century. 'Post-Impressionism' has no foundation in history and no pertinence to, or explanatory value for, that historical moment it is used to possess. This is admitted in the catalogue to the exhibition of *Post Impressionism: Cross-Currents in European Painting* which was held at the Royal Academy of Arts, London, 1979–1980. Nevertheless, its reassertion as the title to the exhibition and its use in the catalogue essays expose its specifiable and significant function within this rhetoric.[1] [. . .]

In Alan Bowness' introductory essay both the purpose of the project and its attendant confusions and inevitable contradictions assert themselves with astonishing insistence. They leak out of the text despite the efforts of his urbane prose to conjure them away. Bowness is at pains to explain that 'Post-Impressionism' was an unhappy neologism. It was a 'somewhat negative label', 'the vaguest and most noncommittal' name which Roger Fry could think of in 1910 and which John Rewald chose to revive in the mid-1950s.[2]

'Post-Impressionism' was derived from a number of particular texts as part of an endeavour to lay hold of the art produced in the period *posterior* to another *lumpen* category, 'Impressionism'.[3] As a chronological description the term designates something after and its use reveals the underlying assumption that sequence is of itself a significant factor in historical processes. The history we are offered is that of a developmental, unilinear progression, an illusion of continuity. It is implicit in the essays wherein the term was first used in 1910 and 1912 that it was meant to indicate a reaction against that which preceded it, a reaction which instantly fragmented into various competing and disparate alternatives. However, the reactions against 'Impressionism' which serve as the point of defining difference do not, and cannot, constitute a unified category. Indeed, as Fry, Rewald and Bowness are forced to admit, 'the unity of an artistic movement is quite simply lacking'.[4] In the absence of any common ground but with some vague notion of an unsubstantiable reaction against an imaginary entity – 'Impressionism' – we are offered merely the spectacle of diverging stylistic and aesthetic tendencies which are held together by the celebration of individualism and genius. But why is 'Post-Impressionism' still retrieved so categorically when both its vagueness as a label and the impossibility of

Source: Art History vol. **3**, no. 3, Sept. 1980, pp. 314–344. Edited for this volume by the authors.

making the works it is used to categorize coalesce into a movement or style are freely admitted?

The will to conjure up a movement, to produce an art historically coherent entity is all pervasive. In Bowness' essay there is a passage which, in the printing, chances to fall directly opposite the paragraphs in which he admits the purely negative value of the term 'Post-Impressionism'; it is a passage of supreme confidence: '. . . Post-Impressionism kept its position as the most challenging form of modern art from its heyday in the late 1880s and very early 1890s until c. 1905'.[5] Our doubts are dispelled, certainty restored as the words summon up in black and white a solid artistic entity complete with a position, a heyday, and what seems to constitute a definition, a particular phase in the continuous development of modern art. No sense here, then, that art is a word which describes a discontinuum of practices and that our own sense of art and the artist is contingent, partial and historically formed. The clues to what is being manoeuvred in Bowness' text come thick and fast in the remainder of this paragraph as the four Great Artists are named as Van Gogh, Gauguin, Seurat and Cézanne whose deaths or withdrawals from Paris created a vacuum within the vanguard from which 'nobody in France was able to go forward into radically new kinds of art until 1905'.[6] The crucial link which reveals the purpose of his project lies in the passage which refers us to the work of Rewald 'that great historian of modern art . . . to whom we are all so indebted, decided many years ago to follow his definitive history of Impressionism with a study of Post-Impressionism'.[7]

Rewald's book *Post-Impressionism from Van Gogh to Gauguin* (New York, 1956) revivified the term and over twenty years after its publication informs the conception of the present exhibition and the organization and contents of the catalogue. Yet one cannot evidence, let along examine, a so-called 'crisis in Impressionism' in the 1880s – as the exhibition claims to do – by hanging works of the four geniuses of the Fry–Rewald–Bowness pantheon amidst a mass of other paintings which are said to constitute 'a fuller context of European painting at the time'.[8] [. . .]

How can we go about reclaiming these works for history? What kind of practices do we, as historians of art practices, need to engage with in order to produce history instead of myth, knowledge instead of cliché and tautology? How can we be sure that our mental appropriations of the world correspond with the real social processes? We have to acknowledge that the world exists outside our representations or appropriations and therefore we need a self-critical methodology for gaining access to the knowledge of its processes. If we begin with the acknowledged precondition for our analysis – in this instance, a range of art practices in a historical moment in the late nineteenth century – we have only an abstract conception of the whole. We have to move from the abstract whole examining the layers and levels of the multiple determinations towards thinner abstractions, simpler concepts. Though reality is complex and cannot be explained in simple terms it is, however, necessary to the mental procedures of analysis to begin with them. They are not the goal. We have to retrace our analysis to a more concrete representation of the whole no longer seen as a chaotic abstraction but as a rich totality of many determinations and relations: not as a static unity but as a series of relations and practices within the constant movement of history.

There was a collective loss of confidence amongst those who had first exhibited together in 1874 at 35 Boulevard des Capucines and a more general crisis in the practices of the self-confessed Parisian vanguard in the mid-1880s. However, it was not because, as Fry imagined, many artists found 'Impressionism' too naturalistic,[9] or, as Bowness asserts, because 'experience rather than appearance [whatever that could mean] became *the* reason for art'.[10] Such accounts, if they merit the term, are unsatisfactory because they explain nothing or because, at best, they are predicated upon a single explanation. The simplistic model of cause and effect renders the category of art labelled 'Post-Impressionism' both over-precise and over-inclusive. It is over-precise in so far as it offers aesthetic or formalist reasons alone for the changes in painting in this period and excludes a vast amount of relevant materials and determinations. And it is over-inclusive because it extinguishes the crucial distinctions which differentiate the practices and paintings which might constitute a category but cause it to be radically questioned.

Initially, one has to recognize that by the mid-1880s the artists who had participated in the 1874 exhibition could no longer sustain their contradictory acceptance and evasion of the modern urban environment or their invention of a particular space for representation within it. Their problem was symptomatic of a more extensive crisis. It was a crisis of representation within the transformed and transforming conditions of artistic practice which was manifested in questions about what to paint, how to paint, whom to paint for, and – as important – where to paint. This crisis raised problems of how to engage with or disengage from the increasing social confusion and incoherence, the insistence of new relations and forces of class while at the same time having to confront disintegrating fixities in the practice of art. The traditions of art, the heritage of grammars and syntaxes of painting, conceptual and practical orthodoxies, were simultaneously undermined, questioned, exposed, displaced, retrieved and reworked. Artists and critics alike tried to force out of the dissolving certainties new conventions for the production or avoidance of meaning, elaborations of supporting critical and theoretical discourses, new systems of exhibition, new publics, and above all new spaces and subjects for art, new sites for artists to occupy. We are studying an intricate network of visual and textual discourses and representations in specifiable and changing historical conditions rather than the mythologies of magical creativity and mythic genius.

Painting is a practice of representation and through its changing systems and codes men and women produce images of, ideas about, and positions on the world they inhabit. It is a material practice in history, in ideology. Paintings are not mere illusions about the world but determined and produced allusions to it. Art history must acknowledge these complexities and work on these real social processes, significations and their interactions and relations. Art history which is also a practice of representation must provide complex accounts. [. . .]

The exhibition is not simply a collection of paintings, it is a spectacle. An exhibition as spectacle is a social relation among people mediated by the paintings on display. The paintings are hung in such a way that superficial comparisons can be made while troubling difficulties and unexpected correspondences can be elided. This spectacle is both the project and the result of the existing mode of production and its dominant art history.[11] The works are intended to be contemplated within false representations which foreclose on the networks of meanings and the real conditions in which they were produced. Van Gogh and Jacob Meyer de Haan, for example, have been evacuated from the Netherlands to France where their importance for the exhibition lies. Gauguin, the focus of the so-called 'School of Pont

Aven' is virtually absented from Brittany. Where is there any question of reconstructing the works in their historical specificity? What were they made for? Whom were they made for? To do what kind of job? What do they mean? Do they achieve meaning? How were they understood by their producers, their first viewers, their first public?

At the Royal Academy paintings are dispossessed of their status as works in and over the histories of which they were a part, from which they were produced. Any consideration of their status as history, as historical representations, and their positions within that complex of social and representational practices we call ideology is completely ignored or avoided. We have to engage with problems of representation within ideology, conditions of life, the work accomplished by art.

Consider this:

> The Large and Small South Rooms are an interlude in the exhibition. They present paintings on a single theme, the French province of Brittany. Brittany had been popular with artists since the 1860s, and between 1880 and 1910 painters came to find distinctive qualities in it – the harshness and ruggedness of the landscape, the costumes and primitive customs of its people and their piety. [12]

And this:

> . . . Brittany's barren, intractable coasts echoed the hardship and danger facing its inhabitants. [13]

And this:

> There was a further aspect of Brittany which appealed to some artists. Springing from its geographical remoteness from Paris, its harsh climate and poor soil, and its social and economic backwardness, Brittany was also a region marked by extreme poverty, intense piety, residual paganism and a fatalism brought on by the bitter struggle for survival. [14]

Brittany is hereby separated from the exhibition's predominant categories and presented as a place of work which attracted artists because of qualities such as remoteness, harshness, poverty, primitiveness and piety.

Paul Gauguin referred to the character of Brittany – other than to comment on how low the cost of living was – only two or three times in his letters. In March 1888 he wrote to Emile Schuffenecker, 'I love Brittany; I find there the savage, the primitive. When my clogs resound on the granite soil, I hear the muffled, dull, powerful tone which I seek in my painting.'[15] Unfortunately he does not say just what it was that he found savage and primitive about Brittany. Later in that same year he wrote to Vincent van Gogh mentioning the effect of 'rustic and *superstitious* simplicity' which he had achieved in the figures in a picture he was working on.[16] Once again, he chooses not to elucidate this remark or offer any clue as to what caused that effect. These unclear and problematic references have contributed to the myth presented above and elsewhere; used without explication they have acted, and still act, as prime movers in the machinery of art history.

Brittany occupies a genuinely problematic place in late nineteenth-century painting, and in attempting to understand what it was, and why and how it was represented by artists as diverse as Gauguin and André Dauchez or Emile Bernard and Pascal Dagnan-Bouveret we have to confront the issues raised above. [. . .]

There is little which is unknowable about Brittany in the nineteenth century but it cannot be understood if it is conceived as a unity of fixed attributes. In place of the historical realities of process, constant movements, changing forces and determinations, bourgeois art history imagines a securable entity with a static, self-evident identity. [. . .]

Let us begin with the obvious. Brittany was a region of France which for specifiable but differing reasons became the object of attention for non-Bretons, a place to visit, and a fit subject for Fine Art. Where will we find those Brittanys, the meanings produced through and for Brittany in representations within the historical processes from which those representations were made? We can get to know it by a little basic historical research but we also have to work over the representations made of it in a variety of discourses. In order to approach any single painting of Brittany we have to analyse a range of materials, networks of discourse which constitute both the conditions of representation in and against which that work was produced and the conditions of its legibility in the circuits of production and exchange of meaning in their historical specificity. In order to contribute to the study of certain paintings made by Gauguin and Bernard around Pont Aven and Le Pouldu in 1888 we have to unpack the history of Brittany and the history of representations of Brittany, and the conditions of a single location within both.

[. . .] Armand Séguin, a Breton-born artist who painted in the province in the 1890s and met Gauguin in 1894, suggested that the 'simplification of the image achieved by Gauguin and Bernard was assisted . . . by the sharply coloured field patterns of the Breton landscape'.[17] What Séguin's remark indicates as much as it does the influence which motif had on style, is the exploited fertility of the land around Pont Aven, fields under cultivation, a well-developed system of agriculture, a man-made landscape. There is no evidence in what Séguin said, or in Gauguin's and Bernard's representations of the Breton landscape, of the harshness of climate, the poorness of soil, or even the social and economic backwardness, which are often regarded as qualities which appealed to these artists and drew them to Brittany. Indeed in most nineteenth-century descriptions of the area around Pont Aven those qualities are noticeable by their absence. In the guide-books Pont Aven is usually singled out for a recommended visit because it is pretty and picturesque not because it has a harsh climate and is socially and economically deprived.

So where does the idea of Brittany as a harsh, rugged, barren and backward place come from? In his journal entry for 3 July 1876, Odilon Redon recorded his strange and subjective responses. He called the province a 'sorrowful land weighed down by sombre colours'.[18] But was he referring to the same place at the same time as Séguin? He was not. Redon was recalling his impressions at Quimper in 1876 and Séguin was describing the area around Pont Aven in the late 1880s and early 1890s. Redon's comment is neither specific to the place nor the date at which Gauguin and Bernard were working. We can derive something useful from these two sources by locating the differences of historical geography contained within them. To do this we have to consult another text from a discursive framework other than artistic practice and tourism which expands our understanding of what Redon and Séguin were unknowingly recording. In the late 1780s an English agriculturist, Arthur Young, made three journeys through France noting as objectively as he could what he saw as he passed through the countryside. The accounts of his trips, made on the eve of the Revolution and just after, were published in 1792. He summed up the region between Quimper and Quimperlé in three words 'wastes – wastes – wastes. . . . The same *sombre* country to L'Orient.'[19] It seems that little had changed between then and the time of Redon's visit. However, in the Introduction written for the 1889 reprint of Young's book Betham-Edwards pointed out the extent to which Young's observations of Brittany were no longer valid.

> Here [Brittany and Anjou] . . . advance has been so rapid within our own time that the traveller revisiting these provinces finds his notes of ten or fifteen years ago utterly at fault.

> 'Landes – landes – landes (wastes, wastes, wastes), a country possessing nothing but privilege and poverty', such is the verdict passed by the Suffolk squire on Brittany in 1788. The privileges were swept away with a stroke of the pen twelve months later; the poverty, though an evil not so summarily dealt with, has given way to a happier state of things. Of no French province can the economist now write more hopefully.[20]

Betham-Edwards then goes on to discuss the various improvements in Breton agriculture and the concomitant improvements in social conditions. It is clear from this that in the late 1870s and 1880s Brittany was undergoing rapid economic developments. Not only had the region around Quimper and Quimperlé probably changed considerably but maybe it even looked something like Séguin's albeit brief description of the landscape around Pont Aven. The comments of Redon and Séguin, Young and Betham-Edwards cannot in themselves be used as proofs or illustrations. They have an historical specificity which has to be understood. In so far as they reveal the mesh of representations and that which is represented in and against the real historical conditions they can function as useful materials for our enquiry.

In the nineteenth century Brittany was caught up in the economic revolution which transformed both urban and rural society. Despite regional variations agriculture and the social orders based on it were dramatically changed by the consolidation of a world-wide capitalist mode of production. Brittany was one of the regions which was extensively and, in terms of productivity and relative prosperity, progressively affected by the economic and social developments. Theodore Zeldin, in his study *France 1848–1945: Ambition and Love*, compares the changes in Brittany and the Garonne in the latter half of the nineteenth century to illustrate the effects of the agricultural revolution in France. Whereas in 1848 the Garonne was one of the richest regions Brittany was one of the poorest. By the turn of the century Brittany had become one of the most profitable and productive regions.[21] One of the factors in this change was the reclamation of waste lands, *les landes*. Between 1840 and 1880 400,000 hectares of waste land came under cultivation, a programme which increased the area of agricultural land by one-third and led to a rise in the production of milk and meat on the pasture land and wine and vegetables from the new arable land. The population increased rapidly; already by 1876 some cantons in Brittany were among the most densely populated in France. Transport systems expanded not only with the building of railways but also with major road building projects (the granite soils offering useful materials for the macadam). By 1900 Brittany had three times more railways than the Garonne and five-sixths more roadways. The areas which witnessed these changes most rapidly and effectively were the coastal regions, especially in the south, so that by 1880 one could speak of a *ceinture dorée*, a golden belt, around Brittany. The intensive exploitation of the fertile soils of South Brittany brought it into the world market. Production was for profit on the capitalist market.

Potatoes, for instance, were one of Brittany's miracle crops and were produced for export as well as for domestic consumption.

The changing methods of farming led not only to more intensive capitalization and consequent profitability for the tenant farmers but also to the dispossession of smaller landholders and the full proletarianization of the landless labourers who then became available for labour-intensive activities, such as harvesting or work in the factories in the neighbouring towns. Some mechanization of farming also occurred. Pont Aven was a rich, fertile and productive place. Several guide-books quote a saying about it, 'Pont Aven, ville de renom: quinze moulins, quatorze maisons'. The fact that fifty-two markets and twelve fairs were held each year is sometimes noted also.

At the same time that the lands along the southern coast were brought under increased cultivation and worked within the market economy, the sea was also intensively farmed. With the development of industrial capitalism the distinction between agriculture and industry, the modes and relations of production and exchange, were increasingly extinguished. Similarly the sites of work, rural and urban or agricultural and industrial, often overlapped. Concarneau, a town with 5,000 inhabitants, seventeen kilometres from Pont Aven, was a centre of one of Brittany's flourishing industries, the sardine and tuna fisheries and factories. At least 1200 boats operated out of the harbour there, and in 1877, even before the impact of the agricultural revolution had been felt, approximately 13,000 people were already employed in the processes of boiling, salting, canning and bottling the huge quantities of fish.[22] A large number of the employees in the fish processing plants, not all of whom were residents of the town, must have been drawn from the neighbouring countryside. The majority were women displaced from agriculture possibly because of the introduction of the scythe or the extinction of rural domestic industries such as weaving or spinning; their numbers increased in the 1880s.

Another harvest from the sea was seaweed. A.S. Hartrick, who shows little understanding of what he saw, describes the way in which it was collected at Le Pouldu.

> Imagine a country of gigantic sand dunes . . . peopled by a savage-looking race who seemed to do nothing but search for driftwood, or to collect seaweed, with strange sledges drawn by shaggy ponies; and with women in black dresses, who wore the great black 'coif' (like a *huge* black sun-bonnet).[23]

The collection of the different seaweeds – *goémon épave, goémon de dérive* and *goémon d'échonage* – was sufficiently important to the French economy to be strictly controlled by law. Anyone could collect driftweed – *goémon épave* – but special permission had to be obtained for the other two kinds of seaweed, and it was only given to those persons whose land adjoined the beach or to maritime municipalities. In the spring and summer four women aided by a man and a panniered ass were able to collect as much as six to eight tons of driftweed in the course of a six-hour day. Gauguin's *Seaweed Gatherers* (1889, Essen, Folkwang Museum) and Dauchez's *The Seaweed Burners* (*c*. 1898, Musée de Moulins, dépôt de l'Etat) both represent the collection of seaweed on the *ceinture dorée*.

By the seventeenth century it was standard agricultural practice to use the nitrogen-rich seaweed as a natural manure to grow crops, especially early vegetables.[24] By the nineteenth century it was also a cash crop. Kelp, the ash which results from burning seaweed, was sold to industry. [. . .] In France kelp making was concentrated on the coasts of Morbihan and Finistère and the manufacture of iodine was carried out at six centres: Le Couquet, Cherbourg, Montsarac, Portsall, Quartrevents, and nearest to Le Pouldu, Pont-l'Abbé. In 1953 iodine was still being produced in Brittany from seaweed gathered on the Breton coast.[25]

Seaweed gathering for manure and the production of kelp for iodine cannot be accurately described as 'one of the manifestations of Breton primitivism'.[26] Nor should it be claimed – even though it obviously appealed to certain artists as a picturesque motif – as representing 'the backward state of Breton farming compared with the rest of France'.[27] As we have seen the state of Breton agriculture was anything but backward. [. . .]

Gauguin, Bernard, Dauchez et al. were tourists, and to become a place for tourists to visit Brittany had to be accessible and hospitable. It was. As so many guide-books with titles such as Ramble into Brittany suggest, Brittany had been accessible before the 1880s, before the spread of railways, the creation of roads and other facilities of communication made travel both easy and comfortable.[28] By that decade tourism had become a major source of income within the Breton economy. It was at that time that conscious and concerted efforts were made to exploit the natural features of such places as Concarneau, Le Pouldu or La Baule so that they could become station-balnéaires, sea-bathing resorts. Tourism is a complex social activity. Changing economic factors make certain places the object of investigation, experience, travel, and in the nineteenth century the site of a search for a new kind of leisure, the summer holiday. The Narrative of a Walking Tour through Brittany by J.M. Jephson, published in 1859, is an instructive document which is introduced to its readers thus:

> The season is approaching when those who have been bearing their part for the last six
> months in the exhausting contest of busy British life, will have to determine where to
> spend their summer holiday . . . Brittany – in its easy accessibility, in the beauty of its
> natural scenery, in its historical and poetic associations, in the abundance of its Celtic
> and medieval remains, in its quaint traditional manners and picturesque costumes –
> possesses unrivalled attractions for the jaded Englishman whose time and means are
> limited, and who yet pants to escape for awhile from the dingy brick walls, dark offices,
> briefs, ledgers, turnpike roads, or Mrs. Grundy.[29]

To the urban bourgeois and petty bourgeois – English and French alike – considering a summer holiday, Brittany offered an escape to something different. It provided a variety of experiences, embracing a whole catalogue of historical threads from picturesque travel to romantic regionalism, consolidated and packaged, which town dwellers could purchase for their summer leisure and pleasure activity. Some of Jephson's particular comments are interesting. After describing the festivities of a village wedding, he pauses to reflect that some people will call these traditional customs barbarous or puerile but then comments that he doubts 'the wisdom of stripping all social events of everything that appeals to the imagination'.[30] Inherent in that comment is the bourgeois traveller's problem of how to understand and respond to the customs of a culture other than his own. Though he can recognize some loss of meaning in his own customs – hence the implicit reference to the control, order and reticence of social formalities which are characteristic of the bourgeoisie – he can have but little comprehension of the meanings within the culture he is visiting.

Within the discourses and practices of tourism not only the natural and man-made landscapes are of interest to the traveller. The indigenous population also provides a spectacle for the visitor to consume according to his or her point of view. In the later nineteenth century the people and their rituals and customs were made available to visitors as part of the experience of Brittany, and the Bretons were not unwilling to put themselves and their way of life on show. In particular, the Pardons and fêtes, and especially the costumes worn at them, were integral features of the province's tourist attraction, features which were open to misreading and misunderstanding seen as they were against the experiences of the mode of life and customs of the town.

There is another, more historically specific level at which we have to locate the spectacle of Breton costume. For many visitors in the nineteenth century Breton costumes were regarded as quaint and picturesque, and perceived as signs of the traditionalness and archaicness of Breton culture. In fact the costumes were neither traditional nor archaic, and such misconceptions as there were about their Celtic origins were the result of ill-informed enthusiasts of Celtomania who were part of a burgeoning Breton nationalist movement. [. . .]

In his book *Les Costumes de Populations Bretonnes* R.Y. Creston provides a history of nineteenth-century Breton costume.[31] Until the French Revolution, the dress of Breton peasants, though different from that worn by peasants in other regions, was a class costume. It signified the wearer's place in the social hierarchy of a still semi-feudal system. It was only with the abolition of the sumptuary laws at the French Revolution, the ending of control over the use of materials, colours and kinds of dress which each class could use, that the distinctive and varied costumes of nineteenth-century Brittany began to develop. It was as a result of the removal of these rigid restrictions that variations between the regions and within individual regions were elaborated. Skirt, bodice and *coiffe*, the main elements of female dress, were subject to minute differentiation which came to signify the wearer's clan or locality. For instance, by the late nineteenth century there were as many as 1200 different kinds of *coiffe* in Brittany, each of which was subject to further variations according to commune.

Furthermore, as a result of the new transport and trade systems, materials such as embroidered cloth and lace became available in Brittany. New decorative fabrics were accessible to Bretons to enhance, elaborate and vary their personal and local costume. These were available to those who could afford to buy embellishing haberdashery or expensive cloth in order to display their wealth and rising social status.

Costume is a social signifying system; it has social meanings. In Brittany costume came to signify region, locality, class, wealth and marital status within a *nouveau riche* peasantry. It was worn by them for display on public occasions; it served both to individualize the wearer and to make his or her place within a part of society recognizable, to separate and to unify. However, what it signified to Bretons within a changing social order was not necessarily understood by non-Bretons for whom it seems to have signified Bretonness in general. It was therefore a site of representation of social and economic change and a site of misrepresentation. In the discourses of non-Bretons, visitors from the town, the signs of dress were appropriated to signify difference, strangeness, otherness. The specific social practices of a rural place and its population were perceived from the urban point of view.

If, as Creston emphasizes, the flowering of Breton popular culture in costume was predicated on the emergence of a more leisured and prosperous section of the peasantry – even though this may not have been explicitly recognized or articulated at the time – it is probable that part of the appeal of Brittany for tourists was precisely that there was a relatively leisured, wealthy, socially acceptable peasantry which was not too strange, not too other. The urban tourist was unlikely to be confronted by Millet's *Man with a Hoe* in Brittany in the 1880s.

The sophisticated system of costume signified a social order no matter how distinct from that of the urban bourgeoisie. That is to say that while travelling in Brittany the distinctive costume would ensure that the visitor would know to whom he or she was speaking, and know who were the Bretons he or she had come to see as distinct from the other inhabitants who may have lived and worked there but were not part of the same tourist experience. Tourism structures what is seen, marks it out, and locates it. It also absents and excludes, and preconditions how things are seen. Activities and events, rituals and customs, sites and peoples are rendered intelligible as signs of Bretonness within the discursive and ideological frames of reference of visitors from the town. Tourism can be understood therefore at two related levels. It is part of the economy of Brittany and a product of the new social and ideological structures that joined town and country, metropolis and region, from which were produced a range of representations.

In 1850 Adolphe Blanqui, a Parisian economist, wrote a report on the conditions in rural France after the 1848 revolution.

> The economic fact which is today most worthy of *our* attention, and which stands out in the most striking way, is the difference in the condition and well being which distinguishes the inhabitants of the town from those of the countryside. One would think that one was seeing two different peoples, living though on the same soil, lives so distinctive that they seem foreigners to each other, even though they are united by links of the most domineering centralisation that has ever existed.[32]

Investigations of this kind – as varied in their forms and purposes as they were numerous – were the product of a particular consciousness of the effects of the decisive changes in the social structures of France in the nineteenth century. They registered a growing concern over the differences between town and country which were perceived from the urban point of view. The differences were posed in terms of relative levels of economic and social development for which the standard of judgement was the level and form attained by the town, especially Paris which was the centre of that centralization, the locus of civilization and urbanity. However, these differences also belong on another axis of difference. At one end of this axis was the increasing similarity of life in the towns of which Paris was the paradigm and on the other end was the continuing diversity of the regions, each distinct from each other and from the metropolis.

The urban point of view brought forth distinct ideological meanings from this recognition of difference. Theodore Zeldin points to at least three ways in which the inhabitants of the countryside were viewed by town dwellers and metropolitans. Firstly, they classified the peasants as savages or barbarians – a view which was as common in the writings of some of those who had recently ceased to be peasants and had come to the city as it was in the work of the aristocrat Honoré de Balzac. Zeldin writes that 'People risen from their [peasant] ranks often attacked the peasants most vigorously, seeing education and peasantry as extreme opposites representing respectively civilization and barbarism.'[33] Difference is being constructed around life-style and, above all, class positions. For another group, the Catholic Revivalists, the peasants and rural society were seen as better than the town dwellers and town life. They projected onto rural society a romanticized view of conservatism, piety and respect for a hierarchical social order based on the pillars of traditional society of pre-capitalist epochs, the Church and the land. Another representation of the countryside grew out of Napoleon III's call for a study of French folklore in 1853. Individuals such as Frederick Mistral in Provence or bodies such as the Celtic Revivalists in Brittany – as well as many other diverse groups – began to study and document regional customs and cultures. This kind of interest was contradictory. It was based in part on an interest in regional difference and diversity, popular cultures and French history, but it was equally motivated by a sense of the threatened extinction and disappearance of such regional customs and cultures in the wake of the same transformation which was producing the dominance of the town, making it different from and generating a concern about the rural world outside its own increasing uniformity.

All these viewpoints, though they have different forms and work from different ideologies, perceived the world from an urban point of view which was based on the recognition of change and an awareness of difference. With this understanding we can locate the prevailing use of such notions as remote, savage, primitive, rustic, simple, or attributions of superstitiousness or fatalistic piety with reference to the peasant population of nineteenth-century France. Their meanings are produced, as are all meanings, within relations of difference. Remote, for instance, could mean a number of things, the physical inaccessibility of a farm far away from tracks, roads and railways, or the difficulty of comprehension of patois or a totally foreign language. All of these levels of differentiation or distance are predicated upon a point, a centre, a given cultural norm, from which something is being seen as removed or distant. Remote means far from civilization. Thus, remoteness in distance metonymically signifies its opposite, the centre of civilization, which, in nineteenth-century France, meant Paris. [. . .]

Brittany represented as remote, savage, primitive, rustic, superstitious or simple signifies within specific historical conditions a nexus of town and country, uneven developments, regional variations and centralization, the history of the dominance of the town and its bourgeois social forms and norms. But by the 1880s Brittany was not geographically remote from Paris. Linguistically only limited parts of the interior of the province remained non-French speaking – the growth in the number of schools built during the Third Republic and military service had ensured that. So why was Brittany presented as it was? Who was representing it in that way? And whose Brittany do we confront in those representations? When we encounter terms such as 'savage', 'primitive', 'rustic' or 'superstitious' in the letters of Gauguin we cannot take them at face value or assume them to be a truth about Brittany, an objective statement of fact, and let them speak as if in explanation of the paintings. We have to recognize them as part of the ideological baggage carried by artistic tourists in those specific conditions of change, relations of difference, and the social and cultural dominance of an urban bourgeoisie.

Gauguin and Bernard went to Brittany from the town, from Paris. As importantly, they went as part of the artistic vanguard which had emerged in the capital. In 1888–1889 they lived well beyond the edge of the metropolis but what they produced there was determined by, and addressed to, the vanguard. The eighth and last 'Impressionist' exhibition, the *Exposition Internationale*, and the *Salon des Indépendants*, all held in 1886, brought into sharp focus the loss of faith amongst the 'Impressionists' and evidenced the beginnings of the attempt to produce what Verhaeren called a 'new art'.[34]

Three years later in his review of the Café Volpini exhibition – where work produced by Gauguin and Bernard during their stays in Brittany was shown – Félix Fénéon noted some of the shifts which had taken place in the practice of art.

> The means of the *tachistes* ['*Impressionists*'] so appropriate for representing *visions disparaissantes*, were, around 1886, abandoned by many painters preoccupied with an art of synthesis and premeditation.[35]

The 'Impressionists' had been faced with a new kind of landscape, man-made, difficult and complicated, invaded by capital and class. They knew it well enough; they were part of it. Yet they evaded it in their pictures. What the 'Impressionists' produced were contrived, expurgated representations of it. [. . .]

In the mid-1880s, Monet, Camille Pissarro and Pierre Renoir passed through a moment of doubt about the whole business. In the end their practices could not be sustained as they were. Only Paul Cézanne, in Aix, realized that that doubt could be made to premise the production of paintings. Fénéon described the moves made after 1886 towards greater premeditation and synthesis. Something was being introduced in vanguard practices to replace phenomenalism – that standing in front of Nature, looking, juxtaposing those broken touches of colour on the canvas standing back again, hoping that in the process of painting an adequate visual equivalent had been made which was in some way a record of a sensation which had already disappeared. The way in which Fénéon suggests that Gauguin and Bernard reacted was by abandoning what Cézanne was determined to maintain, optical fact – *visions disparaissantes* – as the material for paintings.

In his review Fénéon also proposes another crucial difference between the work of the *tachistes* and the new tendencies.

> In as much as M. Seurat, M. Signac, M. Pissarro, M. Dubois-Pillet realised their conception of this art in pictures where episodes were abolished in a general orchestration subject to the codes of optical physics and where the personality of the author remains hidden like that of Flaubert in his novels, so M. Gauguin works towards an analogous end but by different means. For him reality is but a pretext for distanced creations.[36]

The changes Fénéon refers to are visible. The paintings of Seurat and Gauguin do not look like those of Monet and Renoir. However, it is not obvious what those changes mean or how they came about. Fénéon points to the ways in which some artists in the late 1880s redefined their practices and developed new techniques. The position of the artist in relation to that which he represented became obscured, hidden. [. . .] Instead of painting on his motif Seurat visited it, studied it, noted what comprised it, and then returned to his studio to work with those materials. In the studio he worked dispassionately; he applied science. Fénéon sees Seurat's and Gauguin's work as evidencing their apartness from the world they represent.

The emergence of several related but distinct alternatives to the work of the 'Impressionists' suggests that a change had taken place within the social relations of the Parisian vanguard. Towards the end of the nineteenth century it became competitive to an extent not known before as artists and critics contended for positions of importance and leadership within it. Seurat made such a manoeuvre in 1886 when he exhibited his large painting of *A Sunday Afternoon on the Isle de la Grande Jatte* at the 'Impressionist' Exhibition and the *Salon des Indépendants*. The picture represents a scene of metropolitan pleasure. It is not Argenteuil or Le Grenouillère but one of Paris's fast-growing industrial suburbs, Asnières. By 1884–1886 – when the picture was painted – they were not so different. This is not Nature. And it is not an evasion. It is a representation of the kind of crowd which gathered on an island in the Seine on a Sunday afternoon. It is part of the urban landscape, an aspect of public life in the capital. By the mid-1880s the composition of that social gathering was no longer exclusively bourgeois but mixed and confusing. Mass production and distribution of bourgeois fashions blurred the lines of class which dress had helped signify. Maybe that is Seurat's subject: the confusions and contradictions of social relations and encounters which were part of the Grande Jatte at that time. The *Grande Jatte* was so successful as a painting and as a gesture that it helped close that Parisian landscape of pleasure as a subject for vanguard painting. Even Seurat, once he had laid claim to it, moved on to other sites: the artist's studio, a *Café-concert*, a circus, a *boudoir*, the Eiffel Tower – each in their turn came under his scrutiny. There was no alternative for the vanguard to seeing Paris as Seurat revealed it both because of what he showed and because of the way the mode of representation redefined what was represented.

The provinces had always been available to Parisian painters. The 'Impressionists' had made trips away from the capital. In 1870–1871 some of them had fled in advance of another kind of vanguard but that was by definition an evacuation. Most often their outings were respites from everyday life in the town. The trips which many painters made away from Paris to Brittany and Provence in the late 1880s were not primarily motivated by the *bon bourgeois* yen for a week or two of the simple life in the country or at the coast. Of course, that was part of it but by 1886 something had changed. The metropolis was no longer available to them as the main subject matter for vanguard painting. Ambitious artists were directed by necessity to find new spaces to occupy, new areas of representation. Once the *banlieue* had been possible and negotiable but this was no longer the case, and the regions became viable, novel.

Seurat was the figure of authority and centrality in the vanguard, and the *Grande Jatte* was the painting every vanguard artist – no matter where he was working – had to come to terms with. The *Grande Jatte* demanded a reaction and art which remained ignorant of what had been achieved by it looked it. Vanguard painters had to situate their practice in relation to Seurat's current preoccupations; they had to develop along similar lines, take up the issues raised, or challenge his dominance. Van Gogh, in Arles, away from the 'hotbed of ideas' – as he called Paris – acknowledged Seurat's importance. He explored the Frenchman's subject matter without adopting his technique. He even wondered whether his own work was worthy of being exhibited with Seurat's.[37]

Bernard was also preoccupied with Seurat and for a brief moment in 1888 seems to have grasped some of the import and importance of the *Grande Jatte*. He approached Seurat on his own terrain when he produced two watercolour drawings of people relaxing on the banks of a river. Their derivation from the *Grande Jatte* is obvious; and one is actually titled *Idyll at Asnières*. These watercolours certainly explore the same aspect of Parisian life but they are marked apart from Seurat's representation of it by Bernard's almost contemptuous, caricaturing viewpoint. However, these two drawings – they are almost jokes as the ironic title makes clear – were only Bernard's initial, awkward response to Seurat's territory.

Bernard spent several months of 1888 in Brittany, first at the northern seaside resort of St Briac, near Dinard, and then in the south at Pont Aven. It was there he painted *Breton Women in a Meadow* and re-established contact with Gauguin. Gauguin was so impressed with Bernard's painting that he took it with him when he went to Arles. Van Gogh also recognized it as something special, made a copy of it in watercolour, and discussed it in his letters.

> I have seen a Sunday afternoon in Brittany by him [Bernard], some Breton peasant women, children, peasants, dogs walk about in a very green meadow, the costumes are black and red and the coiffes are white. But in this crowd there are two ladies, one in red, the other in bottle green, who make it a very modern thing.[38]

[. . .] Van Gogh drawns a distinction between peasant woman (*paysannes*) and ladies (*dames*), between the women in Breton costumes and those dressed in town fashions (and equipped with parasols) which recalls the confusions of *classement social* in Seurat's *Grande Jatte*. Most significantly, Van Gogh refers to Bernard's painting as 'a Sunday afternoon in Brittany'. [· · ·] *Breton Women in a Meadow* was a Breton motif which, though not identical, was most equivalent to that landscape Seurat represented in the *Grande Jatte*, complex and contradictory, not metropolitan but none the less modern, as Van Gogh realized. It is a representation of what has been called, with reference to Seurat's *Grande Jatte*, the dialectic of pleasure in its bourgeois form: the dialectic of constraint and spontaneity, of ease and unease, pleasure and *ennui*, of awkwardness and informality, of nature and artifice, of the unspoilt spot and the ruined resort, of fashion and recreation. [. . .]

In *Breton Women in a Meadow* Bernard depicts the rural bourgeoisie, the *nouveau riche* peasantry and they are not so very different from the mixed crowd of metropolitans who congregated every Sunday on the Isle de la Grande Jatte. Bernard travelled to what was considered to be a social system different from that to which he was accustomed, to a province which, it was thought, retained much of the character of a bygone civilization. But what Bernard, the vanguard artist, painted in *Breton Women in a Meadow* was a set of social relations very similar to those he knew in the capital. On a Sunday afternoon there was an equivalence between that meadow in Pont Aven and the Isle de la Grande Jatte in Paris. And therein lies at least one level of immediate contradiction in Bernard's picture. He went to Brittany to find difference and novelty, difference from Paris and novelty as an artist. What he encountered there was not remote, strange or backward but in many ways modern. How, therefore, could he signify the difference and similarity, the anticipated archaism and the pressing modernity? How could he engage with and evade the real contradictions of the social and economic developments in Brittany which made that space viable and intelligible for vanguard art practice? [. . .]

The assertion of facture was an important part of the strategy of the vanguard. It had always been so. Seurat presented himself as a technician. He claimed objectivity with his quasi-scientific procedures. And his seemingly mechanical application of paint posed as impersonality. That objectivity and impersonality signified a distance from what he represented. The mode of facture helped distance the spectator from that which was represented. Bernard had to deal with Seurat as much in terms of technique as subject matter. He had found a rural equivalent for the *Grande Jatte* but he had to assert his independence from Seurat technically.

Breton Women in a Meadow is an amalgam of independent groups of figures each in its own area on the canvas. The emphatic outlines seem primarily an aesthetic contrivance, part of a decorative scheme rather than a means of signifying spatial and social relations. Each object has been flattened, made two-dimensional, and depth has been suppressed. There is a lack of coherence, a lack of synchronization between the different parts of the picture. It is a strange painting which holds our attention by its lack of detail and its unreadable space. We are made to see it at once from above, from below, and from our own levels. When Van Gogh copied it he tried to give his model some logical consistency. He changed the intervals between the forms and gave the spectator a positioned space in relation to what was represented. He tried to retrieve a narrative space.

Bernard has dispensed with obvious clues of physiognomy, gesture and space. It is difficult to understand what is taking place and what the people are doing. But it is not without significance. *Breton Women in a Meadow* represents the recognizable *nouveau riche* peasantry behaving in a similar manner to the urban bourgeoise, strolling, conversing, displaying themselves and their wealth in a public place. Most of the people are dressed in regional costume which, as we have seen, was a sign of class and social development. It signified contemporary Brittany but it also marked it apart. The Breton costume was a modern form of dress which at that time was still evolving but the urban population saw it as archaic, medieval. Bernard also included two ladies dressed in town fashions and a young girl in a knee-length dress. Could these be visitors, tourists? The ladies do not mix with the peasants but the girl seems to have made some contact with a peasant in costume who could be someone of her own age. Maybe they are friends. It is possible that the ladies are *Bretonnes* too. Town fashions – not just haberdashery – had become available in the province and it was not unusual for young women to forsake regional costume on special occasions. [. . .] In Bernard's painting the town fashions point to the adulteration of the Breton scene. The unspoilt spot was fast becoming the ruined resort, less rural and more urban in its appearance and manners.

Van Gogh saw these differences of dress in *Breton Women in a Meadow* as signifying a class difference and suggested that this made the picture modern. The ladies are quotations from Seurat's *Grande Jatte*. Van Gogh realized this; as far as he was concerned that was part of the meaning of the picture. As an iconic quotation – and there is at least one other in the painting – it activated a variety of meanings which vanguard artists and critics would have understood. Even now, they signify not only a particular work by another artist but what that painting represented, a specific, confusing, modern social space. Maybe Bernard is trying to make the complexity of his motif clear. He might not have been as certain as Van Gogh was that the difference in dress signified a difference of class. It could also have signified a difference within a class. So how, if at all, did Bernard's *Breton Women in a Meadow* produce the effect of *classement social* and modernity? Could it be in the way Bernard painted the people in Breton costume? They are not so obviously recognizable as quotations from contemporary French painting but they do refer us to other materials which Bernard was drawing on. Bernard was an eclectic. He borrowed devices from Gothic stained glass windows, medieval textiles, enamel work and

Japanese prints in order to represent Brittany. What does it mean to paint the two women who are derived from the *Grande Jatte* as if they are figures in a stained glass window? What does it mean to paint Breton men and women in a manner derived from Japanese prints? What does it mean to medievalize and orientalize Brittany? Does it signify, for example, primitiveness, savageness or simplicity of the region and the people? Or does the use of such stylistic devices assert the modernity of the artist, his vanguardness? And why did Bernard paint in a deliberately naïve, almost awkward way so that the tracking movements of the brush are clearly evident? At the time he and Gauguin were talking of *faire de la peinture d'enfant* [painting like a child]. Why? It was better than painting like *décadents*.[39] In what way was it appropriate for representing *Breton Women in a Meadow?*

The questions multiply. But there are no easy or self-evident answers to them. There is nothing in the picture's complex appearance which affords us the luxury of certainty with regard to its meanings. The longer we spend looking at it, studying it, the more the references to the real social developments of Brittany which rendered that space possible for vanguard painters to represent become occluded. They become obscured, hidden – like Bernard – distanced beneath the assertion of style and the connotations inculcated by the incongruity of the means and materials used. The way an artist represents a scene transforms that which is represented. The mode of representation used for *Breton Women in a Meadow* could not contain the contradictions in the subject matter or in the position of the artist.

In September 1888 Gauguin painted a picture of Breton women in a meadow which has since become known as *Vision After the Sermon*. Many ink-wells have been emptied by the literati of art establishing the priority of Bernard's *Breton Women in a Meadow* and the stylistic influence which it had on Gauguin's painting. Undoubtedly Gauguin's picture was a response to what Bernard had painted. It was part of vanguard practice to surpass a chosen model or an accepted position. Bernard had to go beyond Seurat, and Gauguin had to transcend Bernard. To do that Gauguin had to address the subject matter of Bernard's picture and how that representation was made.

Gauguin's *Vision After the Sermon* has been appropriated by modernist art history as 'the turning point of his entire oeuvre',[40] the 'epitome of his new style'.[41] To give it such a status is wrong. *Vision After the Sermon* is an exceptional painting which stands apart from the main tendencies of Gauguin's work in 1888 and has little relationship to anything painted after it. To try to fix it neatly and assuredly within terms of a personal or stylistic development is to resort to the false security which belief in the cult of the artist and the myth of creativity provides. It negates questions about the conditions of artistic production, and the strategies of vanguard practice, about the complexity of Brittany and representations made of it in the 1880s.

Vision After the Sermon is a particular representation produced in Brittany, in a particular way, to do a specific job. In September 1888 Gauguin described it in a letter to Van Gogh as *un tableau réligieux*.[42] Was Gauguin responding to the debates about the nature of religious painting which Van Gogh and Bernard were pursuing in their correspondence with each other?[43] There is some evidence that Gauguin was intrigued and amused by Van Gogh's evangelical fervour. Did Gauguin's interest in posing as a religious painter stem from his infatuation with Bernard's sister, Madeleine, who was a devout Catholic? Or was the picture a response to the local Pardon? Macquoid regarded the Pardon held at Pont Aven in September as one of the best in Lower Brittany, 'the wrestling and dancing there have quite a reputation of their own'.[44] Wrestling matches were a feature of the day's activities, part of the pleasure of the Pardon, part of the attractions and various entertainments which began, according to Macquoid, after high mass.

> Next we went to the wrestling. The people form a great ring. The judges, consisting of the *maire* and the chief of the townspeople, stand in the midst, and make a point of hiding the performance as much as possible from the lookers on. . . .[45]

Was *Vision After the Sermon* in some way a response to this obscured wrestling match?

We can indicate a variety of possibilities to assist us to locate Gauguin's posture as a religious painter or as a painter of a specific custom associated with Breton religious practice. But is *Vision After the Sermon* a religious painting? It is not an illustration of people or scenes from a religious text. It is a picture which includes an episode from the Bible as if imagined by a number of Bretons as a reaction to a sermon they have heard. Does it inspire religious devotion, faith, or promote an understanding of religious dogmas? How could it? What would be its meaning if that was the case? Is its subject religious experience? Gauguin stated that he had attempted to produce an effect not of piety – goodness, virtue, reverence or veneration – but rustic and superstitious simplicity. How could *un tableau réligieux* have as its content superstitiousness – an ignorant, irrational belief in supernatural forces? Littré cites a passage from Pascal wherein superstition is contrasted with piety: piety destroys superstition. Did Gauguin consider superstition synonymous with Christian piety? In 1889 he wrote to Van Gogh that the Breton costumes were influenced by the superstitions of Catholicism.[46] Perhaps he was aware of, and responding to, the non-Catholic practices associated with the Pardons which took place locally. But did he see the wrestling at Pont Aven in that way?

Vision After the Sermon is not a religious painting. Is it a genre scene? The habit of resting in a meadow close to the church was a common feature of social behaviour at a Pardon. A. Le Braz in *The Land of Pardons* provides this description:

> Only toward evening, when Vespers are over, do the festivities begin. And what simple pleasures they are; how innocent, how primitive! The good folk flock together in the shade of the walnut trees, on the green sward, beneath the spreading elms. And there, under the eyes of the girls, seated demurely on the surrounding slopes, the youths challenge one another to wrestle, to race, to jump . . .[47]

This is like Bernard's motif; it was perhaps Gauguin's starting point. However, if that was the case and Gauguin did base *Vision After the Sermon* on this secular aspect of a Pardon, then the imagined Biblical wrestling match works to dispossess the scene of the connotations of pleasure, leisure, fashion, recreation and commerce.[48] Perhaps this refusal of the specific contemporaneity is the point of the work. Gauguin's representation avoids the space which Bernard had claimed with all its awkwardness and contradictions for his vanguardness.

The only reference – and it is oblique – to modern Brittany is that sign of Bretonness, costume. A year later Gauguin was of the opinion that the Breton peasants had a medieval air and that they showed no sign of thinking for a moment that Paris existed or that they were in 1889. Probably he held the same belief in 1888. In *Vision After the Sermon* Breton costume is deprived of any significance with regard to the social development of Brittany at the time Gauguin worked there.

It was not until the autumn of 1889 when a different critical and artistic situation had emerged in Paris that Gauguin took up some of the issues he had introduced in *Vision After the Sermon*. However, in *Yellow Christ* (1889, Buffalo Albright-Knox Art Gallery) and *Green Calvary* (1889, Brussels Musées Royaux des Beaux Arts de Belgique) his strategies were entirely different. In these pictures the peasants are not visionaries and the religious connotations are made obvious by the use of the crucifix from the Chapel at Trémalo and the calvary at Nizon. There are also references to the exploited, inhabited landscape around Pont Aven and Le Pouldu and to the people who lived and worked there; rich and poor peasants, a shepherdess, a seaweed gatherer, pleasure and religion in a rural society and landscape.

In modernist art history's ideological retreat into stylistic accounts and theories of personal artistic 'expression' and 'experience', *Vision After the Sermon* has been used to safeguard certain fictions about Gauguin and Brittany. The terms in which he described the effects he thought he had achieved in figures in this painting are one of the two fragile threads with which certain notions or *données* of Bretonness have been constructed and sustained. In fact, Stevens manages to use both of them with reference to *Vision After the Sermon*, *Yellow Christ* and *Green Calvary* in one sentence:

> [Gauguin] sought to capture the 'dull, muted, powerful note' of his clogs ringing out on the granite soil, as well as 'the rustic and superstitious piety' [*sic*] of the Breton peasants which he expressed in *Vision After the Sermon* and the two calvary paintings of 1889, the *Yellow Christ* . . . and the *Breton Calvary*. . . .[49]

These phrases – used as if their meanings are transparent – and the verb 'expressed' reproduce a comforting and unproblematic picture of the artist and what he painted. They render redundant, if not unthinkable, any discussion of the historical conditions and structures of representation which determined and mediated the nature of Gauguin's contact – such as it was – with a real historical Brittany and its classed populations. In the 'Literature of Art' these complex social realities are absented, and modernist art history is built upon and structured by that evasion.

References

1   *Post-Impressionism: Cross Currents in European Painting*, Royal Academy of Arts Catalogue, London, 1979, A. Bowness, 'Introduction', p. 11 (hereinafter referred to as *R. A. Post-Impressionism*, 1979).
2   *R. A. Post-Impressionism*, 1979. Roger Fry quoted by A. Bowness, p. 10 and n. 1, p. 12.
3   R. Fry and D. McCarthy, *Manet and the Post-Impressionists*, London, Grafton Galleries, 8 November 1910–15 January 1911, pp. 7–13, and R. Fry, *Second Post-Impressionist Exhibition*, London, Grafton Galleries, 5 October–31 December 1912, pp. 7–8.
4   *R. A. Post-Impressionism*, 1979, A. Bowness, p. 11.
5   Ibid., p. 11.
6   Ibid., p. 11.
7   Ibid., p. 11.
8   Ibid., p. 11.
9   R. Fry and D. McCarthy, op. cit., p. 7.
10 *R. A. Post-Impressionism*, 1979, A. Bowness, p. 11.

11 See G. Debord, *La Société du Spectacle*, Paris, 1967.
12 *Post-Impressionism*, Royal Academy of Arts, 1979–1980, *Exhibition Gallery Guide*, 'South Rooms: Brittany'.
13 *R. A. Post-Impressionism*, 1979, J. House, 'The Legacy of Impressionism in France', p. 15.
14 Ibid., M. A. Stevens, 'Innovation and Consolidation in French Painting', p. 22.
15 P. Gauguin to E. Schuffenecker (February 1888), M. Malingue (ed.), *Lettres à sa Femme et ses Amis*, Paris, 1946, p. 322.
16 'simplicité rustique et *superstitieuse*' P. Gauguin to Vincent Van Gogh (September 1888), *Oeuvres Ecrites de Gauguin et Van Gogh: Collections de Musée National Vincent van Gogh, Amsterdam*, Institut Néerlandais, Paris, 1975, cat. No. G9, p. 22.
17 *R. A. Post-Impressionism*, 1979, M. A. Stevens (p. 22) thus paraphrased A. Séguin, 'Paul Gauguin', *L'Occident*, March 1903, p. 166.
18 O. Redon, *A Soi-même* (1922), Paris, 1961, p. 49.
19 A. Young, *Travels during the years 1787, 1788, 1789 and 1790, undertaken more particularly with a view to ascertaining the Cultivation, Wealth, Resources, and National Prosperity of the Kingdom of France*, Bury St Edmunds, 1792, quoted from M. Betham-Edwards (ed.), *Young's Travels in France*, London, 1913, p. 128, first published in this edition in Bohn's Standard Library, London, 1889.
20 M. Betham-Edwards, op. cit., 'Introduction', p. xii.
21 T. Zeldin, *France 1848—1943 Ambition and Love*, (1973), Oxford, 1979, pp. 176–178.
22 See J. Murray, *A Handbook for Travellers in France*, London, 1877, p. 164; K. MacQuoid, *Through Brittany*, London, 1881, p. 357; C. B. Black, *North France*, Edinburgh, 1885, p. 290; K. Baedecker, *Northern France*, London and Leipzig, 1889, p. 236.
23 A. S. Hartrick, *A Painter's Pilgrimage Through Fifty Years*, Cambridge, 1939, p. 30.
24 V. J. Chapman, *Seaweeds and Their Uses*, London, 1950, pp. 73–74.
25 L. Newton, *Seaweed Utilisation*, London, 1951, p. 46.
26 *R. A. Post-Impressionism*, 1979, M.A. Stevens, catalogue entry No. 59, p. 63.
27 Ibid., pp. 62–63.
28 C. Musgrave, *A Ramble into Brittany*, London, 1870. See also J. M. Jephson, *The Narrative of a Walking Tour Through Brittany*, London, 1859 and J. Murray, *Ramble About France*, London, 1878.
29 J. M. Jephson, op. cit., Preface, p. iii and pp. v–vi.
30 Ibid., p. 161.
31 R. Y. Creston, *Les Costumes de Populations Bretonnes*, Rennes, 1953, vol. 1, p. 15.
32 A. Blanqui, 'Tableau des populations rurales de la France en 1850', *Journal des Economistes*, 1851, **28**, p. 9, translated in T. Zeldin, op. cit., p. 131.
33 T. Zeldin, op. cit., p. 132.
34 E. Verhaeren, 'Le Salon des Indépendants', *La Nation*, reprinted in *L'Art Moderne*, 5 April 1891, translated in J. Rewald, *Post-Impressionism from Van Gogh to Gauguin* (New York, 1956; revised edition, London, 1978), p. 7.
35 F. Fénéon, 'L'Exposition Volpini', *La Cravache*, 6 July 1889 reprinted in *Felix*

Fénéon au-delà de L'Impressionisme, F. Cachin (ed.), Paris, 1966, p. 109.

36   F. Fénéon, op. cit., pp. 109–110.

37   See *The Complete Letters of Vincent van Gogh*, New York and London, 1958, LT 500, LT 539.

38   Ibid., LW 16.

39   Vincent van Gogh, op. cit., LT 527. For a useful introductory discussion of this point see E. van Uitert, 'Van Gogh and Gauguin in Competition', *Simiolus*, 1977, vol. 9, no. 3, pp. 162–163.

40   A. Bowness, *Gauguin*, London, 1971, p. 8.

41   J. Rewald, op. cit., p. 181.

42   P. Gauguin to Vincent van Gogh (September 1888), *Oeuvres*, 1975 (see note 16), p. 22.

43   Vincent van Gogh, op. cit., LB 8 and LB 12.

44   K. MacQuoid, op. cit., p. 260.

45   Ibid., p. 261.

46   P. Gauguin to Vincent van Gogh (1889/90), *Oeuvres*, 1975 (see note 16), exhibition No. G. 32.

47   A. Le Braz, *The Land of Pardons*, London, 1906, p. xix.

48   A. Le Braz, op. cit., p. 265 facing illustration which shows a refreshment booth.

49   R. A. *Post-Impressionism*, 1979, M. A. Stevens, p. 22.

Index A: Names

Index B: Concepts and terms of reference employed in critical writing on art of the period

217-20, 221-31, 233-7, 244, 249-58,
262, 275-83, 287-302
social power, 250, 253, 255-6
social revolution, 135, 210-6, 223-4
sociology, 233-7
spirit, the, 24, 54, 91, 145-8, 160-2,
167-9, 171-4, 235
spontaneity, 54, 55, 59-60, 63, 94, 145,
180
structure, 180, 186-8
style, 57-9, 63, 234, 243-8, 255
subject matter, 135-6, 244-55
symbol systems, 149-56, 177-88,
191-201, 196-201, 255
synthesis, 58, 60, 62-3

technology, 140
tendentiousness, 213, 233-4

theory, 9, 252
three dimensional space, 6, 73, 105-6,
110-1
town and country relations, 285,
297-302
trompe l'Oeil, 8, 54, 106-8, 113
truth, 19, 32-3, 34, 36, 38, 40-1, 42, 43,
45, 82, 110, 120, 160, 171, 173,
174, 180, 197, 200-1, 227, 229, 233,
236-7, 249

universal qualities, 124, 126-7
utility, 138, 142, 207, 210, 250

vanguard, 295-8, 300 (see avant-garde)

working class/proletariat, 211, 213, 216,
227-30, 239-40, 249, 275-83